GREAT GOLF

GREAT GOLF

150 YEARS OF ESSENTIAL INSTRUCTION
FROM THE BEST PLAYERS, TEACHERS,
AND WRITERS OF ALL TIME

Edited by Danny Peary and Allen F. Richardson

FOREWORD BY GARY PLAYER

STEWART, TABORI & CHANG

NEW YORK

For my formidable foursome: Laura, Suzanne, Zoë, and Julianna.
—Danny Peary

For Karen and Samantha, my best girls,
whose inexhaustible patience and support made it possible
and
In loving memory: Rick Greenoe (1955–2001), fellow lefty, friend, brother.
—Allen F. Richardson

Compilation copyright © 2005 by Danny Peary and Allen F. Richardson
Illustrations copyright © 2005 by John Burgoyne

Book Design by Anna Christian

Published in 2005 by
Stewart, Tabori & Chang
115 West 18th Street
New York, NY 10011

Library of Congress Cataloging-in-Publication Data

Great golf : 150 years of essential instruction from the best players, teachers, and writers of all
time / edited by Danny Peary and Allen F. Richardson ; with a Foreword by Gary Player.
    p. cm.
Includes index.
ISBN 1-58479-464-X
1. Golf--Study and teaching. I. Peary, Danny, 1949- II. Richardson, Allen F.

GV962.5.G74 2005
796.352′071--dc22

2005007605

Printed in China

10 9 8 7 6 5 4 3 2 1
First Printing

Stewart, Tabori & Chang is a subsidiary of
LA MARTINIÈRE

CONTENTS

SHOTMAKING

HEAD GAMES

FOREWORD

I am grateful to Danny Peary and Allen F. Richardson for asking me to contribute to their ambitious anthology. Their collection of articles, written by many of the greatest names in golf over the last 150 years, and presented chronologically within the various chapters, confirms that golf instruction and golf history always have been intertwined. Similarly, golf instruction has been part of my history. I have taken instruction, given instruction, read instruction, and written instruction, all to my great benefit.

Undoubtedly, there is tremendous value in reading the essays in this large volume. It's my belief that reading is to the mind what exercise is to the body. While some golfers prefer visual stimulation in the way of video or photographic instruction, others learn more through reading. Learning the basic fundamentals and reading extensively about the game and how it is played is essential during the formative years of an aspiring golfer, and can clearly help an established golfer re-evaluate what he or she is doing. One must always be open-minded to learning more and changing, as I certainly was during my own career.

My earliest golf instruction was received from my father, who worked underground in the gold mines of South Africa. He was a good player and one day he was invited to play with the mining company executives. He asked me to join him, and I was immediately taken with the game. I was in my mid-teens when I took up golf, and my father taught me the basics. I played every chance I got. Over the years I have read most of the authors who appear in this book, but while growing up, I did not read instructional books at all. They simply were not available in South Africa at the time. However, Jock Verwey, the father of my girlfriend Vivienne (who is now my wife), was a golf coach in Johannesburg and became my instructor. Under his tutelage I began to develop into a pretty decent player, and took the job of his assistant pro. The remarkable Ben Hogan and Sam Snead were the other two major influences on me as I set my sights

on a professional career. I admired Hogan for his fundamentals and work ethic; and Snead for his athleticism (and eventually his longevity).

As a club pro, the two things I tried to teach my pupils were patience and my now well-documented mantra, "the harder I practice the luckier I get." Unfortunately, it's easier to get a camel through the eye of a needle than to get the average weekend golfer to practice. It is the hardest thing about being an instructor. However, I have never stopped telling aspiring golfers to practice, and that theme is common to all my books, including the one I'm working on now.

The first book that really influenced how I played was not a golf book, but Norman Vincent Peale's *The Power of Positive Thinking*, which definitely could be applied to the game and its instruction. Positive thinking in golf is a whole lot better than over-thinking. I do believe too many young players, especially today, get "paralysis of analysis." I also think many young players spend too much of their practice time trying to add distance to their drives. In some places it has been written that my philosophy has been to "learn to hit the ball for distance, which always will stay with you, and then learn to golf the ball to score." But that's not my philosophy at all! Seventy percent of all shots are played from 100 yards in and so you must practice your short game with that in mind. *That* is my philosophy—or, at least a major part of it.

Also, as someone who changed his grip and swing early on, I have taught and written that while there are right and wrong things to do in golf, it still must be left to the individual player to find what works or feels best for him or her. This is absolutely true. As long as you have learned the essential, basic fundamentals, what your swing looks like is less important. One only has to look at Jack Nicklaus, Arnold Palmer, Lee Trevino, and me to see how "different" we look when swinging the club. However, our fundamentals are sound and that's what matters. As so many writers in this book stress: Learn the fundamentals before moving on!

I believe that aspiring golfers who read this book will profit greatly from what the old masters wrote on various aspects of golf. Harry Vardon, Bobby Jones, Hogan, Snead, and the others had to be, in many ways, more talented than today's young guns. Just consider the condition of the courses they played on and the equipment and ball they had to use. In fact, the views I expressed in the 1962 essay I wrote on escaping bunkers that is included in this volume, which might have been considered a breakthrough piece back then, have changed in some ways. Today's equipment—wedges with square grooves and over 60 degrees of loft, for example—coupled with the consistency of the sand in any given week on the Tour, have made bunker play much easier than it was forty-three years ago. Unfortunately, a lot of touch, feel, and flare have been eliminated from sand play since I wrote "The Blaster."

Modern equipment, the ball, and impeccably maintained golf courses are the biggest changes that have taken place in golf in the last twenty to forty years. The theories on how to play the game haven't evolved all that much; in the majority of cases, they have simply been—as this book's editors point out—re-examined and recycled using different language. As someone who is called the "World's Most Traveled Athlete," I honestly believe that there has been absolutely nothing new with the golf swing since I began writing instruction. However, the changes in balls, clubs, and courses have resulted in a remarkable depth of talent on the Tour.

With so many players on the Tour having essentially the same skills, now more than ever it's attitude, mental toughness, and the hunger to win that makes the difference. I am pleased that this book's editors also have included essays by the two golfers with whom I've long been associated—Jack Nicklaus and Arnold Palmer—because there are no better models for young players who want to learn what it takes to win. When we competed as the so-called "Big Three," I saw just how mentally tough they were. In my opinion, Jack's strength always has been his mind. Arnold's essay is about course management, but more telling is the title of the book from which it was excerpted, *Go for Broke*, which was the attitude that made him such a tough competitor and champion.

Great Golf is a treasure trove of essays by golf champions as well as the teachers of champions. If you want to become a complete golfer, physically and mentally, then you are sure to find what you're looking for—just begin on page one and keep reading. I am delighted that readers will find me in this book, as one of the individuals who has tried to play a part in the history of golf instruction.

GARY PLAYER

PREFACE

"I love golf, I live golf, I dream golf. If only I could play golf."

This old joke surely sums up the relationship most struggling golfers have with the marvelous but endlessly frustrating game. The supreme joke teller, Bob Hope, insisted he couldn't give up golf because his sweater collection would go to waste, but the rest of us consider it so enjoyable and challenging that quitting is *not* a viable option. All we want is to play better.

As golf has evolved and grown since it was first played in a remote corner of Scotland 600 years ago, all aspiring golfers have desired the same things: a reliable, repeatable swing; a fail-safe short game with a sure putting stroke; a bigger drive; and confidence. In short, we want consistency, touch, *and* power. But, intriguingly, golf always has eluded perfection, and because of that, it has generated endless debate, discussion, and a thousand theories on how best to use a set of oddly shaped clubs and one's physical and mental attributes to register a winning score. The continuing quest for the elusive formula for how to play golf correctly has spawned a corresponding industry devoted to instruction and theory.

The genesis for this book, in fact, was our own obsessive reading of golf instruction. Yes, we had purchased new equipment, and spent countless hours at driving ranges and in our front and back yards making deep divots. We had taken lessons and played as much as our egos could handle. To supplement all this, we felt the need to read as much golf instruction as we could get our hands on, no matter who wrote it. We did it partly because, as sports historians, we were fascinated by the evolution of golf instruction from the mid-1800s, which has coincided with the evolution of the amateur and professional game. More significantly, we hoped to use our new knowledge to upgrade our own games. But as we spent too much time trying to navigate through an endless maze of golf instruction, where there was far less good than bad and ugly material, we realized how convenient it would be if there was *one* book that included only the best essays.

Our goal was to pull together almost 150 years of advice, knowledge, and theory and present it in its original form, as written by the pioneers and influential individuals who followed. Included are both classic essays from famous golfers and gurus and articles by them on aspects of the game for which they are *not* best known; a few forgotten or obscure pieces that deserve attention today; and quirky essays that remind us that golf—and even instruction—shouldn't be taken so seriously that it's no longer fun. Each chapter in the book's five sections is arranged chronologically to show how various golfers and experts during different eras espoused past theory, refined a theory, or came up with something entirely different.

As with art, it appears that each generation of golfers has borrowed from the masters who came before them, modifying an old technique with their own dash of ingenuity, and creating something that both honors the past and is wholly their own. In many instances, the various writers from all eras basically agree on a specific premise. At other times, ideas are reconfigured or cast aside entirely and replaced by vastly different opinions. In some cases, it can be like dueling golf theorists. *Great Golf* is not meant to settle debates; rather, we hope it adds fuel to the fire, leaving to the reader the judgment of how best to proceed.

The authors of the book's 127 passages are a veritable "who's who" of golf history, with essays by renowned golfers who either wrote instruction or actually became instructors, such as Willie Park Jr., Harry Vardon, J. H. Taylor, James Braid, Walter Hagen, Bobby Jones, Henry Cotton, Byron Nelson, Ben Hogan, Sam Snead, Arnold Palmer, Gary Player, Jack Nicklaus, Nick Faldo, Chi Chi Rodriguez, Tom Watson, Ernie Els, and Tiger Woods; legendary teachers such as Ernest Jones, Percy Boomer, Paul Runyan, Davis Love, Bob Toski, Jim Flick, John Jacobs, Jimmy Ballard, Gary Wiren, Jim McLean, Bob

Rotella, David Leadbetter, and Butch Harmon; and great writers such as Sir Walter G. Simpson, Horace G. Hutchinson, Grantland Rice, P. A. Vaile, George Plimpton, and Michael Murphy.

The names listed above are only of men, but *Great Golf* also provides a needed forum for female golfers and instructors whose contributions to the body of golf instruction have long been unfairly neglected. Celebrated players such as Genevieve Hecker, Cecil Leitch, Joyce Wethered, Patty Berg, Babe Zaharias, Mickey Wright, Nancy Lopez, and Annika Sorenstam, and teachers such as Vivien Saunders, Beverly Lewis, and Kellie Stenzel take their rightful places with their male counterparts. Indeed, we wonder how different this book would have been if the bored, male, Scottish shepherd of legend, hitting a rock with his crook, had been out in that meadow with a female companion, and they had said, *together,* "Ah, let's invent golf." Perhaps if women had been there at the beginning, the skill, creativity, and art would be even more enhanced in this best of all games, whose appeal reaches to both the heart and the mind.

DANNY PEARY & ALLEN F. RICHARDSON

PART ONE

PRE-SWING FUNDAMENTALS

THERE IS NO GREATER SATISFACTION in golf than hitting the ball precisely as intended. But as the greatest players and teachers have preached for over a century, to hit successful shots consistently, aspiring golfers must spend countless hours mastering the *pre*-swing fundamentals. Indeed, most duffers fail to improve because they don't work on their grips, setups, and pre-shot routines. In the late 1800s, golfers began experimenting with new grips that moved the club from the palms into the fingers, encouraging the hands to work together. The three grips that evolved and are still taught today were the ten-finger "baseball" grip, the interlocking grip, and, most notably, the overlapping, or "Vardon," grip. Around 1900, golfers also broke away from the setup associated with the classic St. Andrews swing. Since then, instruction emphasizing the proper setup has evolved into a set of standards applying to the width of the stance, posture, balance, alignment, and ball position—in relation to the clubs being used and the desired shot. The pre-shot routine was the last of the pre-swing fundamentals to be codified in golf manuals. However, even early champions like Jim Barnes and Joyce Wethered urged golfers to *first* "visualize" their shots, and Bobby Jones stressed the importance of combining that mental aspect and a flawless setup. Decades later Jack Nicklaus also instructed to use imagination with a meticulous setup to produce consistently good shots, and many more golfers bought into the concept.

~ 1 ~

THE GRIP

ART IS IN THE EYE
OF THE BEHOLDER

Of Style in Driving

1887   SIR WALTER G. SIMPSON

As young men Walter Simpson and Robert Louis Stevenson canoed through Belgium and France, inspiring Stevenson's maiden book, *An Island Voyage*. Ten years later, Simpson, a member of the Scottish bar, also contributed to English literature with a seminal early work in the evolution of golf instruction. *The Art of Golf*, inspiration for such future luminaries as Ernest Jones and Henry Cotton, was the first serious book of golf theory (and the first with photographs) and set down prevailing grip methods, some centuries old. Simpson's contemporaries grasped the era's thick handles loosely in their palms, but he radically promoted a firm grip and argued, somewhat mysteriously, that for every inch the hands were apart the ball would fly a corresponding number of yards less. While his "baseball" grip would be discredited by Harry Vardon, Simpson anticipated a major theme of Vardon's: The proper grip compels the hands to work in unison.

———

"How ought I grip my club?" is a question which causes lifelong trouble to, and bars the progress of, many players. Addressing the ball means working their hands into some cramped position. They arrange the left hand tight, the right loose or tight, in the palm or in the fingers, under the club, over it, or with knuckles pointing in some prescribed direction, according to whose disciple they are. There is scarcely a modification of holding with two hands which someone has not adopted as his grip, each giving its owner a sense of command over the club, so long as it is at rest, behind the ball. That a player should give attention to this important matter is right enough; but the mistake usually made is to get the hands into the most efficient position for dealing a heavy, instead of a swift blow, without reference to the most essential point in a grip—namely, that it be so arranged as to prevent the club either slipping or twisting in the palms during any part of the swing. If a player gets his hands under the club-handle . . . it is impossible to take more than a half swing without letting go. If . . . he have the right more under than the left, and tight (a grip one is apt to adopt when a "screamer" is contemplated), anything but a swing round the waist must bring the clubhead back to the ball turned in (which is the secret of the screamer when it comes off, and also the cause of its failing so often).

If anyone by chance has read this last paragraph carefully, he will feel pretty certain that I am about to describe the proper position and tightness of each hand. But he will be wrong. On the contrary, my view is that players may take great liberties with their grip—at least with that of their right hand—without affecting driving. The club may be sunk in the palm, to save a sore finger, or held in the fingers if the palm be painfully horny, without prejudice to play, so long as it is so held as not to slip or turn one hair's-breadth throughout the shot. Nay! in the right it may be even allowed to turn. In fact, if a player grip [with the right hand under the club] he must hold loose with the

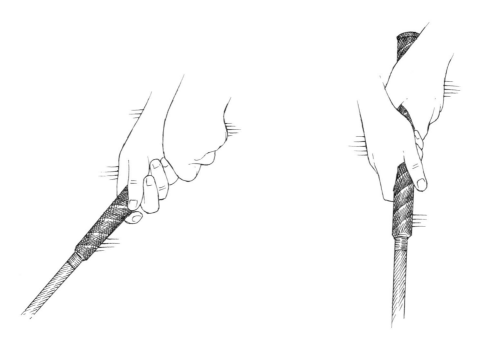

Sir Walter Simpson's variation on the "palm" grip of the early Scots anticipated Harry Vardon's modern grip.

right, and allow the club to slip round if his swing be perfect, otherwise his wrist becomes locked. Of this a trial swing will convince anyone. It is only possible with a grip [where both hands are "over" or "above" the club] for the right hand to remain glued to the club throughout a perfect swing. "How is the grip to be tested for adherence during the swing?" is the real question, which the address ought to solve thus: Having placed himself opposite the ball, let the player take hold of his club loosely, but so that, if held short, the end of the shaft would pass under the wrist bones … Let him swing it backward and forward freely over the ball, describing an elongated eight, whose length is limited by the locking-point of the wrist joints. After two or three such continuous figures have been described, the hands, still holding loosely, will settle themselves into a proper relation to each other, and to the shot. The club will then be placed behind the ball, the grasp tightened just as it is, and the blow delivered. Whether both should be tightened, or only the left—whether it is into the fingers, or the palm, these movements are to adjust the club—are immaterial points, which may be left to individual taste. Nor ought the amount of tightening to be treated as important. Some only tighten a little, some as much as they can; all that can be said is, that the limit of permissible looseness is overstepped when, in the course

of sweeping away the ball, there is any slipping or turning in the left hand at the very least. The preliminary flourish under discussion will be detected in the driving of the best and freest players. Should an elongated eight be found on any ancient Egyptian monument, it is certainly the symbol for golf, and will prove that venerable nation to have played the game. I say this flourish can be "detected" in a good style; but a practiced player does not require to pass over his ball more than once, or he may even pretermit all, except the merest rudiment. He has a proper hold at once, without searching for it, and can at once proceed unhesitatingly to strike. There is no pause, after the club has been placed behind the ball, to allow a final and fatal alteration to be made. It is interesting confirmation of the soundness of what I am advancing, that fine players, many of whom are proverbial for the instantaneousness of their address, are often more elaborate in a big match. Whereas a mere rudiment of a flourish is all they ordinarily indulge in, this becomes one or more complete eights, when a single mistake might be fatal. It is as if they said, "I am almost certain to grip rightly; but it is as well to test it."

Whether this plan of preliminary flourish is or is not the best, there is no doubt the grip should be found by some sort of trial swing, not by placing the club behind the ball, and settling down as comfortably as possible. The true grip is that which accommodates itself to a free swing, not to a commanding stance. Indeed players may be divided into two classes, according as they act upon or ignore this principle. The one arrives at the position of the hands typified in [a good grip]. The other is prone to [a faulty grip with the hands too far round or under the club]. The one makes its flourishes, places its club for an instant behind the ball, and without hesitation strikes. If they allow it to dwell longer, it is not comfortable perhaps. Nor need it be. Ease while swinging, not while at rest, is the essential thing. The other finds its grip while the club is at rest, and then proceeds to flourishes. Take the case of a player of this class who makes the orthodox figure-eight gyration. He takes his grip, makes a motion over the ball, and, unless by chance it is a true one, disturbs it by so doing. You may see him pause a moment to rearrange it; the other accepts the disturbance as a proper correction. Whatever the prowess of the player, his class in this respect can be detected by watching whether, after putting his club finally behind the ball, he hesitates or strikes at once. Nearly all bad players belong to the class which does not arrive at its grip by experiment but dogmatically; not that all in it are bad, however. Their grip may by chance be good, or they may have the tact to accommodate their swing to the conditions they have imposed upon it. But assuredly this common error of taking hold of the club in the most comfortable way for aiming at the ball, rather than for the blow, has to answer for many monstrous styles, efficient and otherwise.

From *The Art of Golf*, by Sir Walter G. Simpson. David Douglas, Edinburgh, Scotland.

The Grip of the Club: Two Hands Like One

1905 ⚒ HARRY VARDON

Great Britain's "Great Triumvirate" of Harry Vardon, J. H. Taylor, and James Braid dominated golf from the early 1890s to World War I. That Vardon surpassed the fame of his two rivals is due equally to his links legacy—"The Stylist" won six British Open titles and was a tremendous success touring America—and his popularization of the overlapping grip that had been pioneered by Scots Johnny Laidlay and F. A. Fairlie and was being used by Taylor and other golfers to make their hands work together. Vardon's seminal *The Complete Golfer* is still widely read because he explained his influential swing and other reasons he was his era's best all-around player, but the starting point continues to be the "Vardon" grip. Although its early detractors feared it might break players' thumbs, it became the foundation for "modern golf" and remains, 100 years later, the grip of choice.

Now comes the all-important consideration of the grip. This is [a] . . . matter in which the practice of golfers differs greatly, and upon which there has been much controversy. My grip is one of my own invention. It differs materially from most others, and if I am asked to offer any excuse for it, I shall say that I adopted it only after a careful trial of all the other grips of which I had ever heard, that in theory and practice I find it admirable—more so than any other—and that in my opinion it has contributed materially to the attainment of such skill as I possess. The favor which I accord to my method might be viewed with suspicion if it had been my natural or original grip, which came naturally or accidentally to me when I first began to play as a boy, so many habits that are bad being contracted at this stage and clinging to the player for the rest of his life. But this was not the case, for when I first began to play golf I grasped my club in what is generally regarded as the orthodox manner, that is to say, across the palms of both hands separately, with both thumbs right round the shaft (on the left one, at all events), and with the joins between the thumbs and first fingers showing like two Vs over the top of the shaft. This is usually described as the two-V grip, and it is the one which is taught by the majority of professionals to whom the beginner appeals for first instruction in the game. Of course it is beyond question that some players achieve very fine results with this grip, but I abandoned it many years ago in favor of one that I consider to be better. My contention is that this grip of mine is sounder in theory and easier in practice, tends to make a better stroke and to secure a straighter ball, and that players who adopt it from the beginning will stand a much better chance of driving well at an early stage than if they went in for the old-fashioned two-V. My grip is an overlapping, but not an interlocking one. Modifications of it are used by many fine players, and it is coming into more general practice as its merits are understood and appreciated. I use it for all my strokes, and it is only when putting that I vary it in the least, and then the change is so slight as to be scarcely noticeable.

. . . I do not grasp the club across the palm of either hand. The club being taken in the left hand first, the shaft passes from the knuckle joint of the first fin-

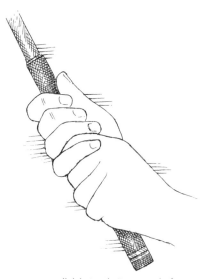

Ben Hogan called the "Vardon" grip a work of art.

ger across the ball of the second. The left thumb lies straight down the shaft—that is to say, it is just to the right of the center of the shaft. But the following are the significant features of the grip. The right hand is brought up so high that the palm of it covers over the left thumb, leaving very little of the latter to be seen. The first and second fingers of the right hand just reach round to the thumb of the left, and the third finger completes the overlapping process, so that the club is held in the grip as if it were in a vice. The little finger of the right hand rides on the first finger of the left. The great advantage of this grip is that both hands feel and act like one, and if, even while sitting in his chair, a player who has never tried it before will take a stick in his hands in the manner I have described, he must at once be convinced that there is a great deal in what I say for it, although, of course, if he has been accustomed to the two Vs, the success of my grip cannot be guaranteed at the first trial. It needs some time to become thoroughly happy with it.

. . . I have the strongest belief in the soundness of the grip that I have thus explained, for when it is employed both hands are acting in unison and to the utmost advantage, whereas it often happens in the two-V grip, even when practiced by the most skillful players, that in the downward swing there is a sense of the left hand doing its utmost to get through and of the right hand holding it back.

There is only one other small matter to mention in connection with the question of the grip. Some golfers imagine that if they rest the left thumb down the shaft and let the right hand press upon it there will be a considerable danger of breaking the thumb, so severe is the pressure when the stroke is being made. As a matter of fact, I have quite satisfied myself that if the thumb is kept in the same place there is not the slightest risk of anything of the kind. Also, if the thumb remains immovable, as it should, there is no possibility of the club turning in the hands as so often happens in the case of the two-V grip when the ground is hit rather hard, a pull or a slice being the usual consequence. I must be excused for treating upon these matters at such length. They are often neglected, but they are of extreme importance in laying the foundations of a good game of golf.

From *The Complete Golfer*, by Harry Vardon. Methuen & Company, London, England.

Evolution of the Hogan Grip

1948 ⚍ BEN HOGAN

Ben Hogan's Power Golf was published in 1948, soon after the driven, introverted Texan won the U.S. Open, and a few months before his career almost ended in a nearly fatal car crash. Although less detailed and sophisticated than Hogan's 1957 instructional masterwork, *Ben Hogan's Five Lessons, The Modern Fundamentals of Golf,* it gave readers insight into how the period's most dominant (with Sam Snead and Byron Nelson) and obsessive player never stopped figuring out ways to improve. In the book's first chapter, the lefty who became a right-handed golfer as a boy revisited how he altered his grip to have more success, coming up with an overlapping grip that had a different finger placement than Harry Vardon's model, and, like Bobby Jones's, differed from Vardon's in regard to pressure points. The result was that from 1946 until the accident in early 1949, he would win a remarkable thirty-two tournaments!

The grip I now use was arrived at by a series of trial-and-error experiments which began when I first took up the game. As recently as the fall of 1945, when I got out of the service, I made a radical change in my grip which I had been experimenting with whenever I got a chance to play golf while in the Army.

I had been aware for some time that if I wanted to make a comeback as a successful golfer after I was discharged from the Army that I would have to make a change in my grip to correct a tendency I had always had to over-swing on the backswing. . . .

Formerly I used a grip in which I had what might be best described as a long thumb when speaking of the position of the thumb of the left hand on the shaft. During the course of the backswing that thumb used to slide down on the shaft and as a result I was always guilty of a certain looseness at the top of my swing which prevented me from getting the maximum of control.

In correcting this I pushed the left thumb back up on the shaft. The entire change couldn't have amounted to more than half an inch in the movement of the thumb, but it was enough to restrict my backswing so that it no longer is loose. . . .

It took me some time to get accustomed to that new grip, but I had . . . it in working order when I resumed tournament play in 1945. . . . I've used it ever since.

The nearest publicized grip to which my grip can be compared is the overlapping grip made famous by Harry Vardon, the great English player, and adopted by so many top players in this country. Strictly speaking, however, my grip is not the same.

My grip differs from the conventional overlapping grip in the relationship between the little finger of the right hand to the index finger of the left hand and the position of my right hand on my left.

In the conventional overlapping grip the little finger of the right hand overlaps the index finger of the left hand. Whereas I have found that I am able to get a firmer grip, transmitting more power to the clubhead, by gripping the little finger of my right hand around the knob of the knuckle of the index finger of my left hand.

My grip also differs from that of other golfers in that my right hand rides higher on the outside of my left hand. This enables the two hands to act as a single unit, thus imparting considerably more hand action and consequently more clubhead speed at the moment of impact.

Getting the proper grip at the start is one of the most important steps in learning how to play golf. For that reason let us first consider the intents and purposes of the grip in relation to golf.

One reason why the grip is so important is because by means of it we telegraph our energy and our desires to the club. To do this with a maximum amount of efficiency we've got to have a grip which will permit our hands and wrists to work properly as one unit and not against each other.

The idea is to have free and uniform hand action throughout the swing while still maintaining the clubface at the proper angle when it strikes the ball. The objective is to make a solid contact of the clubhead with the ball at the exact moment you are telegraphing your greatest amount of energy to the club via the grip. . . .

As I favor my own version of the overlapping grip, naturally that's the one I'm going to talk about. . . . Starting with the left hand, my grip is very definitely a palm grip. The leather or rubber grip on the shaft of your club will lie diagonally across the palm of the left hand just above the callus pad.

In folding the left hand around the club the left thumb will be slightly on the right side of the shaft. As you look down on your left hand in gripping the club you should be able to see the first three finger joints on the outside of that hand. It also should be apparent to you that your left hand is well over the shaft.

In gripping with the left hand there is definitely more pressure on the last three fingers of that hand than there is on the index finger and thumb. While gripping with these three fingers you should also push down on the top of the leather or rubber grip of your club with the butt of your hand. This will assure you of a firm grip. Try it and you will get the sensation of having the club locked in that hand.

As far as the right hand is concerned my grip is definitely a finger grip. By that I mean that the club lies diagonally across the fingers of the right hand below the callus pad. When you fold the right hand over the grip on the shaft you will find that if you have gripped the club correctly there is a cup formed in the palm of the hand that will allow space enough for the left thumb. The thumb of the right hand is slightly on the left side of the shaft and not on the top.

Make sure that the right hand rides high on the left hand. The purpose of this, of course, is to mold the two hands together so that they can act as one unit and not two. The greatest pressure in the right hand is in the two middle fingers. That is because the club is well down in the fingers of the right hand with a lot of hand left over.

From *Ben Hogan's Power Golf,* by Ben Hogan. Copyright © 1948 by A. S. Barnes and Company, Inc. Reprinted with the permission of Writers House, LLC, as agent for the Ben Hogan estate.

How to Hold the Club

1961 ✦ DAI REES

Arguably, the best British instructional books of the 1950s and early '60s were written by Dai Rees: *Golf My Way*, *Dai Rees on Golf*, and *The Key to Golf*. That the Welshman was a four-time British PGA champion and Ryder Cup captain and hero in a thirty-year career added to their validity—even when he was promoting something as suspect as his own two-handed grip, which he insisted was back in vogue in America for the first time since Harry Vardon's day. With hindsight we know that the ten-finger grip would never catch on in a big way in the States—Art Wall and Bob Rosburg were among the most prominent players to use it—but even today anyone writing a "complete" essay on the grip is forced to include a description of the "baseball" grip. At least it can be a "handy" tool for kids and most other beginners.

The function of the grip is to hold the golf club in such a manner that it will be fully controlled and will execute the swing properly. That can only be done if each hand transmits an equal amount of force at exactly the right moment. It is necessary, therefore, that the club is held properly. In this respect you will notice I used the word "held" instead of "gripped," because I feel that the word "grip" suggests to some people that they must hold the club so firmly that they are almost frozen.

But to the other extreme, and this is most important, the hands must not be independent of each other. They must work as a pair or a team, and they must allow the wrists to flex as required because the wrists are the hinge on which the whole swing depends.

There are several kinds of grip, and I dare say that the devotees of them all can put up a good reason why their grip is the best. I always listen to such enthusiasts, because after all they have thought things out for themselves and decided that their particular grip is the one for them.

Undoubtedly the most common one is the overlapping or "Vardon" grip. It was made fashionable by the famous professional who was once at the South Herts Club which I now have the honor to serve.

Its popularity lies in the fact that the little finger of the right hand overlaps the forefinger of the left hand, thus linking the hands together. Many golfers like the confidence such a grip gives them, for it keeps the hands as close together as they can be. That is a very good thing, believe you me, because if the hands are loose then you are in trouble from the word "go."

There is a snag with the overlapping grip, and the snag is that it does not suit those golfers with rather short fingers.

If you have been overlapping and have not been getting as much power into your shots as you think you should be getting—this over a long period—then you might do worse than think about the one I use, the two-handed grip.

I've played with this all my golfing life and it feels comfortable to me, consequently it works. Nowadays it is growing in popularity in the United States and

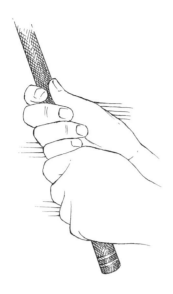

Dai Rees found success with the "baseball" grip.

club with the left forefinger and the thumb. Do not grip tightly but, all the same, grip it firmly. The next move is to close the last three fingers of the left hand over the shaft.

If you look down you will now see that two knuckles of the left hand should be showing. Some teachers insist that you should see three knuckles of the left hand, but I think this is wrong. You will see also that the V formed by the thumb and the forefinger is pointing toward the right shoulder. Do not listen to any club-bar lawyers who tell you that the V should be pointing a good deal to the left. They are quite wrong.

Now add to it the right hand on the shaft below the left hand, and remember one important point. It is only the fingers of the right hand which go round the shaft. That is where so many people go wrong. I think the most important finger of the right hand, or of either hand if it comes to that, is the forefinger. It should nestle round the shaft, caressing it in much the same way as the forefinger caresses the trigger of a rifle. If you look down you will see that the V formed by the forefinger and thumb of the right hand also points toward the right shoulder.

After that the grips vary slightly, but they should all do the same job of work—transmit the necessary power to swing the club.

When you check up on your grip from time to time you will find that one or other of the hands has moved out of position. Usually it is the left hand which is the culprit. It often wanders toward the right and the result is a vicious hook. The best thing, even though it is risking the amused looks of your friends, is to check the grip before *every shot.* . . .

Once you have taken your grip you must not change it or loosen it. It is part of the whole swing system, and a very important part too, for it is when the hands move back at the start of the swing that the other parts of the body start working as well.

The hands are the only parts of the body which are in contact with the club, and consequently their role in the game of golf is tremendous. If more average golfers paid attention to the hands, there would not be so many long faces in the golf club in the early evening.

several of their best golfers now use it, in addition to many thousands of the rank-and-file. Incidentally, I have my hands very close together and my hands do work in unison.

There is another grip, but not in such wide use now. That is the interlocking grip, in which the little finger of the right hand is interlocking with the forefinger of the left hand. Some long-handicap players use this but I fancy if you are to get results from it you need very long and flexible fingers.

I have suggested that if you are uncomfortable with overlapping, think about using the simple two-handed grip; but on no account change unless you are desperately unhappy and feel there is something very wrong. Too many golfers experiment for the sake of experimenting and it gets them nowhere. . . .

I have said that both hands should be in control of the club. I do not mean by that that you should hold the club as you hold a hammer. I have often likened the golf grip to the hold you have on the steering wheel of your car: firm, but not vice-like. The hands should always remain flexible and there should be no tenseness at all.

To get the correct grip, put the head of the club on the ground and lay the shaft in your left hand, so that it lies diagonally across the fingers between the center of your forefinger and the base of the other three. Having done that, you take the shaft of the

How to Grip

1977 ⚬ JACK NICKLAUS
WITH KEN BOWDEN

Dai Rees claimed the interlocking grip was almost passé by the 1950s. In America, Lloyd Mangrum and, for a time, Julius Boros were the only PGA golfers of note using the grip once employed by Francis Ouimet and Gene Sarazen. In the '60s only one notable new golfer on the Tour used it, but since it was emerging superstar Jack Nicklaus, the interlocking grip was legitimized once again as a viable alternative to the overlapping grip. Tom Kite and even Tiger Woods would later use the interlocking grip, but Nicklaus is still the golfer most associated with it. In this essay written with *Golf Digest*'s then editorial director Ken Bowden, Nicklaus asserted he used the interlocking grip because of his small hands, but he argued convincingly that any golfer desiring a natural, firm, easy-to-learn grip that assures the hands will work in unison should give it a try.

⸻

My grip today is the one I started with—the interlocking grip, in which the little finger of the right hand and the forefinger of the left hand intertwine. I've nothing against either the overlapping grip or the ten-finger grip, but I really can't understand why the interlocking grip is not more popular. It has, in my view, three big assets. First, it is more natural than the overlapping grip, where the hooking of the small right finger over the knuckle of the left forefinger seems to me to be an artificial linkage. Second, the interlocking grip is the easiest to learn—beginners find it much easier than the overlapping grip. Third, it automatically locks the hands together—you try pulling mine apart! However, the correct grip for you is the one that works best for you. You should experiment to discover which that is, then stick to it.

The right hand grip is primarily in the fingers, for two reasons. First, a finger grip promotes maxi-mum "feel" or "touch." Second, a finger grip allows the right hand to whip the clubhead through the ball with a powerful slinging action. Imagine the way a baseball pitcher generates speed by grasping the ball near the end of his fingers. . . .

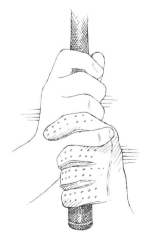

Jack Nicklaus was known for his interlocking grip.

I grip the club firmly with all my fingers, but I feel pressure particularly in specific areas of each hand. In the left hand, these pressure points are the last two fingers and the pad or butt of the hand. In the right hand, the pressure points are my thumb and index finger. . . .

Whatever style of grip you choose, keep it as natural as possible. I believe that for most golfers the most natural grip is one in which the *back* of the left hand and the *palm* of the right hand and the *clubface* are square to the target when the player takes his address position. I grip the club this way because I know that with it, if the rest of my swing is correct, the clubface will be square to the target at impact. . . .

Don't be mislead into thinking that big hands are essential for good golf. My hands are small and not particularly strong, but I still get reasonable power into my shots. I do so much more through *leverage* than hand action. I create the leverage through my arms and the club, as a result of proper body action and timing. My hands serve primarily as a connection, or hinge, between my arms and the club. As such, they transmit, rather than generate, power.

Especially if you have small hands, your left thumb can form a valuable anchor for your grip. Push the left thumb down the shaft as far as it will go— this is what the pros call a "long left thumb." You'll find this will firm up your grip and also increase your "feel" and control.

Hold the club firmly, but don't squeeze it. I think of my grip pressure as "firm but passive."

From *Jack Nicklaus' Lesson Tee*, by Jack Nicklaus, with Ken Bowden, from a collection of articles in *Golf Digest*, 1972–76. Copyright © 1972, 1973, 1974, 1975, 1976, 1977, and renewed © 1992 by Golden Bear, Inc. Used by permission from Jack Nicklaus and Ken Bowden.

Toward a Stronger Grip

1993   HARVEY PENICK
WITH BUD SHRAKE

Harvey Penick's Little Red Book probably produced as many converts as Mao's treatise of the same name and established him as a cross between Confucius and Obe Wan Kenobe in the golf world. A welcome mix of wise observations and reassuring advice that the gentle Texan (who died in 1995) had accumulated while teaching collegians and pros like Tom Kite, Mickey Wright, Ben Crenshaw, and Kathy Whitworth, it deservedly became a perennial best-seller. Yet the famed teacher's green-covered follow-up offered as many gems, including this take on the grip. Note that Penick described how the modern player combines "feel" and "body motion" while using the slightly stronger "Vardon" grip, rather than Hogan's neutral one. Many thoughtful current teachers have picked up on his suggestion that players practicing new grips should wait until they are completely comfortable before actually hitting balls.

For a number of years during Ben Hogan's prime and thereafter, many golf teachers taught the neutral grip—in which the Vs of the thumbs and forefingers point more or less toward the nose or right eye.

This was Hogan's grip, and it was the right thing for him because he was always fighting a hook. In fact, most good players tend to be hookers. This neutral grip worked well for the good players and still does.

For players who are not so good, the neutral grip encourages a slice.

Recently, some gentlemen from Tokyo came to visit me at Austin Country Club. We were sitting in the grassy patio, nibbling at hors d'oeuvres from a tray, drinking ice tea, and chatting about golf through an interpreter.

Mr. Tsuyoshi Honjo, editor in chief of *Baffy* magazine, asked if I would look at his grip. He removed his jacket, rolled up his sleeves, and placed his hands on a 7-iron that was sent out from the golf shop.

His Vs pointed straight at his nose.

"I see you have read Ben Hogan's book," I said.

"Oh yes . . ." he beamed. "Everyone has read Mr. Hogan's book."

"I imagine you are quite a slicer," I said.

"Oh yes . . . " he said, not so happily. "[I have a] very big slice."

I asked him to roll both his hands to the right until his Vs pointed at his right shoulder. I tossed a little tiny carrot off the tray, into the grass at his feet.

"Hit the carrot," I said.

We kept it up for half an hour, Mr. Tsuyoshi Honjo hitting tiny carrots off the patio grass with a 7-iron and a strong grip.

The reason I wanted him to hit the carrots instead of golf balls is that he would have no expectation about hitting carrots, and so his mind would be free to concentrate on the grip and the swing. If we had put a golf ball in front of him, he would probably get tense. . . .

"How does the grip feel?" I asked my Japanese visitor.

"I think I hit it much harder and farther." He smiled.

"Please practice that grip and that swing, hitting carrots or leaves or twigs, until you feel good about it," I said. "Then go to the practice range and use the grip and swing on some golf balls. I think you will be pleased."

. . . In the last few years I have noticed that the golf grip is evolving back toward a stronger position. In the days of Vardon, the Vs pointed at the right shoulder. During the era of Hogan, the Vs moved to point at the nose. Now [with such players as] Freddie Couples, Davis Love III, John Daly, and others, the grip has once again moved the Vs toward the right shoulder.

I believe this is because of all the good modern players who have learned to combine the hands-and-arms swing of the strong grip with the big muscle swing of the neutral grip.

Without a doubt, the strong grip is better for the average player. As Mr. Tsuyoshi Honjo said, a less-than-expert player soon feels he can hit the ball harder and farther with a strong grip.

Reprinted with the permission of Simon & Schuster Adult Publishing Group, from *And If You Play Golf, You're My Friend*, by Harvey Penick, with Bud Shrake. Copyright © 1993 by Harvey Penick, Bud Shrake, and Helen Penick.

The basic factor in all good golf is the grip. Get it right, and all other progress follows.

TOMMY ARMOUR

— 2 —

THE SETUP

THE STARTING BLOCKS OF GOLF

Advice to Beginners—The Stance

1897 · H. J. WHIGHAM

In the decade after golf was introduced in America, Scot H. J. Whigham helped spread its popularity, both through his play and by writing about the fundamentals for those learning the sport. The son-in-law of Charles Blair Macdonald, the first official American amateur champion, Whigham won back-to-back American Amateur titles, in 1896 and 1897, and then published America's first true instructional book. In advising on the setup, he was old-fashioned only in favoring a wide stance; otherwise, he opposed the key setup elements of the classic St. Andrews swing. Advocating a more modern square or slightly open stance, even weight distribution, and placing the ball nearer the left foot, Whigham offered a blueprint for hitting the high, controlled fade suitable for American courses. Anticipating Jack Nicklaus by seventy years, he also urged his readers to concentrate less on swing mechanics than the pre-swing fundamentals that are compulsory for hitting good shots.

Let the novice grasp his club . . . and stand square to the ball, not stooping too much, nor yet uncompromisingly rigid.

The books tell him that he may stand, as regards the ball, in one of two ways, basing their arguments on the best form. But driving from the left leg has gone out so much in the last few years that the open style may be regarded as the only one which is worthwhile to teach to beginners.

He must take his position, then, with the ball placed rather more toward his left than his right leg, and at such a distance that he can place the head of the club comfortably behind it without stooping or stretching out the arms, and leaving as obtuse an angle as possible between the arms and the shaft of the club.

The feet should be from two to two and a half feet apart, according to height, and the right, if anything, advanced a trifle in front of the left.

CLUB DEFINITIONS

Here are the names of now antiquated clubs with roughly their modern equivalents.
Brassy — 2-wood   Cleek — 4-iron   Driving Cleek — 1-iron   Mashie — 5-iron
Mashie Niblick — 7-iron   Niblick — 8/9-iron   Spoon — 3-wood

This style has generally been referred to as driving off the right leg, as opposed to the method of driving from the left leg, already mentioned. But that is in reality an abuse of language.

When the right leg is advanced so far that the weight of the body rests almost entirely upon it, the expression is perfectly correct; but that is not what is at present intended. The beginner must accustom himself to stand fairly erect, with the weight of the body equally distributed between each leg; he will then drive not from one or the other, but from both, and that is the only correct method.

In swinging back he will let the weight fall naturally upon the right foot until the top of the swing is reached. In coming forward again, the weight will follow the club, and when the drive is finished it will rest almost entirely upon the left foot.

But this must be done unconsciously. As soon as the beginner allows himself to think about changing his center of gravity his swing is sure to get out of gear. It will be quite sufficient, then, if he will stand correctly in the first place, and swing as I shall instruct him.

From *How to Play Golf*, by H. J. Whigham. Herbert S. Stone & Co., Chicago, Illinois. Copyright © 1897/1902.

H. J. Whigham pioneered the modern stance.

GET THE DISTANCE JUST RIGHT

Two-time PGA Champion and Ryder Cup hero Leo Diegel offered a timeless piece of advice for how to determine if golfers are standing the correct distance from the ball. Using the right hand (fingers spread), golfers can measure the space between the left leg and the end of the clubshaft. If the hand doesn't fit into the space, they are crowding the ball, and if the hand doesn't "span the gap," they are standing too far away.

The Stance

1904   GENEVIEVE HECKER
(MRS. CHARLES T. STOUT)

Slender, blue-eyed, twenty-year-old Genevieve Hecker was America's first female golfing sensation, "a wonder" as one magazine portrayed her. After winning two national amateur championships, she published America's first instructional book written specifically for women—as British champ May Hezlet simultaneously published *Ladies' Golf*—with chapters taken from the magazine *Golf*. Her book was reissued recently because of its historic significance, charm, and still-valid instruction. At a time when men were formulating theories on how everyone should play the new American sport, Hecker told women to follow their own instincts because "how can a man understand the ways and moods and means which must be taken into consideration when a woman prepares to golf?" Like Whigham, she observed the stance from behind and said not to obsess over mechanics, yet she had a unique style of teaching that was at once feisty, funky, and a mix of old-fashioned femininity and feminism.

After settling the question of the proper method of gripping the club to one's entire satisfaction, the next step in order is the determining of the relation the position of the feet shall bear to the ball, and the direction it is wished that the ball should take.

This is technically called the stance, and there are almost as many ways of standing as there are of gripping the club.

The stance may be divided into three classes, which are called:

I.—Off the right foot.

II.—Off the left foot.

III.—Standing square.

The most common method is the first, and probably so because the player can see the direction in which she wishes the ball to go better, and consequently feels more confidence that it will go there.

In adopting this stance, the right foot is placed in advance of the left, the exact difference depending upon the player's fancy. In other words, if a line were drawn on the ground parallel to the line of flight, the left toe should be just touching it, while the right would be anywhere from one to ten inches over it. The extent to which the right foot is advanced determines the proportion of the weight of the body it should hold; the farther it is advanced, the greater amount of weight is rested upon it.

In driving "off the left foot," the right foot is withdrawn in almost the same proportion as it is advanced when driving "off the right foot," and the stance is virtually the inverse of the former.

In standing square, the stance is as its name implies. Both feet are on parallel line, and the weight of the body is equally divided between them.

Genevieve Hecker was a role model for female readers.

The distance which the feet should be apart is another matter which must be decided by the individual, and should be regulated by both feeling and physique.

Roughly speaking, the feet should be from 18 to 24 inches apart.

The knees should be bent in the smallest degree, just so that the knee-joint is not stiff, and the arms, when the clubhead rests behind the ball, are bent in an equally small degree at the elbow.

The position of the ball and its relation to the feet are most important.

When the "standing square" stance is adopted, the ball should be nearly opposite the left heel—that is, within two or three inches of the line which a right angle drawn by the feet and ball would make.

When playing "off the right foot" the ball should be more to the right, and as the foot is advanced, so proportionately should the ball be moved to the right.

When playing "off the left foot" the ball should be inversely moved to the left.

I favor using a stance in which the feet are practically on a line. . . . I do not, as I said before, try to place my feet in identically the same position for each shot, and therefore the position of the right one may occasionally vary an inch or even two inches, both in its distance to the right of the left foot and its distance ahead of the left.

Again, I try to have my feet approximately twenty inches apart, but I let the matter settle itself instinctively, and only try to get a stance which seems natural. The majority of the men who have written books on golf, and also the professionals, agree that it is only the position of the left foot which is really important, and that the right may vary in its place several inches without affecting the result of the shot; my experience has been that this is true.

Another point, perhaps a minor consideration, but one which many a beginner on the rocky pathway to golfing fame stumbles over, is the position of the toes. Some think that they must be turned out as nicely as a dancing professor insists upon in the first position; others think that the feet should be straight, and some imagine, or at least a casual observer would so suppose, that a good drive can only be secured by turning the toes in.

No one need worry over this point, however, for as good drives may be made in one way as in another. Ordinarily I place the ball and I tee about three inches to the right of my left heel, and I rest the weight of my body equally on each foot. I have found that by adopting this stance I can obtain a full, easy backward swing, and that I can swing my club in a sweeping circle much farther and straighter in the line of flight of the ball. . . .

Never make the mistake of taking up a certain stance simply because some celebrated golfer uses it. Be a law unto yourself, for, unless you stand so that you feel natural and easy and as though you were going to hit the ball exactly as you wish, you never will be able to do so. Confidence in golf is at least half the battle. If you find that some champion uses the same stance that you do, well and good. Say to yourself, he uses good judgment and is a legitimate champion, and feel well satisfied that the champion follows you, but never follow him. When I say that, after finding the stance which seems best, one should continue using it, I do not mean that one should worry over getting in exactly the same position each time. I take up a stance which is substantially the same, but I do it instinctively, and never think of looking to see just how many inches one foot is away from the other, or how many inches one is in front of the other.

There is no surer way of producing foozles or of acquiring a stiff and awkward, to say nothing of an improper, swing than to continually worry over getting in identically the same position for every stroke.

The ball should be teed at whatever place the clubhead lies when it is gripped in the proper way, and then allowed to fall naturally to the ground straight in front of the player. The whole idea is to get it at such a distance that it will be directly in the line of a *natural* swing. There is a great diversity of opinion about the distance one should stand away. Some of the best drivers in the country stand so far that the toe of their club, when addressing the ball, is quite two or three inches behind the ball, while others have the ball even with the neck of the clubhead. I do not favor either of these extremes.

If the ball is too far away and the player has to *reach* for it, as it were, the whole position is quite apt to be cramped, and the swing is consequently without snap, or else, in endeavoring to have it free and easy, the player does not always "reach" the exact fraction of an inch which is necessary for the perfect performance of the shot, and a bad slice or pull results.

From *Golf for Women*, by Genevieve Hecker (Mrs. Charles T. Stout). The Baker & Taylor Co., New York, N.Y.

The Stance

1931 ✦ T. PHILIP PERKINS

During the late 1920s and early 1930s, *Golf Illustrated* didn't have the following of its competitor, *The American Golfer*, and it wouldn't be remembered so fondly, but it invariably featured well-written, detailed articles that proved useful to readers trying to understand the basics of the game. Its contributors included golfers and expert writers like T. Philip Perkins, who could be counted on for serious instruction on numerous aspects of the game, including the fundamentals. There is nothing groundbreaking in this excerpt, but that's the point; in telling readers that they should take a natural stance by first squaring the clubhead to the target line, and then planting their feet, Perkins emphasized things so simple that undisciplined golfers tend to overlook them.

The simplest things in golf have to be thought out, and the method of standing and taking the stance are no exceptions to the rule. To my mind, the stance should be as natural as possible. It is a good plan first of all to stand facing the line of play a little way behind the ball, to take aim, then to step forward with the objective in one's eye, and next to place the club to the ball. The stance then fits in easily. While arranging one's feet (which is automatic) one again looks along the line to the objective. If all this is faithfully carried out one should be in a position to complete the follow-through in the proper direction without feeling in any way tied up or cramped. The wrong method of taking the stance is to attempt to plant the feet in position before squaring up to the ball, which in actual practice is always more or less difficult from the point of view of aiming straight. The correct method, as above described, of taking up the stance, sounds simple to carry out, but really it has to be cultivated. It is so easy to slip back into the old way. I do not wish to recommend any particular method of standing. The best stance for each individual is usually the one that is comfortable and allows a free swing with the follow-through along the line of flight. The wise instructor prevents his pupil from adopting a freakish position, but at the same time allows him to use his individuality. Moreover, small adjustments have an immense bearing on the swing and the shots. . . .

From *Golf Illustrated* (April 1931), by T. Philip Perkins.

Ready for Action

1940   RICHARD BURTON

This Englishman named Richard Burton didn't marry Elizabeth Taylor, but he did win the 1939 British Open when American Johnny Bulla 7-putted the final two holes. His fame was so short-lived that Sam Snead said, "I beat the hell out of him in the Ryder Cup, but other than that, I can't recall the name." Burton did capitalize on his big win by writing an instructional book with the very British title *Length with Discretion* while golf courses in his country were being converted into airfields. It drifted into obscurity along with its author, which is a shame because as this excerpt illustrates, Burton wrote practical instruction and was quite entertaining. He was one of the first writers to present himself as a teacher working with the reader on the course, rather than just giving impersonal how-to tips. One can envision Burton today on the Golf Channel or starring in instructional videos.

Let me see you take your stance. Remember that you are not bracing yourself to withstand the shock of an oncoming train. . . . Walk up to the ball. Now . . . grip the club. There is no need consciously to turn your toes inward or outward. As you have walked quite naturally up to the ball, spread your feet to the width of your shoulders, or a little beyond. As in everything else in golf you must be natural. If you walk with your feet turned slightly outward, they should still be pointing outward when you address the ball. To turn your feet square or inward because you have seen someone else do so is not a sufficient reason for a conscious act that serves merely as another distraction. It will not cure a hook or slice, and will not of itself stop swaying of the body. Your feet, like the rest of your body, have a natural function to perform in the golf swing, and the more readily they are allowed to do it the more easily they will react to your demands without forcing themselves on your consciousness. You must always remember that your main purpose in playing the game is to eliminate as many considerations as possible in order to concentrate on the main essential of swinging the club the right way.

No, don't stiffen your legs. You did not walk up to the ball with stiff legs. In fact you would not dream of doing so. In walking your legs give you the best service when they are used freely to carry your body forward. Used freely they will carry the body round as far as it wants to go in the golf swing. Loose and supple. That's right. Avoid all tension, for it is your worst enemy.

Don't push the balance of the body on one leg or the other. Your weight must be carried evenly on both. Each must do its share.

We have at last, I hope, got you standing naturally. Now put the clubhead down to the ground. There is no ball there at the moment, so you need not bother how you are going to reach for it. Most golfers commit the original sin of reaching for the ball, arms poked out toward it, an action in itself which ruins their intention of being relaxed. Immediately their shoulders are jerked forward instead of being slightly bent, and tension is once more again set up in hands, wrists, arms, and the shoulders themselves. That tension increases as the club is swung back until the whole position is cramped and stiff as the clubhead nears the top of the backswing.

Let's try it again. Remember there is no ball. You have taken a stance, the club in your hands. Now place the club on the ground so that the head of it lies flat on the surface of the ground. Your shoulders have come forward slightly, though there is no discomfort in the movement. Your shoulders, in fact, feel as free as the rest of your body. If you let your arms and hands drop into the correct lines you will find, too, that your wrists are already cocked, and that is all you need bother for the moment about the cocking of the wrists, because I shall not ask you to perform some fanciful evolution at the top of the swing. . . .

With no ball to fascinate or distract you, you should now feel comfortably placed in the address. Don't try tucking your head in between your shoulders or holding it up as if you are being offended at some slight. If you hold yourself too erect you will only draw away from the ball when you begin to swing, and it will need a desperate lunge forward to get you back to it again. Which will mean that if you hit the ball correctly you will surprise me. And you are not likely to do it twice in succession.

If you have followed these instructions carefully you are in a position to swing freely, giving all your muscles full play. How different from nine out of ten players you see on the first tee, braced by the do-or-die feeling which makes them adopt all attitudes but the right one. If the average club player would realize that by addressing the ball naturally, and *only* by that method, can he hope to make consistently successful shots he would save himself from half his worries. Watch any professional addressing the ball. He does not look as if the cares of the world rested on his shoulders. He does not stiffen and hunch up his left shoulder in expectation of some imaginary strain it is about to undergo. Nor must you. It is a common fault that immediately a player addresses the ball up goes his left shoulder. Probably this movement is inspired by the fear that he may not get the ball into the air. What it does is to upset immediately the balance of his stance. He is now leaning away from the ball toward his right side and the result of the swing will be a scooping motion that will get the ball into the air all right—it will either balloon it or send it to the right or left. There will be no control. . . . Don't be afraid that the ball won't get up. In the case of the driver, the arc of the swing will take care of that; in the case of the irons, the loft of the club is sufficient to give the ball the correct height providing it is struck properly.

It has always been a mystery to me why the average golfer is so concerned about the air above him. . . . We professionals think in altogether different terms. We have got our thoughts not in the clouds but on the ground before us. We think of getting the ball *forward* and not *upward*. Thus we are always playing forward at and through the ball.

If you like, take a stone in your hand. Your object is to throw it as far as possible. Do you look upward, or even aim the stone upward? No, you look ahead, and throw the stone forward. It goes into the air all right. If you aimed to get it into the air you would lean back to throw it up, but all you would achieve would be height—not length. . . .

[W]hen next you come to address the ball . . . give your shoulders a forward shrug. In this way you will get rid of [any] tension you have set up [and] keep the shoulders relaxed as you address the ball. By doing so you [also] will adjust the balance that you [may] have carried off its correct plane, and the new position should of itself make you feel more comfortable and give you a greater sense of security.

When you are waiting for your turn to go off the first tee at weekends, notice how many of your club colleagues stand easily in addressing the ball. They may know that it is a sin to stiffen their muscles, but few of them are conscious that they are committing it. In anticipation of having to knock the ball some 200 yards they have automatically braced themselves for a supreme effort. The necessity for relaxation has been forgotten. Yet if you asked them to sit down and relax they would not sit bolt upright and cling on to the arms of the chair. They would quite naturally sink into it and feel at ease. That is the principle I want you to adopt on the first tee.

Until you have mastered this ability to relax it is no use my asking you to go on with the task of improving your golf. It is essential to my idea of the swing that it should be begun in this atmosphere, because, as I have said, preliminary tension serves to increase as the swing develops. And anything that tends to interrupt the flow of the clubhead is bad.

And this is a point to keep in mind always. If, when you have reached the top of the swing, you feel tension in the shoulders you will know that you began wrongly, and that unconsciously there was some stiffness when you addressed the ball. You must seek the cause and root it out. . . . Get used to the *feel* of the club, to the *feel* of standing naturally until you are so used to both that eventually you will do both without thinking about them. . . . You will realize that it requires no conscious effort to behave naturally. It should, in fact, come naturally to you.

And now I have, I hope, at last got you into the proper frame of mind. . . .

From *Length with Discretion*, by Richard Burton. Hutchinson & Co. (Publishers) Ltd., London, England, and Melbourne, Australia.

THE EYES HAVE IT

In the classic book *How to Become a Complete Golfer*, Bob Toski and Jim Flick advised golfers to align their eyes properly, claiming many players either ignore this simple setup fundamental or do it wrong by cocking the chin at an angle that sets the eye line to the right of the target. The eye line must be parallel to the target line, and the head should be straight as the golfer addresses the ball. They added that when golfers want to sight their target, they should *rotate* the head to the left rather than tilting it up and down to make sure the head and eyes get back into proper alignment before the swing starts. The same advice applies to putting.

Balance

1962 · SAM SNEAD
WITH AL STUMP

Sam Snead was fifty years old when he wrote his classic instruction book *The Education of a Golfer* with the estimable sportswriter Al Stump (of *Cobb* fame). The living legend from Hot Springs, Virginia, still hadn't won the last of his record eighty-two PGA tournaments and would play another nineteen years on the Tour. No one had more natural talent than Snead, but that didn't mean that every facet of his game wasn't the product of countless hours of practice and analysis. True, the following excerpt in which he audaciously tells President Eisenhower to stick out his butt more and corrects "Stardust" composer Hoagy Carmichael's footwork at address is characteristically full of disarming wit. Yet in his homespun, direct fashion, Snead makes it clear that the balance he maintained during his famously graceful, rhythmic swing was possible only because he practiced—with *serious* intent—balance in his stance.

———————

Once, when I played with President Ike Eisenhower at White Sulphur Springs, he remarked that his restricted backswing was causing him to lose sleep. "They tell me to turn, turn," said Ike, "if I want more distance off the tee."

I said nothing, and when we finished, Ike asked, "What do you think?"

"Stick your butt out more, Mr. President," I said. Some of Ike's bodyguards were shocked, but he only blinked.

"I thought it *was* out," he said.

Well, it wasn't—not enough, anyway. The big hitting muscles are located in the back of the legs, shoulders, and in the middle back, and that's one reason your weight shouldn't be forward on the balls of your feet or toes but back through the heels. When these muscles are in full play, your rear end sticks out. Another reason is that the force of the downswing may pull the body forward, throwing the clubhead into a shank or scuff position. Ike wasn't settled back enough where he could dig in with good balance. His turn was on the short side, but some of the reason for that showed up when I spoke to his doctor. I mentioned that Ike wore glasses with small lenses, so that to keep his eyes on the ball he was forced to reduce his turn. Shifting his weight back a little and wearing larger lenses helped Ike later—or so I was told.

Stepping, rocking, and swaying are all caused by an off-balance stance. Hoagy Carmichael played "Celebrity Golf" with me, and I said, "You're taking a left step forward at the address; then on your forward press you're stepping back with the right foot." Hoagy said he wasn't. At a running of the TV film he was proved wrong. It astonished him, for he thought balance was one problem he'd licked. He was an example of a golfer who can't believe what you're telling him because he doesn't feel like he's doing a specific wrong. You must prove it to him.

Footwork, balance, is everything to me because of my life-long theory (and Ben Hogan agreed) that the more you minimize hand, wrist, and arm action, the better. I believe the body pivot launched by the feet is the *big* factor. Many golfers get too much wrist leverage into their shots, where I have as little as possible. If your pivot is good, a gradual speeding up of the club-head as it nears the hitting area will follow without any forehand wham or rushing of the shot with the arms.

If the head and body stay behind the ball and the hips don't move in there too far and waste power before contact, you are set up to knock the cover off it. One of the ways I get distance is in the way my knees bend into position on the downswing.

And the knees can't put you into a power-hitting position unless the feet are working for you.

- ↠ It's automatic with me that, in taking my stance, slightly more weight is placed on the right foot than the left and I feel an easy sort of loose-ness from the bottom of the foot clear up to my hip socket. I'm relaxed with no chance of a hip lock.
- ↠ I'm in a slightly closed stance—about ten degrees on tee shots; the closed stance gives me more traction than any other.

From *The Education of a Golfer*, by Sam Snead, with Al Stump. Simon & Schuster, New York, N.Y. Copyright © 1962 by Sam Snead and Al Stump. Reprinted with the permission of Jack Snead.

The Stance or Address

1963 ✏ PAUL RUNYAN

"Little Poison" was five feet seven and weighed just 130 pounds, and rarely hit a ball more than 230 yards off the tee, yet he won twenty-nine PGA titles, including the PGA Championship in 1934 and 1938, when he stunned the long-driving Sam Snead. His attributes were his accuracy on drives and perhaps the greatest short game in history. Paul Runyan would be a Hall of Fame player, but his real contribution came during a Hall of Fame teaching career that lasted until his death in 2002, at the age of ninety-three. He's so associated with the short game that it's often forgotten he taught every component of golf, including the fundamentals. In this obscure, helpful essay, which was hidden in the *preface* of a *Golf Digest* book, he wrote clearly but with refreshing sophistication about the stance and ball position in relation to the swing arc.

In the stance or address position, we are attempting to encourage two fundamentals.

First and most important, the address position should provide a "suspension point" that remains constant during the swing. This "suspension point" is found at the base of the player's neck. It represents the center of the swing arc, the radius of this arc equaling the length of arm and clubshaft.

Second, the stance or address position provides the distance the player's head is situated from an imaginary line that extends upward vertically from the ball.

The taller and thinner the player, the closer his head will be to this imaginary vertical line. The shorter and stouter the player, the farther away his head would be. Also the head's position, either behind or in front of the ball, is influenced by the stance or address. This makes it possible for the player to either pinch or lob the shot as the need arises.

With a driver you play the ball opposite the inside of the left heel with the weight evenly balanced on the insides of the feet. Thus the head is positioned somewhat behind the ball. This is correct because with the ball teed, the player will strike it about two or three inches after the clubhead reaches the bottom of its arc. This reduces the backspin on the ball to provide maximum distance.

When the ball is lying on the turf as in the case of the 2-, 3-, and 4-woods, it is advisable to strike the ball nearer the bottom of the swing's arc. If fairway woods were to strike the ball well after reaching the bottom of the arc, as with a driver, a portion of the ball would be below the bottom edge of the clubface. The result would be that full compression of the ball could not be obtained and some power would be lost.

If the ball is played about even with the left heel on the drive, the bottom of the swing's arc comes at a point about two to three inches behind the ball. Thus if we moved the ball back toward the center of the stance by about two inches, this should cause the bottom of the arc to come directly at the ball. This is what we want with the fairway woods, with the 3- and 4-woods being fractionally farther back in that order.

The long irons are almost as straight of face as the 3- and 4-woods. However, these irons do not generate the same velocity of propulsion on the ball as do the woods. It is not easy for most light hitters to get the ball airborne with long irons as readily as with fairway woods. Therefore, it is inadvisable to play long irons any farther back toward the center of the stance than the fairway woods unless the player desires a very low, hard-flying type of shot.

I advise that the 2-iron be played about two inches inside the left heel with the weight fractionally more on the left foot than on the right. Then each succeeding iron from the 3 to the 9 should be played slightly farther toward the center of the stance until, with the 9-iron for an ordinary type shot, we would find the ball at about the very center of the stance with the weight remaining fractionally more on the left foot than on the right.

If the player desires an unusually high-flying shot for any of the irons, he should move the ball farther forward toward the left foot, keeping the weight evenly balanced between the left and right foot. In this way the ball is swept up off the turf in what is known as a lob shot. Generally this type of shot requires a reasonably good lie. . . .

On the other hand, should a lower-than-average flight of the irons be desired, the ball should be played back toward the center of the stance, with the weight slightly more on the left foot than usual. Then the ball is pinched more into the turf, giving a lower flight with more backspin. One advantage of this type of shot is that it works well from a great variety of lies off almost any type of turf from the soft-lush to the hard-packed.

The Setup, Aim and Alignment, and Ball Position

1992 · TOM WATSON
WITH NICK SEITZ

Tom Watson's extraordinary playing career is well known to anyone who has watched golf over the last thirty years. He was the PGA Player of the Year six times and the PGA Player of the Decade for the 1980s, and counted among his victories two Masters, one U.S. Open, and five British Opens. Moreover, since 1977, the popular Kansas City native has been a playing-editor for *Golf Digest* and written several excellent instructional books. His instruction has been consistently smart, sound, provocative, and creative. Note that in this excerpt, in which he took a fresh look at long-established setup theory, Watson presented the classic "railroad-tracks" image, telling readers how to square their alignment by imagining that their feet are on the inside track and the ball and target line run along the outside track. Watson also echoed Snead on posture and balance, and explained how (and why) to vary ball position for different clubs.

I almost always can predict when my 15-handicap friends are going to hit a good shot, because they will be set up well. Their posture will be good. Your posture virtually dictates how you will strike the ball.

Posture is a problem for most players, but it is probably the simplest problem to correct. Since posture directly affects your balance and the plane of your swing, it is extremely important. I advocate an elementary 1-2-3 approach to establishing good posture.

→ Stand up straight, with your feet slightly wider than your shoulders. Open—toe out—your right foot about 15 degrees and your left foot about 30 degrees. This is so you can turn more away from the ball and back through it.

→ Bend from the waist. Now you have created a sound spine angle and can swing down at the ball. You will want to maintain this spine angle throughout the swing. It stabilizes you and keeps your head from bobbing up and down. . . .

→ Flex your knees and stick out your rear end. This final stage balances you and puts ballast in your swing. You should almost feel as though you're sitting down. If you fall forward as you swing, you know that your butt isn't sticking out enough. Stick it out until you feel a little tension in the small of your back.

Your weight will still be toward your toes, but not too much. You're poised to move. Your lower body can work easier. You'll be able to stay down on the ball making contact. No good athlete gets his weight back on his heels. A fast runner is on the balls of his feet. . . .

I'd rather see you put too much weight toward your toes than err toward your heels. If you're back on your heels starting your swing, there's no way you can turn your hips correctly. You'll have to just lift the club with your arms and make a weak swing. You'll straighten up and fall back. If you fall forward, at least you can swing your arms down the line with some speed. . . . Your knees should be flexed enough that they are just about over your toes as you look down. Your legs will be flexible from that position. . . .

There's another positive result of flexing the knees and setting your weight on the balls of your feet. An active lower body keeps the head quiet. . . . If your legs are stiff—if you have "cement" legs as I call them—and your weight is back toward your heels, your head is going to move way too much.

Your weight should be distributed about equally between your feet. I like the way Jack Nicklaus exemplifies that and also how he positions his weight toward the insides of his feet. Jack's in wonderful balance.

. . . From [the setup posture I've described] you can let your arms hang naturally and comfortably, and that's where you'll grip the club. Your wrists will be semi-cocked already. If your left arm and the club form a straight line, your wrists are too high and you will swing stiff-armed.

You should never feel you have to reach for the ball, even with a driver, and you should never feel cramped either. Your arms should be able to swing in front of you in a relaxed manner, and from the setup posture we've talked about they will. . . .

COMMON SETUP FAULTS

The most frequent setup mistake I see is standing too erect. It happens typically with people who are short or who have weak legs or both.

If you are too erect, your arms hang too close to your body and you cannot swing them freely in front of you. Your arms might hit your legs. The club will go around behind you too soon and you won't be able to make a full, easy turn and coil on the backswing. Your swing is dominated by the arms having to work too hard without much help. You probably will spin out.

You must have enough bend at the waist to make an easy shoulder turn. The shoulders have to stay on plane. That means you cannot stand too erect.

At the other extreme, crouching and bending over too much results in a swing that's too upright.

About all you can do is stick your arms straight up in the air. The club wants to move too vertically instead of around the body. . . . When you are bent over too much, you are apt to lift up coming into the ball and make poor contact.

AIM AND ALIGNMENT

How you line up a golf shot pretty much determines where it will go. Aim and alignment are factors you can control before you swing and they deserve extra care. You aim the clubface and align your body, in that order.

Aiming the clubface is like aiming a gun. If you don't aim the face accurately, you won't hit your target. I recommend the Jack Nicklaus method of spot-aiming. I don't use it completely myself, but I'm convinced it's the best way. It's like spot-bowling. Instead of concentrating on a distant target (the pins), a bowler focuses on a close-in target (a spot on the lane).

. . . You should start from a few yards behind the ball and pick out your intended target line. You are looking out over the ball at your target. You get a much clearer picture of the line from behind the ball than from the side, where you will address it. You'd aim a gun sighting down the barrel, right?

. . . You have identified your target line and are still standing behind the ball. Now you want to identify an intermediate target or aiming spot just a few feet in front of the ball. It might be a light blade of grass or a leaf or a small stick. You build your aim and alignment off this spot.

Keep referring to your spot as you move into your stance from behind the ball. Aim the clubface first, then align your body. Too many people align the body first, which causes faulty aiming. . . . You circle into the ball from behind, checking your intermediate spot as you do. Aim the clubface squarely at your spot. Aim the bottom line of the clubface to make sure it's square.

Your right foot is roughly in position. Spread your left foot out into place, and adjust your right foot so you're comfortable. Be sure as you take your stance that you do not change the attitude of the clubface. . . .

Look up and check to see that your clubface, your spot, and your ultimate target off in the distance are all

Proper posture and balance are essential for a good swing.

in line. If you fear they are not, back off and start your aiming and alignment process all over again. . . . [Y]ou have to get this part of the game right or you cannot play acceptable golf. Be brisk, but be exacting.

THE BODY IS PARALLEL LEFT

Basically your body should be aligned to your target line at address. Imagine a pair of railroad tracks. The ball and your target line are on the outside track.

Your feet are lined up on the inside track. Your feet, hips, and shoulders are aligned parallel or square to the target line.

. . . A common fault is aligning the body at the target. . . . If your body is aligned at the target, then your clubface almost certainly is aiming to the right of the target! Your body should be aligned somewhat left of the target, so the clubface can aim straight at it. Then you can make a natural swing without having to compensate and try to pull your shot back in the proper direction.

. . . Your eye position is also important. It's possible to align your body accurately, but cause yourself problems when you look at your target before you start your swing, especially if you lift your head. Your eyes must be parallel like your body. If your eyes are cocked to the right of the target, that's most likely where your swing and the ball will go. If your eyes are cocked left, your swing and shot are prone to go left.

Even good players have trouble with their eye alignment. . . . I suspect it has something to do with a player's dominant eye, and it might make sense to get your eye doctor's thinking. But the point is to align your eyes the same as your feet, knees, hips, and shoulders. It's [also] helpful to swivel your head when you look at the target instead of lifting it. If you lift your head, you probably will lose your eye line.

. . . Your overall head position is worth mentioning, too. Some amateurs sink their chins down into their chests as they line up a shot. They are defeated before they ever start to swing, because it's impossible for them to make a good turn. You want to swing your left shoulder under your chin on the backswing, and that's impossible if your chin gets in the way.

BALL POSITION

I advocate varying your ball position. The hitting zone is from the middle of the stance forward, and that's where you should put the ball. The longer the club, the farther forward you play the ball.

For a normal shot with a driver, I want the ball opposite my left heel. For a wedge it will be back almost in the center of my stance. . . . You move the ball back in your stance for a shorter club because you make a more descending swing. You cannot hit down on the ball effectively if it is off your left heel.

I know there are some great golf minds that advocate one standard ball position, just inside or opposite the left heel—Jack Nicklaus and Ben Hogan

for two. But you have to be very athletic in your lower body to go down and get the ball. If it's in a bad lie, all the more reason to put the ball back in your stance. If you have trouble driving your legs and shifting your weight through the shot, you almost surely shouldn't play everything off your left heel. Most older players fall into this category. I've heard that Hogan moved the ball back as he got older, and I wouldn't be surprised to see Jack do it one day.

. . . My left foot is essentially constant for every swing, driver through wedge. I change the width of my stance, and open or close my stance, by adjusting my right foot.

My stance narrows and also opens as the club I am using gets shorter. With the driver, my right foot is about an inch back of my stance line and 20 degrees toed out to the right. With the wedge, my right foot is about an inch in front of my stance line and a bit less toed out. I never want my right foot perpendicular to the line. It's too hard to turn my body on the backswing.

The essential reason for changing the right foot is to promote or restrict hip turn. A shorter club requires a more vertical swing, with less body pivot and more arm swing.

You use different swings in this game. Your rhythm should stay the same, but your arc changes. Golf is difficult for a tall man because he has to swing so vertically, and the body doesn't want to. It's easier for someone my size (5′9″, 160 pounds) to swing every club freely. . . .

How far should you stand from the ball? I get this question a lot. . . . You'll be farther from the ball with a driver than a 5-iron, but if you set up soundly that takes care of itself. Don't reach for the ball or feel cramped.

~ 3 ~

THE PRE-SHOT ROUTINE

LIKE CLOCKWORK

Visualizing the Shot

1931 ⚒ JOYCE WETHERED

Tall, shy Joyce Wethered succeeded rival Cecil Leitch as the queen of British golf in the early 1920s, and became perhaps the greatest female golfer in history. Bobby Jones claimed she was the best golfer he'd ever *seen*—men included; Henry Cotton wondered if she was the best *ever*, period. In her articles and books, it's evident that a major reason for her success is that she was ahead of her time in believing physical play is impacted by what goes on in the mind. She has been credited, wrongly, for being the first to write about "visualizing shots"—Jim Barnes and others did so years earlier—but she was responsible for fleshing out the concept. As she contended in this famous essay, good players have a better chance for a great shot if they first visualize the ball landing where they wished to hit it and rolling exactly as they wanted.

———◆———

There is a great deal of talk about temperament. We understand that it counts for so much in competitive golf, just making the difference between the first- and second-class player, and deciding the issues that depend on the closest margins. Temperament is concerned with our thoughts, and the player has two or three hours of thinking before him while he plays a round. It is interesting to consider the nature of some of these thoughts, either while the strokes are being played or during the longer intervals that divide them.

In watching a big match the spectator can probably learn very little from the demeanor or the expression of the players; but at the time it is evident that their minds are exceptionally alert and keyed up. This is a state which can produce inspired moments, and can, at the same time, produce chaos. The part that the mind plays in imagination is extremely varied and differs with each individual. There is the time spent while the player is walking after his ball, or waiting through what may seem interminable ages while his opponent studies his putt and meditates upon the green. At these times it may be a matter of great difficulty to keep the mind still and at rest.

To many the mind is a racing, revolving machine that cannot be quieted when once it is roused. A few favored individuals may possibly be ignorant of these difficulties and may experience no trouble in keeping their minds evenly concentrated on the match undisturbed by what has happened or what is likely to happen presently. But I suspect that they are rare exceptions even among those who declare that they have no nerves. Calmness can be cultivated, and without it the technique of hitting the ball can be seriously affected. If consistent accuracy is to be expected, stroke play must be largely mechanical; the mind must be as free as possible from technical worries and able to concentrate upon visualizing what has to be done.

This personal vision of the shot is a thing which everyone experiences, and it would be of the greatest interest to be able to get behind the minds of some of the most distinguished players and see the shot as

Texan Kathy Whitworth won eighty-eight titles, the professional record for both men and women. She said that one reason for her amazing success was her ability to narrow her target. In her 1990 book *Golf for Women*, written with Rhonda Glenn, she stated: "The smaller your target, the straighter you are going to hit the ball." ∾

they see it. I believe it would be a different vision every time; the elevation and degree of run or back-spin would vary, although probably the ball would finish in very much the same place.

Joyce Wethered's pioneering writings on visualizing shots had immediate and lasting impact.

By vision, I include the whole feeling of the shot, as you are going to play it. Personally, I find that certain contours—for instance, in the shape of the greens—have an effect on the imagination, suggesting either a sliced or pulled shot. I must definitely allow for it or correct the feeling in the making of the stroke. The most subtle of golf architects are well aware of this force of suggestion and quite rightly make full use of the fact in order to puzzle the player and get him in two minds.

It is surprising how difficult it is sometimes to hit a straight shot at a hole where perhaps some hill or contour—not affecting in any way the actual flight or landing of the ball—makes one feel that the ball must curve in its flight also. In most cases you must play the shot as you visualize it in order to make it convincing; but there is a danger also that, if you see the shot wrong or allow the influence to overpower you, you will be led astray.

This leads to another factor. The mind is always conscious of the weakness which we know to exist in our game and we often consciously, and sometimes unconsciously, look at an approach in a way we should avoid, simply because we want to save ourselves from the necessity of playing a shot which we distrust.

If we have a tendency to slice the ball, we are apt to see the shot drifting from left to right; we may even see it running away from us across the green. If we take our golf seriously, we shall not feel satisfied, if we allow ourselves to yield to the inclination to play the shot in this way. We must resist and counteract the tendency by visualizing the shot as being held up firmly with even a suspicion of draw in order to strengthen our resolution. The club generally follows the inclination of the mind. We must positively see the ball flying as we wish it to, and the time will come when our technical ability will triumph over the weakness which previously would have mastered us.

The first-class player, when in full practice, is certain of what he is trying to do. He knows where his ball is to pitch, what it will do when it lands, and how it will find its way to the hole side. He sees it all, and his power over the club makes the result inevitable. But should he waver and be undecided, the ball will answer the mental vacillation to which he has yielded.

On the putting green, also, the mind can be a grave source of trouble. Begin to dislike the look of a putt, and the chances of holing it at once become less. The sight of a slippery patch can weaken our determination; or a particular slope may make us feel that we are uncertain of the strength of the putt. How many putts are affected by our thoughts about them while we are waiting to play! How sensitive we are to likes or dislikes on the green!

I can recommend only one frame of mind which might help us. We can, if we wish, pretend to enjoy the shots which frighten us. We can positively make ourselves look forward to playing as many of them as possible. Instead of fearing them we can stimulate an interest in them. A delicate pitch over a bunker can be converted by a little judicious mental effort into a delightful adventure. We can assure ourselves that we enjoy using our putter, even if we feel incapable of holing a putt.

You may say that is only a method of self-deception, but if we can make ourselves believe what we wish to believe, we shall in a very short time have restored our confidence. Our pitches will then be deadly and the two-yarders will drop satisfactorily. There is more in the question of liking and disliking than one thinks. We all enjoy the shots we can hit successfully and it is only a step further to approach unpleasantly doubtful shots in the same spirit.

From *The American Golfer* (September 1931), by Joyce Wethered.

Now, It's Up to You

1948 🏌 BEN HOGAN

Ben Hogan scholars in search of brilliant instruction usually go directly to his 1957 book, *Ben Hogan's Five Lessons, The Modern Fundamentals of Golf*. However, to find Hogan writing about his pre-shot routine, they must go further back to his less-acclaimed first book for this very brief, but often cited excerpt. The story goes that Hogan once didn't even notice when his playing companion made a hole-in-one, and that's not surprising after reading here that his goal was absolute concentration before striking the ball. However, unlike Patty Berg, Hogan didn't say to concentrate solely on hitting the ball, but echoed Joyce Wethered in using a pre-shot routine to conjure up images of shots hitting their final targets. He also came up with the idea of backing off the shot if somehow he was distracted—a tactic now widely taught and used without apology by both professionals and smart amateurs.

While I am practicing I am also trying to develop my powers of concentration. I never just walk up and hit the ball. I decide in advance how I want to hit it and where I want it to go.

Try to shut out everything around you. Develop your ability to think only of how and where you want to hit the shot you are playing. If something disturbs my concentration while I am lining up a shot I start all over again.

An ability to concentrate for long periods of time while exposed to all sorts of distractions is invaluable in golf. Adopt the habit of concentrating to the exclusion of everything else while you are on the practice tee and you will find that you are automatically following the same routine while playing a round in competition.

Naturally, on the practice tee you don't get the variety of golfing problems you get in competition and it is more difficult to keep interested. My solution is to play each shot . . . as though it were part of an actual round. . . .

While playing an actual round I sharpen up my concentrative powers and stimulate my interest in each shot by sizing it up as I walk up to where my ball lies. Make a habit of doing this and you will increase your powers of concentration threefold while also speeding up your play.

Addressing the Ball

1 9 6 0   R O B E R T   T Y R E   (B O B B Y)   J O N E S ,   J R .

Bobby Jones's first instructional book with material not first written for magazines or newspapers was published thirty years after he retired with a justified claim that he was the greatest golfer ever. In an eight-year amateur career, he had won thirteen national championships, including golf's only Grand Slam in his final year of competition. Jones was a tremendous student of the game and continued to write brilliant, influential instruction as well as make eighteen shorts teaching Hollywood celebrities, produced by Warner Bros. for a then-whopping one million dollars. Back then, nobody really talked much about a "pre-shot" routine, but it's clear from this excerpt that Jones thought in those terms for himself and his pupils. He advocated a fluid, economical, and almost continuous motion leading up to the ball, a method to eliminate tension that applied both when he played and when he wrote his book, and is still valid today.

It is [essential] to standardize the approach to every shot, beginning even before taking the address position.

It is far easier to maintain a complete relaxation if one keeps continually in motion, never becoming still and set. It sounds far-fetched, I know, but I have had a few players tell me that after taking great pains in addressing the ball, they have reached the point where they simply could not take the club back. It is a manner of freezing and is well know to tournament players as a form of the "yips."

Long ago, and with no remembered intention, I standardized my approach in the following way:

Having decided upon the club to use and the shot to play, I could see no reason for taking any more time in the address than was necessary to measure my distance from the ball and to line up the shot. The more I fiddled around arranging the position, the more I was beset by doubts which produced tension and strain.

I began then to approach every shot from behind the ball looking toward the hole. It was easier to get a picture of the shot and to line it up properly from this angle than from any other. Ordinarily, coming up from behind, I would stop a little short of what my final position would be, just near enough to the ball to be able to reach it comfortably. From there, the club was grounded, and I took one look toward the objective. The club gave me a sense of my distance from the ball; looking down the fairway gave me the line, while my left foot swung into position. One waggle was begun while the right foot moved back to its place. When the club returned to the ground behind the ball, there was a little forward twist of the hips and the backswing began. I felt most comfortable and played better golf when the entire movement was continuous. Whenever I hesitated or took a second waggle, I could look for trouble.

The little twist of the hips I have mentioned is a valuable aid in starting the swing smoothly, because it assists in breaking up any tension which may have crept in. Often referred to as the "forward press," it has been regarded by many as the result of a movement of the hands. In actual fact, the hands have nothing to do with it. The movement is in the legs, and its chief function is to assure a smooth start of the swing by setting the hip turn in motion. Without it, the inclination is strong to pick up the club with the hands and arms without bringing the trunk into use.

I do not think it wise to prescribe any definite number of waggles. This depends too much upon how long is required for the player to settle into a comfortable position and obtain proper alignment. But it is important to make the movement easy, smooth, and comfortable and to form the habit of getting the thing done without too much fussing and worrying.

MODERATION

In *Hints on Golf* (1886), Horace G. Hutchinson counseled golfers to use the "waggle" for "acquiring the requisite freedom and play of wrist," but not to overdo it. He also warned against staring at the ball for too long—lest it "weary the eye"—advice that would be incorporated into the crisp, consistent pre-shot routines later described by Bobby Jones and Ben Hogan, and now followed by good golfers throughout the world. ❧

The Waggle

1967 · GEORGE PLIMPTON

George Plimpton, the erudite founder of the *Paris Review,* had already written *Paper Lion,* about trying out with the NFL's Detroit Lions, and *Out of My League,* about pitching to a team of major league all-stars in Yankee Stadium, when he decided to fulfill another fantasy and spend a month on the PGA Tour. *The Bogey Man* is correctly regarded as one of the most amusing and edifying golf tomes, as Plimpton, an 18-handicapper, represented all hackers who make valiant efforts to fill their heads with golf "wisdom" before their next time on the links. In this excerpt, the confused Plimpton tried in vain to answer that age-old question, "To waggle, or not to waggle?" in order to relieve tension or trigger the swing. Although he mixed up a few names, it's obvious he did some homework, because he brought up famous figures from golf's distant past who came up with answers.

I came to a sheaf of notes under a paper clip which seemed . . . worthy of study. I had put them together some months before. They dealt with the "waggle"—namely, the movement of the clubhead before beginning the swing. Could my trouble lie here? It seemed far-fetched, but then I had collected the waggle material because many golf authorities believe that a very specific type of waggle is not only helpful but essential to the execution of a great golf swing. Bernard Darwin, in an essay engagingly entitled "Some Reflections on Waggling," felt that a change in waggle, if things were going badly, was a definite help.

The purpose of the waggle, of course, is to see that everything is perfectly adjusted for the stroke. It is simply impossible to hit a golf shot without some sort of preliminary physical action. In his chapter Darwin speaks of two schools of wagglers. In the first, there are those who indulge in the quickest action possible (three examples of his time were Taylor, Duncan, and Ray). Doug Sanders would be a con-

temporary example of this school. There is a slight jiggle that moves the material of his golfing trousers as he sets himself, but his club stays right behind the ball until the actual process of his shot begins. In the second school are those who rely heavily on the waggle to get started, who simply cannot begin without it—". . . like the toy animals," Darwin writes, "who have to have a key inserted in their stomachs before they will walk around the floor." Braid and Herd and Hilton were representatives of this latter school. Darwin wrote of Herd's waggle as being a cumulative preliminary, and that, gradually, with his waggles, he lashed himself into a "sort of divine fury before hitting the ball."

In more recent times Tommy Armour was noted for his waggle—maneuvering as many as fifty times before getting his shot off. He also thought of it as an exercise which "accumulated" power.

Perhaps the oddest waggle notion was that suggested by Eddie Loos. He was the author of the famous theory "Let the club swing you," in which he urged golfers to forget about balance and arms and forward press and where the elbows are, and so forth—just forget all that doctrinaire advice and concentrate instead on getting the "feel of the club." To do this he suggested waggling one's name in the air, writing it out as if the club were a gigantic pen, the longer the name the better, and doing it as often as one could, not only as a waggle but while walking down the fairway or waiting for one's partner to hit. "Feel the clubhead and let it swing you." That was what Loos kept telling people. He evolved his theory from watching the golf game of a one-legged player who shot consistent rounds in the low 70s—Ernest Jones (a relatively short name to waggle in the air), a flier who had lost a leg in the war, and who could sit in a chair and hit the ball 200 yards. There were many golfers who subscribed to the theory. Leo Diegel, just as an experiment, shot a round in the 70s standing on one foot. The father of Manuel de la Torre of our foursome—Angel, his name was—was employed as a professional at the Lake Shore Country Club in Glencoe, Illinois, where the experiment started. I had to ask Manuel if he was a proponent of the system. He said that he had been started off in the system, willy-nilly, because he was only eighteen months old when he was given his first club, cut down to a foot and a half, and since he couldn't talk or understand very much, certainly not the arcane instructive phrases of golf, at the beginning he was surely a natural student of the "Let the club swing you" school.

I set my notes aside and left the room for the lodge and a nightcap. I sat down at a small iron garden table in the bar and ordered a drink. The place was crowded.

"Mind if I sit down?"

I looked up. A long-faced man was standing by the table. He had a drink in his hand.

"Not at all," I said. "Have a chair."

He sat down and put his legs straight out.

"Had a good round today?" he asked. "I take it you're in the tournament."

"Yes," I said. "But I had a rotten round."

"Too bad." He had a very sunburned face, too pink for the almost leathery copper color of the pros. So I took him for an amateur. Probably a very good one. He had said "Too bad" with a certain superior sense of pity.

"I've just been sitting in my room reading about the waggle," I told him.

"The waggle?"

"Some people think it's important. You can see I'm reaching for straws. You're supposed to write your name in the air with your club."

"I'll say," he said. "The waggle? Hell, a waggle's a waggle."

"Darwin says . . ."

"Darwin? That old guy." He held up a hand. "Hold on," he said. He turned and gulped down his drink and ordered another. "I'll tell you what my philosophy is. What you need is confidence. Pure and simple. That's what the game is. Confidence. Concentration. Control. The three Cs. That's all the game is about."

"I see," I said. . . .

From *The Bogey Man: A Month on the PGA Tour*, by George Plimpton. Harper & Row. Reprinted by the permission of Russell & Volkening as agents for the author. Copyright © 1967 by George Plimpton, renewed in 1995 by George Plimpton.

Cultivate a smooth waggle for, as the old Scotch saying goes, 'As ye waggle so shall ye swing.'
TOMMY ARMOUR

Pre-Shot
and
Going to the Movies

1974 — JACK NICKLAUS
WITH KEN BOWDEN

In the introduction to his celebrated pupil's classic book *Golf My Way*, Jack Grout testified that Jack Nicklaus became, arguably, the greatest player ever because he paid equal attention to what came before his famous swing as the swing itself. Nicklaus always stressed the critical importance of a meticulous, consistent pre-shot routine and, in this well-known essay, coauthored by noted writer-editor Ken Bowden, he, interestingly, contends that *the shot he visualizes each time determines his exact setup*; and that his mind refuses to let him swing until his setup is correct. Even more noteworthy is that he took Joyce Wethered a step further, equating his form of visualization to "Going to the Movies," a concept he made famous. Significantly, in his Hollywood spectacular it isn't enough to picture the next shot, but to picture it as a *perfect* shot—which Nicklaus accomplished more than any other golfer.

———————

I am sometimes accused of being a slow player. Well, the truth is that I walk very fast up to the ball, make a fairly fast decision about what I want to do when I get there, but then sometimes set up to the shot slowly.

There are some good reasons for my being so methodical about my setup. I think it is the single most important maneuver in golf. It is the only aspect of the swing over which you have 100 percent conscious control. If you set up correctly, there's a good chance you'll hit a reasonable shot, even if you make a mediocre swing. If you set up incorrectly, you'll hit a lousy shot even if you make the greatest swing in the world. Every time I try to deny that law by hurrying my setup, my subconscious rears up and beats me around the ears. . . .

I feel that hitting specific shots—playing the ball to a certain place in a certain way—is 50 percent mental picture, 40 percent setup, and 10 percent swing. That's why setting up takes me so long, why I have to be so deliberate. In competition I am not simply trying to hit a *good* shot, but rather the *perfect* shot for the particular situation. I frequently fail, of course, often because I've mentally pictured the wrong shot. But unless I can set up *exactly right* in relation to the shot I have pictured, I know I have no chance of executing it as planned. Therefore, I *must* get perfectly set—it's almost a compulsion—before I can pull the trigger. My mind simply *will not let me* start the swing until I'm "right," no matter how long it takes. . . .

I am usually the last golfer in a group to play his fairway shots. At one time, out of courtesy, I would

Jack Nicklaus has written that a meticulous setup and an established pre-shot routine are most valuable when putting.

ing the shot, aiming and aligning the clubface and your body relative to your target, placing the ball relative to your intended swing arc, assuming your overall address posture, and mentally and physically conditioning yourself just before pulling the trigger. . . .

GOING TO THE MOVIES

I never hit a shot, even in practice, without having a very sharp, in-focus picture of it in my head. It's like a color movie. First I "see" the ball where I want it to finish, nice and white and sitting up high on the bright green grass. Then the scene quickly changes and I "see" the ball going there: its path, trajectory, and shape, even its behavior on landing. Then there's a sort of fade-out, and the next scene shows me making the kind of swing that will turn the previous images into reality. Only at the end of this short, private, Hollywood spectacular do I select a club and step up to the ball.

It may be that handicap golfers also "go to the movies" like this before most of their shots, but somehow I doubt it. Frequently those I play with in pro-ams seem to have the club at the ball and their feet planted before they start "seeing" pictures of the shot in their mind's eye. Maybe even then they see only pictures of the swing, rather than of what it's supposed to achieve. If that's true in your case, then I believe a few moments of moviemaking might work some small miracles in your game. Just make sure your movies show a perfect shot. We don't want any horror films of shots flying into sand or water or out of bounds.

stand by while the others played, then go to my ball and assess my shot while they waited for me. Now, as unobtrusively as possible, I walk ahead to the region of my own ball to make my decisions while the others are playing their shots. So far as is possible, I do the same thing on the putting greens. And, if you care to notice next time you're at a tournament, I also walk pretty darn fast on the golf course.

The point I'm stressing is the vital importance of the setup on every shot you hit. This includes pictur-

Abridged from *Golf My Way*, by Jack Nicklaus, with Ken Bowden. Copyright © 1974, and renewed © 2002 by Jack Nicklaus. Used by permission of Simon & Schuster Adult Publishing Group. *Golf My Way* is available in an updated, expanded edition (2005).

Don't be in such a hurry. That little white ball isn't going to run away from you.

PATTY BERG

Developing a Routine

1999 ✦ MICHAEL CORCORAN

Shotmaking Techniques, a condensed volume of *The PGA Tour Complete Book of Golf*, is one of the most reader-friendly instructional books of the last twenty-five years. Popular golf writer Michael Corcoran (whose other books include one on the flag) clearly advances his own theory and supports it with those of numerous PGA members, and the result is an entire book that makes sense. In this excerpt Corcoran provides a recommended checklist for a solid pre-shot routine, which if it had been published seventy years earlier would have made all future writing on the subject superfluous. Also he presents former British Open champion and 2006 American Ryder Cup captain Tom Lehman discussing his own pre-shot routine, which includes finding an intermediate target and waggling the club. Significantly, Lehman points out that one's routine should never vary in *any* way, including taking the same number of clock ticks before every shot.

Without question, preparing to play the shot is more important than anything you do once the club is in motion. If the beginning is not right, there is not much chance of achieving the hoped-for end results. Chances are you have heard or read a description of a Tour player's pre-shot routine and how important it is to his game. It can be—and should be—just as important to your game. The word *routine* is used here in the purest sense—that is, a sequence of thoughts and movements that are repeated with great efficiency. The routine is significant and should not be glossed over.

The basic elements of a pre-shot routine are:

→ An assessment of the lie of your ball. Is it going to interfere with clean contact?
→ The selection of a target.
→ Accurate determination of the yardage between your ball and the target.
→ The selection of an intermediate target (from behind the ball) to aid in aiming the clubface.
→ The setting of your body into place (or alignment and posture).
→ A single key swing thought—for example, "Take the club away low and slow." You should have only one swing thought as you prepare to play a shot. Tour players often say things such as "I wasn't really thinking about anything when I played that shot," because they concentrate on choosing the right club and getting aimed properly. After that, they trust their swings to get the job done.
→ A practice swing that matches the swing you would like to make when actually playing the shot.
→ A visualization of the shot as you expect it to fly. "Seeing" the shot before it is played is a hallmark of almost every great player.

TOM LEHMAN: WAGGLING THE CLUB MAKES IT EASIER TO START YOUR SWING

"I think the most important thing about my pre-shot routine is that it always takes the same amount of time. I think if someone were to time me on every shot over the course of a season, there would be a variation of no more than one second—which means the same number of waggles, the same number of looks at the target, etc.

"You should be completely comfortable with your routine. It should be second nature so that you're not even conscious of how you do it. I couldn't tell you exactly what I go through to play a shot. It's one of those things like, 'How do I breathe?' I know it's the same every time, because I've done it so many times that I just know I'm doing it right.

"If I don't do my routine correctly, I'm aware of it because I've done it thousands and thousands of times. There's an immediate feedback that says, "Hey, this isn't right!" At that point you should always step back and start over. Everyday players seem reluctant to do this, but on Tour the players don't hesitate to back off if something doesn't feel right.

"I start from behind the ball, and I take a couple of practice swings and visualize the ball in flight. When I walk up to the ball, I take a little half swing and then get over the ball and shuffle around until I feel comfortable. I waggle the club a few times and look at the target and then I swing.

"When my wife is watching me play, she says she knows exactly when I'm about to hit the ball because my last waggle is always a little bigger than the others. I never come to a complete stop between that final waggle and the start of my swing. I've always found that if I get to a point where I'm totally static—where I'm not moving at all—that the chances of my hitting a good shot are dramatically decreased.

"If you watch any athlete who is good at something—someone shooting free throws or getting ready to steal a base—they're always wiggling their hands or bouncing the ball or looking at the basket. They bend their knees, they breathe, they shrug their shoulders—they do something so that they don't become totally frozen. I think it's because it's easier to get a big motion going if you already have a little motion going. I know I take the big waggle, make a little forward press with my hands, and away I go. It's just my way of initiating my swing without coming to a dead stop."

From *The PGA Tour Complete Book of Golf*, by Michael Corcoran. Henry Holt and Company. Reissued in condensed form as *Shotmaking Techniques*. Copyright © 1999 by Mountain Lion, Inc. Used by permission of Michael Corcoran.

DON'T SHORT-CIRCUIT YOUR BRAIN

In his book *Natural Golf*, Seve Ballesteros, while advocating the pre-shot routine, explained that professional golfers understand that once the brain comes to recognize the exact moves the body makes in the precise order they each will be executed, then the swing will be automatic. "Apparently," he wrote, "only when something out of the ordinary occurs, such as extra waggles added to the normal quota, does the subconscious become perplexed. When that happens, the fellows say, the swing short circuits."

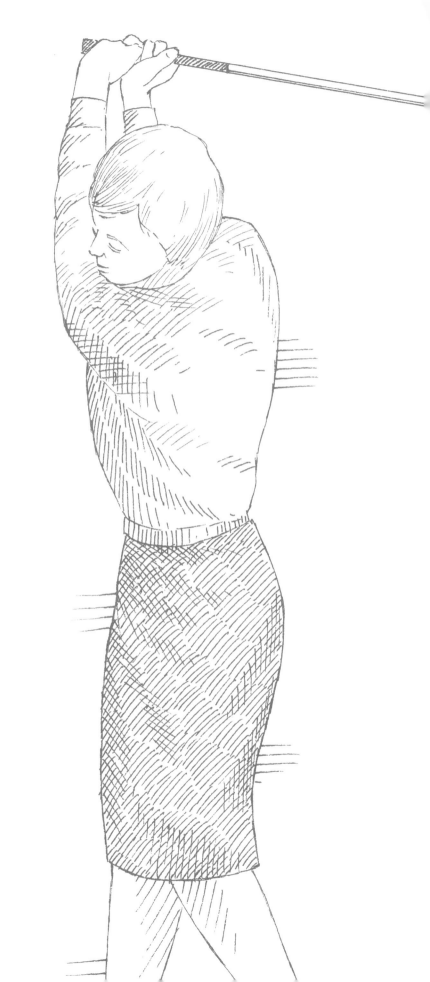

THE SWING

IN 1857, H. B. FARNIE wrote that driving the ball was the most "dashing and fascinating" part of golf, *and* its "principal difficulty." That central paradox is still true today. The swing lies at the heart of the game, yet constitutes its central mystery. Ever since that legendary ancient shepherd first hit a rock with his crook, golf theorists have offered numerous, and conflicting ideas on the best way to swing a golf club, with some teachers emphasizing feel and others mechanics. As the swing evolved from the "handsy" St. Andrews method of the early Scots to the big-muscle power swings of Tiger Woods and Michelle Wie, the disagreement only intensified. At the same time, golf instructors broke down the swing into individual components, such as the swing plane and the "delayed hit," and then asked golfers to practice each before blending them into one continuous, athletic motion. Traditional instruction also split the swing into the backswing and through-swing, and then told the golfer to reconnect them—although in the best swings these two elements may overlap. But the main arguments remained over what to emphasize in teaching the swing, as well as to whom. For the average golfer to "dig the thing out of the dirt," as Ben Hogan called it, "feeling" the club-head with the hands, or "small muscles," is recommended. For the better golfer, relying on the big muscles of the torso and legs may be the way to go. However, the best golfers might strive for an ideal "mix."

— 4 —

SWING THEORY

FROM GADFLYS
AND GARDENERS
TO GURUS

Elementary Instruction

1890 ✦ HORACE G. HUTCHINSON

Bernard Darwin once said that Horace Hutchinson might have disappeared from the pages of time—dismissed as yet another upper-class dilettante—had his youth not coincided with the beginning of interest in golf in England. Hutchinson embraced the new game, winning two British Amateur championships and then staking out his own library section by writing sixteen books on various aspects of golf. Despite a rather stiff upper lip, Hutchinson possessed a deft touch in his instructional writing, making the difficult and complex "Scottish game" comprehensible to aristocrat and commoner alike. Although his prose may seem slightly archaic today, including this essay from an early book, many of his swing concepts are refreshingly modern and useful. Asserting that the golfer must think about *swinging through the ball,* rather than "hitting at" it, Hutchinson's idea anticipated Bobby Jones and such diverse current instructors as David Leadbetter and Jim Flick.

Above everything, the golfing drive is a swing, and not a hit. These are very short and simple words, and contain a truth universally admitted—universally, almost, forgotten. If only a man can show practical full appreciation of their depth of meaning, he is not far from a finished driver. It may be almost termed a sweep; the ball is to be met by the clubhead at a certain point in the swing, and swept away; it is not to be *hit at*. The word "hit" ought to be a misnomer for the stroke—too often it is not—and the word "drive" should be scarcely less so. There is much in a name, in its effect upon those to whom it appeals; and the golfer, holding fast to the idea of "driving"—as if driving in a pile, or, at all events, driving through a dense medium, which is really the notion which the word suggests—is unconsciously misguided into errors from which the idea conveyed by a "sweep" or "swing" would have probably preserved him.

But what precisely is the difference, it may be asked, between a hit and a sweep or swing? Just this, that the former is delivered with a jerk and with tightened muscles, the latter is a motion whose speed is gained by gradual, not jerky, acceleration, with the muscles flexible. This is, to a golfer, an enormously important truth; and one whose full appreciation would probably go far to improve the play of even the very best of golfers. It does not in the least preclude the application of great strength and great effort to the swing; it only precludes their misapplication. The muscles of the left hand are the sole exception to this rule of general flexibility; for the grip of the left hand must be firm, since it is the main connecting link between the human swinging machinery and the hickory machinery it wields. There must be no such weakness in this important joint between man and club as to permit the slightest falling out of gear on the concussion consequent on the meeting of club and ball.

. . . Now what, after all, is the meaning of the word "swing," which we have so often had occasion to use? It has a meaning which is useful to fully realize. The upward swing should be slow and even, downward swing even and swift. But though the upward swing should be slow, it should . . . be a swing and not a lift. And the essential difference between a swing and a lift, and between a swing and a hit, is this: that in a swing one is all the while conscious of—one can all the while feel in one's hand—the weighty thing, the head of the club, *swinging* upward or downward, at the end of the shaft. We are to feel that the weight of the head has its influence upon the movement of the club—we must rather try to follow and be guided by this influence than to interfere with it with our tautened muscle; for this it is that produces jerkiness, and unevenness, and misses, and disaster.

Encouraging and accelerating the speed of this swinging thing at the end of the club means hard driving, in its true sense—above all, accelerating the pace to its utmost at the moment that the clubhead meets the ball. But directly we begin to force the swing out of its harmony—to over-accelerate the pace—from that instant it loses the true character of a swing and becomes a hit, a jerk—and this is "pressing." *Festina lente*—"Don't press." Let the club swing *itself* through. Help it on, on the path of its swing, all you can, but do not *you* begin to hit with it. Let it do its work itself, and it will do it well. Interfere with it, and it will be quite adequately avenged.

From *The Badminton Library: Golf*, by Horace G. Hutchinson
Longmans, Green, and Co., London, England.

The Styles of Champions: Walter Hagen

1 9 2 3 ⚷ O. B. KEELER

Walter Hagen tore into golf balls with a slashing swing that mirrored his flamboyant personality. As stylish as was Hagen's lifestyle—he said he never wanted to be a millionaire, but wanted to live like one—he also walked the walk when he played. This is clear in this article by O. B. Keeler, the *Atlanta Journal* writer who became Boswell to Hagen's early rival, Bobby Jones. Using an unusually wide stance for stability, "Sir Walter" displayed a bigger-than-life swing that drew admiration from galleries, while intimidating opponents. Remarkably, his lower body made the transition into the downswing before his upper body completed the backswing. This move by the man in knickers and a tie was ultramodern—Jim McLean contends only the *best* players master this exquisitely sophisticated power move. When Hagen's shots were wild it was only because the whippy, wooden shafts of his day couldn't handle the surge.

Walter Hagen, rated the premier professional match play golfer of the world, has been about all the kinds of champion a professional golfer can be in America—National Open, Western Open, Metropolitan Open, PGA Champion, North and South Open, Florida West Coast Open, and a good many more. But his winning of the British Open in 1922 probably was the crest of his championship career to date, being the most noteworthy by reason of a startling contrast. In his first venture in that classic three years previously, he finished a sorry 55th in the great field, so his bound into first place caused even our staid British cousins to raise their eyebrows a bit.

Hagen is a thoroughly interesting type to study, on the course and off it; and before the end of this little sketch is reached I hope to let you in on a factor of his amazing success as a golfer that, to my way of thinking, has at least as much to do with that success as his fine, sound style and his powerful play. Perhaps more, you can't tell about such things. No man can be a golf champion these days without a sound style and plenty of power. But there are many who possess both these requisites and are not champions, and have not been champions, and very possibly never will be champions. . . .

A Slashing Style

The first impression you get of Hagen's golfing style is that it is free, slashing, and of enormous power. I was interested in the views of Damon Runyon, the well-known sport writer, who saw his first golf at the National Open Championship at Skokie in 1922. It was getting the view of an intelligent chap and a good writer utterly unsophisticated in that particular line. He called Walter Hagen "The Big Fellow" in his articles.

And it was easy to see where Mr. Runyon got the idea. Hagen is not a "big fellow," in the sense that Dempsey and Firpo and Ted Ray are "big fellows."

Hagen is a well-proportioned man of about five feet ten, weighing, I should guess, around 175; not a "big fellow" at all.

But watching him tear into a golf ball for a full shot, with the tremendous drive of his right side carrying all his weight far forward onto his left foot, it is impossible to escape an impression of bulk; the vast power of the man seems to dilate him; the action is expansive, in a way. I do not wonder that Runyon called him "The Big Fellow."

And this dynamic style is most interesting to analyze; easy, too, if you go about it the right way, taking the swing by sections and not allowing yourself to be dazed by the smashing effect of the stroke as a whole.

Walter shoots from a firm foundation. He employs an exceptionally wide stance; I know of no golfer of his height whose feet are more spread for a full stroke. The stance is fairly open; it has to be, to permit the astounding use of his right side that is one of his leading characteristics.

As he takes his stance and addresses the ball, you may note another Hagen characteristic. Since you took up golf you have been told to keep your eye on the ball; but have you ever paused to wonder which eye? There is a master-eye in golf, the same as in rifle shooting; and in most golfers, as in most riflemen, it is the right eye. With Walter Hagen it is the left eye, as with Bobby Jones. Offhand, they are the two leading exponents, so far as my observation goes, of the left-eye style of address—and it is the style that favors the right-hand golfing swing, because with the left eye lined on the ball the head naturally is turned slightly in the direction the body must turn in the pivot that brings the club back; hence, there is less strain in keeping the head in one place as the backswing progresses.

Hagen and Bobby Jones, when concentrating on a stroke to the limit, give the impression of "cocking" the head, so immobile is the cranial pose as the club starts back. You may see this in any photograph of these players at the moment of address.

A golf swing is a collection of corrected mistakes.

Carol Mann

A Medium Swing

Hagen's swing is neither upright nor flat, but is nearer the former. He takes the club back smoothly to a position just dipping past the horizontal; a full swing, it would be called these days, though far short of the "St. Andrews swing" of a generation ago. The left arm all through the stroke, until the ball is gone, is rigidly straight; but that is a characteristic of all first-class players, practically; only Harry Vardon, the Old Master, eases the backswing at the top by a slight bend of the left elbow, and he brings it out straight again early in the downswing.

At the top of the swing, Hagen's right leg is rigidly braced and his weight seems to have moved back on to it, but the left foot is gripping the ground firmly; the foundation is solid all through the stroke. But once the downswing is under way, Hagen does not hesitate to shoot the left hip into a leading position, and at impact his right heel is well off the ground—his weight is coming through with a rush as his right side goes driving on. But his . . . head remains still, the pivot of the swing, until the ball has gone and the rush of his right side fairly yanks it from its position. I never have seen Walter play in a hat or cap, but I firmly believe that that terrific snap would flip his head from under its covering. He finishes the stroke with his right shoulder the nearest portion of his anatomy to the objective, and his weight is so far forward that a photograph of his finish looks as if he were running after the ball.

This is his big shot, and it is a grand effort, and an impressive one. He is one of the greatest wood-club players of our generation; perhaps of golfing history. . . .

From *The American Golfer* (May 19, 1923), by O. B. Keeler.

Getting Distance on the Drive

1924   TED RAY

In 1913, Ted Ray, a huge Englishman with an outsized personality, joined Harry Vardon for his famous promotional tour of the "New World." It ended when Francis Ouimet, an unknown amateur, stole the show at the U.S. Open in Brookline, Massachusetts, but Ray returned in 1920 and captured America's top prize. Despite the restrictions of a tweed waistcoat and a pipe clenched in his teeth, Ray used his bulk to muscle golf balls thirty yards past his contemporaries, making crowds gasp like John Daly would decades later. Ray occasionally invoked Zeus to describe his driving talents, but in this essay about the age-old quest for length he was more reserved. Ray analyzed common errors that modern golfers will recognize, including the "reverse pivot," and stressed concepts their instructors will second, including proper weight transfer and body coil. In this regard, his ideas provide an early prototype for "big muscle" theory.

Long driving is of prime importance in golf. It need not be long enough to make the world gasp. But it must be long enough to give the golfer some chance against bogey, and to put him on good terms with himself.

I think this can be done almost in every case as soon as the underlying principles of long driving are correctly understood. The intelligence must play a part in this branch of the game as in every other branch. There may come a day when habits have been so permanently established that good golf is played mechanically. I suppose, like other leading professionals, I may be said to have passed the thinking stage.

Of the great bulk of amateurs, however, this cannot be said. They are still thinking and thinking very hard; wondering, in fact, what every shot is going to be like, and too often wondering why things do not happen as they should.

When amateurs talk over their games it will generally be found that the length of their drives—or the lack of length—forms the chief topic. When a man is able to say that he has carried a bunker at some prodigious length, he is very well pleased with himself. So when golfers talk of others, who are noted for the length of their drives, they do so with a mixture of admiration and envy. Professionals who go playing before the public all over the country would attract very small gatherings if their tee shots belonged to the commonplace, no matter how scientifically executed the iron or mashie shot might be.

There is a spectacular charm about long driving alike for those who look on and those who play the shots. To see one's ball soaring into the air and gathering what looks like a new lease on life on its journey is indeed a rare pleasure, even to those of us who are more or less addicted to drives of this description.

We have all seen amateurs, not necessarily of scratch quality, make magnificent drives once or twice in a round. It must be particularly tantalizing to these gentlemen when drives of this description are followed by very indifferent specimens. It is here that the need for knowledge comes in and brings with it good reason for hope. It has always seemed to me that that the greatest of all drawbacks to long driving is the tendency to lean forward on the left foot while taking the club back, and then to fall back on the right foot in bringing the club through again. The ball is not driven in this way, but might be said to be scooped into the air.

So again one often sees another common error in operation. I refer to the over-tightening of the right leg at the top of the swing, bracing oneself, so to speak. It can never be possible to drive a ball a long distance in this fashion. Everything becomes too taut. There is no play in the knees, wrists, or shoulders; at least, not the necessary amount of play which goes to the making of a long tee shot. In dealing the blow with the clubhead—and I am an advocate of hitting—both knees should be slightly bent, so as to permit of the right shoulder coming well through after the ball, just as the left shoulder has been swung under the chin in taking the club back.

Everything in the nature of tightness must be eliminated from the swing of the driver. I do not mean that slackness cannot be overdone. I rather mean there is much greater danger of tightness being overdone. I suppose I am one of the most powerful golfers in the professional ranks today, and one of the longest drivers. That, at any rate, is how they speak of me, and I cannot see any reason for differing from the popular belief.

I am supposed to hit with all my might. So I do. What better use can "might" be put to? What is the use of having driving force if you allow yourself to be theorized out of employing it? But don't let it be imagined that mere brute force could be relied upon without the careful direction of it.

Sometimes it is said of me that I belong to that class of golfers who rely on swaying—and the timing of it—for length. I do not sway so much as may be thought. In fact, I should say that the camera would support my contention that all the swaying I do is after the ball has been dispatched. Then I often feel myself, not only throwing the right shoulder through and the head with it, but actually getting off my right foot and walking after the ball. That may be called swaying, but it is the kind of swaying that a boxer uses in delivering a blow, or a cricketer in making a forward stroke.

It is necessary to get the weight of the body slightly on to the right leg at the top of the swing; for only then can one be in a position to heave the body at the ball. The whole weight then comes into play. Of course, perfectly exact timing is required here, and the art of perfect timing is not acquired in a day. There is nothing in all golf that is so much deserving of study as timing.

Another danger to be guarded against as one of the reasons for short driving, is that of over-pivoting on the left toe. The grip of the ground has then practically gone and the player is almost reduced to the physical handicap of standing on one leg.

I have always been known as the unorthodox golfer. But I am not so unorthodox as some people think. My method of playing golf is one which might with advantage be adopted by the generality of golfers. The underlying principle of my style, if it may be called style, is that of attacking the ball without taking too much account of grace. I am not advocating anything in the nature of clumsiness, and I am not pleading guilty to that offense.

What I am trying to get at is that the clubhead must be, so to speak, flung at the ball without any conscious restraint. I should say that a very large percentage of players, who find their handicaps rather stationary, would at once discover an element of progress coming into their game if they would let out more at those shots, whether from the tee or the fairways, which call for length.

. . . A humorist once described my method of teaching golf in these words: "Keep your head down and hit as if you meant to knock the cover off the ball." In principle he was not far wrong. But there is hitting and hitting. The kind of hitting I am speaking about is no mere punch and done with it. It is rather a blow and on with it. The right arm and right shoulder cannot follow too far after the ball, but they can easily fail to follow far enough.

Well, now, how is this hitting of a golf ball accomplished? What position must be taken up by the player when he wishes to drive the longest ball of which he is physically capable? Suppose him to be a strongly built man, or a lankily built man, which involves strength as the term is applied to golf.

First of all, he must get into the right relation to the ball at the top of the swing, whether it be a full or a medium swing. Speaking for myself, I always know one thing; that if I get my body in the right position when commencing the downward swing a good drive becomes a practical certainty. . . . [And as the downswing is executed] the body must not be "pulled through." It must swing through, giving the player the feeling that he has been released from a spring.

From *The American Golfer* (February 9, 1924), by Ted Ray

KEEPING A LEVEL HEAD

Seymour Dunn told golfers to take an address position near a wall, and then lean their heads against those walls while practicing the pivot, or body turn. The idea is to keep centered during the exercise. Jim McLean and others teach the modern version of this drill (which McLean attributes to Paul Runyan), which is for golfers to take a pillow and put it against the wall and lean the head into it, keeping it in place as they take an imaginary swing. ❧

Style and How to Form It

1931 ✒ T. Henry Cotton

When he published *Golf*, Henry Cotton was still three years away from ending America's stranglehold on the British Open, but was already regarded as the best British golfer since Harry Vardon. And although his body was misshapen from endless practice in a golfer's crouch, Cotton, whose family was upper-middle class, was already rubbing crooked shoulders with the super-rich and celebrated. Explaining he "had to live like a champion to be a champion," Cotton understood "style," the now archaic term for a golfer's individual technique, and decades before television, videos, and computer simulations, "the Maestro" advocated watching great players and adopting their methods. The approach is now standard orthodoxy, but, ironically, Cotton didn't develop into who Henry Longhurst called "the greatest striker of a golf ball I ever saw," until he stopped imitating and evolved his own style that emphasized hands, concentration, and no-frills shots that rarely missed the fairway.

What is style, and why should you endeavor to acquire a style of your own? These are questions which you will ask, for surely there must be a right and wrong way of playing a shot. There are many correct methods and probably more ways of playing wrongly, so that what may be right for you is wrong for the other player. Therefore, you must build up an individuality in the game—that is, a personal method of playing which, while fundamentally correct, may differ in some aspects from another player's methods. That is what you will call your style, which may be judged from appearance, ease and grace, and results. What may be a good or bad style may be left to your critics. Providing it gives good results, is endowed with a certain amount of grace and easiness, it should be a good style; but I regret to say that sometimes a very businesslike defective swing is passed over as being unstylish as compared with a dashing swing which gives poor results. Frankly I do not believe there are two identical styles in the world. Why should there be? Golf is a game of individuality. Every person is differently built, and there are no two people with exactly similar temperaments.

For that reason I say cultivate a style of your own, but to be right you must believe in it. You must take the advice of your teacher and work out the style for yourself. All the time, however, you must remember that just because a method looks attractive it is not necessarily right. As a matter of actual fact, style does not count at all in the game of golf, because style means method, and method is a result of practice. A golfer who practices will discover a style of his own. This may fall short of his ideals, but possibly he will have copied, unconsciously perhaps, several points from his model golfers.

When you are young it is almost second nature to imitate, and the game of golf is no exception to this. There have been players who formed the foundation of a successful golfing career upon the style of another player whom they imitated. It is possible that they adopted a style which suited them and improved upon it, just as you can. But it must be remembered that no player should sacrifice results for style.

Some players think so much of a stylish swing that they destroy their chances of success for it. It may be all very well to go on to the first tee and cut the heads off daisies with your driver in a glorious free and easy manner. You may make the spectators envious, but you will get very little satisfaction when you know that you did not hit your first drive just as you wished to.

By adapting your play to your physical abilities you will cultivate a style, and it must follow that a method which gives the best results is more useful than one that merely looks pretty. It is very nice to have a perfect style in golf, just as it is in swimming or running or any other game, but if the results do not justify it, then it is wrong and you must find another style. It is possible to have a good-looking swing which, when analyzed, is bad in effect because it is full of faults. Results matter far more than appearance. If

you asked me a question which has so frequently puzzled me, "Who should I copy?" I should say, "Copy as much of Bobby Jones, Tommy Armour, George Duncan, Miss Joyce Wethered, and Harry Vardon as you possibly can. Copy them all, and from these great players build up your style without entirely imitating any one of them, because you will remember that it is your own style which will always be the most effective so far as *you* are concerned."

I think the reason that almost everybody agrees that Harry Vardon, Bobby Jones, and Miss Wethered are the world's greatest stylists, without doubt, is primarily because of their excellence as actual champions, but also because of their accuracy and beautiful swings.

You must not think I am not an admirer of the great stylists, but I wish to impress upon you the importance of an effective swing rather than a stylish one. Style is necessary because a player who looks ungainly when making his stroke is very frequently wrong in his methods, while most frequently the golfer with a good style is the better player. For instance, there are many players with a bad style caused by a curtailed follow-through. They do not time the ball properly, and they hit the ball too soon. This is just one of many instances of a bad style resulting in a bad shot.

I found that the club most always move in a circle making ane angle of 45 degrees with the horizon. I found that in bringing down the club ye most turn your body as farr about towards the left following the swinge of the club as it had been turned before towards the right hand.

Thomas Kincaid, *Diary of an Edinburgh Medical Student* (1687)

Having raised the point about the follow-through in connection with style, I must answer again the question, "How far must I follow through?" The query itself is really a little stupid, because if you hit the ball at the right moment, that is at the proper part of your swing, you cannot check the club, and it will go on its way without any effort. You see, therefore, that a stylish follow-through simply means that you play the shot correctly.

On the other hand, I have seen players who insist upon allowing the club to fall to a horizontal position at the top of their swing solely because it looks nice. If you discover that your wrists will not bend sideways sufficiently far to permit of the club going back to the horizontal position, please do not try to make them in your efforts to obtain a stylish pose. Hold on to the club. Never mind about appearance, for if you lose your grip you may have cause to remember what I said in an earlier chapter about "piccolo players." Do not think it necessary for a club to travel a complete circle to give the best results.

When you are trying to imitate a great golfer whom you admire, you must realize that your physique may not permit you to adopt precisely the same style, for your hero may be built on very different lines from yourself. You cannot all imitate Bobby Jones. He is extremely strong, heavily built, in spite of his inches, and very supple. Unless you are similarly equipped you cannot expect to succeed merely because you slavishly follow his style. Imitate someone of similar build to yourself. If you are tall and thin choose your model from the tall golfer and imitate him. I have seen people of this build trying the opposite in using a close stance because they thought it looked well or perhaps because their favorite golfer plays like that.

But it would be foolish of me to advise who you should imitate. . . . I like the style of [certain] players . . . for their elegance and their results. But I admire the effective crispness of Abe Mitchell's style [as well], the simplicity of Charles Whitcombe's, the forcefulness of Archie Compston's, the deliberation of Ed Dudley's, the obviously studied style of Leo Diegel, the rhythmic swing of Johnny Farrell, Horton Smith's short, controlled, backswing, and Walter Hagen's poise and adaptability. If you can take something from the methods of each of these and build your own personality into them, you will have a style which for you is perfect.

From *Golf*, by T. Henry Cotton. Eyre & Spottiswoode Publishers, Ltd. London, England.

NO PEEKING

When pressed, most modern gurus will admit there aren't that many new ideas about how to groove a swing. In a 1990 article for *Golf Digest*, Jim Flick advised golfers to hit balls with their eyes closed, and was pictured scorching a shot with a wood while wearing a blindfold. Similarly, Chick Evans, the first man to win a U.S. Amateur and U.S. Open in the same year (1916), recommended hitting golf balls in "pitch darkness" in his 1921 tome *Chick Evans' Golf Book*—which he dedicated to his mother. He said he got the idea from four-time U.S. Open winner Willie Anderson (1901; 1903–05), who practiced hitting 200-yard drives blindfolded. ꝏ

Swinging the Clubhead

1934 ✎ VIRGINIA VAN WIE

Sickly as a child, Virginia Van Wie heeded her doctor's suggestion to take up golf for exercise and fresh air. It was a splendid prescription because by the time she was a healthy teenager, her game was drawing the attention of sportswriters—one called her swing "perfection"—and competitors like Glenna Collett Vare. But under pressure, Van Wie often buckled, and she labored in golf's wilderness—famously thumped by Vare in her first U.S. Women's Amateur Championship final—until she met the charismatic teacher Ernest Jones. Surrendering to his feel-good swing theories and chant of "Swing the clubhead!" Van Wie came back the following year (1932) and defeated Vare. With Jones's help, she learned to erase the competing swing thoughts that raged in her head—what modern golfers call "paralysis by analysis." Once she learned to play by "feel," the fundamentals she'd once agonized over fell into place.

Golf is so simple it is difficult. That may be a strange statement, but I believe a true one. When Mr. Ernest Jones tied a jackknife in a corner of a large handkerchief and proved to me what swinging actually meant, what a real swing felt like, I proceeded to forget a multitude of so-called fundamentals and worked solely on one thing—to learn to swing the clubhead with my hands and let the rest of my anatomy follow the swing.

From that day on, not only did my golf improve to the extent that I was able to win the National Championship, but I learned that the game could be a joy and a pleasure, instead of a mild form of torture, and an aggravation to a none too docile temper.

For years, every time I missed a shot, I would immediately take inventory of my well-memorized list of fundamentals; had my elbows been in the proper position at the top of the swing; were my wrists cocked at some point; had my head remained stationary while the rest of my body turned, or hadn't I pivoted enough; was my weight distributed correctly? Possibly I had just turned my body too fast during the downswing. I would try next time to remember all of these things, and perhaps, if I didn't die from brain fever, my next shot would be a good one.

You can imagine what a pleasure it was to learn that all of this was as unnecessary as it was impossible. I do not mean to say I promptly knew what swinging meant, not at all. I had as much difficulty as anyone making that jackknife in the handkerchief travel in an arc instead of figure eights. But once I could swing it, the sensation was such a delightful one I could hardly wait to get my club in my hands to swing it the same way. So much concentration was necessary to feel the clubhead swing as I had felt the knife swinging that I had no time to remember any list of fundamentals.

Besides, this was fun. I was getting a sense of controlling that clubhead which was an entirely new experience. There is no sensation in golf quite so delightful as feeling the clubhead swing. I have had days when I did swing it and consequently played very well, but I was not conscious of what I was doing, the result being, that the next day my shots might go wild, and I did not know quite how to straighten them.

If a slice had crept up on me, I could stop it by applying a little trick which, in a short while, would develop a hook and then I would be no better off than I was before, because I discovered that just as many trees, traps, and other hazards were waiting to catch hooks as slices.

Any trick in golf can be exaggerated, and though it might cure a fault at first, when this happens it becomes a fault in itself. Tricks are very tempting because they are quick cures, and at first give the impression that you have solved your problem, but I have served my time trying them. There is no trick to swinging. It is definite action and not too quickly understood and acquired. But anything that can add yardage and accuracy to my golf shots, and give me such a sense of control is well worth the time I have spent learning it.

The most amazing, as well as amusing, thing about it to me is this: Since I have made a practice of forgetting fundamentals and tried only to learn to swing, professionals and good golfers have repeatedly told me how apparent these very fundamentals now are in my swing. This, above all else, has proven

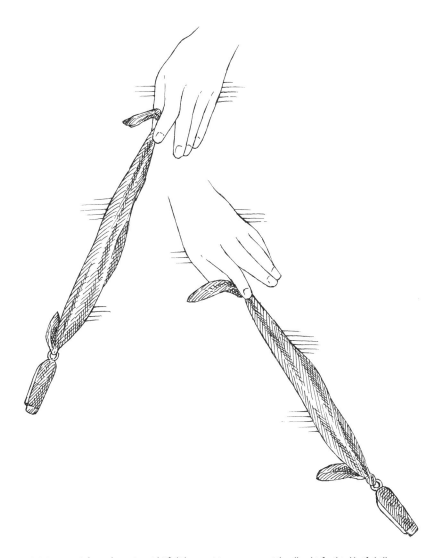

Virginia Van Wie learned to swing with "feel" by practicing Ernest Jones's handkerchief and jackknife drill.

to me that the fundamentals of a golf swing, which are taught the world over, are undoubtedly correct, providing you forget them, learn to swing, and just allow them to happen.

All of this applies to my everyday golf, and has meant a great deal to me, but the result it has had upon my tournament golf is no less important. Tournament golf is far more difficult where the psychology of it plays a large part. One is under a terrific mental strain, and a week of such strain pulls one down physically. When my mind was encumbered with many fundamentals, I found myself under a great tension. One of some twenty things might cause a shot to be missed, and the natural tendency is to try and guard against them. No brain is capable of concentrating on more than one thing at a time, so when I discovered that swinging the clubhead was the one fundamental to concentrate on in order to possess the others, a large portion of the mental disturbance was eliminated.

The first tournament I entered after adopting this method, I won. It was the first time in my life I had been able to win a 36-hole final. A weak back has been a handicap to me for years, and when I would tighten my muscles in an effort to keep my head still, my left arm straight, etc., the strain upon my back was too much. I would tire quickly and could not last 36 holes. By trying only to swing and allowing my body to follow that motion as it naturally will, if not forced to do otherwise, this strain ceased and I discovered that 36 holes were not that difficult. I also discovered that I could practice three times as long without tiring.

The mental advantages proved just as great. Anyone who rode to the Wentworth Club with the American team on their way to the International Team Matches against Great Britain would never say that a top-class golfer has no nerves. . . . There is no nervous strain in golf equal to playing an International Match. A true champion, however, regardless of whether her nervousness is apparent or otherwise, plays better golf under a strain. It rather keys one up for the battle. . . .

In the singles played that afternoon, I was paired against Miss Wanda Morgan, and I found myself three down at the end of nine holes, and two down going into thirteen. Here was a splendid opportunity to see if concentrating upon swinging alone would prove . . . sufficient. . . . By putting all my efforts at concentration on one thing, I discovered I stood a far better chance of succeeding in it. It worked, and I won two and one.

This last national championship in which I played the final against Miss [Helen] Hicks was another test. I [was] four down on the fifteenth green with a ten-foot putt to sink to keep from being five down. . . . That putt dropped fortunately and we ended the first eighteen holes with myself still two holes behind. I still refused to concentrate on anything but swinging the clubhead, and with my share of good fortune managed to win the championship.

When any method proves itself so successful under two such circumstances . . . I am not inclined to cast it aside lightly. I shall never again try to do anything but swing the clubhead.

From *The American Golfer* (April 1934), by Virginia Van Wie.

In any full swing, correctly performed,
the trunk will begin to unwind
while the hands and the club are still going back.
As the down-stroke begins, one should have
the feeling of leaving the club at the top.

BOBBY JONES

The Matter of Control

1935 ✦ ROBERT TYRE (BOBBY) JONES, JR.

By most accounts, Bobby Jones had the sweetest, most consistent swing of any golfer past or present. Yet he admitted that even he didn't always have control of his swing, and wasn't always sure how it worked when he made a good shot. But Jones certainly had all the tools needed to analyze his mechanics and those of others—an engineering degree from Georgia Tech to assess the components and structure, a literature degree from Harvard to articulate his findings, and a law degree from Emory to argue his case. So it was only appropriate that in this essay and others, Jones waded into the debate over whether the swing is controlled by the hands or the body, the most significant discussion in the evolving field of golf instruction. In contemporary lingo, it's "small muscle" theory versus "big muscle" theory, and the disagreement continues to this day.

◆

The average golfer of twenty years ago had to take a lot of punishment. If he happened to be seriously concerned with his progress in the game, and made any special effort to keep informed of the latest theories of the leading players and writers, he might reasonably have come to believe almost anything. The idea of throwing the clubhead from the top of the swing was only the most absurd of the conceptions prevalent among players who had never seen their swings in slow motion.

Today there is very little excuse left for argument about what actually happens during any particular swing. And because so many of these swings have been found to include similar movements, we are justified in asserting that the fundamentals of a correct swing have been established. But the battle has only been transferred to another sector. The question now is one of control. Upon what does one direct one's thought in order best to cause one's muscles to accomplish a correct swing?

In brief, the contest is one of hand action against what we call body action. One side of the argument is that if the hands swing freely and are used correctly all else will follow; that if one swings the club with the hands the winding and unwinding of the body will take care of itself. The other side is that the action of the swing should originate in the center of the body, initiated by the muscles in the waist and back, that it is in this way that the average golfer will have the best chance of building up a sound and complete method.

Upon each side there is eminent authority of both players and instructors. A perfectly reasonable difference of opinion exists upon a question which is wide open to argument. The only unfortunate aspect has been supplied by certain extravagant and patently thoughtless statements to the effect that hand action or hip action accounted for 70 percent or 80 percent of the golf swing. Such statements have confused the real issue, and made it appear one of mechanics when it is not so at all. Whether a person may learn more rapidly in one way or the other to accomplish a swing that is correct according to standards accepted by both sides depends in great measure upon the pupil.

There is no conceivable way in which the relative importance of two functions, both essential parts of a correct swing, can be evaluated. For purpose of study we sometimes find it to advantage to consider the hands or the hips alone, but even then, in any discussion, it is always assumed that the action of either must always be in proper relation to the movement of the other parts of the body. Obviously if the rest of the body is held immovable, the hands and arms, in order to bring the club against the ball, must do something different from the performance which would be correct when supplementing an ample body turn.

Gene Sarazen is one of those who place great emphasis on the hands. Gene has made the statement that the grip is the most important thing in the golf swing. That it is a first essential without which a correct swing is utterly impossible there can be no doubt. Until the hands are placed on the club in something like correct positions there is no need to go on.

But when one begins to talk of hands and body in the swing one runs up against something like this. In describing the familiar swing which hits up at the ball by means of an awkward lift of the body, it can be said correctly that the faulty body movement was induced by incorrect hand action. In other words the shoveling action of the shoulders was made necessary because the hands straightened out too soon and put the swing so out of gear that the body chose the only means of completing the stroke. But it could have happened just as well that the hips by refusing to lead the unwinding from the top of the swing had made it necessary for the hands and arms themselves to begin the movement.

Sarazen, of course, recognizes the question as one of where to apply the control. Apparently he believes in following his hands, for he says that he starts his backswing with them. Even though to make a similar effort would destroy my swing, as long as Gene accomplishes a sound swing in this way I agree that he applies control in the best way for him.

One cannot say that the average golfer is deficient in either hand action or body action. He is deficient in both, or he would not be an average golfer. But in most cases his hands are at least active. The player tries to use them and it seems to me would be likely to succeed fairly well if his body movement gave him a chance.

On the other hand one finds any number of players who are so tied up that they cannot make use of their hips and legs. Having started the swing by picking the club up with the hands, no suggestion is ever received that an important source of power is being neglected. Only among really expert players does one find even an apparent attempt to assure an ample use of the muscles in the waist and back.

It is for this reason that I prefer a control that will start the hips to moving. The power available from a full windup of the hips is the cheapest power in terms of effort that a golfer may come by. As Abe Mitchell puts it, a good golfer plays a lot of golf "beneath himself," that is, with his hips and legs. The average golfer can afford to run no risk of leaving these important members on the sidelines.

From *The American Golfer* (September 1935), by Robert Tyre (Bobby) Jones, Jr.

FEET TOGETHER NOW

Bobby Jones is generally credited with creating perhaps the most commonly taught drill to this day for enhancing a golfer's ball-striking ability. Jones hit hundreds of practice shots with his feet close together to instill the proper feeling for timing, balance, and proper swing path. If the golfer tries to swing too hard, he or she will not be able to stay poised and will, literally, fall over. According to more modern pros, the drill also teaches connection, forcing the golfer to match his upper torso to his arms and shoulders in the swing. ⚭

The Swing Technique

1946 · ERNEST JONES

Before becoming the most famous instructor of his time, Ernest Jones was forced to rethink his own swing after losing part of his right leg during World War I. He came up with the mantra he'd preach for forty years and that would be the title of his 1952 book *Swing the Clubhead*. Armed with his trademark props—a pocketknife and a handkerchief—the English expatriate lectured at five dollars a pop to professional champions and seemingly hopeless amateurs in a loft space in Manhattan. Jones popularized the idea of the swing as a pendulum-like action while readily dismissing those who would emphasize body and brawn over *feel*. In this excerpt from his popular first book, Jones insisted that if the hands and fingers lead the club, the body (and mind) naturally will follow—a swing philosophy that still inspires prominent instructors such as Manuel de la Torre, Bob Toski, and Jim Flick.

———

One of my duties as a professional was to teach others to play. From my first effort, I realized that I had not the slightest idea of how to go about it. . . . I read books by the leading professionals, and many others besides, but I am frank to confess that, with a single exception, these, instead of helping me, merely added to my confusion, because of their many contradictions.

There was among these a volume, *The Art of Golf* by Sir Walter Simpson, published in 1887, which proved very helpful because it set me to thinking along a line entirely different from anything I had encountered up to this time. It pointed out, among other things, that in golf "there is one categorical imperative, 'Hit the Ball,' but there are no minor absolutes."

[But] I think "Swing the Clubhead" is preferable to "Hit the Ball" because there are more ways than one of hitting it. . . . And I claim nothing new or revolutionary in "Swing the Clubhead," because the identical term "swing" is used to designate the player's effort to wield the club, whether it bears any resemblance to a real swing or not. Yet I am convinced that very few players indeed can explain satisfactorily just what is meant by swinging the clubhead, and further that few high-handicap players really swing in making a stroke. . . .

The longer I teach golf, the more I realize how very little the average golfer understands by what he or she refers to as "my swing." The term, of course, relates to the action of moving a golf club in striking the ball. But just what is implied in referring to the action as a swing is to most golfers a field wholly unexplored.

. . . [L]earning to swing the clubhead is the one essential to laying the foundation on which is built all permanent, consistent development of skill in playing this ancient game . . . [and] there is only one thing that you are allowed to use in hitting the ball—the clubhead. To hit the ball effectively with the clubhead, you must move the clubhead, in a manner which will develop the greatest force in striking the ball. The greatest force you can develop with a given amount of power is centrifugal in nature, that is, it is achieved by swinging. There is no need to enter here into a study of physics to establish that fact. [Even] in the time of David and Goliath men realized the value of using a swinging action to develop maximum force.

Further, there is only one medium through which you can transmit to the clubhead the power which you possess. That medium is your hands. . . . Various parts of your anatomy function in the action of playing a golf stroke, but what the rest of the body does is wholly responsive to the initiating action of swinging the clubhead through the use of the hands and fingers. . . .

[T]he good golfer has a feel of what he is doing with the clubhead. He does not see the successive movements that different parts of his anatomy execute through the stroke. Moreover, he never learned to play well through thinking or giving conscious consideration to the working of these different parts, other than to learn how to hold the club properly and how to stand correctly to the ball.

Let me begin by calling attention to the fact that swinging is a definite action in itself, and subject to its own peculiar laws. It is entirely free of, and distinct from, leverage. Swinging and levering are diametrically opposed methods of applying power. In a swing the connection medium between power and the object swung has both ends moving in the same direction; in levering, the two ends of the medium move always in opposite directions. It is no more possible to join up the two in one unified application of power than it is to mix oil and water. . . .

Moving a weight back and forth on the end of a string . . . is possibly the simplest demonstration of a swinging action. A pocketknife attached to the corner of a handkerchief serves the same purpose. Since the handkerchief is flexible, it cannot transmit power through leverage. . . . [W]hen the knife is swung through approximately half a circle . . . the handkerchief is drawn taut, because a swinging action is always an expanding action, with the weight exerting an outward pull . . . and this condition will prevail whether the swing be short or long.

[Now, if I swing] a club along with the handkerchief, executing a swing through approximately half

a circle . . . the handkerchief in its movement serves as a check on whether there is an actual swing of the clubhead. If I push or pull on the shaft of the club, it may still be moved through a similar arc, but the movement of the knife and the handkerchief will not coincide. Leverage, replacing swinging, may produce a result that appears to the eye as being quite similar, because the shaft of the club is stiff and therefore a suitable medium for levering. But you cannot apply leverage through a highly flexible medium, such as a string or handkerchief.

I should like to emphasize again the fact that feel of the action, and not seeing it, is the necessary essential to its correct understanding. . . . It requires something of an experienced eye to detect at once the difference between a true swinging movement, in moving the head of a golf club through the arc [described], and the result that may be attained in a movement brought about through levering. The casual observer may be unable to detect any difference. But the check afforded by moving the club and the string with a weight on the end together is complete and convincing. Furthermore, continued experimentation with this test will finally enable the player to distinguish between the two methods, not only by the sense of sight but by the vastly more important method, so far as learning golf is concerned—that of feeling the difference.

The action [described] is, of course, that of a pendulum. Its fundamental and distinguishing characteristic is the same whether the pendulum is swung through a small arc or a large one. The maximum arc is a complete circle, assuming that the power is applied at a fixed center. The golf stroke actually is not a circle, because the center of the stroke, which is the center of gravity of the body, is not fixed throughout. . . .

"Yes," says one, "all that you have said may be true, and I understand when you say 'Swing the clubhead,' but I still do not understand exactly what you mean by 'swinging.' It is clear enough that, when you whirl a weight on the end of a string, you are swinging it, but I don't see just how this kind of swing can be made to coincide with a movement that has to change direction." . . .

However, a little reflection will reveal that the same agency which enables a person, swinging a weight on the end of a string through less than half a circle, to expand the arc conveniently to a complete circle without physical hindrance also makes possible the change in direction in the path traveled by the clubhead, without interference with the characteristic quality of swinging. This agency is the flexible wrists, or more properly, the unified action of the two wrists.

The wrists supply a factor in swinging a golf club that is impossible in a purely mechanical device, for, whereas the arms are in part stiff and rigid, they are also in part flexible. This flexibility in the wrists makes it possible for the golfer both to extend the arc of the swing and to bring about a change in direction without disturbing the rhythmic action characteristic of swinging. A sense of feel of what is being done with the clubhead takes care of this . . . [And] the sensation, felt in the hands, of what is being done with the clubhead, is the guide by which conscious effort should be directed. All other physical actions on the part of the body should follow as responsive movement. . . .

The distinction I have drawn between the mechanics of swinging and levering will, I hope, help clarify [the golfer's] understanding of just what is meant by swinging. But he must go further than that. He must learn to know a swing by its feel, and no one can exercise his sense of touch or feel for him.

The Force-Center

1 9 4 6   P E R C Y   B O O M E R

Like his father, Percy Boomer was a village schoolmaster who golfed as a hobby. But after winning three European championships in the 1920s and having his dad's former students Harry Vardon and Ted Ray seek his counsel, Boomer decided it was time for a career change. For the next thirty years, mostly in France, Boomer taught golf royalty, true royalty, and commoner alike. His only book, *On Learning Golf* (for which the Duke of Windsor wrote the foreword), remains in print and is considered a classic. Modern golfers will recognize a number of phrases in this excerpt—such as "muscle memory" and "connection" in the swing—which Boomer either coined or popularized. But perhaps his most significant contribution was providing the historic link from the Ernest Jones school to the more modern "big muscle" theorists, by arguing that the clubhead shouldn't swing the body, the body should swing the clubhead.

I think that few experienced golfers will disagree with the dictum of that great teacher Ernest Jones that our strivings to attain a good swing will have been largely in vain unless at the end we have learned "to feel our clubhead."

Now this is a difficult thing to feel and an exceedingly difficult thing to teach a pupil to feel, though I have often succeeded in teaching it. The real difficulty is that you cannot teach it by teaching skill in the physical movements of the swing—yet this physical skill is a basic necessity before the feel can be induced. So we have to build up the swing and then seek for "the feel of the clubhead" somewhere in its cycle.

. . . Incidentally, I should hate to tell you how long I had played golf before I did really feel that the club had a head to it! . . . In some great players this feel is so pronounced that you can actually see them seeking it and using it. Walter Hagen approaching and on a tee was a lovely example of this and so today is Henry Cotton—no other modern player gives so strong an impression of the clubhead feel as does Cotton in his drive. . . .

Now after years of study of this matter of clubhead feel, I came to a very conscious conclusion about it, and it was this conclusion which enabled me to be quite exceptionally successful in imparting clubhead feel to my pupils. Here it is: We do not feel our clubhead with out hands; we feel it with our bodies.

What I mean is that, though the hands, being the "railhead" of our feel, do of course play an important part, yet the feel does not stay in them—the hands (and arms of course, though less consciously) *transmit this feel to the body* to the central organization of our golf mechanism. And arising from this the most common mistake we make in trying to feel the clubhead is to look for the feeling of it in our hands instead of at the center.

This matter of feel at the center is so important that I have coined a name for its seat, for where it is felt. I call it the "force-center." I cannot give you an exact anatomical definition of where the force-center *is*, because its position varies with different shots. As the shot (and the swing) become *longer*, so the force-center rises; as they become shorter, the position of the force-center drops. Yet there is always the feeling that we swing from a center, wherever that center may be. And where it is, there also must be the feel of the clubhead.

. . . This is obviously a difficult feel to fix, and the best way I have found is by making the pupil stand in [an] imaginary barrel. . . . Swinging in this barrel gives him the feeling of keeping his hips up; at the same time he must now *stretch down* (even when his hands are up chest high). Because the body is braced, there will no longer by any tendency for the knees to sag in towards one another; they will roll round at a constant height as he pivots and this is a very essential feel in the backswing. . . .

The good swing is based on a pivot with the minimum of to-and-fro movement. Both hips and shoulders are held up and braced, and they move in the same circular path—except that the turn of the body slightly inclines the shoulders as they go round. Now if you stand before an imaginary ball, holding an imaginary club, with your arms stretched down but held lightly (with little tension, I mean) as if you were ready to play a shot, and then turn first right and then left, rather briskly and getting the movement from the knees, calves, and feet, you will begin to feel the pull on your arms from the force-center. *The power is largely produced by the feet and legs, but it is the force-center (somewhere in the pit of the back) which collects it and is responsible for its transfer to the arms and then out to the clubhead.*

Now take a mashie and do very short swings to and fro with it. Soon you will begin to detect the *center* which you will feel controls both the setting up of power and the guiding of the club. Do not break the wrists or lift the clubhead during this experiment. The hands do nothing but keep the club straight out in front of you; let the arms feel supple and yet pushed down as the clubhead is down, while all the time you are moving to and fro from the legs. You begin to feel connected right through, from legs to center and from center to clubhead. Though you make this experiment first with a mashie (that being an easy club to feel), the full drive is simply a big edition of the same movement and must be just as connected.

What I think you will find different in this braced pivot movement as compared with an uncontrolled swing is this: As your hips turn without sag, you will feel you are getting more power and getting it in a different way. You develop rotary power, largely from the legs. This is what I want you to feel, because, when you feel it, you may know that you have got your nether regions well fixed in space. . . .

So I have told you how to build up a force-center, and that when you have built it up, you should be able to feel the clubhead in it. You will be able to do this only if there is no break in the connections between the clubhead and the force-center, but one of these connections—the arms—is the most liable to disconnection of any in the whole swing.

At first glance this would seem easy enough to control, because the arms should work in exact relation to the shoulders and chest. The thorax and biceps should become one in movement. But things do not work out this way, because we do inherently—and in spite of ourselves—consider golf as being played with the arms. So we *use* our arms, ever so little it may be, but enough to make us disconnected. Now this is a fine and most delicate point in which lies most of the difference between a good, a very good, and a superlative golfer. It is by the management of the arms that championships are won and lost.

For it is no use to have built up perfect connections to bring coordination to the whole body throughout the whole swing if we then *break* the connection at a vital point by allowing our arms to work independently of our chest and shoulders. They must be not independent but reactive. The body in the swing must be a unity. . . .

I must remind you again, because it is fundamental to this book, that *learning by a sense of feel* is something quite different to learning by the intellect. Intellectual memory may be of use in learning golf, but it is never paramount. What is paramount is what I have called muscular memory, a memory for the right *feeling* of a movement which enables the muscles to repeat that movement time after time, without directions from brain or will.

From *On Learning Golf*, by Percy Boomer. Copyright © 1942, 1946 by Percy Boomer. Used by permission of Alfred A. Knopf, a division of Random House, Inc.

Playing the Drive

1953 LOUISE SUGGS

Louise Suggs learned golf from her father at the age of ten and six years later was the Georgia Amateur champion. After an outstanding amateur career, she turned pro and promptly won the 1949 U.S. Women's Open by a record fourteen strokes. She described her immediate rivalry with fellow LPGA charter members, Babe Didrikson Zaharias and Patty Berg, as "cats fight[ing] over a plate of fish." She'd eventually win fifty-eight titles, including eleven majors, writing *Golf for Women* soon after capturing her second Open. Ben Hogan, usually terse and cool, raved about Louise Suggs's "beautiful" swing in his introduction, recommending it as *the* "model" for women golfers. Explaining the swing that allowed her to "knock the cover off the ball," Suggs offered advice that is as seamless, precise, and powerful as her technique. There was good reason Bob Hope called her "Miss Sluggs."

The drive, more than any other shot in golf, is the one that seems to invite everyone to "knock the cover" off the ball. The objective *should* be to get good, average distance that is within one's own physical capabilities, while striving for accuracy. The longest hitters off the tee are not necessarily the best scorers, particularly when they are "powering the ball" to the extent that they are wild in their direction. . . .

START OF THE BACKSWING

I have a mannerism with my hands and wrists just before the start of the backswing that is designed to break tension and pave the way for a smooth-flowing, rhythmic backswing. What I do is carry my hands forward in unison just an inch or two while the clubhead remains stationary. My right knee flexes slightly at the same time. The return of my hands and knees to their original position at the address of the ball develops in a continuous motion into the backswing. This "forward press," as it is known, is essential to avoid the jerking motion that is apt to result from a cold, rigid start on the backswing.

[At the start of] my backswing, [t]he clubface is still square to the ball and is being pushed back in a low trajectory. My weight is just beginning to go over from my left to my right foot. . . . [T]he clubhead has not been "picked up" by my right hand, for my left arm and the shaft still form a straight line. My hands are working together, but I have the feeling that my left hand is *pushing* the club back away from the ball. My right hand is just "riding" at this point.

Every part of my body is working as a unit. . . . [T]he left knee is beginning to flex to accommodate the turn of the hips and the shoulders which starts at this point. My right leg is bracing (not becoming rigid) so that it can bear the weight of my body as the transfer to the right side takes place. This transfer continues during the backswing.

At [the] point in the backswing [when the club is just past parallel to the ground] the wrists are just beginning to "cock." This is not a conscious effort. It is caused by the upward pull resulting from the momentum of the clubhead. At this point, as well as all others in the backswing, the motion is a rhythmic, graceful one. During the course of the backswing there should be no thought of how you are

Louise Suggs's "model" takeaway.   *Halfway back: toe pointing at the sky.*

going to "murder" the ball when you finally get back to it. The best insurance for a well-hit ball is a backswing that puts you in position to have full control of the downswing and thus insure maximum hitting efficiency.

The turn of my hips and shoulders continues, as does the transfer of weight from my left to right side. While my head is turning with the shoulders as it must to avoid rigidity and tenseness, it remains in its original position and my eyes are fixed on the spot on the ball I expect to hit.

My left arm remains straight and firm, but not tense. My right arm is breaking at the elbow, but remaining comparatively close to my body.

[Near the top of the backswing] my weight is pronouncedly over on my right side, and the inside of my left foot is now carrying what weight remains on my left side, and my left knee continues to give with the turn of my hips and shoulders. My head is still turning, but remains in its original position and my eyes are fixed on the ball. . . .

TOP OF THE BACKSWING

[When I arrive] at the top of my backswing . . . I have set the pattern for my downswing into the ball. It is the opinion of every golf authority that if the backswing is properly executed, it is virtually impossible to hit the ball poorly. About the only thing that could cause you to do so, if you have gotten to the top of your backswing correctly, is for your footing to give way.

Remember this: the ills that throw a golf swing out of kilter develop in the course of the backswing. It is virtually impossible to cure them by remedies in the downswing. If the backswing is faulty, it is impossible to hit the ball consistently straight and far. Any good results obtained under these circumstances are purely accidental.

My back is now turned toward my objective. The turn of my shoulders has pulled my head seemingly out of position. Such is not the case. It has had to turn on its own axis with the turning of my shoulders, but out of the corner of my left eye, I can still see the point on the ball at which I am aiming.

Many golfers have entirely the wrong notion of what the head is supposed to do. They have been warned: "Keep your head down." "Keep your eye on

An elegant weight shift to the right.

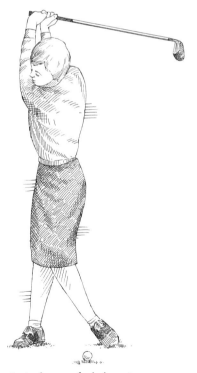

Setting the pattern for the downswing.

The power angle.

The moment of truth.

the ball." "Don't move your head." This leads them to keep it in a fixed position which is completely unnatural. It is humanly impossible to [complete your shoulder turn], and still keep your face pointed straight down at the ground. In doing this, you would disastrously restrict the backswing. However, your eyes should still be on the ball.

It is TRUE that you must *not* MOVE the head. It is UNTRUE you must not TURN it. It helps you to understand the head in relation to the rest of the golf swing if you think of it as the hub around which revolve the spokes (which are in this case the arms). If the clubhead is to travel in the desired trajectory the head must not deviate from its original relationship to the ball. . . .

[M]y left arm remains straight and firm. This is an important factor in keeping the clubhead in the desired downward trajectory, and in bringing it into the ball SQUARELY. If the left arm bends or collapses, the clubhead automatically deviates from its intended course. When this happens a missed or badly-hit shot is sure to result.

[M]y hands are [also] still firmly on the clubshaft . . . and in full control of the club . . . [with] my right hand . . . under the shaft. In this position the hands are set to deliver the clubhead into the ball with the greatest possible efficiency.

The transfer of my weight to the right foot is now complete. . . . My left foot serves merely as a balancing point at this stage. I am well balanced and ready for the downswing.

START OF THE DOWNSWING

At the start of the downswing my sensation is that of *pulling* the clubhead with my *left hand* back to the ball in the same arc as that described by the clubhead during the backswing. The position of my hands and wrist in relation to my arms is practically the same as it was at the top of my backswing.

THE DOWNSWING

The transfer of weight from my right side to left side starts at the same moment my arms and hands begin their downward course . . . [and] my body has already

The ideal finish, with poise and balance.

followed the turn of my shoulders back into approximately the same position as at the address. My left leg has become the foundation of my left side which is firm as it must be to permit me to lash at the ball with full power and still remain completely in balance. [Finally] my right elbow is hugging my right side, without being restricted by it.

IMPACT WITH THE BALL

[At impact,] I have the feeling that I have "slapped" the ball off the tee with the back of my left hand . . . [while] the palm of my right hand is facing my objective. This is always evidence that the clubhead has met the ball squarely—that is if you have taken the proper grip and stance at the outset.

My clubhead . . . follows the flight of the ball, but will soon start to turn upward and inside the line of flight. My weight has transferred well over on to my left foot. Because I have not tried to slug at the ball or "kill" it I am in good balance.

After contact with the ball the essential points to note are:

→ [M]y head turns to follow the flight of the ball. This is caused by the natural pull of the shoulders as they rotate to a full finish.

→ My hands [finish] well up, slightly above the top of my head. This is a normal consequence of a correct swing, and shouldn't be forced. There is no tendency to lose control of the club, even at this point.

→ My weight is now completely over on my left foot, but there has been no tendency to fall away from the ball and I am still well balanced.

[At the finish of the swing] my shoulders and hips have completed a full turn from their positions at the top of the backswing. Because my head has followed the turn of my shoulders, as it must to avoid tension and a conflict in muscular function, my eyes are now directed toward my objective.

[An imaginary] straight line [could be drawn] running from my left ankle to my right shoulder, indicating that I am still well-balanced. Even though the finish has been full, my hands are still in control of the club.

completed much of the uncoiling process. However, let me precaution you against making a conscious effort to rush the turning of the hips. This should be part of a coordinated motion in which the hands, wrists, arms, shoulders, hips, legs, and feet work together to get the clubhead back to the ball with the face square to the intended line of flight, and with a maximum of controlled velocity.

[At this stage of the downswing] my hands lead the clubhead. My wrists have not yet begun to start their "lash" at the ball, and my weight is almost evenly distributed between my right and left feet at this point. My left arm remains an accurate guide to the clubhead in describing its intended arc, because it is still straight.

[When the club is back to near parallel with the ground] my hands are in position to throw their full power behind the clubhead as it nears the "hitting area" which with me is approximately the final foot and a half before the impact of the clubhead with the ball.

My weight is now over on my left side . . . [and] my right heel is well off the ground. My head has now

Reprinted with the permission of Simon & Schuster Adult Publishing Group, from *Par Golf for Women,* by Louise Suggs. Copyright © 1953 by Prentice-Hall, Inc.

The Trouble with Women

1962 ❧ MICKEY WRIGHT
WITH JOAN FLYNN DREYSPOOL

Mickey Wright retired at the age of thirty-four with little left to accomplish in golf, after eighty-two wins and thirteen major championships. But it was the pressure of being Mickey Wright that led to the decision. While playing in thirty tournaments a year—sponsors often threatened to cancel if she didn't show—and promoting the women's game full-time as the LPGA president, the articulate but somewhat shy protégé of Louise Suggs finally had to step back. In this excerpt, the former Stanford psychology major talked about her admiration for the extroverted and hard-hitting Babe Zaharias. To Wright, Zaharias (like Suggs and Patty Berg) should have been the model for golfers on the Tour, not an exception. Other female players, often self-conscious about exhibiting "non-feminine" play, didn't hit the ball hard enough to leave their imprint—or divot—on the earth. Today's long-hitters like Laura Davies, Annika Sorenstam, and Michelle Wie, who play with controlled aggression, apparently got Wright's message.

———————

On the golf course, we women are definitely The Weaker Sex.

It's muscles, not mentality. From a standpoint of pure physical strength we cannot compete with men. The lady pros, pitted against the male pros, cannot overtake the 50-yard difference in a driver and two-club length difference in an iron shot.

Someone once explained it to me this way. A human muscle is like a rope of fibers that contract. A woman's muscle is a comparatively little rope, and a man's muscle is a bigger rope with stronger contractual power.

All humans have two kinds of muscles, the voluntary which execute movements prompted by the will and the involuntary which perform independently of will. We recruit the voluntary muscles for the golf swing. They have to work when we tell them to and if we don't put them to work, they'll just be there doing nothing.

To compensate for this lack of strength, a woman golfer should have no wasted motion in her swing so she can utilize all those voluntary muscles to their maximum efficiency.

Good women golfers do. This is why I believe a woman can learn more from a good woman golfer. I believe, too, that if a woman understands more the whys and wherefores of the basic mechanics of a swing she can capitalize on that knowledge.

Apart from our comparative lack of strength, I think too many women golfers possess an even greater weakness on the golf course. *Women don't hit the ball as hard as they can.*

Too many women are so concerned that they won't look graceful swinging hard at the ball that they end up with a most ungraceful powder puff caricature of a swing, looping, lunging, limp.

A psychiatrist and a golf addict, who liked to relate the two, cornered me once after a tournament to expound his theories, Freudian, of course.

"Do you know why women are afraid to take a divot?" he said to me so menacingly that if I were on a couch I would have slid down.

"Are they?" I said, completely intimidated.

"Are they!" he challenged. "I'll say they are! Women are afraid to take a divot because they don't want to damage the earth."

I'm no psychiatrist, but I am a golfer and a woman.

Dr. Freud isn't to blame, but the women are. Too many don't hit the ball hard enough to leave the imprint of their swing on the turf, let alone know when or why they should take a divot.

The late Mildred "Babe" Didrickson Zaharias was the strongest woman I ever knew. An Olympic star in javelin, hurdles, and high jump at the age of eighteen, she was also the greatest woman athlete of this or any century.

Golf was the Babe's greatest love and she succeeded in it despite the fact she didn't take it up until she was nineteen. Analytically, Babe's swing was not the best. She didn't transfer her weight properly to the right side, but she offset that by her magnificent power and coordination, her gentle touch around the greens, her putting prowess and her supreme confidence in her ability to perform. No shot was too tough for her to try. She was a great scrambler—and champion.

Babe hit the ball as hard as she could every time, with all that superb muscular power behind it. Not content with that, she practiced, practiced, practiced, especially on her short game and putting.

Even for her, there were no miracles in golf. She knew she couldn't wish herself into a good game. She worked at it and tried to understand how to get the most of each shot.

The Babe was something unto herself, as far as I was concerned. I could keep up with her and out-hit her, but the Babe was the Babe with her glorious history of sports. Today, I am consistently the longest hitter among the women pros. I average around 225 yards a drive, a most satisfying average for a woman. I had a drive once in a Texan tournament that went ten yards over the green on a 385-yard hole, but everything was in my favor; a 40-mile wind behind me, the Texas hardpan to assist me, split-second timing, maximum power and clubhead squareness in the hitting area.

But, I frequently say to myself, if hitting the ball long were the only secret of good golf, why don't I win every tournament?

I don't. I win often, more often than most, but it is my swing, plus my savvy, plus my strategy, plus my short game that puts me in the winner's circle. I can out-hit many men, much to their embarrassment, for suddenly they are pitting their masculinity against my femininity; their strength against mine. That's foolish. They aren't competing with my strength; they're competing with the efficiency of my swing.

Another Mickey, Mickey Mantle, and I have adopted Dallas, Texas, Big "D," as our hometown when we're not swinging elsewhere for a living. Mickey and I have played golf together two or three times. He's a good example of why a golf swing is important in hitting the ball.

When Mickey connects with a golf ball, he hits it a ton, but usually he doesn't hit the ball much longer than I do because he doesn't contact the ball solidly. He tends to slice it. He moves the club to the outside; has his right elbow in the wrong position at the top of the swing and has the clubhead coming outside in across the ball. He has a surprisingly good short game considering he doesn't have much time to work on it. He's a high 70 or low 80 shooter.

We have girls on our tour who win tournaments and don't average more than 200 yards on a drive but a 200-yard drive is a good average, especially if the ball is straight. . . .

Women worry too much about the wrong things in golf. Some of their golfing values are false. When I swing a club, I am not consciously aware of my hands or my hips or my head or how I look swinging, factors which give other women undue—and hampering—concern.

For instance, a woman doesn't have to swing a heavy club to get better results. Most women, especially beginners, should use lighter clubs with whippy shafts which have greater flexibility and are designed as a substitute for strength to facilitate feel of the clubhead and allow for more clubhead speed at the hit. I use a lightweight men's club . . . [with a stiff shaft] but I am a pro.

Women should rely upon their woods more, without fear of being criticized. We're after results and whatever club will put us where we want to be is the club to use.

A wood doesn't have to be swung as fast to loft a ball. A long iron, a 2 or 3, commands great expertness in the hit. There is the same loft on a 5-wood as there is on a 2-iron, but if a 5-wood is easier to hit, then hit it.

It's how we get there, not what we use to get there, that's important.

I've given hundreds of clinics for women and told them what I feel are the basic mechanics of the swing and demonstrated the swing itself. As always, when I wind up a clinic, I recommend to the gallery to consult their club pro, whenever possible. After one clinic, a woman came up to me and said, very pleased with herself, "Mickey, I do exactly what you say, only instead of going to one pro, I go to two."

"Why two?" I asked.

"I go to one pro for my woods and the other pro for my irons," the golfing enthusiast explained, as if to say, "Doesn't everybody?"

She didn't realize it, but she was making the game of golf twice as difficult for herself by not accepting the idea that a swing is a swing is a swing and that she should swing the same way with every club; that only the club itself and the position of the ball change.

This is absolute truth. The entire game of golf is built upon this principle.

What Not to Do

1975 ✏ HOLLIS ALPERT, IRA MOTHNER, AND HAROLD C. SCHONBERG

Many people have stated that golf seems to have more teachers than players. What's worse, most of them write instructional books and articles. Even worse, their editors are so intimidated by these famous personages that they leave their indecipherable manuscripts intact. Desperate readers, searching for the one bit of helpful instruction that will allow them to play at the local course without a disguise, either decide they are too stupid to understand the game's nuances or go out on the links with a new "understanding" that results, disappointingly, in eighteen double bogeys. In their hilarious book, annoyed film critic Hollis Alpert, journalist Ira Mothner, and music critic Harold C. Schonberg, who obviously had read too much, captured the hacker's frustration trying to interpret golf writers whose convoluted prose, hastily derived ideas, and recommended drills simply make no sense.

I t takes guts. It's like kicking cigarettes, booze, and chewing gum all at once. It is like forswearing peanut butter. It is like going off sex. But it has to be done.

Don't read instructions by pros or teaching pros. Or if you haven't got the manhood or determination to stop reading them, at least don't take them too seriously. If you do take them seriously, the result is like going to a quack shrink. You'll end up in knots.

It's madness. One pro says your right hand is too strong. The other looks you square in the eye and says it's too weak. One says you play the ball too far to the right. Another says you play it too far to the left. One says you're leading with the shoulders. Another says you're not leading enough with the shoulders. One says the club is over-controlled. The other says it's under-controlled. A guy can go crazy reading this stuff.

Fortunately for the Double Bogey Golfer, most of it is as undecipherable as Second Dynasty cuneiform. In the first place, you have to be an anatomist to understand it. In the second place, most anatomists themselves don't understand it. In the third place, those who claim they *do* understand it break a couple of blood vessels laughing over the mistakes. In the fourth place, once a Double Bogey Golfer starts getting himself twisted up with the various exegeses of the golf writers, he will suddenly find himself a triple bogey golfer or maybe even a quadruple bogey golfer. In the fifth place, it asks the Double Bogey Golfer to perform unnatural acts. In the sixth place, it fills the head with confetti. In the seventh place, it confuses him. In the eighth place, it just doesn't work.

Hard words, you say? Exaggerated, you say? Well—

In an issue of a certain popular magazine, a teaching pro tells you how to overcome the six most common faults of the golf player. The first fault is misaiming the clubface. The cure: "Draw a straight line to your target and another that intersects the first at right angles. Then practice hitting balls off the first line while aligning the leading edge of your clubface parallel with the second."

Fault No. 2: Playing the ball too far right in your stance. Cure: "Draw the intersecting lines in the turf as described in the previous cure. Place the ball at

the intersection of the lines and position your feet so the second line extends to the inner edge of your left heel. Be sure you do not allow your shoulders and thighs to turn open to the left as you place the clubhead to the ball in its new up-forward position."

Fault No. 3: Right side too high at address. Cure: "Cock your knees laterally toward the target . . . and place about 60 percent of your weight on the inside of your right foot. This tucks the right knee inward, . . ."

And so on, and so on. The cure for Fault No. 5 has an entrancing poetry of its own. Fault No. 5 is leaving the line too soon on takeaway. The cure: "Draw a line straight back from the ball. Then make another line back from 'four o'clock' on the ball. Swing the clubhead back for several inches along the first line, then return it along the second. . . ."

All this is undoubtedly great and good advice written by a great and good man. But its only real value, aside from contributing to the gaiety of the nations, is whatever the pro got paid for writing it. Let the Double Bogey Golfer try to put these nuggets of wisdom into effect. Just let him try. His head will be so full of lines, angles, weight shifts, and other impedimenta that by the time he gets up there he's going to *miss* the damn ball.

If, indeed, he can even begin to follow the directions. Ever try putting 60 percent of your weight on the inside of your right foot? I mean, are you *kidding*?

Or what is the Double Bogey Golfer to make of this kind of prose:

> When the right hand is dominant, the grip end of the club is dragged back at the start of the takeaway as the clubhead remains stationary and the left hand is put into a broken or submissive position. In effect a reverse single hinge is created. Harry Vardon and Bob Jones are examples of top players who used this method.
>
> Equal use of the right and left hands approaches the true "one-piece" theory in which any wrist hinging is inhibited until the player is well into his backswing. Byron Nelson was one of the top players utilizing this method.
>
> There are, according to Toski and Flick, basically three ways to set the angle: (1) a set and swing; (2) a swinging set, and (3) a swing

and a set. There are advantages and disadvantages to each, but the pendulum swings in favor of the first two because they get the angle set earlier, forcing the right hand to become more submissive and overpowering. . . .

Once you reach the top, your left side is still in control, your hips and legs must control the forearms and hands into and through the forward swing, maintaining the smooth body flow that helps retain the angle. The left knee works in a lateral rotation toward the left of the flight path. The right side stays soft and exerts no influence until the left side pulls it into position and centrifugal force brings it into play without any conscious help from you. Yeah.

The only parallel in the history of human thought to this kind of writing is the long section on the transcendental unity of appreciation in Kant's *Critique of Pure Reason*. In the original German, of course.

Forget all this. There is a much simpler way to understand the nature and dynamics of the golf swing. Simply, let x equal the right side; y equal the left side;

z, the left hand; t, the right hand; a, the right knee; and d, the left knee. The elements of the golf swing are then easily obtained by putting for space of four dimensions the equation for the spherical golf ball:

$$x^2 + y^2 + z^2 + t^2 = R^2 \ldots \ldots (1)$$

and for the distance ds between the points (x, y, z, t) and $[(x + dx)\ (y + dy)\ (z + dz)\ (t + dt)]$ the value

$$ds^2 = dx^2 + dy^2 + dz^2 + dt^2 \ldots \ldots (2)$$

It is easily found by means of the methods used for three dimensions that the shortest lines are given by equations of the form . . .

$$\left. \begin{array}{l} ax + by + cz + ft = 0 \\ \alpha x + \beta y + \gamma z + \phi t = 0 \end{array} \right\} \ldots \ldots (3)$$

in which a, b, c, f, as well as $\alpha, \beta, \gamma, \phi$, are constants . . .

Or, as Srinivasa Ramanujan so wittily put it:

if $\alpha\beta = \pi^2$, then

$$\alpha^{-\frac{1}{4}} \left(1 + 4\alpha \int_0^\infty \frac{xe^{-\alpha\chi^2}}{e^{2\pi\chi} - 1}\, dx \right) = \beta^{-\frac{1}{4}} \left(1 + 4\beta \int_0^\infty \frac{xe^{-\beta\chi^2}}{e^{2\pi\chi} - 1}\, dx \right)$$

GENERATE REAL PUNCH

In the 1959 book *Golf Magazine*'s *Pro Pointers and Stroke Savers*, three-time Masters winner Jimmy Demaret answered questions sent in by golfers with problems. A 20-handicapper asked the colorful Texan, who was as famous for his flamboyant attire as his thirty-one PGA titles, how he could use his wrists to get more distance on his shots. Demaret replied: "Forget about your wrists. 'Wrist-action' is strictly duffer talk." Demaret went on to explain that real power is generated from the ground up, through the legs and arms, and then transmitted to the clubhead by the hands. "This is the way a fighter generates punch," he added, "and it is the way a golfer should generate distance. I suggest you erase the thought of the 'wrist' from your mind and concentrate instead on using your hands." ꙮ

The Modern Swing: How It All Began

1976 ✒ BYRON NELSON
WITH LARRY DENNIS

Modest to a fault, Byron Nelson did not assess his considerable impact on the game until years after retirement. But as the record shows, the moniker *Lord* Byron is more than apt. In an era when most pros were still wielding hickory-shafted clubs, the young Nelson embraced the future, in the form of steel-shafted weapons, and redesigned his own swing to cope with the new technology. In doing so, he not only "invented" the modern swing, but also provided the prototype for a flurry of new theories about how the swing worked. Nelson completed the transition, started by Harry Vardon, from the flat swing of the St. Andrews school. He provided the bridge to the modern era by relying less on the hands and more on the body. In this excerpt—written with former *Golf Digest* associate editor Larry Dennis—Nelson describes the great leap forward.

———————

All I was trying to do was find a better way to swing so I could make a living at the game. I found a better way and, as a result, I've been credited by most experts with developing the modern way to play golf. But I sure wasn't thinking about that at the time.

I started playing golf in 1925, when I was 13 years old and a caddie at Glen Garden Country Club in Forth Worth, Texas. . . .

Back in those early days I had the typical old caddie swing. The hickory shafts I used then in my iron clubs had a lot of torque, or twist, in them. So you had to roll the clubface open on the backswing, then roll it closed coming through the shot. If you didn't, the force of your swing would leave the face open when you struck the ball. Naturally, you had to swing flatter, because you couldn't roll the clubface open and swing upright at the same time, the way we do today.

So the swing was loose and flat. "Turn in a barrel" we called it. There wasn't the foot and leg action you see today. The feet were kept pretty flat, and coming through we would hit against a straight left leg and side, kind of throwing the clubface into the ball to get it square again.

That swing worked pretty well with the irons. But all this time I was using steel-shafted woods and was hooking them something terrible. I never could figure out why. Then, about 1930, I got my first set of steel-shafted irons, and I began hooking with them as badly as I had with my woods.

I realized finally that the reason I was hooking was because the shaft didn't have as much torque, but my hands were still opening and closing as much as ever—pronating and supinating are the technical terms for this. I was rolling the steel-shafted club closed too quickly, and this was causing me to hook the ball.

When I discovered what was happening, I decided not to roll my hands so much. But I was still using that old caddie swing—low and around the shoulders. And I couldn't play as consistently. I'd play a 67 or 68, and all of a sudden I'd shoot 75 or 76 or 77. I didn't know where the clubhead was or what it was doing. I couldn't hit the ball as far, either, and I didn't like that at all.

Everybody else was in the same boat at the time, and nobody knew exactly what to do, but I kept on thinking. I decided that if I were going to take the club back without any pronation, then I'd have to start swinging more upright. So I began taking my hands back higher. But I was still using my feet and legs in the old way—which is to say not much at all—and that didn't work very well.

Then I decided I had to learn to take the club straight back. When I got to the top of the backswing, I felt as if I would just let it fall, with my feet and legs helping to carry it straight back through the ball and keeping it on line toward the target. This would eliminate the hook that was troubling me.

About that time I also developed the idea that I had to keep my head still, and with that discovery everything began to fall into place. Keep my head still . . . take the club right straight back through the ball . . . keep my feet and legs very active, leading the club and helping me carry it through the hitting area . . . keep the legs going straight through toward the target instead of doing any twisting . . . just back and through.

I started making this change in my swing in 1930, when I was 18 years old, but it sure didn't happen all at once. I hit a lot of golf balls trying to make it work. One thing that helped me was practicing against the Texas wind. Keeping the ball down against the wind helped me learn to take the club straight back and straight through. I also think my pronounced leg drive developed from trying to keep the ball low against the wind. I was trying to swing through the ball with as shallow an arc as possible at the bottom and keep the club going down the target line as long as I could. You need strong leg action to do that.

. . . I think I was the first player to make the complete change from the old way of swinging to the modern method we use today. Of course, the older players weren't making many changes, even with the steel shafts. They had played their way for so long that they probably were afraid to. As we get older, we tend to resist change.

But I feel the younger players did start to copy me. Most people, I guess, like to copy somebody who is successful and after a while I began to have pretty good success with that swing.

I turned professional in November, 1932, went to Texarkana, and played in a little $500 tournament. . . . I finished third and won $75. I was 20 years old by then.

The next spring they hired me as the pro at Texarkana Country Club. There was so little money in the tournaments in those days that you had to make your living at a club. In fact, the only time I ever stayed on tour full time was in 1945 until the day I quit in August, 1946. . . .

I began playing in tournaments right away, though. In 1933 I tried to play in two or three without any money and ended up hitchhiking back home from California. I returned to the winter tour that fall, but in the summer of 1934 I played in only a few local tournaments. By then I had made enough of a reputation so that I was invited to the second Masters tournament. . . .

So I kept working on this theory of keeping the face of the club square with the back of the left hand, just as though I was trying to hit the ball with the back of that hand.

I felt I was controlling the swing from the left side. But I knew I was getting some power from the right side, not early in the swing, but late. That was something that just kind of happened. I wouldn't recommend that anyone deliberately try to hit with the right side, because if you do you'll be in trouble. Even though I felt I pushed off the right foot, I don't believe you should think about this, because you'll do it too much ahead of time. The right-side power builds up because of the proper use of the feet and legs. When you move to the right in the backswing and then back to the left you automatically generate the proper use of the right side.

Finally, in 1937, I had developed this style of play to my satisfaction . . . I also started winning consistently that year. I won the Masters and three other tournaments, and I played on the Ryder Cup team. I never tried to change anything in my swing from that time on. . . .

The modern players have carried the improvements in the swing even further, I feel. They tie the whole swing together better than I did. They combine the use of their feet and legs with the whole turn of their bodies.

They stand reasonably close to the ball—closer than we did in my time—and they push the club straight back. Even if some of them break their wrists immediately, they hold it, and by the turn of their shoulders they carry the club high into the air. They make a big shoulder turn, but they don't let their hips turn as much as their shoulders. As a group, the players today get their hands much higher on the backswing than I did. Over the years they have developed a longer, fuller arc, a fuller extension going back and coming through. And they do it more smoothly.

As a result, they hit the ball harder and farther, yet they hit it amazingly straight. They do this because they have such good control of the left side. I don't know a good player out there today who doesn't control his swing with the left side. They also keep the club more on line with the target during the swing, and they keep their heads very still.

. . . When you're driving it 255 yards as the boys are today, you've got to be straighter to keep it in the fairway than when you're hitting only 225 or 235. It's simply a matter of angle.

That's why I tried to keep my head still. And that's why I kept complete control in the left side, the left hand and arm, never letting that clubhead get past my hands until I'd passed the hitting area. After I made my swing change, I began driving the ball about as long as most of them do now—but I had to do those things in order to stay on the fairways.

From *Shape Your Swing the Modern Way,* by Byron Nelson, with Larry Dennis. Published 1976 by Golf Digest, Inc. Reprinted with permission of Byron Nelson, individually, and Byron Nelson, Trustee, of the Byron Nelson Revocable Trust.

Long driving, if it be not the most deadly, is certainly the most dashing and fascinating part of the game; and of all others the principal difficulty of the golfer to acquire, and his chief delight when he can manage it.

H. B. Farnie

Triangle and Center

1981 ✦ JIMMY BALLARD
WITH BRENNAN QUINN

Jimmy Ballard's star ascended in the 1980s when he wrote his groundbreaking book, from which this excerpt is taken, and two of his pupils, Hal Sutton and Curtis Strange, became stars. Established as an original thinker and vital link in the development of "big muscle" theory, Ballard offered his notion of "triangle and center," which flows directly from Percy Boomer's theories of "the force-center." Both men were trying to stress the idea of "connection," meaning that the big muscles of the upper and lower body work together to lead the swing. Ballard updated that by having golfers throw a heavy shag bag at a target, emphasizing the leverage and power created by the big muscles working together and transmitting energy and force to the hands. The "triangle-center drill," which is based on his theory, and is described in this piece, remains a staple of teaching pros around the world.

The triangle and center are reference points to help you both understand and feel connection in its role as the moving constant in the golf swing.

When a golfer assumes the braced connected address position, the relationship between the shoulders, arms, and hands forms a triangle, when viewed from straight on. During the swing, from waist high to waist high, back and through, this triangle remains clearly visible. As the club passes waist high on the backswing, it may appear that the triangle breaks down. From a side view, however it can be seen that as the club moves toward the top, the right arm and shoulder work up and back, with the right elbow pointing down and behind the golfer, but the right arm folds within the triangular shape. So also, at waist high, on the follow-through, the left arm begins to fold on the body, but again, the triangle shape is maintained into the completed finish. Ideally, a player wants to stay with the triangle throughout the swing.

To experience the triangle-center feeling, try the following exercise. Take a driver, and grip down on the shaft until the butt of the club touches the middle of the chest about an inch up on the sternum. This point I call center. Keeping the butt of the club touching center, swing the triangle of arms, hands, and club back and through, waist high to waist high. Repeat this exercise several times being particularly aware of the feelings generated. It should become apparent that center coils in an arc back and slightly up, down through, and back up. Also, center never stops moving throughout the course of the swing. Center represents the middle of the upper body mass. With repetition, you should have the sensation that you are swinging the triangle with center. This insures that the large muscles of the legs and torso initially control the arms and hands—another way of introducing the feeling of connection into the swinging action.

Center is merely a point of reference and does not lead the swing. The swing should begin with a rhythmic kick of the left foot and left knee which immediately introduces the sequential coiling of the left side, the triangle, and center. In other words, the backswing operates from the ground up, through center with connection. This interrelationship happens so rapidly that it is difficult for the untrained eye to appreciate the sequence. . . . So also the downswing begins from the ground up with a kick of the right foot and right knee immediately followed by the sequential connected recoiling of the right side and center.

Center is always the reactor, never the initiator. If the golfer mistakenly tries to move behind the ball, through it, and past it with center only, the result will be a disconnected waving of the upper body back and through. A fixation on using center improperly destroys the leg brace and the coiling and recoiling activity which is the hallmark of the great ball strikers. The idea of swinging the triangle with center is a reference to provide an awareness of what the upper body actually does in a connected swing, in response, or as an immediate natural reaction to the coiling and uncoiling of the legs.

At waist high in the backswing, the connected coiling of the triangle causes the left knee to break in well behind the point where the ball would be addressed. You should be able to feel the large muscles on the inside of the legs, and as you conclude the

Jimmy Ballard has taught golfers to form a perfect triangle with their hands, arms, and shoulders at address, and then maintain that connection throughout the swing.

abbreviated backswing, also notice that your weight is predominantly on the inside of the right foot.

As you swing through to the waist-high finish, keeping center and triangle moving together, notice that your weight has shifted completely to your left side—you could pick your right foot off the ground. During the through-swing, you should experience much the same feeling encountered when you [throw a] shag bag [at a target.] The point is, you can't swing the triangle with center correctly without incorporating the entire body from the ground up.

As to upper body sensations, notice that at waist high on the backswing the right arm has moved away from the body and is just beginning to fold naturally. The left arm is not rigid or stiff, but comfortably extended from the lat muscle. If you held this position and had someone pull the club, moving it to the place where you would normally grip it, you would have maximum extension of the clubhead with connection.

What if you find that this exercise feels uncomfortable or restrictive, or both? In the first place, you've probably never tried to take an abbreviated swing with the butt of the club touching your chest, so it has to feel different. But, and this is more important, you have probably never taken the club away from the ball with your hands, arms, shoulders, . . . and body, all working in concert.

If you are a student of the game, the term one-piece takeaway probably crossed your mind when you preformed the exercise correctly. For years, players have had difficulty with this move because of the manner in which it was taught. "Take the hands, arms, and shoulders away in one piece," was the usual instruction. The practical result was that the club was pushed back with the hands, arms, and shoulder joints. At this point, the only way to raise the club up is to produce an abrupt and unnatural cocking of the wrists, and lift the arms across the chest, continuing to operate from the shoulder joints. It felt restrictive or dead because the move was not made with either center or connection. So even though the fanning open of the club, or the early set of the wrists was avoided, the body center didn't go with the hands and

arms, and in an attempt to prevent one kind of disconnection, another was created.

The initial move in the golf swing can't be performed properly unless the player swings the triangle back *with* center.

Your next question might well be, "Now that I've got the triangle waist high what do I do?" The answer is you shouldn't *have* to do anything. At approximately waist high, the folding of the right arm and the momentum of the club cause the natural hinging of the wrists. Years ago, one of the old touring pros was quoted: "You're in the locker room changing your shoes and you hear two guys discussing 'wrist action.' . . . You don't have to look, you know they're amateurs!" I agree. There should never be any conscious effort to cock or un-cock the wrists during the golf swing. If the club is gripped correctly, and the triangle is taken back with center while maintaining connection, the wrists will do their job perfectly without your assistance. Allow it to happen. The pick and roll has a definite place in basketball, but no place in golf. . . .

If we are to return the clubface square to the ball consistently, the best way to achieve this is with no conscious manipulation of the wrists, but with connection. . . .

The average golfer who pre-sets the wrists or hinges early disconnects. Pre-setting or hinging the wrists, or picking up the club allows not only the butt of the club but the hands, as a unit, to be worked independently of center. From here, there is never the proper coil behind the ball. The arc is shortened and the swing loses its connection. This is why I stress the butt of the club in the center of the chest. By keeping this in mind, along with the idea of the triangle, the golfer will have the best chance of minimizing the extraneous movement and thus avoid the connection-breakers during the swing.

From *How to Perfect Your Golf Swing: Using "Connection" and the Seven Common Denominators*, by Jimmy Ballard, with Brennan Quinn. Golf Digest/Tennis, Inc. a New York Times Company. Copyright © 1981, by Jimmy Ballard. Used by permission of Jimmy Ballard.

Feeling Your Hands

1988 ⚬ BOB TOSKI AND DAVIS LOVE, JR.
WITH ROBERT CARNEY

Bob Toski and Davis Love, Jr., sometimes taught together, penned a book together, and entered *Golf Magazine*'s World Golf Teachers Hall of Fame together in 1999. Toski, the first living inductee, was briefly a 118-pound pro, prior to spending the last forty years teaching 100,000 pupils, writing books and articles, and dispensing tips on television (originally NBC) and videos. A student of Harvey Penick, Love—the father of PGA star Davis Love III—also became a revered instructor, before dying in a plane crash, at age fifty-three, in the same year as the publication of his book with Toski. The renowned duo expected golfers to learn how the various parts of the body should feel during the swing; and in this excerpt they paid tribute to "small muscle" theory, quoting mutual influences Seymour Dunn and Ernest Jones on how golfers should use their hands to generate clubhead speed and let the body follow their lead.

"Some players might as well stick their hands in their pockets," said the great golf instructor Seymour Dunn, "for all the use they make of them." . . . The hands start the clubhead moving, keep it on its natural path and sustain its centrifugal motion. . . .

The hands, Dunn said, are the leaders of the swing. And that surprises most golfers. You see them on the practice range struggling to lift the club with their arms or pull it with their shoulders or help it along with their legs and trunk. They twist and turn and slap and hit, clutching the club in a grip so tight their hands lose all of their natural power. "Most golfers," Ernest Jones said, "merely use their hands to hold the club. They don't understand that it is through the hands and fingers alone that they can influence the behavior of the club."

If that shoe fits you, here's some good news: The golf swing is easier than you thought, much easier when you master the movement of the hands. . . .

First, because your hands generate clubhead speed. Second, because your hands impose the greatest influence on the face of the club. Third, because your hands lead your arms in creating clubhead path. And finally, because they control the amount of tension in your swing. (If your hands are tight, your forearms become tight, your shoulders become tight, and so on.) In short, your hands are the boss. They control the speed at which you can swing and therefore the distance you can hit the ball. They control the accuracy with which you hit it.

. . . [F]ollowing Ernest Jones's example, swing a pen knife at the end of a kerchief. As you . . . learn the movements of the hands during the swing, try to duplicate that free-swinging motion. Your hands' job is to allow the club to swing . . . And through your hands [you] let the club swing. . . .

You'll note that we have not yet used the word "release" in [regards to] hand motion. In the golf swing, release means the rotation of the hands, wrist, and

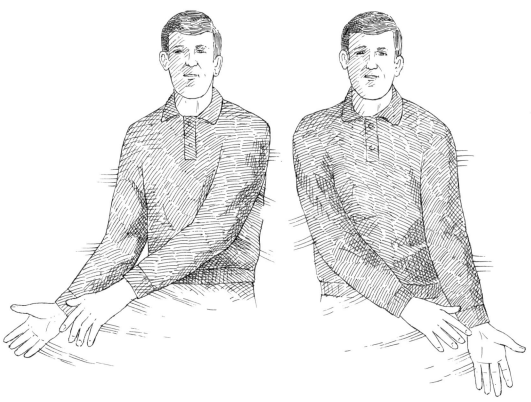

The classic drill for "feeling" proper hand action and increasing clubhead speed.

forearms from their position on the backswing, back to a square position at impact, to their position on the follow-through. Some books spend a great deal of time talking about release. . . . Release will occur naturally when your hands and forearms are working in tandem.

Here's an exercise by master teacher Paul Runyan, the former PGA Champion, that promotes efficient hand, wrist, and forearm coordination. It will also increase your hand and, therefore, clubhead speed. You can do it while you're watching TV. Stand up and put your left hand in front of you, palm facing toward you. Now flip the palm as fast as you can so that it faces away from your leg. Repeat it again and again, keeping your hand, wrist, and forearm as loose and flexible as you can. Then do it with your right hand and arm, starting with the palm facing away from you and flipping back toward you. Now place both hands in their starting positions, move them together to your

The "click" of a solid wood shot soaring down the fairway is worth all the hours of practice.

JIMMY DEMARET

right and swing them back to your left, flipping the palms as quickly as you can as you go. . . . Repeat the movement over and over, starting slowly and increasing the speed of the "flip" of the wrists. Without touching a club, you've learned the correct movement of hands, wrists, and forearms during the swing. You've also learned that the "softer" your hands, the faster they flip. Which begins to explain why tight grip pressure decreases, not increases, clubhead speed. Stiff hands and wrists are slow hands and wrists.

Also great for "release" is the Baseball Drill, especially if you tend to slice the ball. Grip your club normally and begin to swing it at waist level the way you would a baseball bat. Gradually bend forward and lower the club to ground level, still thinking of a "level" swing. We've seldom seen a player who could slice the ball while trying to swing level. . . .

FEELING THE CLUBHEAD

Hold a club between your thumb and forefinger and let it swing. Feel the weight of the clubhead, notice how it slows down on the way up, picks up speed on the way down.

HAND MOVEMENTS DURING THE SWING

HITCHHIKE DRILL. With no club, make a full turn and swing your left hand back from an imaginary address position until it points at your right shoulder. Then swing it down and across your body until it points at your left shoulder. Do it again and again in a swing-like motion, observing the movement of your hand.

The Pivot

1990 ✦ DAVID LEADBETTER WITH JOHN HUGGAN

Born in England but raised in Zimbabwe, David Leadbetter dropped out of business school to follow the dodgy path of aspiring golf pro. He never made it as a player, but he quickly found a niche, spending the next thirty years building an international empire of golf schools, churning out best-selling books and videos, and tutoring top professionals. His childhood friend Nick Price was an early client, but it was the complete "make-over" he gave Nick Faldo in the 1980s, resulting in his winning the first of an eventual six Majors, that established Leadbetter's reputation. In this excerpt, Leadbetter took yet another step in the evolution of "big muscle" theory by advocating a pivot around two "axis points" and relegating the hands and wrists to mere followers. For such advice from the influential instructor, rising pros like Charles Howell III and Michelle Wie, and thousands of hackers, pay top dollar.

Learning the pivot motion of the body is [a key] step toward building an athletic golf swing. . . . Without making a good pivot you can never fully control the swinging motion of the club.

What Is a Pivot?

The dictionary defines a pivot as a "movement around a fixed point." This is a fair description of the athletic swing except that, as we shall discuss, the transfer of your weight from its original static position at address to your right side and back to your left side is around two axis points rather than one. . . .

What the Pivot Does

Your pivot motion provides three vital ingredients in your athletic swing:

- a coiling and stretching effect where your torso is wound up and loaded like a spring ready to unwind;
- a transfer of your body weight from one side to the other;
- consistent tempo or speed.

That, in a nutshell, is what your pivot motion is all about. A clear concept of how and what your body does will put you well on your way to becoming an athletic swinger.

For now, understanding the pivot action does not require you to use a club, not in the conventional sense anyway. You will need one only when working through some of the drills. This chapter describes the movement of your body—nothing more. *You must know what your body does during your swing before learning the roles played by your arms, hands, and club.* Indeed, it is my experience that most golfers feel the benefits of a proper pivot more quickly when the club and, perhaps more importantly, the ball are removed from the equation. . . .

Youngsters who start the game at an early age learn by imitation. Give them the opportunity to see some good, athletic swings and it is likely that their body motions will be fairly athletic in turn. However, it is my contention that most golfers never totally understand what constitutes a correct body pivot. As a result, they play all their lives with swings requiring constant patching, giving no thought to its inner workings. . . .

Centrifugal Force

The term "centrifugal force" is used increasingly by teachers when discussing the golf swing. But I have found that only a few golfers really know either what it means, or what it does.

It is a force created away from the center of your swing. Transmitting from your body, out through your arms and hands, it creates leverage, width of arc, and clubhead lag. In turn, they create clubhead speed and maintain the club on a steady orbit or arc.

So how do we harness this important force found in the swings of all good ball-strikers? Simply, *it is the efficient coiling and uncoiling of your torso in a rotary or circular motion which maximizes centrifugal force.* Think of it this way: Holding a piece of string with a weight on the end, begin to spin your wrist in an anti-clockwise direction. As long as your arm stays steady, the weight moves into a constant orbit. The quicker you spin your wrist, the faster the weight moves. The weight, though, will always be moving much faster than your wrist—the centrifugal force created will see to that.

This centrifugal force or outward pulling of the string is maintained by the movement of your wrist. It is that which keeps the weight in orbit. If your wrist moves out of its original position, the weight moves out of orbit. Your golf swing displays identical characteristics. If your body does not move correctly, the club will not move on the correct plane or orbit. It will also lose speed. That means shots lacking in both distance and direction.

In the same way, the relationship between body and club during the golf swing is very much like a pair of ice skaters. I'm sure you've seen this on television; the lead skater (representing the body in the golf swing) is the hub around which his partner rotates. He revolves quite slowly while the female skater (representing the clubhead) is moving at a tremendous speed. This is a perfect example of how centrifugal force can be built up around a relatively slow moving axis and transferred to another, much faster object. [In other words] . . . the dog must wag the tail.

Your golf swing starts from the address position, where the club is virtually static. It then gathers speed as it changes direction and culminates in a whip-like action through the ball. This acceleration stems from the turning or pivotal motion of your torso—the power base or engine room of every athletic swing.

That is how centrifugal force is maximized. Through the motion of your body, power is built up; power that flows through your arms and hands into the clubhead. The impression that the power in your golf swing stems from the motion of your hands and arms is a false one. Just like a discus thrower who builds up power through the coiling motion of his or her body, you use your hands and arms merely as conductors of your torso-created power.

That is not to say your hands and arms play no part in your golf swing. They most certainly do. Even the most efficient pivot motion could not generate a great deal of clubhead speed operating alone. But there is a definite chain of command—your hands and arms must react to, not dominate, the movement of your body.

It should be clear to you that maximizing the centrifugal force in the clubhead requires a certain amount of physical ability. That is why it is very difficult to play golf well with a bad back. A lack of mobility or flexibility in your back reduces the rotary motion of your spine and cuts the supply of power to your arms, hands, and club. When forced to take over the task of moving the clubhead, they are less effective.

As proof of how important your body motion is, try hitting some balls when sitting on a stool, your feet off the ground. To hit the ball any distance is all but impossible because the only source of power is the swinging motion of your arms. Remember: *the power base in every athletic golf swing is the turning motion of your body—your pivot.*

As you work on your pivot motion, realize that you do not rotate around only one fixed axis point, your head. Imagine a line drawn down the inside of your right shoulder, through your right hip joint and past the inner part of your right thigh into the ground.

Now imagine the same line traveling down the left side of your body. These are the two axis points around which every athletic swinger rotates, back and through.

Rotating around your right axis point, then your left, will encourage what I call a "turning weight transfer" in both directions. Your body weight, from a fairly even start at address, moves to your right heel on your backswing and toward your left heel on your downswing. It is quite normal for your head, especially on the backswing, to move a little laterally as you turn. It should certainly be free to swivel. Keeping your head overly still can only restrict your motion around your two axis points.

An incorrect rotation around your two axis points can, in fact, lead to a so-called "reverse pivot." This occurs when, on your backswing, your weight does not move around your right axis point, but hangs on your left side. On the downswing, that translates to your weight moving onto your right side instead of your left. By severely reducing the ability of your body to correctly control your hands and arms, this causes all manner of bad shots.

Although your pivot motion should not include any pauses or breaks in motion . . . for the sake of clarity, [I can describe it as] . . . three pieces:

→ your backswing or pivot motion to the right;
→ the transition from backswing to downswing as the body changes direction;
→ your downswing or pivot motion to the left.

This, I feel is the best way for you to attain a clear understanding of the complete motion.

I don't really believe there is an orthodox golf swing.

GARY PLAYER

The Pendulum-Like Swing

1997 *Jim Flick*
WITH GREG WAGGONER

For over a half century, Jim Flick has built a reputation as one of the country's top teachers through frequent magazine articles and television appearances and, since 1992, as the principle instructor for the Nicklaus-Flick Golf Schools. Focusing on how to swing the clubhead and the pendulum-like nature of the swing, he has taught golf as a game of *feel*, rather than mechanics. If that sounds vaguely familiar, it might be because of his long association with Bob Toski, with whom he wrote the popular book *How to Become a Complete Golfer*—and their mutual admiration for past masters Ernest Jones and Seymour Dunn. But Flick is hardly a throwback. While a stickler for the fundamentals, he decries the "big muscle" approach for the average, slice-bound hacker. He believes in clearing the mind of competing theories and focusing on natural movement—*playing* the game, rather than *working* at it.

The first time I talk to students about the pendulum-like swing I see a lot of skepticism in their eyes. Some of it disappears after our first short-game session because the stroke for the basic chip and pitch shots is certainly pendulum-like and the square contact "feels" right. But the unspoken—and sometimes spoken—reaction is, "Okay. A pendulum's fine, but I'm not going to hit my ball far enough."

And I have to convince you that you will.

The term is "pendulum-like," as in similar (but not identical) to a pendulum. Unlike a true pendulum on a grandfather's clock, of course, the golf swing doesn't keep going back and forth, through the same arc indefinitely. But if we examine the properties of how a pendulum swings and then liken it to golf motion, you'll see a lot of similarities.

For most golfers, the pendulum-like swing is the simplest, quickest way to achieve consistent repetition of motion—the much coveted, much pursued, always elusive Repeating Swing.

Attach a golf ball to a string, let it hang from a fixed point, get it swinging, and—presto!—a demonstration pendulum. Question number one, Is there any acceleration? The answer is yes: pendulums accelerate as long as they're swinging down. There is a bottom point—actually, in physics I believe it's called the zero point—where there is no more acceleration. But that is also the point where you've got maximum velocity.

How good is that? You've got your clubhead picking up speed, picking up speed, then hitting *maximum* speed at contact. That would actually be an optimum transfer of energy.

Next, almost always, comes a question that—*invariably*—sends one of my teaching colleagues, Martin Hall, up the wall, off the charts, and into orbit: "If the pendulum stops picking up speed, that means I have to make sure to accelerate and follow through, right?"

Now, everyone has his hot-button issue. Mine is "One-Piece Takeaway." For Martin . . . the thing that drives him craziest is "accelerate and follow through."

Listen to him on the subject:

I can't think of anything worse to try to do with a golf club in your hands than "accelerate and follow through."

Does the swing accelerate? Yes. What's making it accelerate? Gravity. Let me repeat: it's accelerating because of the pull of gravity.

Now, is there a follow-through? Of course, there is. Why? Because of the swing, because of momentum.

So with the pendulum-like swing, we have acceleration, and we have follow-through as a consequence of momentum. If you think "accelerate and follow through" when you swing, then you are going to try to help momentum.

Believe me, momentum doesn't need any help.

Martin's right. There is a follow-through in the golf swing, but it's caused by momentum, not a conscious effort. If you go into the golf swing thinking about accelerating at impact to create a big follow-through, you'll undermine the principle of the pendulum-like swing, inevitably cause your muscles to tense up, and almost certainly disrupt the swing's arc with the midpoint increase in effort, thereby reducing the likelihood of a square clubface at impact.

Not only that, but you will really annoy Martin Hall.

NOT ONE, BUT TWO

There are actually two pendulums at work. The first is formed by the hands and wrists cocking, un-cocking, and re-cocking. The second is created by the forearms and upper arms swinging from the shoulder sockets.

My former colleague from *Golf Digest* school days Peter Kostis called them the first swing and the second swing. I think of them as two pendulums.

What permits the two pendulums to work together is the combination of the weight in clubhead, centrifugal force, the good old law of gravity—and the golfer. These pendulums supply about 80 percent of the distance in your golf shot—provided the swinging elements of your body drive the turning elements and not vice versa.

If your grip pressure is too tight, the weight at the end of the club is restricted from doing its job.

If you try consciously to turn your shoulders and shift your weight, you destroy the natural harmony of those two pendulums.

If you try to accelerate at impact and follow through, well you know what happens there.

But if your posture is good, and your grip pressure—fingers secure, arms relaxed—is correct, you give those two pendulums a chance to work in harmony.

A LITTLE CHIN MUSIC

Alex Morrison, the Los Angeles pro who influenced several generations of golfers and their teachers, told players to think about keeping their chin pointed behind the ball through impact. Doing so, of course, keeps the head behind the ball, and is a better method than the old admonition to "keep the head down," or "keep your eye on the ball," ancient advice that often led golfers to freeze over the ball and contributed to any number of errant shots when incorrectly applied. ❧

"Your" Golf Swing

1 9 9 8 ✑ R I C K   S M I T H

A former assistant to Dick Harmon, the influential Rick Smith is consistently ranked among the country's top teachers by both *Golf Digest* and *Golf Magazine*. He is an instructor who can't be labeled. As the word "Your" in the title of his impressive *How to Find Your Perfect Golf Swing* indicates, he adapts to his pupils rather than the other way around. That's why he has been able to work with such diverse swingers as Lee Janzen, David Duval, Vijay Singh, Phil Mickelson, and Jack Nicklaus. When teaching, he likes to put his clients in front of mirrors to check body positions in the swing, while at the same time emphasizing the importance of clubhead "feel." Some might call this "*mixed* muscle" theory, but Smith prefers to describe his approach as one that "matches" the swinging of the arms and club to the coiling and uncoiling of the body.

Here are some golf sayings that can be easily misinterpreted by many players. Depending on a golfer's problems, they can be helpful. But, ironically, they have hurt more people than they've helped.

- → Keep the left arm straight.
- → Turn.
- → Lift the left heel.
- → Keep the left heel down.
- → Make a one-piece takeaway.
- → Cock the wrists.
- → Rotate your left shoulder under your chin.
- → Stay down.
- → Clear the hips.
- → Slide the hips.
- → Pause at the top.
- → Keep the right elbow close to or against your side.

Do you think there is room for misinterpretation or confusion with any of these sayings? Some are even contradictory. Allow me briefly to address some of these sayings.

- → *Keep the left arm straight.* Ideally, the left arm is straight at the top of the backswing, which is what this saying deals with. However, the arm doesn't have to be straight; a slight bending at the elbow is permissible. Furthermore, straight does not mean rigid, which is how many golfers interpret it. What should be avoided is a left arm that has bent so much at the elbow it approaches a 90-degree angle. The most important point of any discussion about the straightness of the left arm, however, is to say that it should be straight at impact. It is far better to have a soft left arm (slightly bent) at the top and then have it straight at impact than to have a rigid (or even straight for that matter) arm at the top and then have it bent at impact.
- → *Turn. Turn* usually refers to the body in the backswing: specifically the shoulders, and to a lesser degree, the hips. If you don't turn enough, chances are you are outside-in down.

Work on flexibility and by all means try to turn your shoulders. But an equally common problem is turning too much too soon after initiation of the backswing. This focuses attention on the questions, Turn what, when, and how much? The shoulders really don't turn that much during the first part of the backswing. When the left arm moves up to horizontal to the ground, the shoulders will have turned only about 30 degrees of the full 90 degrees desired. In addition, such movement is in response to the movement of the arms, not the result of conscious effort. The hips are responding to the movement of the upper body and, therefore, have turned even less. Frequently, I will see a golfer so intent on turning, the hips and shoulders begin doing so abruptly—immediately and excessively—as soon as the backswing begins. The unfortunate result is a movement out of sequence and a body motion that forces the arms to take the club back too much to the inside.

→ *Lift the left heel/Keep the left heel down.* Whether the left heel comes up or not depends on the flexibility of the golfer and individual preference. Either can be correct. The issue here, however, deals with the words *lift* (lift the heel) and *keep* (keep the heel down). Both imply conscious effort on the part of the player, independent of other factors. This is not correct. For an inflexible golfer to turn the shoulders correctly and sufficiently in the backswing, the left heel may have to rise; but both that it does so and to what extent are caused by prior movement of the body, not by a conscious effort to lift the heel. . . . A golfer who is supple enough to turn completely with the heel down but who artifi-cially lifts the heel will invariably over-swing at the top and lose all hope of an accurate, powerful swing.

→ *Make a one-piece takeaway/Cock the wrists.* . . . [O]ften a student will ask, "When do I cock my wrists?" By the very nature of the question, I know he or she doesn't have the proper concept of how this should occur. You should never cock the wrists. Rather, the swinging motion of the club and the weight of the clubhead cocks them for you, which will most certainly occur as long as nothing is done to interfere with the accomplishment of the task. Such interference might come from excessive grip pressure, an incorrect grip, an overzealous attempt to control the backswing, a backswing plane that is too flat, or from exaggeration of the one-piece takeaway.

→ *Rotate your left shoulder under the chin.* This phrase is supposed to ensure a full shoulder turn in the backswing. The turn of the shoulders was discussed earlier, but let me assure you this thought, or even the accomplishment of it, will not ensure your shoulders will be fully turned—particularly if you start moving your chin down and/or left in the backswing, as many do.

→ *Stay down.* The adage . . . usually applies to the downswing and the through-swing. Those who attempt to follow this directive are usually pulling up and away with their upper body at the finish. However, this is an effect of another problem—either the posture, the swing itself, or a combination of both. Most often, such golfers are over-the-top, outside-in swingers. This type of swing will often force the golfer up. It will not do you any good to

The right way to play golf is to go up and hit the bloody thing.
GEORGE DUNCAN

tell yourself to stay down. You may indeed try to do so. But you will not succeed until you fix the real cause of the problem, which is the swing itself. Lower handicap players who are too inside on the downswing can also experience this raising of the spine as well. But again, it is the result of the swinging motion, usually, not vice-versa.

- *Clear the hips/Slide the hips.* These sayings refer to the motion of the hips in the downswing. . . . The major problem here is that the average player who tends to cut across the ball and who, therefore, already clears his hips, or rotates them through impact, does so excessively. However, he or she is constantly hearing on television how the professional is working on this move or makes this move beautifully, and so on. . . . For the average player who slices, trying to clear the hips would only make him or her slice more. Thinking of sliding the hips would be more helpful. The idea of clearing the hips is more beneficial for the player who is too inside-out and tends to hook or push the ball.
- *Pause at the top.* Again, the pause is not something you make happen, but rather it happens naturally as a consequence of a correct swing, it's pace and proper sequence of motion.
- *Keep the right elbow close to or against your side.* People often get confused about when this should happen. The right elbow moves away from the side throughout the backswing, at the top, and initially down. It is only when the downswing has been half completed that the elbow moves in against the side. Too often I see golfers forcing their elbow into the right side immediately during the takeaway then keep it there throughout the backswing, which makes the club come back too inside and the backswing too flat.

These are just some of the sayings to think about before adopting them as part of your swing. It is not to say they are always wrong. Depending on the nature of the golfer's mistake, indeed any one of them could be helpful. Here are some other phrases that can be misconstrued, but let me identify when they could also be helpful.

	Could be helpful if:
Extend back.	right elbow too close to side in takeaway.
Extend through.	left arm chicken-winging at impact.
Swing the club toward the target.	through-swing too left or right.
Finish high.	follow-through is too low due to an outside-in path.
Release.	for a good player who has too much lag.
Employ a late Release.	for a poorer player who un-cocks prematurely.
Take the club back slowly.	it is your nature to be deliberate.
Hit against a firm left side.	left knee sags at impact.
Rotate.	you slice and arms fold and separate at impact.
Maintain a firm grip pressure.	wrists are excessively active in the downswing.
Maintain a light grip pressure.	wrists are too rigid in backswing.
Keep your head behind the ball.	upper body moves laterally past the ball prior to impact.

The obvious point I'm making is to be wary, careful, and inquisitive when it comes to golf's phrases, sayings, and adages. If you are taking lessons, make sure you ask for, and get, a satisfactory, understandable explanation for anything said that might be unclear to you or subject to interpretation. If you read something that is unclear, ask your professional for an explanation.

From *How to Find Your Perfect Golf Swing*, by Rick Smith; edited by John Andrisani. Copyright © 1998 by Smith Management, Inc. Used by permission of Broadway Books, a division of Random House, Inc.

— 5 —

SWING COMPONENTS

THE DEVIL IS IN
THE DETAILS

The Delayed Hit

1919 · JAMES M. BARNES

"Long Jim" Barnes stood six feet four, towered over his more famous rivals, like Walter Hagen and Gene Sarazen, and consistently out-hit them. Capitalizing on his victories in the first two PGA Championships, Barnes (who would later capture U.S. and British Opens) published the landmark book *Picture Analysis of Golf Strokes*. With full-page, stop-action photographs of his swing at various stages—and a minimum of explanatory text—it was a "How to Do It" alternative to teaching manuals that featured long, descriptive, and often hyperbolic prose, and presaged today's instructional videos. Barnes's book would be important if just for a photograph of his seemingly delicate wrists, freezing the moment *before* they snap the clubhead into the ball. This concrete image of the "delayed-hit" launched more theories than Helen did warships—the most common being: If golfers can maintain that power angle, they can increase power and distance.

DRIVER OR BRASSY

In starting the downward swing of the club the body begins to turn and in unison with it the left wrist starts the clubhead. The left arm remains straight and pulls the club down simultaneously with the body turn. The right elbow comes in close to the body, still retaining the same bent position as at the top of the swing.

The left heel drops to the ground, so that both feet are firmly supporting the stroke.

The right knee starts to bend in toward the ball and the left knee to straighten.

THE DOWNWARD SWING

The hands continue to drop with the turn of the body until the arms are about vertical by the time the club is horizontal. The right elbow is still bent and well in to the body, and the right wrist is still bent as far back as it can go.

Both feet are flat and firm on the ground.

WHERE THE REAL HITTING BEGINS

The body turn has reached a point almost the same as at the address. Although the left arm is almost straight down, the right hand has made as yet but little effort, but is now in position to begin its real work. The right wrist has retained practically the same bent position as at the top of the swing. The wrinkles in the flesh at the wrist [indicate] the bend to be still there.

From this point the right hand does the hitting—gets the head of the club through—while the left arm is pulling straight through with all the strength at its command.

The pressure is [now] taken off the right heel and transferred inwardly to the ball of the foot and toes. The principal difference [as the swing nears impact] is in the position of the right wrist [which now starts to move forward].

[At the moment just before impact] . . . the left arm is still straight and pulling hard, while the right hand is whipping the clubhead through. The thumb and forefinger of the right hand are playing a very prominent part in the work.

It is interesting to note . . . where the maximum speed of the clubhead occurs. . . . [As] the clubhead itself is just above the left foot . . . the shaft is almost unbelievably bent from the speed which is imparted to it. At this point the speed of the swing is reaching its maximum and results mainly from the whip of the right wrist.

THE IMPACT WITH THE BALL

The concentration at this point is very intense, which is largely the secret of a successful shot. It keeps the head still and prevents looking up.

All the muscular movements which make up the stroke reach their climax at this point, and that comes from a perfectly even and smooth development of the power. This feature is commonly called timing and the success of the stroke is directly proportional to the accuracy with which it is accomplished. . . . The body, arms and hands [are] at maximum effort and in perfect unison.

The right knee is bending and turning inward to accommodate the turn of the body.

For many years the question of how long the ball remains on the head of the club after the impact has been written about and discussed. [Photography at 1/1500 of a second now] answers that question. The ball is . . . in contact with [the clubface] for a distance about equal to the width of the clubhead.

While the left arm is practically straight throughout the whole swing, the right arm does not become straight until just as the ball is leaving the clubhead.

. . . The clubhead has been thrown out after the ball, which action keeps both arms straight out from this point until practically the finish of the stroke.

CONCLUDING REMARKS

. . . All the various parts of the body which make up the turning movements [in the swing] operate smoothly in unison, easily and deliberately, without any semblance of jerkiness or hurried action, but firmly and with a feeling of complete control. The club is started back with a simultaneous bending of the left knee, swinging of the straight left arm, and a bending of the right elbow, the shoulders and hips turning smoothly with the movement right from the

Jim Barnes first captured the "delayed hit" in photographs.

start. The wrists delay their bending action until the club has reached a horizontal position, where they begin to lift and turn the clubhead, harmonizing their action smoothly with the other movements. All through the backward swing there is a distinct feeling of firm support on the right leg without transferring too much of the weight to it. It gradually tightens to the top of the swing. At the finish of the backward swing the left shoulder has turned underneath without disturbing the position of the head.

When the club starts its downward movement the previous relaxation disappears and in its place a distinct feeling of tenseness ensues. The grip is tight in both hands and the various movements, although still in complete unison, are fast and decisive. At the start the right knee begins to bend in toward the ball and the left knee to straighten. The body turns around very rapidly and with it the left arm pulls straight down and the right elbow comes in close to the body, still in its bent position. The wrists delay their action until the clubhead has reached a horizontal position, at which point they begin to put their power into the stroke, and that power is the final climax toward speeding up the clubhead and timing the force so that it is at the maximum just as the clubhead meets the ball. Before this final action of the wrists throws the clubhead into the ball the body has advanced in its turning movement until it is facing considerably ahead of the position of the ball. The arms are thus permitted to stretch straight out and away, forcing the clubhead to continue its motion close to the ground and along the path of the flight of the ball. The impetus of the stroke carries the clubhead to its final position at the finish, where relaxation again occurs.

From *Picture Analysis of Golf Strokes: A Complete Book of Instruction,* by James M. Barnes. Copyright © 1919 by J. P. Lippincott Company.

Swing Club in a Proper Oblique Plane

1922 ⚑ SEYMOUR DUNN

Seymour Dunn was an early transatlantic commuter, ferrying back and forth across "the pond" on business ventures. In 1900, the Scotsman established the world's first indoor golf school in England. (He'd open another in Madison Square Garden in 1929 with thirty instructors and eighteen pitch-and-putt holes.) Eventually settling in Lake Placid, New York, he worked as a golf pro and opened a mail-order clubmaking business. Dunn is best remembered as an early golf guru because of his well-known adherents—Jim Barnes, Walter Hagen, and Gene Sarazen—and his classic, self-published book *Golf Fundamentals*, which, like Barnes's earlier success, used photographs to illustrate points. He was one of the first writers to focus on the swing plane, using what looks like a frayed clothesline strung across the frame. Significantly, almost forty years later, Ben Hogan would update this little-articulated idea, substituting his famous imaginary pane of glass for Dunn's primitive prop.

The golf swing is all on a slope, i.e., it is Oblique.

Right arm controls obliquity.

Clubhead travels in an obliquely elliptic course about the player's head. Obliquity is determined by distance of ball from player, and the style of the player's swing, i.e., flat, orthodox, or upright.

Club should travel not merely in an oblique course but in an oblique *plane* which must pass thru the center of the ball. To be orthodox, hands and clubhead should be in the same plane with the swing center and the ball.

The oblique plane of the swing varies greatly in the matter of style. A short player of powerful physique using longish clubs would stand further from the ball than a tall player of slender physique using shortish clubs. The degree of obliquity would be more upright for the tall player, and flat for the shorter player, and in every case if the clubhead, hands, swing center, and ball be all in the same plane, the swing is orthodox on this point whatever the degree of obliquity may be.

The degree of obliquity varies not only with different players, but with each individual. With the shorter clubs such as the mashie, we make a more upright swing because we stand nearer the ball; swing center is more nearly over the ball, and therefore the plane from ball to swing center is more upright, and the clubhead, and hands should work in this same plane.

[In the flat swing the] clubhead, hands, and ball are all in the same plane though not in a plane with the shoulder center. This kind of swing is all right; it will produce good results, because it is mechanically correct, merely slightly unorthodox in style.

Restricted vertical arm action is the cause of the flat swing. . . . Had there been a little more upward action of the right arm in the swing . . . the swing would not have been flat.

I emphasize the right arm because while the left arm must necessarily also rise with the right, the right arm is the controlling arm so far as the oblique plane of the swing is concerned.

Too upright a swing is frequently the cause of over-swinging, i.e. swinging the club back over the shoulder beyond horizontal. When over-swinging is due to this, the cure is obvious—restrict the upward action of the right arm. Over-swinging is never caused by excessive backward bending of the wrists, but only by bending the left elbow or raising the hands too high. You cannot bend the wrists back too far.

[An overly flat swing that is considerably off plane] is worthless, being both unorthodox and mechanically incorrect. The club [may not even] connect with the ball. [But if it does, such a fault constitutes] the common cause of topping the ball with the heel of the club. . . . The club always follows in the plane of the arm action . . . [and when] the clubhead and hands are not in the same plane with the ball . . . the swing is mechanically incorrect and it would be unreasonable to expect satisfactory results. . . . Err ever so slightly [by taking the swing off plane] and the resulting ball's flight will be unsatisfactory.

Players sometimes fall heir to a persistent malady, and for lack of understanding cannot cure it. "*Socketing*" the ball with iron clubs is frequently due to too flat a swing.

From *Golf Fundamentals*, by Seymour Dunn. Saratogian Printing Service, Saratoga Springs, N.Y.

Swing tempo has been the most important factor in my career. It relieves the pressure and stress of the game.

NICK FALDO

The Swing Plane

1957 · BEN HOGAN
WITH HERBERT WARREN WIND

Ben Hogan tirelessly sought new angles to explore and explain golf, so it's not surprising that he invented the most famous geometric image in instruction history: the swing plane as a pane of glass, extending from the ball to the shoulders. Hogan believed his concept could help golfers find that elusive "slot" at the top of the backswing—golf's "G" spot—so that the clubhead is primed for an ideal downswing. Moreover, he thought it might satisfy golf's enduring quest for a consistent swing. As he explained in this excerpt from *Ben Hogan's Five Lessons, The Modern Fundamentals of Golf*, the golfer's goal is to keep the club parallel to or just below this imaginary pane. Dropping the arms too far below it, Hogan contended, would produce an overly flat swing and result in a vicious hook, while going too high—and "breaking" the glass—would result in a nasty slice.

———

Over the period I've been in golf, oceans of words have been devoted to the arc of the swing, but only the merest trickle to the plane. This is unfortunate, for in the dynamics of the golf swing the plane is extremely important, far more important than the arc.

What precisely is this plane? To begin with, there are two planes in the golf swing, the plane of the backswing and the plane of the downswing. . . . [T]he plane of the backswing . . . is most simply described as an angle of inclination running from the ball to the shoulders. The pitch of the angle is determined by two factors: the height of the individual's shoulders and the distance he stands from the ball at address.

On the backswing, the plane serves the golfer as sort of a three-dimensional road map. *His shoulders should rotate on this plane, continuously inclined at the same angle (with the ball) they established at address.* En route from address to the top of the backswing, *The arms and hands (and the club) should also remain on this same angle of inclination as they swing back.* (Use your left arm as your guide.) When your shoulders, arms, and hands follow the appointed route the plane sets up, it insures you that your upper body and arms will be correctly interaligned when they reach that crucial point where the backswing ends and the downswing begins. Then, when the downswing is inaugurated by the hips and the turning hips unwind the upper part of the body, the shoulders and then the arms and then the hands flow easily and powerfully into the swing. In other words, by staying on the backswing plane, the player pre-groups his forces so that each component is correctly geared to work with the other components on the downswing. . . .

There is no such thing as an absolute and standard plane for all golfers. The correct angle for each person's plane depends on how hc is built. A fellow whose legs are proportionally shorter than his arms, for example, necessarily creates a shallow angle for his plane. At the other extreme, a man whose legs are proportionately longer than his arms sets up a very steep angle for himself. Neither plane, let me repeat, is incorrect. Technically, it is wrong to term the man who properly swings on a shallow plane a "flat swinger," or the man who properly swings on a steep plane an "upright swinger," simply because their planes happen to be flatter or more upright than the plane of the man of more average proportions. However, if any golfer permits his arms and his club to drop well below his established plane, then, whether he normally possesses a shallow or steep or an average plane, he would be swinging too flat. Similarly, if he hoists his club above the line of this plane, he would be swinging too upright.

Perhaps the best way to visualize what the plane is and how it influences the swing is to imagine that, as the player stands before the ball at address, his head sticks out through a hole in an immense pane of glass that rests on his shoulders as it inclines upward from the ball. *If he executes his backswing properly, as his arms are approaching hip level, they should be parallel with the plane and they should remain parallel with the plane, just beneath the glass, till they reach the top of the backswing. At the top of his backswing, his left arm should be extended at the exact same angle (to the ball) as the glass.* Actually, his left arm would brush against the glass. As for his shoulders, as they turn on the backswing, the top of the shoulders will continuously be brushing against the glass.

As golf faults go, it is not too injurious if your club and arms travel on a plane a little flatter than the ideal one. *However, you are heading for disaster if you thrust your arms up above the plane so that they would shatter the pane of glass.* Poor golfers make this error at any and all stages of the backswing, but it occurs most commonly when they are nearing the top of the back-

The swing plane theories first advanced by Ben Hogan have influenced instruction for fifty years.

swing. Then, when their hands are about shoulder high, they suddenly lift their arms almost vertically toward the sky—crash! goes the glass . . . and their shot. They conclude the backswing on an entirely different and far more upright plane, with their hands and forearms and elbows pretzeled all over the place. Hopelessly out of position, they struggle to right themselves on the downswing. Invariably, they can't and they mis-hit the ball in every conceivable way and in all directions. There are quite a few fairly talented golfers who also make this mistake of looping their arms above the plane as they approach the top of the backswing. It explains their frequent erratic spells. They cannot groove their compensations, and they make errors on both sides of the fairway.

. . . Try to visualize your proper plane and to keep your arms traveling on that plane as you swing the club back. Quite a few of my friends have told me that once they got the idea of the plane in their heads, it worked wonders for them. Like nothing else, it got them out of their old bad habits and made the correct movements come so naturally they could hardly believe it. ·

I can believe it. I really never felt that my own backswing was satisfactorily grooved, or could be satisfactorily grooved, until I began to base my backswing on this concept of the plane. Up to that point—

this was in 1938—I had been struggling along with a backswing that was a lot less uniform and, consequently, a lot less dependable than I wanted it to be. I began to wonder whether or not I could find a set "slot" for the club to hit at the top of the backswing. Then, if I could swing the club into the slot on every swing—well, that would solve my problem of inconsistency.

I began to think more and more about the golfer's plane. After some experimentation, I found to my enormous relief that, if I swung back along this plane, my club would, in effect, be traveling up a set slot *throughout* my backswing, on swing after swing. I practiced swinging on this plane and started to gain confidence that my backswing was reliable. It helped my whole swing, my whole game, my whole attitude. I can honestly say that for the first time I then began to think that I could develop into a golfer of true championship caliber.

The Swing Arc

1965 ◖ JULIUS BOROS

Although he didn't become a pro until he was thirty years old, Julius Boros won eighteen PGA titles, including the U.S. Open in 1952 and 1963, and the PGA in 1968, when the forty-eight-year-old former Connecticut accountant became the oldest player to win a Major. Diagnosed early on with heart trouble, Boros controlled his emotions and played with ease and efficiency, employing an elegant, silky-smooth swing. During his prime, he wrote exceptional instructional books, including *Swing Easy, Hit Hard*, in 1965. Ben Hogan's almost snide dismissal of the "swing arc" as an unimportant concept in golf instruction in his 1957 classic didn't deter Boros from devoting a few interesting words to it in this thought-provoking excerpt. His fluid description of the swing arc contains a handy tip for finding where the bottom of the arc touches the ground, which is key to putting the clubhead squarely on the ball.

The arc of your swing is the loop or invisible line made in the air by swinging your clubhead. Your arc has a shape that has many variations. The long full arc is made with your woods and long irons; the medium with the middle and short irons; and finally, the very short arc with the pitch shots, chip shots, and putts. In the first few feet of the swing your arc may follow the ground or pick up abruptly. These first few feet determine whether the clubhead will come into the ball on the downswing, the upswing, or on the level. Adjustment in stance will help bring about this change. For example you play the woods off the left foot so that you hit them on the upswing. On the short irons you play the ball back, causing the club to hit the ball on the downswing. Shifting your center of balance forward onto your left foot, or back onto your right foot, moves the low point of your arc forward and back also.

The arc your clubhead makes influences the flight of your ball, dictating whether it flies high or low, and to some extent, the amount of backspin you can apply. A common fault on short shots is to shorten your backswing arc too much by not turning your shoulders, which then necessitates an exaggerated punching hand action to generate sufficient power. This invariably leads to poor distance control.

DETERMINING THE LOW POINT OF THE ARC

To determine the low point of the arc of your swing, take a number of practice swings on the same spot, then carefully note where you start taking a divot. This will show you where your clubhead makes contact with the turf. This is also the lowest point of your arc. Do this in several spots with different length clubs to determine the variance with each type of club. Remember where your feet are in relation to that spot so you will know what correction should be made. If it is too far back you may have too much weight on your right foot and if too far forward you have too much weight on your left foot. . . . [T]he center of balance changes the axis of the arc from front to back. When you have developed a fine control over your swing, you can alter this arc at will to meet the needs of the shot you choose to produce, whether it be high or low.

The lengthening or shortening of your arc by just a few inches makes a difference in the distance you hit the ball. Make sure you swing back far enough. I didn't say over-swing.

[It is also important to note that] the forward swing does not follow the same arc as the backswing because your hips shift forward and your right elbow drops into your right side.

From *Swing Easy, Hit Hard*, by Julius Boros, illustrations by Lealand R. Gustavson. Copyright © 1965 by Julius Boros and Lealand R. Gustavson. Reprinted with permission from Armen Boros.

Swing Concepts: Timing and Tempo

1989 ⚬ BEVERLY LEWIS

Beverly Lewis, a former playing pro, became one of Britain's foremost golf theorists and, until recently, was a monthly columnist for and only woman on the teaching panel of the major U.K. publication *Golf World*. In her spare time from giving lessons, doing golf commentary for the BBC, and her new appointment as the first female captain of the British PGA, she writes outstanding instructional books that take a blended approach to "big muscle" versus "small muscle" theory—with a special emphasis on the needs of women players. Golfers, like baseball hitters, are always talking of timing and tempo, but as Mark Twain said about the weather, few do anything about it. In this excerpt, Lewis does, going where remarkably few have in the last 150 years. After defining the terms, and showing their interrelationship, she tells readers how to find their personal tempo and offers drills to hone their timing.

You have probably realized by now that golf necessitates using all the body's muscles. However, muscles do not all work most efficiently at the same pace. So there has to be a compromise, where the faster muscles, such as those in the hands and arms, work only at a pace that accommodates the larger muscles, such as those in the back and thighs. Beginners sometimes think that the ball can be hit further by swinging their arms faster, but this reduces the contribution that the back and shoulders can make, and the swing is denied power and direction. Similarly, if the downswing is rushed, the thigh muscles do not have time to work, and the tautness experienced at the top of the swing is dissipated. Some golfers try to copy top professionals who accentuate their leg action but, because they do not possess the same strength of hand action as the professional, the outcome is usually a thin or cut shot. Correct timing of the golf swing calls for a balance of pace between muscles which take time and practice to achieve. Beginners need to concentrate on making what seem to be very mechanical movements, and until such time as they acquire a little more fluency they must just accept that they will hit their share of poor shots.

For the more experienced player, who perhaps feels that she swings the club quite well but without due reward, here are two simple guides to analyzing and correcting timing.

If your shots tend to fade and slice, or you thin quite a few, then your leg action is too strong for your hand and arm action. You must concentrate on a stronger arm swing, practicing hitting balls with your feet together until the strike improves.

If your shots draw or hook, and you hit a lot of fat shots, then your leg action is not lively enough. You should put more emphasis on *pulling* with your left arm, and moving your left knee more emphatically from the top of the swing. With your arms hanging in front of you, take a club and hold either end of the shaft horizontally with your feet shoulder-width apart. Now make a swing, and you should find that your legs work more fluently.

Remember that you swing the golf club about 20 feet in an arc before you strike the ball. If you are half an inch or one degree out, you have hit a less than perfect shot. As your strength increases so the timing of your swing may alter slightly, so don't be too hard on yourself. By paying a little more attention to the timing of your swing, you may get closer to that perfect strike.

TEMPO

Timing and tempo are very much inter-related in the swing. Timing is the sequence in which different parts of the body move. Tempo is the pace at which all this movement takes place, and has a direct bearing on the timing of the swing. So, what is the correct tempo for you, and how do you find it? It has been said that your tempo reflects your character, that a person who is always dashing about will swing the club quickly, and vice versa. To some extent this may be true, but the overriding factor, whatever your character, is clubhead control.

It is self-defeating to swing the clubhead faster than you can control it, no matter whether you are by nature the tortoise or the hare. But what you are trying to achieve is a golf *swing*, and to that end there must be a certain degree of pace, or else all sense of rhythm is lost.

The pace of the backswing will have a direct effect on the pace of the downswing and, as already mentioned, this is likely to change as your swing and strength develop. I have to advise many more male players to slow down their swing than I have to ask to speed it up. With the extra strength men possess in their hands and arms, they are often guilty of making short, quick backswings without turning their shoulders.

This is naturally not such a common error in women, but for them a quick backswing will result often in a long backswing, where control is lost. On the other hand, I have found women players who I

believe swing the club too slowly. They seem to *take* the club back instead of swinging it back. They fail to create any rhythm in the swing, which leads to a very uncoordinated downswing, and usually lack leg action.

The backswing not only positions the club, it serves to create the pace and rhythm. Golf teachers spend a lot of time trying to get a pupil into a good position at the top of the swing. You might ask, if this position is so important, why don't we start from this point? Well, we don't because a good backswing helps to create good rhythm and tempo.

HOW TO FIND YOUR BEST TEMPO

Take a 6-iron and hit some shots from good lies at your normal pace, noting distance and accuracy. Now hit a similar amount of shots with first of all a faster and then a slower tempo, and again note where the balls land. From this you may be surprised to find that, by swinging at what feels to be three-quarters of your normal pace, you have hit the balls further and straighter. On the other hand, a slightly faster tempo may reveal that your control of the clubhead is now good enough for you to put a little more speed into the swing. Of course, you may already swing at your optimum tempo. Whatever the outcome it is always an interesting exercise to return to from time to time.

You may also benefit from making a few swings without the club, by just interlocking your two hands. You will find it easier to make a smoother unhurried swing without the club or ball to distract you.

Here is one last example of good timing and tempo, to which I'm sure many of you can relate. Imagine a shot from the fairway that has to carry a hazard and for which you need a good 3-wood. To be safe you decide to lay up short of the hazard, so you select a 6-iron, and make a smooth, unhurried swing. To your surprise, the ball zooms off into the distance and lands in or very near the hazard, and you wish you had been more courageous and hit the 3-wood. This has happened because during the swing you relaxed and made what felt like a three-quarter-paced and -length swing. In fact, you achieved perfect timing and tempo. Had you used the 3-wood, you might have tried to thrash the ball, resulting in poor timing and tempo and a bad shot.

Keep this example in your mind when you play and see if, with improved timing and tempo, the mechanics of your swing take a turn for the better. Top class golfers are always searching for good rhythm. Even for them it is something that can be perfect one day and gone the next, so don't worry if this happens to you, just keep persevering.

. . . What women lack in strength, they can compensate for with good timing and tempo. I have played many pro-ams with men who are usually quite surprised just how far I can hit the ball, with seemingly little effort. I would expect to hit a 5-iron shot about 155 yards (I am five feet three inches tall, and weigh only about 125 pounds). I enhance my sound technique by concentrating on maintaining good timing and tempo, which results in maximum clubhead speed at impact.

From *Golf for Women*, by Beverly Lewis. Gallery Books, an imprint of W. H. Smith Publishers, Inc., New York, N.Y. Copyright © 1989 Sackville Books, Ltd. Reprinted with the permission of Beverly Lewis.

Your Swing Plane—The Foundation

1 9 9 9   H A N K H A N E Y
W I T H J O H N H U G G A N

A bit of a cowboy, renowned instructor and *Golf Digest* writer Hank Haney runs seven golf schools in Texas, including the Hank Haney Golf Ranch, which is located on a converted horse farm. Even the title of Haney's book carries a certain Texas swagger: *The Only Golf Lesson You'll Ever Need.* As this chapter's title attests, Haney has made the swing plane the foundation of his teaching. Significantly, he has taken Ben Hogan to task for insisting that the golfer stay on only one plane during the swing: Haney says if you follow Hogan's advice, you'll "hurt yourself and your game." In the perfect swing, Haney argues, the club actually passes through several planes, but always stays parallel to the plane *angle*, an imaginary line formed by the clubshaft at address. Ideally, you will reproduce that angle at impact.

———————

Swinging on the correct plane is the most difficult thing in golf because it is the most important thing. In fact, the swing plane isn't just the most important thing it is the only thing.

Now, that's a pretty powerful statement when you consider that golf is ultimately supposed to be about posting the lowest score you can. But you can't do that consistently if you can't hit at least semi-decent shots.

Which is where the swing plane comes in. Let me explain.

In golf, you don't hit the ball. The way you stand to a shot doesn't hit the ball. The way you hold the club doesn't hit the ball. Your swing doesn't even hit the ball. No, only one thing hits the ball: the golf club. And the only things influencing that collision and the flight of the resulting shot are the angles on which the club is swinging into the ball. Specifically, the angle of the clubface and the angle of the shaft. So, to my mind, the swing plane is everything in that it is the one thing that has a direct bearing on the way in which club meets ball and therefore how the ball flies. . . .

Of course, you don't swing every club on the same plane. As the club in your hand changes, so does the plane of your swing. The longer the clubshaft gets, the further you have to stand from the ball, so the flatter your plane will be. For example, if you have a wedge in your hands, you want a little more of a descending blow so you will automatically stand closer to the ball and swing on a more upright plane than you would with a 5-iron. But your thoughts and your feelings don't change. The length and lie of the club makes any changes for you.

The swing plane is the cornerstone of my teaching and, it must be said, perhaps the most misunderstood aspect of the golf swing. It has been explained many times in print, most notably and memorably by Ben Hogan in his book, *The Modern Fundamentals of Golf*, but, I don't believe it has ever been explained correctly. Hence all the confusion.

LET ME EXPLAIN

Everything you do in your golf swing has one basic aim—sending the ball to the target. Easier said than done, of course. Achieving such a goal on a consistent basis requires that you get a few things right.

A straight, solidly hit shot results when the golf club moves along the proper path, when the angle of the clubhead's approach into the impact area is correct and when the clubface is square, or squaring, as it contacts the ball. Thus, the key to any golf swing is the plane on which the club moves from address to impact. In reality, it is the only thing that matters.

As with so many other aspects of golf, there are three possibilities when it comes to swing plane. Your club is either on plane, too upright (above the plane), or too flat (below the plane). . . . Every golfer has [his or her] own swing plane. Everyone is built differ-

Hank Haney has focused on reproducing the "plane angle" at impact.

ently and has different length arms, heights, setups—so each person has a swing plane unique to them.

WHAT DETERMINES THE SWING PLANE

The perfect swing plane for you is largely determined by your posture at address, the length of your arms, your height, and what percentage of that height is made up by your back versus your legs.

Having said that, swing planes of short and tall individuals are usually not that much different. They do vary some, but the real key is that you swing on your swing plane. The plane of someone else's swing is of no concern to you. In other words, everyone has a swing plane but there is no one swing plane for everyone. In general, tall people stand closer to the ball and have more upright swing planes. Those who are shorter tend to stand further from the ball and have flatter swing planes. Look at, say, Jeff Sluman and Nick Faldo and you'll see what I mean.

The swing plane is nothing new. As I said, it was the basis for Ben Hogan's *Modern Fundamentals*. In fact, in order to explain his swing plane philosophy, he created what may be the most famous and enduring image in golf instruction—the pane of glass angled through his shoulders and down to the ground. Hogan's theory was that you should swing the club below and parallel to the glass from address to the end of your follow-through. And that is how countless golfers have tried to swing on plane ever since.

Hogan produced a great image, but unfortunately he was wrong in this assertion. There is more than one plane in the perfect golf swing, but only one plane angle.

THE PLANE ANGLE

The plane of your swing is dictated by the angle at which the clubshaft lies at address, provided your clubs are fit correctly. Ideally, you want to reproduce that angle at impact. That would be perfection. And the best, easiest, and most repeatable way to achieve that—as you'd expect—is to swing the club on the plane angle from start to finish.

Notice I'm saying that the club swings on the same plane angle, not the same plane. If you remember nothing else from this chapter, take that sentence home with you. The most important thing to understand about the swing plane and swinging on plane is

that although there is one plane angle—the angle at which you set the clubshaft at address—the club must travel through more than one plane throughout the swing.

At first glance that can seem confusing. But it isn't. Here's how it works. The club starts back along the original angle of the shaft. You swing back along that plane. Then the club swings up and is above but parallel to the original angle of the shaft. So it is passing through different planes.

CONGRUENT ANGLES/DIFFERENT PLANES

As you move the golf club back it consistently goes up and in, the plane of your swing constantly changing as it does so. What doesn't change is the relationship between all those planes and the original angle of the clubshaft at address. They are always parallel.

Then, as you swing down, the club passes through those same planes on the way back to the ball . . . , all the while maintaining that parallel relationship.

It's up through the planes on the backswing, down through the same planes on downswing, and up again on the same planes on the follow-through. Achieve that and the angle of the clubshaft at impact will be the same as it was at address. That is the perfect swing, one which should produce a little draw. Unfortunately, most people don't follow that path or produce that ball-flight. Most golfers have a bunch of different loops in their swings and a seemingly infinite number of different shots.

Those parallel angles are called congruent angles. In other words, they are numerically the same angle but have different points of origin as the club moves back and through. Therefore, the clubshaft does not always point to the target-line at all stages of the swing, as some teachers have argued in the past.

As for Hogan's pane of glass, Ben's idea is doomed from the start. Because your arms have a slight droop in them as they hang down in address, you never actually swing the club on the plane established by this imaginary pane of glass. It would be physically impossible. So, don't try it. You'll hurt yourself and your game.

— 6 —

THE
BACKSWING

WAKING UP
THE CADDY

Elementary Instruction:
The Upward Swing

1890   HORACE G. HUTCHINSON

In this charming, if antiquated, essay, "Horatio" Hutchinson, who won his first of back-to-back British Amateur titles at St. Andrews in 1886, described the "St. Andrews Swing," the dominant technique of the era. Made popular by those who played on the gale-swept links of Scotland for four hundred years, this backswing had a flat, around-the-body motion designed to make the ball fly low under the prevailing winds and roll forward with topspin after it landed on hard, crusty fairways. The technique is long outmoded, but readers will find antecedents for concepts embedded in current swing theory, and recognize ideas furthered by swing experts from Bobby Jones to Butch Harmon. Hutchinson, a barrister, Oxford man and staunchly upper-class Brit, could write with common appeal, but also revert to form, once sniffing: "We borrowed golf from Scotland as we borrowed whiskey . . . not because it is Scottish, but because it is good."

The swing is, of course, made up of two parts, the upward and the downward swing; and the downward swing has a wonderful tendency to be, in point of direction, a reproduction, in reverse order, of the upward swing—that is to say, that the clubhead will tend to trace the same course in its downward flight as it did in its upward. This is a fact so well known that professionals take every pain to see that the learner gets the upward swing correctly, knowing by experience that a correct downward stroke will naturally follow. . . . So true is this, that an experienced observant player can nine times out of ten foretell, by watching the course of another's upward swing, whether or no he will make a correct swing of the downward stroke—that is to say, whether or no the shot will be a good one. Let us then give every due attention to this upward swing. . . . In leaving the ball, therefore, the clubhead should swing back as far as possible, but without too forced and painful straining after this objective. . . . The clubhead ought to sweep back along the ground, away from . . . the player. And how is this to be accomplished? By allowing the arms to go to their full length as the clubhead swings away from the ball, or as nearly to their full length as is possible without forced stretching. In order to prolong this horizontal sweep back of the club some players fall into the error of swaying the body toward the right as the club swings away; but this is a mistake, for the extended sweep is thus attained at too great an expense—at a sacrifice of accuracy. The driver's body should move on its own axis only; the shoulders working round as if the backbone were their pivot. Let the club, then, be swept well away from the ball, the arms swinging freely away from the body, the left hand gripping firmly, the right hand holding lightly. . . .

Now, when the club, in the course of its swing away from the ball, is beginning to rise from the ground, and is reaching the horizontal with its head pointing to the player's right, it should be allowed to turn naturally in the right hand until it is resting upon the web between the forefinger and the thumb. At the same time the right elbow should be raised well away from the body until, when the club is horizontal *behind* the head, this right elbow is considerably above the level of the right hand. The club will have turned so freely in the right hand that the right wrist will be straight—in a natural easy manner—and the back of the right hand will be uppermost. The slight crook which will have been given to the left elbow, as a natural result of the slight upward turn of the back of the left hand, will have allowed the left hand to come up above the level of the right shoulder without any fumbling of that elbow against the striker's chest; and the left wrist will have been turned back to allow the club to come to the horizontal behind the head—for it is behind the head and above the right shoulder, not *round* the shoulder, that the club must be allowed to swing. To let the arms swing well away from the body, and to let the club turn freely in the right hand, are the two great points to bear in mind.

Such, then, should be the course of the upward swing—roughly approximating to an arc of a circle with a somewhat flattened circumference toward its base. And—remember this—it is a *swing*.

How many times has it been inculcated upon the young player that he is to bring his club slowly back, and how many has it led astray? For the golfer, hearkening to these words of his mystic oracle, "Slow back," has a tendency to lift his club with a stealthy painfulness of motion, as of a man—as Sir Walter Simpson humorously has it—striving to grab a fly upon his ear. So slow, so painfully slow, deadly slow—and then—whang! with a jerk. This is fatal: a cruel instance of the vile uses to which an excellent maxim, misunderstood, may be turned. There should be a certain even harmony about the golfing swing. The club should swing back quietly, without jerk or effort—slowly if you will; but it must be a swing, and not a lift. It must swing quietly back, and it must not be arrested before it has done swinging back. The real meaning of the advice "slow back" is that the club is not to be hurried back so that it cannot travel well out

from the body. The advice called "quick back" means being in such a hurry to get the club up that it is swung too perpendicularly. The tiro who has this advice drummed into him is apt at last to turn in desperation and say, "Why, every good player brings his club up quick!" This is true, but he does not bring it up so quickly that he has not time to sweep out his arms, as the tiro will inevitably do if he tries to raise it equally quickly. Whether the swing be long or short, let the gentle force of the swing expend itself naturally, without effort of your muscles. . . .

At the Top of the Swing

Now as the club came to the horizontal, behind the head, the body will have been allowed to turn, gently, with its weight upon the right foot. The knees, when addressing the ball, should have been slightly bent, at an easy natural angle, and in order to allow the body to make this half turn, without effort, the left heel should be allowed to rise slightly off the ground, so that, with an inward bend of the left knee the whole body will turn, naturally, upon the left toe. This raising of the left heel should not be an artificial action,

The St. Andrews swing, favored for six hundred years.

so to speak—it should not be exaggerated with the view of *encouraging* the club to come round, but it should rather follow, as a natural sequence of the disposition of the rest of the frame. Some good drivers do not raise the heel at all, but this immobility is very little short of fatal to freedom. As in most other cases, the virtue is in the mean.

. . . When the club is at the horizontal, roughly speaking, behind the back—i.e., at the top of the swing—the left forearm will be almost vertical from elbow to wrist, with elbow the lowest point, and will be brought round to what was the striker's front, as he stood when addressing the ball. It will be seen, too, that the left shoulder has been allowed to swing round underneath the head, while the right shoulder is above.

. . . The backbone must be steady, approximately speaking—for the body is not to be swung back, away from the ball (that, as has been pointed out, is a frequent error), but rather the shoulders are to swing round, upon the backbone, between the shoulder blades as their pivot—working freely on a steady pivot.

From *The Badminton Library: Golf*, by Horace G. Hutchinson. Longmans, Green, and Co., London, England.

Slow Back—The Line of the Clubhead in the Upward Swing

1905   H A R R Y   V A R D O N

The father of modern golf—in whose honor a trophy is awarded annually to the PGA golfer with the lowest stroke average—not only popularized the still-dominant overlapping grip but also developed a swing that changed the game. In *The Complete Golfer*, which includes numerous photographs of Vardon in action, he furthered the democratization of the sport, saying that he was trying to help "improving golfers of all degrees of skill"—and presumably, on all rungs of Britain's social ladder. This excerpt begins with a familiar maxim, as Vardon suggested players take the club back slowly. But then he staked out new ground. Rather than urging his followers to then sweep the club away in the old St. Andrews style, Vardon told them to continue taking it back along the target line—the same move taught by swing teachers today and put into practice by all good golfers.

As a first juncture, it may be stated that the club should be drawn back rather more slowly than you intend to bring it down again. "Slow back" is a golfing maxim that is both old and wise. The club should begin to gain speed when the upward swing is about half made, and the increase should be gradual until the top is reached, but it should never be so fast that control of the club is to any extent lost at the turning-point. The head of the club should be taken back fairly straight from the ball . . . for the first six inches, and after that, any tendency to sweep it round sharply to the back should be avoided. Keep it very close to the straight line until is halfway up. The old St. Andrews style of driving largely consisted in this sudden sweep round, but the modern method appears to be easier and productive of better results. So this carrying of the head of the club upward and backward seems to be a very simple matter, capable of explanation in a very few words; but, as every golfer of a month's experience knows, there is a long list of details to be attended to, which I have not yet named, each of which seems to vie with the others in its attempt to destroy the effectiveness of the drive. Let us begin at the top, as it were, and work downward, and first of all there is the head of the golfer to consider.

The head should be kept virtually motionless from the time of the address until the ball has been sent away and is well on its flight. The least deviation from this rule means a proportionate danger of disaster. When a drive has been badly foozled, the readiest and most usual explanation is that the eye has been taken off the ball, and the wise old men who have been watching shake their heads solemnly, and utter that parrot-cry of the links, "Keep your eye on the ball." Certainly this is a good and necessary rule so far as it goes; but I do not believe that one drive in a hundred is missed because the eye has not been kept on the ball. On the other hand, I believe that one of the most fruitful causes of failure with the tee shot is the moving of the head. Until the ball has gone, it should, as I say, be as nearly perfectly still as possible, and I would have written that it should not be moved to the extent of a sixteenth of an inch, but for the fact that it is not human to be so still, and golf is always inclined to the human side. When the head has

been kept quite still and the club has reached the top of the upward swing, the eyes should be looking over the middle of the left shoulder, the left one being dead over the center of that shoulder. Most players at one time or another, and the best of them when they are a little off their game, fall into every trap that the evil spirits of golf lay for them, and unconsciously experience a tendency to lift the head for five or six inches away from the ball while the upward swing is being taken. This is often what is imagined to be taking the eye off the ball, particularly as, when it is carried to excess, the eye, struggling gallantly to do its duty, finds considerable difficulty in getting a sight of the ball over the left shoulder, and sometimes loses it altogether for an instant. . . .

In the upward swing the right shoulder should be raised gradually. It is unnecessary for me to submit any instruction on this point, since the movement is natural and inevitable, and there is no tendency toward excess; but the arms and wrists need attention. From the moment when the club is first taken back the left wrist should begin to turn inward (that is to say the movement is in the same direction as that taken by the hands of a clock), and so turn away the face of the club from the ball. When this is properly done, the toe of the club will point to the sky when it is level with the shoulder and will be dead over the middle of the shaft. This turning or twisting process continues all the way until at the top of the swing the toe of the club is pointing straight downward to the ground. . . . The left wrist [should finish] the upward swing underneath the shaft. . . . When the wrist has not been at work in the manner indicated, the toe of the club at the top of the drive will be pointing upward. In order to satisfy himself properly about the state of affairs thus far in the making of the drive, the golfer should test himself at the top of the swing by holding the club firmly in the position which it has reached, and then dropping the right hand from the grip. He will thus be enabled to look right round, and if he then finds that the maker's name on the head of the club is horizontal, he will know that he has been doing the right thing with his wrists, while if it is vertical the wrist action has been altogether wrong.

During the upward swing the arms should be gradually let out in the enjoyment of perfect ease and freedom (without being spread-eagled away from the body) until at the top of the swing the left arm, from the shoulder to the elbow, is gently touching the body and hanging well down, while the right arm is up above it and almost level with the club. . . .

In the upward movement of the club the body must pivot from the waist alone, and there must be no swaying not even to the extent of an inch. When the player sways in his drive the stroke he makes is a body stroke pure and simple. The body is trying to do the work the arms should do, and in these circumstances it is impossible to get so much power into the stroke as if it were properly made, while once more the old enemies, the slice and pull, will come out from their hiding places with their mocking grin at the unhappy golfer.

The movements of the feet and legs are important. In addressing the ball you stand with both feet flat and securely placed on the ground, the weight equally divided between them, and the legs so slightly bent at the knee joints as to make the bending scarcely noticeable. This position is maintained during the upward movement of the club until the arms begin to pull at the body. The easiest and most natural thing to do then, and the one which suggests itself, is to raise the heel of the left foot and begin to pivot on the left toe, which allows the arms to proceed with their uplifting process without let or hindrance. Do not begin to pivot on this left toe ostentatiously, or because you feel you ought to do so, but only when you know the time has come and you want to, and do it only to such an extent that the club can reach the full extent of the swing without any difficulty. While this is happening it follows that the weight of the body is being gradually thrown on to the right leg, which accordingly stiffens until at the top of the swing it is quite rigid, the left leg being at the same time in a state of comparative freedom, slightly bent in toward the right, with only just enough pressure on the toe to keep it in position.

To the man who has never driven a good ball in his life this process must seem very tedious. All these things to attend to, and something less than a second in which to attend to them! It only indicates how much there is in this wonderful game—more by far than any of us suspect or shall ever discover. But the time comes, and it should come speedily, when they are all accomplished without any effort, and indeed, to a great extent, unconsciously. The upward swing is everything. If it is bad and faulty, the downward swing will be wrong and the ball will not be properly driven. If it is perfect, there is a splendid prospect of a long and straight drive, carrying any hazard that may lie before the tee. That is why so very much emphasis must be laid on getting this upward swing perfect, and why comparatively little attention need be paid to the downward swing, even though it is really the effective part of the stroke.

From *The Complete Golfer*, by Harry Vardon. Methuen & Company, London, England.

PAUSE AT THE TOP

Tommy Armour created perhaps the most famous and useful tip in the history of golf instruction when he came up with "pause at the top," a technique he used himself to become a deadly skillful iron player. Realizing that many golfers often hurry the start of the downswing, and thus botch their shots in a variety of ways, Armour was looking for an image that would force them to move more slowly into the transition from backswing to downswing. Whether there is actually a "pause" or not, the idea is to wait for the lower body to start the downswing, rather than using the hands first and thus coming over the top.

Jock Hutchison:
An Upswing in Three Parts

1924 ✑ R. ENDERSBY HOWARD

St. Andrews–born Jock Hutchison finished second to Jim Barnes in the first PGA Championship in 1916, won in 1920, and became the first naturalized American citizen to capture the British Open in 1921. Years later, the dour, nervous Scot starred in a three-dimensional "stereopticon" instructional slide series—called "Corte-Scope Golf"—that was a sensation and foreshadowed the sequential teachings of modern instructors like David Leadbetter and Jim McLean. Judging from this oddity by British golf writer R. Endersby Howard—a rare early instructional piece to analyze a golfer's swing—Hutchison's technique would seem to be a strange choice for study and emulation. Howard related that Harry Vardon taught the swing in three parts, but said Hutchison was the only golfer so deliberate during the backswing that the three stages were evident to the naked eye. Decades later Leadbetter and McLean would teach the continuous swing by breaking it down into stages.

Jock Hutchison of Chicago, British Open golf champion of 1921, is like no other first class player I have ever seen. He's the only champion who seems to hide none of his art. If he tried deliberately to make it all perfectly clear by showing it in installments, even during the most thrilling struggles, he could not achieve a greater success. He is a living, working model of the golf swing—or, rather, the uptake of the club, which is where most people go wrong—dissected into three parts. Each part has its perceptible beginning and ending, although the three sections merge into a whole.

When Vardon was endeavoring once to drill into my head the correct principles of the upswing, he said: "You know that mechanical figure whose hand goes up to the salute, when you pull a string? The hand rises with three jerks: it starts out and pauses, goes up and pauses, and then comes in and finishes by the side of

the head. Well, that's the idea of the golf swing, except that the hands move up to the head in an arc and there are no jerks. But the idea of the three movements is a good one to remember so long as you swing with a rhythm that makes the whole movement continuous, and do not create any complications by disconnecting when you finish the one section and join on the next."

Jock Hutchison makes this principle plainer to see than anybody else ever has done. Watch him playing a drive or a nearly full iron shot. His first movement is to take the clubhead away from the ball—back about two feet. That is an operation all to itself. I will not say he does it in the same manner as most other golfers, for whereas they nearly all keep the clubhead close to the ground and follow a line straight behind the ball for two or three inches, Hutchison appears to lift the clubhead up the instant he starts it.

It is an abrupt looking trait in his methods. It probably explains why, having completed the first section, he permits himself a semi-pause—not a complete stoppage, but an unmistakable slowing down, as though he were steadying the clubhead and himself for the second section.

He gathers pace again—although his backswing is never fast—until the club reaches the stage where it is ready to fall into position behind his head, preparatory to starting the downswing. There is another slight pause; and then the club falls into position with, perhaps, a very slight relaxation of the grip and the upswing is complete.

It is the most manifest operation in three parts that I have ever seen, and the first time I watched Hutchison I recollected instantly the analogy that Vardon had drawn some years previously between the mechanical figure that saluted in three parts and the golfer's upswing, accomplished also in three stages.

To try and do it with the deliberateness with which Hutchison does it would lead the ordinary player into disaster. To make these distinct joints in the swing without causing the whole movement to become disjointed must be very difficult. There is obviously considerable danger of a disturbance of the poise or a lowering of the head toward the ball in a carefully thought out scheme of raising the club stage by stage.

In connection with this point, one is reminded of a peculiarity in the methods of that very excellent lady player, Miss Cecil Leitch. She reaches what we may term the second stage without any perceptible change of balance or head. Then she pauses before completing the upswing, and as the club goes farther back her head goes forward an inch or so. There are good judges who think this last little movement puts her swing out of gear, and keeps her on the fringe instead of being in the midst of the group of champions.

Hutchison goes through with his three parts without ever sacrificing one iota of his physical balance or head-position. I dare say he does it naturally; that is, he is unconscious of the dissection of the swing that he is throwing into such bold relief. Probably the average golfer who decided to try this system would have to train himself to be no more than subconsciously aware of the three stages of the upswing. But, then, the subconscious influence is always the best influence in golf. To endeavor literally, methodically, and with that knowledge which the mind has of its own acts and feelings to do exactly what a famous player does is hopeless. Perceptions which are not allowed to become oppressive rules of action undoubtedly do help.

Whether Hutchison honors the traditional theory that the clubhead must come down by exactly the same track as that which it follows when going up I do not know. Whether, indeed, this belief is supported in practice by any of the leading golfers of today is open to question. The downswing is so very fast by comparison with the upswing that nobody can tell. Hutchison, having recovered the clubhead from the top of the swing and started it gently downwards, seems simply to sling it at the ball.

"Sling," I think, is the right expression if by it can be conveyed the idea of a smooth swing with a punch in it, a combination, indeed, of swing and hit.

From *Lessons From Great Golfers*, by R. Endersby Howard. Methuen & Company, London, England.

I want the sensation that I've turned my upper body over my right leg with my back to the target.

KARRIE WEBB

The Backswing

CIRCA 1930 ✑ ROBERT TYRE (BOBBY) JONES, JR.

In the 1966 book *Bobby Jones on Golf*, Jones and *Golf Magazine*'s Charles Price reworked Jones's articles from the years before and after his retirement in 1930. In this excerpt, golf's first matinee idol advanced several ideas modern readers will recognize. Jones, the last great golfer to use hickory-shafted clubs, had a swing that was by necessity "handsy," but, like today's pros, employed a fully integrated body turn and relied on exquisite rhythm. Jones asserted that the left side of the body dominated the action, and that the left arm should be kept straight in the backswing—concepts that evolved into the "one-piece takeaway." He also advanced the notion that the upper body "coiled" like a spring against the resistance of the legs. In effect, these ideas led to Byron Nelson's invention of the modern swing and opened new avenues that theorists from Ben Hogan to Butch Harmon would explore.

———

It is often urged that a person playing golf who worries about how to take the club back, how to start it down, and what to do at this stage and at that, ultimately loses sight of the only important thing he has to do—to hit the ball. We, who write on the game and those who attempt to teach it, are told often enough that we should give more attention to the contact stage and less to the details of the preparatory movements.

. . . [T]he backswing has for its purpose the establishment of a perfectly balanced, powerful position at the top of the swing from which the correct actions of the down-stroke can flow rhythmically without the need for interference or correction. In the end, on the basis of consistent reproduction of the successful action, the preparatory movements become just as important as the actual hitting—the entire swing, a sequence of correct positions, following naturally and comfortably one after the other.

ORIGINATING THE BACKSWING

. . . The moderate flatness of the swing that I like must result from a correct body-turn, and not from manipulation of the club by the hands and wrists. Many players begin the backswing with a sudden pronation of the left wrist that whips the club sharply around the legs, opening the face very quickly. This is just as bad as a swing straight back, carrying the arms away from the player's body.

The initial movement of the club away from the ball should result from forces originating in the left side. The real takeoff is from the left foot, starting the movement of the body. The hands and arms very soon pick it up, but the proper order at the very beginning is body, arms, and lastly clubhead. It is always easier to continue a motion than to begin it; this order has the virtue of originating the hip-turn; it goes a long way toward assuring a proper windup of the hips during the backswing.

It is easy to think of the golf swing entirely in terms of the clubhead, and, after getting set, more or less painfully, to begin the backswing by some sort of movement of the hands to start the clubhead going. Regardless of what this movement may be, it is bound to result in neglect of the all-important turning movement.

ARGUMENTS FOR A LONG BACKSWING

. . . One of the characteristics of the true swing, and the one that most often escapes the inexpert player, is the ample sweep of the backward windup. The average golfer, partly because he is unfamiliar with the movements that will accommodate a long backswing, and partly because he does not trust himself to go so far, almost always favors a short, hacking stroke. Quickly back and quickly down, employing a sudden acceleration almost amounting to a jerk, there is scarcely any chance of obtaining power or accuracy.

The most usual argument in favor of a backswing of good length is that it allows a longer arc and more time to attain the maximum clubhead speed at the instant of contact. But there are others of less equal force. It is certain that the more gradual acceleration made possible by the longer backswing is bound to make the swing much smoother and less likely to be yanked out of its groove; also, it is certain that it makes it possible to attain an equal speed with less sudden effort and therefore less likelihood of introducing contrary forces detracting from the power of the stroke. . . .

If we liken the backswing of a golf club to the extension of a coil spring, or the stretching of a rubber band, I think we shall not be very far off the mark. The greater the extension or stretching, the greater the force of the return. In the golf swing, every inch added to the backward windup, up to the limit at which the balance of the body can be easily maintained, represents additional stored energy available to increase the power of the downswing. It may be possible for a player with a comparatively short windup to make up this difference by an extraordinary hitting effort, but he will never be able to do so without more than a proportionate loss in smoothness and precision.

Bobby Jones's backswing motion and theories gave birth to the "one-piece takeaway."

It seems to me likely that too much stress has been laid upon the desirability of compactness in the swing, especially when the impression is that such compactness demands an abbreviated stroke. Many players have come to believe that a short backswing, by eliminating some of the body turn, simplifies the stroke to such an extent that grave errors will be avoided. I have always held the contrary view, and am convinced that a great many more shots are spoiled by a swing that is too short than by one that is too long, and this applies in the use of every club, from the driver down to and including the putter. . . .

Roll of the Left Foot

Many players, for one reason or another, form the habit of arriving at the top of the swing with too much of their weight supported by the left leg. This is usually evidenced by the heel of the left foot being firmly planted on the ground at this stage. Not only in such a swing is the player prevented from shifting his hips forward as he begins to unwind, but the necessity of maintaining his balance will always force him to fall back upon his right foot as he swings through.

The raising of the left heel during the backswing must not be considered to be an end in itself; rather, it is to be looked upon as the result of handling the backward windup of the body in a correct fashion. The body simply turns, with the weight either moving back toward the right foot, or, if enough of it is already there, without any lateral shift whatever, and the heel comes up as the leg action accommodates the turning movement.

One thing should be emphasized—that there must be no pivoting on the toe of the left foot. The weight supported by this leg at the start of the backswing should be felt to roll across the foot until it is resting upon the inside of the ball of the foot and the great toe. The player who swings his foot around and pirouettes upon his toe until the entire sole of the shoe is exposed to the hole is guilty of a very serious mistake. By doing so, he puts his left leg entirely out of commission and otherwise upsets any possibility of correct body movement. . . .

The Position at the Top

There is no part of the golf swing that consists of one simple movement. The whole thing is a process of blending, correlating, and harmonizing simple movements until smooth, rhythmic motion is achieved. When actually swinging a club, there is no way to complete the body turn and wrist movement separately, having done with one before the other is commenced.

Now there are a number of important things to be watched in the position at the top of the swing. It is possible to write many pages on this phase of the stroke. But the one feature I have in mind now is the one the duffer ignores entirely, and yet it has everything to do with the success of the stroke.

At the top of the swing the shaft of the club, which for the long shots is in a position approximately in a horizontal plane, should at the same time be pointing to a spot slightly to the right of the object at which the player is aiming. This will be found to be a uniform practice among the best professional golfers. It is the result of swinging the club back to the top, rather than lifting it up as so many beginners do. . . .

The Straight Left Arm

Good form in any physical activity must be valued in terms of efficiency. The efficiency of a thermal engine, for example, is measured by the ratio of the work done by the engine to the heat energy supplied to it. The efficiency of a golf stroke must be measured, in the same way, by the ratio of the work done on the ball to the amount of physical energy used up in the swinging. The expert golfer drives far with little apparent effort because of the high rate of efficiency of his performance. The duffer, though he strains himself to the utmost, falls far behind because so much of the energy expended goes to waste.

A high rate of efficiency, and hence good form, in golf, depends upon three things: the development of the greatest possible clubhead speed at contact, with whatever energy or power the player can supply; the achievement of a precisely accurate contact between club and ball, directing the blow along the line upon which it is intended that the ball shall travel; and consistency in performing approximately according to these standards.

Although these are obvious generalities, it is helpful to do a little thinking along these lines in order to appreciate the importance to a golfer of a proper use of his left arm. For it is in this particular that all duffers are most appallingly deficient, and here, too, that the better players most often go astray.

For some persons, a straight left arm is a physical impossibility. So let us say that an extended left arm is one of the prime requisites of good form. In many ways, it contributes to clubhead speed, accurate contact, and consistency of performance—the three components of the efficiency rate.

Just now we are interested chiefly in the backswing. The backward movement is merely the means of storing up power to be used in the hitting—but to increase the amount of this stored-up energy is of first importance. We have seen that the beginning was made in the hips in order to assure that the windup of the body would at least be started. When this has progressed a short distance, we began to force the club back with the left arm.

Now with the club having completed about half of its backward travel, the left arm has become almost straight, and is pushing the club as far back as it can comfortably go. The arc of the swing is thus made wide so that the space and time for adding speed to the clubhead coming down will be as great as possible.

The player who allows his left arm to bend perceptibly is sacrificing width of arc and power. His swing, because it is not as wide as it could be, is that much away from the ideal of efficiency that he could make it.

There is nothing in the straight left arm that, of itself, increases the power of the swing. It is a part of a sound method, for those who are able to keep it straight, because it is the factor which definitely limits the arc of the backswing. Consequently, when the arm is straight, this arc is as wide as it can be made, and the swing can then be more easily repeated time after time in the same groove. Except that the bending of the arm reduces the width of the arc, and hence the time and space within which the speed of the clubhead may be built up, the chief loss from the bend is in precision.

At that, few players keep the left arm rigidly straight during the backswing. I like to have the feeling of pushing the club back with the left arm because this assures that it will be reasonably extended, but the arm does not become completely straight until it is stretched out by the beginning of the reverse turn of the hips, back toward the ball, while the club is completing its backward movement.

In order to complete a backswing of full length, at the same time keeping the left arm even approximately straight, there must be a good bit of movement in the hips and waist. Naturally, a good free turn of the hips is not so easy for the player past middle age, whose waistline lacks some of the suppleness of former years. If he wants to get the club back at all, the left elbow simply must give a little. There is no other way.

The important thing, so far as the left arm is concerned, is that it should not collapse in the act of hitting. In the motion pictures of Harry Vardon, made when the great Englishman had passed his sixtieth birthday, a bend of almost ninety degrees could be seen in the left elbow at the top of the swing. Yet as soon as the hip-turn had stretched out the left side, this arm became straight and remained so until after the ball had been struck. The bend at the top, then, is by no means fatal if the succeeding movements are performed correctly.

What will help most is complete relaxation. Timing and rhythm can make up a lot in power. By all means, swing the club freely, both backward and forward, and avoid the tightening a short backswing must produce.

From *Bobby Jones On Golf*, by Robert Tyre (Bobby) Jones, Jr. Doubleday & Company, Garden City, New York. Reworking of material from 1927–35 published by the Bell Syndicate and in *The American Golfer*. Copyright © 1966 by Robert Tyre Jones, Jr. Reprinted with permission of the family of Robert T. Jones, Jr.

The First Part of the Swing

1957 ✎ BEN HOGAN
WITH HERBERT WARREN WIND

Ben Hogan won nine Majors, including a career Grand Slam, had sixty-four PGA Tour victories overall, and wrote instruction to explain why he was so good. In this classic lesson from his second book, he described what many golfers consider the ideal backswing model (except, possibly, for the notion of the hands starting the sequence). Hogan's key concept was to inhibit the movement of the hips, thereby building dynamic tension between the upper and lower parts of the body in order to unleash a powerful downswing. The germ for that idea had come from Bobby Jones and today is most dramatically visible in the swings of Tiger Woods and Michelle Wie. Hogan also provided the still defining image of how to "finish" the backswing, advising golfers to wait until they feel their left shoulders come under their chins. As this piece makes obvious, Hogan was a true technocrat of the game.

———————◆———————

This phase of the swing requires some instinct, a sense of organization, some thought, and a fair control of muscular action. It is, however, much less involved than this makes it appear. Learning the backswing actually consists of getting a few movements clear in your mind and then learning to execute them. This is where the golf shot begins to be played.

The first point about the backswing (and the swing in general) I want to emphasize is this: If his body, legs, and arms are properly positioned and poised to begin with, any golfer with average physical equipment can learn to execute the proper movements. This is why you must build on a correct grip and stance, for the golf swing is an accumulative thing. All the actions are linked together. . . .

The backswing is . . . initiated by the almost simultaneous movement of the hands, arms, and shoulders. . . . [T]he golf swing is, in principle, a continuous chain of actions. Like the component parts of the engine of an automobile, the component parts of the swing fuse together and work together in a purposeful sequence. As each component performs its part of the operation, it sets up the proper operation of the other components with which it is connected. I bring this up at this particular point, for if a golfer clearly grasps the interrelationship of the hands, arms, shoulders, and hips, he will play good golf—he can't help but play good golf.

On the backswing, the order of movement goes like this: hands, arms, shoulders, hips . . . On the backswing, the hands, arms, and shoulders start to move almost simultaneously. *Actually, the hands start the clubhead back a split second before the arms start back. And the arms begin their movement a split second before the shoulders begin to turn. As a golfer acquires feel and rhythm through practice, the hands, arms, and shoulders will instinctively tie in on this split-second schedule.*

Ben Hogan believed that finding the elusive "slot" at the top of the backswing assures a powerful through-swing.

The main point for the novice is to know that they do start back so closely together that their action is unified.

On the backswing, the shoulders are always ahead of the hips as they turn. The shoulders should start turning immediately. The hips do not. *Just before your hands reach hip level, the shoulders, as they turn, automatically, start pulling the hips around, as the hips begin to turn, they pull the left leg in to the right.* Now let us examine these actions in closer detail.

THE SHOULDERS. You want to turn the shoulders as far around as they'll go. (Your head, of course, remains stationary.) When you have turned your shoulders all the way, your back should face squarely toward your target. . . . Most golfers think that they make a full shoulder turn going back and they would challenge you if you claimed they didn't, but the truth is

that few golfers really complete their shoulder turn. They stop turning when the shoulders are about halfway around; then, in order to get the clubhead all the way back, they break the left arm. This is really a false backswing. It isn't any backswing at all. A golfer can't have control of the club or start down into the ball with any power or speed unless his left arm is straight to begin with. When he bends his left arm, he actually performs only a half swing and he forfeits half his potential power. More than this, he then is led into making many exhausting extra movements that accomplish nothing for him.

An excellent way to check that you are making a full shoulder turn is this: *When you finish your backswing, your chin should be hitting against the top of your left shoulder.* Just where the chin contacts the shoulder depends on the individual golfer's physical proportions. In my own case, it's about an inch from the end of the shoulder. My golf shirts have a worn-down spot at this particular point.

THE HIPS. Turning the hips too soon is an error countless golfers make, and it's a serious error. It destroys your chance of obtaining the power a correctly integrated swing gives you. As you begin the backswing, you must restrain your hips from moving until the turn of the shoulders starts to pull the hips around.

Some prominent golfers advocate taking a big turn with the hips. I don't go along with this. If the hips are turned too far around, then you can create no tension in the muscles between the hips and the shoulders. A golfer wants to have this tension; he wants the mid-section of his body to be tightened up, for this tension is the key to the whole downswing. . . . [I]t is so important to have this torsion, this stretching of the muscles, that results from turning your shoulders as far as they can go and retarding the hips. It's the difference in the amount of turn between the shoulders and hips that sets up this muscular tension. If the hips were turned as much as the shoulders, there'd be no tightening up at all.

THE LEGS. When the hips enter the swing, as they are turned they pull the left leg in. The left knee breaks in to the right, the left foot rolls in to the right on the inside part of the sole, and what weight there is on the left leg rides on the inside ball of the foot. *Let me caution you against lifting the left heel too high off the ground* on the backswing. *If the heel stays on the ground—fine. If it comes up an inch off the ground—fine.* No higher than that, though—it will only lead to faulty balance and other undesirable complications.

The body and the legs move the feet. *Let them move the feet.* As regards the left heel, how much the left knee breaks in on the backswing determines how much the heel comes up. I never worry about the left heel. Whether it comes off the ground a half-inch or a quarter of an inch or remains on the ground as a result of my body and leg action on the backswing—this is of no importance at all. I pay no attention to it.

As regards the right leg, it should maintain the same position it had at address, the same angle in relation to the ground, throughout the backswing. That is one of the checks the average golfer should make when he's warming up and when's he's on the course. When you have a stable right leg and the right knee remains pointed in a bit, it prevents the leg from sagging and swaying out to the right and carrying the body along with it.

Nicklaus: 22 Years at Hard Labor

1972 ✎ ALISTAIR COOKE

Alistair Cooke, the one-time U.S. correspondent for England's *Guardian* and host of *Masterpiece Theater*, was a man of letters and a man of the links. Among his writings on golf was this sharp examination of how Jack Nicklaus, who had just captured his thirteenth of an eventual eighteen Majors, developed his distinct backswing under the tutelage of his inspirational, long-time mentor Jack Grout. Cooke viewed Grout as strict but smart enough to recognize this pupil was capable of adding creativity to the basics. There's no mention of Nicklaus's famous flying elbow, but Cooke suspected young golfers already would flame out trying to emulate the powerful, exaggerated body turn and enormously wide arc Nicklaus employed to trigger a vicious, leg-driven through-swing. Content that his pupil was fundamentally sound, Grout didn't make Nicklaus temper his tendency to swing for the fences, confirming that *great* golfers have unique styles that can't always be imitated.

Jack Nicklaus, 32, of Columbus, Ohio, is the best golfer in the world, and he means to improve. That, in brief, is what sets him apart from the other giants of the game, and perhaps from the giants of most other games also. He first picked up a golf club when he was 10 and for the past 22 years has been laboring over his game, in the flesh by day and in the mind by night. He is certainly the most cerebral golfer since Ben Hogan, whose *Fundamentals of Modern Golf* is practically an advanced text on human anatomy and aerodynamics. And he is the coolest, the least fooled, analyst of his own game since "the immortal one" of golf, Robert Tyre Jones, Jr., who, since he is now dead, is more immortal than ever.

"The golf swing for me," Nicklaus told Herbert Warren Wind, his Boswell in the best golfing biography that has appeared so far, "is a source of never-ending fascination. On the one hand, the swings of all the outstanding golfers are decidedly individual but, on the other, the champions all execute approximately the same moves at the critical stages of the swing. . . . There is still a lot about the swing we don't know and probably never will. . . . In any event, scarcely a day goes by when I don't find myself thinking about the golf swing." . . .

Jack William Nicklaus (pronounced Nick-lus, not Nick-louse) is the great-grandson of an immigrant boilermaker from Alsace-Lorraine and the son of a prosperous Columbus, Ohio, pharmacist whose hobbies were Ohio State football, golf, fishing, and telling his son of the miracles of St. Robert Tyre Jones, Jr. Jack was born in 1940, the year of Dunkirk and the Fall of France, when the British were plowing up their golf courses and planting land mines against the anticipated Nazi invasion. . . .

He had started to toddle, and hack, around a golf course after his father injured his ankle badly, prompting the doctor to suggest that henceforth, Father Nicklaus forgo volleyball and take to gentler exercise, "the sort of movement you get when you walk on soft ground." Father turned to golf but found himself something of a lagging invalid to his regular partners so he haled in his 10-year-old son as a walking companion. The youngster got his first set of cut-down golf clubs just as the Scioto golf club, to which Father Nicklaus belonged, acquired a new pro, Jack Grout, then a taut, tanned 42-year

old. Nicklaus to this day has had no other teacher except himself, who is probably the more exacting of the two.

So on a Friday morning in June 1950, the golden bear cub lined up on the practice tee with 50 other youngsters. It is clear from the record that the perfectionist strain in the Nicklaus character at once took over to refine the normal, rollicking ambition of small boys to bang out rockets. The first time he played nine holes, he had a creditable 51. . . . He supplemented the Friday morning regimental drill with private lessons from Grout. The knobbly-jointed stripling began to develop a golf swing. . . .

If there was any luck in the time and place of his initiation, it was in having Grout newly arrived at Scioto. Grout was a teacher with some firm convictions, one of which, however, was that every golfer is an individual. This runs counter to the insistence of many young pros—and most of the textbooks—that every pupil must be broken in to the mold of a favorite dogma. For instance, 998 golfers in 1,000 use the Vardon grip, which has the little finger of the right hand resting on top of the cleft between the first and second fingers of the left. The 999th manages, don't ask me why, with a baseball grip, the two hands completely separated. Nicklaus was the 1,000th oddity who was more comfortable interlocking or hooking the little finger of the right hand securely around the forefinger of the left. Nicklaus indeed, the big bear of the broad beam and the 27-inch thighs, has small hands so surprisingly weak in their grip that he swears he has often asked his wife, a girl svelte to the point of fragility, to unscrew pickle jars for him. Grout let him stay with this eccentricity, and he uses it today.

But Grout's tolerance of idiosyncrasy had severe limits. He insisted from the start on two fundamentals. Since they apply to every golfer, young and old, they may help us all, if only we can absorb them well enough to let them pass over into what Ben Hogan memorably called "the muscle memory." Nicklaus avows that his game is rooted in these two fundamentals.

The first is that "the head must be kept still" throughout the swing. Nicklaus figures it took him at least two years to master this simplicity, sometimes under the duress of having Grout's assistant hold on the hair of Snow White's head to make him, in J. H. Taylor's fine phrase, "play beneath himself." Anyone who has ever had his head gripped while trying to repeat a serviceable swing will have quickly learned the painful truth that we are all "natural" jumping jacks. I once had an easy-going friend, a cheerful hacker who refused to take any lessons on the down-to-earth assertion that "I simply try to be a pendulum." Unfortunately, the human body is constructed with marvelous ingenuity, not to be a pendulum. . . .

The second fundamental, which Nicklaus maintains gave his game its early solidity, was Grout's insistence that "the key to balance is rolling the ankles inward," the left toward the right on the backswing, the right in to the left on the downswing. Here . . . the picture in the mind has been painted many different ways. Some talk of keeping the left heel down while "bracing the right leg." Jones hit off a sharp poetic image when he said that golf is played "between the knees." Nicklaus more recently said, "If you go over beyond your right instep on the backswing, if you relax the pressure there, you are dead." And George Heron, the little 80-year-old Scot who, as a boy made clubs for Vardon, is still telling pupils down in St. Augustine, Fla., "A knock-kneed man is going to be a better golfer than a bow-legged one."

Well, on these two fundamentals alone, Nicklaus calculated he spent four or five years, in the meantime working through the range of clubs for hours on end on the practice tee. He says today "whenever anything goes wrong," he goes out and hits a thousand balls "flat-footed," neither lifting his heels nor moving his ankles, as a drastic way of restoring his sense of balance. . . .

There was a third fundamental taught to the young Nicklaus which decidedly does not apply to golfers of all ages and which, in Grout's day, was condemned for golfers of any age. The general practice was to force youngsters to resist the urge to go for distance and to teach them precision first. Grout felt that a boy should begin at once to stretch and develop the back muscles that would let him take the club as high, and as far behind, as a straight left arm would allow. The longer the arc of the club on the backswing, and the more acute the angle between the clubshaft and the left arm as the hands come down and go ahead of the ball: this, not the blacksmith's mighty muscle, is the secret of distance. Nicklaus achieves it with a vast arc at the top of the backswing, his left shoulder bulging beneath and almost beyond the set of his chin, while his left arm and hands are poking into the stratosphere. I have walked along with him even on practice rounds when only a lynx could follow the trajectory from the clubhead through the sky.

It is a sight whose result produces flattering gasps from the crowd around the tees. It has nothing to do with Hercules and everything to do with centrifugal force. Nonetheless, it is an act which most of us over 40 had better not try to emulate, unless an ambulance is on call. . . .

From *The New York Times Magazine* (July 9, 1972), by Alistair Cooke. Reprinted by permission of the estate of Alistair Cooke.

SHAKING HANDS

Glenna Collett Vare, "The Queen of American Golf," won eight international championships in the 1920s. In *Golf for Young Players*, she devised a drill to teach women the proper weight shift in the backswing. Advising them to stand before a mirror, she told them to put their hands on their hips, and then turn to look at something beside them. "Your hips have made a turn such as they will make in a full swing of golf," she wrote, "and the whole scheme of balance, or equilibrium, are then felt and understood." A modern variation, taught by such diverse instructors as Bob Toski and Butch Harmon, is for the golfer to imagine turning to shake hands with or hand the golf club to an imaginary person standing to the right. ❧

The Backswing: Coiling Behind the Ball

1981 ✑ JIMMY BALLARD
WITH BRENNAN QUINN

Jimmy Ballard's teaching approach includes finding the "common denominators" in the eye-candy swings of superstars from Walter Hagen to Seve Ballesteros. According to Ballard, "connection" is a significant common element and in this excerpt from his influential book, he describes how the "connected backswing" helps the golfer coil behind the ball and trigger a powerful downswing action. It's a concept he learned from Sam Byrd, a Yankee teammate of Babe Ruth who became a successful PGA pro and instructor. Byrd, who gave Ballard his first job in golf, taught him his "handkerchief" drill, inspired by Byrd and Ruth's technique of keeping towels under their left arms throughout their swings at batting practice. The idea was to keep the arms close to the chest and utilize the big muscles of the upper body. Today, numerous PGA pros, including Vijay Singh, religiously do a version of this exercise using a golf glove.

Hardly a day goes by when I don't meet at least one student who complains of a lack of distance and admits to having spent many frustrating years of trying to make a better weight shift, or a more positive move through the ball.

Almost without exception, these golfers have spent all of their time and energy after the fact. They can't swing the club through the ball correctly because they didn't swing it back correctly. It's as simple as that. Only by making a sound backswing can the player create the position and leverage that will produce a sound golf shot. In this respect, we might say that a golfer is only as good as his backswing. . . .

Although it is relatively simple to illustrate and explain the connected backswing, some players have difficulty trying to produce the necessary changes. For the most part, the reason lies in the vast difference between what the great ball strikers actually do when they swing the club back, and what most instructors teach in this critical area. Here again, there are a number of misconceptions that have been accepted as gospel by a large majority of players. Several are so familiar that golfers are hesitant to disregard them; but as long as they remain, they represent mental and physical excess baggage that impedes any chance to approach one's potential.

Almost to the word, the terminology generally applied to the teaching of the backswing fails to convey to students the essential elements that are readily observable in all of the backswings of the great ball strikers. [For example], I've found that the word "turn" does so much more harm than good that I have stopped using it entirely. The word "sway" is universally misunderstood. "Pivot" seems to mean more things to more people than the word democracy. Very few players have a clear understanding of what a reverse pivot is. Fewer yet can feel one.

While we are erasing the damage such words have done, we must also change our mind's image of the very shape of the backswing. In this regard, the video camera has been a godsend to me. . . . On a number of occasions, I've had students with excellent eyesight, three feet from a screen as big as some windows, witness their own backswing only to turn to me seriously, and say, "Who was that?" I had a pretty good amateur once, who upon seeing his own backswing position compared to those of Snead and Nicklaus, asked, "Do you have an airline sickness bag handy?" . . .

THE MOVE BEHIND THE BALL

. . . On any standard full shot, where the ball is played approximately off the left heel, all of the great ball strikers have coiled totally behind the ball at the top

Great ball strikers coil fully behind the ball.

of the backswing. By this I mean that if we draw a vertical line through the center of the ball, at a right angle to the ground, and extend it six feet in the air, at the completion of the backswing all of the great strikers are totally behind that line.

How did they achieve this position? From a braced, connected address, they have taken the triangle with center and coiled the entire left side (the left foot, left knee, left hip, and left shoulder, in a chain reaction—a straight line) into the "brace" or "set" of the right leg.

A player could feel this in reverse (left shoulder, left hip, left knee, left foot), or, as I've had players tell me, they feel as if they take the right shoulder and pull the left side into the right side; or they may feel the left lat moving level to a position behind the ball as they swing toward the top. How an individual golfer feels the move is not important, provided he has moved to a place behind the ball in a strong connected position so he can recoil and hit it with authority. I often refer to this move as "loading the gun." . . .

Most of the mistakes players make on the backswing immediately or ultimately result in a reverse pivot, golf's unforgivable sin. Why do so many golfers commit the sin? The idea of turning is one reason. If a player thinks in terms of a turn, he or she will stop [the] center from coiling laterally back, and level, as it should, or worse yet, move it down and forward. Why? Once players assume the braced connected address position, they are working from both hip joints. If you were to stand on one foot, like a flamingo, you could turn on the ball and socket of one joint until you lost your balance. But once you've braced the legs, at about shoulder width, and you're working from the insides of the legs, if you then try to turn, you will succeed only in turning against the left hip joint. . . .

Let me now create a clear conceptual understanding of what coil is. Suppose you took your address position with your right foot touching the end of a brick wall, waist high, with the understanding that you are going to coil the whole left side toward the wall during the backswing. If you tried to turn you would simply twist or spin (turning against the left hip joint) and the upper body would move away from the wall. You want to coil the upper body toward the wall, as deeply as you can, while maintaining the brace of the right leg.

If you went to the outside of the right foot in making this move, you would both lose the brace of the leg and send the upper body over the plane of the wall. Frankly, I wish I had students initially moving over the wall (I don't think I've seen six beginners move over the wall in 20 years), rather than turning *away* from it, as is so common. If a student moves over the wall, he or she at least has a feeling for attempting to coil or move behind the ball, and we can realize immediate improvement by simply bracing up the right leg. . . .

The whole idea is to coil as deeply as you can, toward the wall, while making certain that your weight is on the inside of the right foot, leg and hip joint. . . .

The bracing of the legs creates an opposing feeling from the waist down. There is equal pressure on the inside of each leg. This feeling must never be destroyed. It would be like coiling a spring that was attached to the ground. You are taking your hand and coiling the upper part of the spring as tightly as you can against the fixed resistance of the lower part so that you can create the strongest possible recoiling action when you release the spring. Because of the design of the spring, you could simply turn it to create the recoil. However, the human anatomy is infinitely more complicated than the spring, and if we are going to create a coiling and recoiling action, this action, as we have seen, involves more than we generally mean when we think of turning.

"But," you are saying, "if I coil toward the wall, won't I be moving off the ball? Won't I sway?" The answer is no. In fact, the biggest problem is that most golfers have such an ingrained fear of moving off the ball or swaying, that they actually sway forward. The word "sway" has been used improperly for years. Jimmy Demaret, in analyzing Ben Hogan's swing, once said: "Ben sways a little as he moves back, which I think most good golfers do—he moves back to the right of center at the top of the swing." . . . Hogan didn't sway. He coiled the entire left side into the brace or set of the right leg. He never moved away from the ball—that would be a sway. . . .

[A]ll the great ball strikers coil back to the right. You must wind to unwind. A boxer couldn't set his weight on his right foot and then draw back his arm and throw a punch that would stagger his grandmother. And a baseball player can't just set his weight and the bat back to the right and move forward without hitting little popcorn jobs that could hardly back up an infielder. Natural rhythm and coordination, the obvious dynamics of hitting an object properly, dictate that the boxer, hitter, or golfer coil and recoil in order to obtain leverage and power. . . .

When golfers reverse-pivot on the backswing, they automatically unload the gun. Since they arrive at the top with the weight predominantly on the left foot or toe, it must move to the right foot during the downswing. In others words, the reverse-pivoter changes directions in the backswing. It is impossible to shift weight to the left, when it is already there! With the disconnection and the tilt forward, the opportunity to coil behind the ball has been destroyed, all leverage and resistance leaves the legs, and all of the large muscles of the legs and body are immobilized.

The failure to coil into the inside of the right leg and hip joint prevents the proper, sequential recoiling from the ground up, and the player has no option but to begin the swing from the top—that is, with the smaller muscles of the hands and arm. As the hips are simply spinning and, in fact, the weight is transferring to the right foot, the player throws or casts the club from the top—an out and over feeling—which forces the path of the swing to be across the intended line of flight. Generally, the player drags the club across the ball with the face open and hits a weak slice. When this is done to any degree, the

Nobody ever swung the golf club too slowly.

BOBBY JONES

player can sense the absence of solid, square contact; he feels he has hit the ball a sort of glancing blow. We call it a "wipe." However, from exactly the same beginnings, the player might occasionally flip the hands over and hit a dead pull. . . . When the golfer throws, drops or drags from the top of the swing across the intended line, the hands will disappear in the impact area. They have been pulled out of the center of the chest. . . .

SUMMARY

At the top of the backswing, the weight should be on the inside of the right foot, and right hip and the balance point should be six to eight inches behind the

ball. Try to exaggerate the coiling motion—to go as deep as you possibly can with connection, and without the weight going to the outside of the right foot or hip. I suggest this because I know from experience that unless you make a definite point of it, you will cut the coiling short, and come up with some degree of twist and a reverse. In Demaret's words, I want you to "sway" like Hogan.

From *How to Perfect Your Golf Swing: Using "Connection" and the Seven Common Denominators*, by Jimmy Ballard, with Brennan Quinn. Golf Digest/Tennis, Inc. a New York Times Company. Copyright © 1981, by Jimmy Ballard. Used by permission of Jimmy Ballard.

Drill: Clip the Tee Going Back
and
Drill: Put a Brace Behind the Right Knee

1 9 9 9 ✑ B U T C H H A R M O N

Claude "Butch" Harmon is part of the royal family of golf instruction, which includes his younger brother Dick, and their late father, Claude, the 1948 Masters champion and a legendary club pro and teaching professional. Butch is best known for shepherding Tiger Woods through his career Grand Slam, but his work with other superstars and hot newcomers like Aussie Adam Scott assures he will remain at the top of the teacher rankings. His popularity is partly due to his ability to tailor his lessons to each pupil rather than preaching a fixed philosophy. The first part of this *Golf Digest* excerpt tells golfers how to master the crucial initial step in the takeaway, a lesson that echoes Harry Vardon and Bobby Jones, yet is pure Butch. In the second part, Harmon offers a tip for a backswing fault that is often overlooked—straightening the right knee.

MISTAKE: POOR TAKEAWAY

There are two faults you can make in the takeaway. You can pick the club up, or you can pull it back inside.

When you pick the club up, your left shoulder drops. You tilt but don't really turn your shoulders. You hang on your left side, reverse pivot, and either top the ball or chunk it.

When you take the club back inside, your left arm goes out away from your body, and halfway back it's above your right arm. The club goes behind your body, and you have to loop it up and over on the downswing, causing slices or pulls.

A GOOD TAKEAWAY

When your club is halfway back, the shaft should be exactly in line with your toes, and your right arm is slightly higher than your left.

DRILL: CLIP THE TEE GOING BACK

I believe strongly in a one-piece takeaway. That means that until your hands are waist high, you maintain the triangle formed by your arms and shoulders at address. It helps to think about taking the club back low and slow. Here's a good drill: Place a tee about a grip-length behind the ball, then try to clip the tee on your takeaway. That will help you learn a low one-piece takeaway.

MISTAKE: THE STRAIGHT KNEE

Many amateurs straighten or even lock the right knee immediately as they start their backswing. That causes their hips and shoulders to turn the same amount, so they aren't building any coil for power. They end up throwing the club over the top to get back to the ball, which further reduces power and leads to slices or pulls.

Instead, maintain the flex of your right knee throughout the swing. This encourages the shoulders to turn more than the hips, storing power. On the downswing you'll be more on plane and can release the club later for a more powerful hit.

DRILL: PUT A BRACE BEHIND THE RIGHT KNEE

Knee flex is something Tiger Woods and I have worked on for years. He has perfect posture at address and tries to maintain the posture of his right leg all the way back in the swing.

If you tend to straighten your right leg on the backswing, try the drill . . . in which a partner pushes a club into the back of your right knee as you swing. If you're by yourself, bury the head of your wedge in the ground so the shaft is angled at 45 degrees upward, place a head cover over the grip end, then back your knee up to it before you swing.

From "The Eight Stupid Mistakes Every Golfer Makes," by Butch Harmon, in *Golf Digest* (December 1999). Reprinted with permission from Butch Harmon and Golf Digest®. Copyright © 2005 The Golf Digest Companies, which is a subsidiary of Advance Magazine Publishers, Inc. All Rights Reserved. Golf Digest is a Registered Trademark of The Golf Digest Companies, which is a subsidiary of Advance Magazine Publishers, Inc.

When your hands reach a point somewhere level with your hips [in the backswing], the wrists will want to hinge, or cock. Let it happen.
PETER ALLISS

The Backswing

2 0 0 0 · VIVIEN SAUNDERS

Before becoming a top teaching pro, Vivien Saunders won the 1977 British Women's Open, became the first English golfer to qualify for the LPGA Tour, and helped found the first European women's pro tour in 1979. Off the links, she earned a degree in psychology and a master's in business administration, and practiced law for five years, qualifying her as an heir to Bobby Jones's legacy of the sophisticated, literate golfer. In this excerpt from one of her many books, Saunders offered pure, modern orthodoxy on every stage of the backswing. It is notable for its succinct, practical advice, including her instruction to use the left thumb to maintain a proper swing path—a classic idea that goes back to Ernest Jones, and today is taught primarily to women golfers in order to firm up their wrists and help them avoid dipping the club past parallel in the backswing.

———

The address position prepares you for the backswing. The left arm is straight, though not stiff, and the right is relaxed. The left shoulder is slightly up and the right shoulder is down and relaxed. The knees are very slightly flexed and knocking in toward each other. The eyes focus on the back of the ball, with the head behind it.

At the top of the backswing, your back has turned to the target with your left arm swinging across and upward, supporting the club on the left thumb. The hips and legs move just enough to let this happen. The right leg should stay slightly flexed, not locking and straightening. The clubshaft should be horizontal or just above the horizontal. The left arm ideally stays straight, swinging across toward the right shoulder. The right arm should naturally form a right angle.

In the perfect position, the back of your left wrist should be almost flat with the club more or less parallel to the line of your shot.

Your weight starts slightly on the balls of your feet. Professionals often swing to the top of the backswing without lifting the left heel, but most women playing club golf will find they need to. Let the left heel lift slightly, while keeping the ball and toes on the ground. The foot should simply fold and bend as the heel rises up.

THE LEFT ARM IN THE BACKSWING

Though golf is very much a two-handed game, with the left and right working as one with as even a strength as possible, the harder you make your left arm work in the backswing the better it will be.

The beginner needs to develop the correct takeaway in order to produce a perfect backswing. Swing the club to hip height. The back of the left hand should face forward and the toe of the club directly upward. Feel your left thumb on top of the club. Hinge up on the left thumb to form the backswing.

The club should be supported on the left thumb at the top of the backswing. The left hand should be in control without opening in a "piccolo" grip. For a useful exercise, trap a tee peg between the club and your hand and keep it there throughout the swing.

Left Arm Practice

Swing the club to and fro with only your left arm . . . to get used to feeling your left arm really working in the swing. The left thumb should be slightly down the side of the club [at address]. From here feel yourself swing the club round and onto the left thumb.

Balance the club between the left index finger and the pad of your hand.

Practice holding the club in you left hand only and swinging it across your body and up to the top of the backswing. Then swing it back down slowly but no further than your starting position. Twenty left-handed swings a day works miracles. Remember to keep breathing!

Hold your left arm out in front of you, palm down, with your right hand holding your left elbow. Pull the left arm across your body to your right shoulder. Repeat this until you feel freedom in the shoulder.

At the top of the backswing the left shoulder turns, rounding in toward the right one. This is very different from opening and turning the right shoulder away. This error usually produces an unwanted "flying" right elbow. Think of your backswing as being dominated by turning the left shoulder, swinging the left arm and supporting the club on the left thumb.

Perfecting the Backswing

The backswing is a turn of the body and a lift of the arms. Try to make it one smooth movement. The simpler you make it, the more you can focus on striking the ball to the target.

To start the backswing, everything should ideally work together. However, every golfer usually needs a little movement of some sort to get started. Most professionals just make a slight kick forward with the right knee, which then acts as a trigger for everything to start back in unison.

Don't let your trigger movement be a little forward press with the hands. This can cause problems. Worse still, but very common is to let the fingers of the right hand open and close and the grip alter as your way of saying, "Let's go!"

Much better to stick to that little right knee movement and set everything off together.

At address, the clubshaft should point to your navel—maybe up or down a bit. The clubface faces you. As you start to turn, the club should turn with you

Tame and train the left arm.

with its face always square to you. As it gets to about hip height both wrists should naturally hinge and cock upward. You shouldn't feel the wrists hinge. If you make the left thumb support, it happens naturally.

You will notice that better golfers make a little waggle of the clubhead before they commence their backswing. This is simply a way of loosening the wrists slightly. If you learn to waggle the club backward and forward before your takeaway, it helps to achieve a perfect backswing where the back of the left wrist is flat. This is the position we aim for with advanced and championship golfers.

Of course, you need to be confident that you aren't going to touch the ball accidentally as you return from the waggle.

As you turn in the backswing, your head must move very slightly to the right to allow your shoulders to turn.

If you keep your head too still you can restrict the backswing. Give yourself just enough freedom, letting it move an inch or so. If you find you have this fault, think of "right ear down" in the backswing!

At the top of the backswing the shoulders should be near to horizontal with the left arm always lifted above the shoulders.

— 7 —

THE THROUGH-SWING

MOMENT OF TRUTH

The Downward Swing
and
Finishing the Stroke

1906 | JAMES BRAID

James Braid, the lone Scotsman in the "Great Triumvirate," won his first British Open at Muirfield in 1901, besting Harry Vardon and J. H. Taylor by a comfortable margin despite hitting his opening drive out-of-bounds. A clutch putter and a hard-hitter off the tee, he was thirty-one when he won that first Major, but he rattled off four more Open Championships before turning forty-one. Braid was famous for his "sudden, furious" downswing, which Horace Hutchinson memorably likened to a "divine fury." In an initially successful but now obscure British pamphlet that was soon reissued in America by Spalding, Braid counseled the golfer to view the downswing as a sweep through the ball, rather than a "hit" at it. He also offered a valuable tip that is standard in today's teaching canon: If you hold the finish it will help establish balance, or what Braid delightfully called "this pleasant position."

THE DOWNWARD SWING

The downswing, which, though it is all-important in that it is the really active part of the stroke, the one that makes the ball go, is in many of its features one which in the nature of things affords less scope for effort and care than the upward swing. . . . One might say that the upswing is really the first half of the downswing, and the half that settles what the whole thing is going to be.

The chief thing to bear in mind is that there must be in the case of play with the driver and the brassey no attempt to *hit* the ball, which must be simply swept from the tee and carried forward in the even and rapid swing of the club. The drive in golf differs from almost every other stroke in every game in which the propulsion of a ball is the object. In the ordinary sense of the word, implying a sudden and sharp impact, it is not a "hit" when it is properly done. When the ball is so "hit," and the club stops very soon afterward, the result is that very little length comparatively will be obtained, and that, moreover, there will be a very small amount of control over the direction of the ball.

While it is, of course, in the highest degree necessary that the ball shall be taken in exactly the right place on the club and in the right manner, this will have to be done by the proper regulation of all the other parts of the swing, and any effort to direct the club on it in a particular manner just as the ball is being reached cannot be attended by success. If the ball is taken by the toe or heel of the club, or is topped, or if the club gets too much under it, the remedy for these faults is not to be found in a more deliberate directing of the club on the ball just as the two are about to come into contact, but in the better and more exact regulation of the swing the whole way through up to this point. . . . The object of these remarks is merely to emphasize again . . . that the dispatching of the ball from the tee by the driver in the downward swing is merely an incident of the whole business. The player, in making the down movement, must not be so particular to see while doing it that he hits the ball properly as that he makes the swing properly and finishes it well, for—and this signifies the truth of what I have been saying—the success for the drive is not only made by what has gone before, but it is also due largely to the course taken by the club after the ball has been hit.

On the whole the player will be, and must be, far less conscious of all the details of his action in the downswing than when he was taking the club upwards. Having brought the club with the utmost care and thought and attention to detail to the top point, there is only one more thing to do, and that is to finish off the swing and get the ball away as rapidly as possible. It is only after the ball has gone that consciousness will begin to fully assert itself and enable the player to give thought to the manner of finishing. In time, and when the man is on his game, the whole thing, from start to finish, should be to a certain extent mechanical.

The initiative in bringing down the club is taken by the left wrist, and the club is then brought forward rapidly and with an even acceleration of pace until the clubhead is about a couple of feet from the ball. So far the movement will largely have been an arm movement, but at this point there should be some tightening up of the wrists, and the club will be gripped a little more tightly. This will probably come about naturally, and though some authorities have expressed different opinions, I am certainly one of those who believe that the work done by the wrists at this point has a lot to do with the making of the drive. It is merely an assertion of power on their part, and if it ever comes to the player it will come naturally and in the course of experience. Directions about it cannot be laid down. Just when the wrists begin to

take their part in the stroke, when the face of the club is approaching the ball, the body begins to turn and the left knee comes in quickly from its pivoting position, so that at the moment of striking the player is quite firm on both his feet and faces directly to the ball, just as he did when he was addressing it before he began the upward swing. Anyone who thinks out the theory of the swing for himself will see that it is obviously intended that at the moment of impact the player shall be just as he was when he addressed the ball, which is the position which will afford him most driving power and accuracy.

FINISHING THE STROKE

The second the ball is hit, but not before, the player should begin to turn on his right toe, and to allow a little bend of the right knee, so as to allow the right shoulder to come round until the body faces the line of flight of the ball. When this is done properly the weight will be thrown on to the left foot, and the whole body will be thrown slightly forward. The whole of this movement needs very careful timing, because it is a very common fault with some players to let the body get in too soon, and in such cases the stroke is always ruined. . . .

A word about the varying pressure of the grip with each hand. In the address the left hand should just be squeezing the handle of the club, but not so tightly as if one were afraid of losing it. The right hand should hold the club a little more loosely. The left hand should hold firmly all the way through. The right will open a little at the top of the swing to allow the club to move easily, but it should automatically tighten itself in the downward swing.

There is only one point now in regard to the finishing of the stroke to which one feels that one should direct attention, for if everything has been done properly up to this point the accurate performance of the rest is almost inevitable. But there is a great tendency on the part of some players to twitch in their arms and nip the drive after the impact with the ball. The hands are pulled in and come to a stop close to the left breast-pocket of the coat, and when this is done the clubshaft either points forward or straight up. The most immature player will feel by instinct that there is something wrong about this, and that it is a rather weak and uncomfortable way of finishing what was a very even and powerful movement. The fact is that the hands have no business in this place, and their being there has prevented the arms from going out and the club from getting right through with the stroke. When the ball has been swept from the tee the arms should to a certain extent be flung out after it, and they should be carried through well clear of the body until they come to a natural and easy stop and not a forced one, just about shoulder-high but some distance from the shoulder. When this is done the club will have passed the perpendicular and will have traveled a distance toward the back, which varies in the case of different players. Some men go in for rather exaggerated finishes, and carry the club so far through that it comes almost back to their right heel, but I cannot see that there is any advantage in this process, so long as the finish is fully executed up to the point I have indicated. When the arms get well through, and the hands finish high up in the place I have indicated, the player will find that he experiences a sense of completeness and satisfaction, even of exhilaration, which will be denied to him if his drive is nipped. It is a very pleasant thing when, having followed well through and finished the stroke properly, the ball is watched speeding onward on the proper line and with just the right angle of flight to make it travel well.

It is appropriate to mention at this point just a word of warning about style. When you have followed through and finished the stroke properly, get into the habit of retaining this pleasant position until the ball has pretty well run its length and the time has come for your opponent to take his place on the tee, or, if he has already driven, for you both to be moving on. Some players, generally those of a somewhat excitable disposition, get into the way of dropping their club, or releasing one hand from the grip and dropping it to the side, and of moving their feet and bending their body as soon as the ball has been struck. Perhaps if they quite realized how badly the appearance of such a proceeding compares with that of a finish in the proper manner they would be more anxious to get out of the habit than they often are.

As a final injunction, one would again urge the importance of keeping the body perfectly steady not only during the upward swing, as already emphasized, but during the downward swing until the ball has gone, and the head all this time should be perfectly motionless with the eyes glued on to the back of the ball. If the body keeps to its original position and turns from the waist, and the head remains still, it should be found that at the top of the swing the eyes are looking over the left shoulder which will be in a direct line between the head and the ball.

From *Golf Guide and How to Play Golf,* by James Braid. Copyright © 1906 by the British Sports Publishing Company, Ltd., London, England.

THE MAGIC MOVE

Harvey Penick said that there was no one "magic move" in golf, but spent a lifetime teaching a basic swing key that would enable the golfer to hit the ball as if by "magic." At the start of the downswing, he advised, golfers should shift their weight back to the left foot and drop the right elbow back down to the side, explaining that this was one move, not two. ᴄᴅ

Like James Braid and J. H. Taylor, Harry Vardon could finish off a swing with as much aplomb as he used to beat his opponents.

His instructional book, The Complete Golfer, *has endured longer than the writings of his two rivals.*

Analyzing the Downswing

1931 ✑ HELEN HICKS

In 1931, twenty-year-old Helen Hicks won the U.S. Women's Amateur title, ending Glenna Collett Vare's three-year run. As a member of the first Curtis Cup team a year later, she, Vare, Patty Berg, and Virginia Van Wie led the Americans over a formidable British team that included Joyce Wethered and Enid Wilson. But it was Hicks's unprecedented act in 1934—when she became the first notable female golfer to turn pro—that secured her place in history. In addition to continuing competitive play, Hicks became the first female to tour the country giving clinics and promoting equipment after signing an endorsement contract with Wilson Sporting Goods. In this magazine article, "Hard-hitting Helen" also broke new ground as one of the first "left-side" theorists, arguing that rather than the hands and arms, the unwinding of the hips triggers the downswing. Ben Hogan and countless others would adopt this as gospel.

The downswing is one of the very important factors in golf because it is during this phase of the swing that the clubhead comes in contact with the ball; and it seems to me the main idea of the game is to "hit the ball." In order to write about the "Downswing" we must start from the beginning of the objective, that is to say, at the top of the backswing. I favor the hands being held high which will assure one of a more full and rhythmic swing, instead of being flat, caused by the hands being too far around the shoulder at the top of the swing. One hears so much about the "straight left arm." All right—the left arm should be straight, nearing, and at the point of contact with the clubhead and the ball. But if one tries to keep the left arm too straight at the top of the swing, one will find that it is very tense and rigid, therefore, this arm should be slightly bent, to feel relaxed, but also feel, "all powerful." The left wrist should be cocked or bent under the shaft. The right arm should be in a position somewhat resembling that of a waiter carrying a tray. I mention this

as it is the tendency of many players to let this elbow point skyward.

. . . After a careful and intensive study of the golf swing, I feel that what I am about to say (though it may prove contrary to popular theories), is undoubtedly correct. Heretofore, the general belief has been that the first movement from the top of the backswing is the starting of the arms toward the ball. However, up to this time very little consideration has been given to the movement of the body and I feel that in the correct shifting of the body lies the secret of timing and power.

While the left wrist and forearm should feel the power and control of the club, the initial effort at the beginning of the downward swing is caused by the necessity of getting the body, or the "right side" out of the way, so that the arms and club may have a free and uninterrupted passage on the way to the ball. The body action is a lateral motion of the hips, often referred to as the forward shift, and has laid the foundation for the now well-known axiom of golf—"hitting against the left side." The left heel, by reason of this shift, has now come back to the ground and the right knee begins to twist inward toward the ball. The left arm, which up to this point may have been slightly bent or relaxed, now begins to straighten and become taut. This is the beginning of the arm and wrist work, and it must never come into action before "the shift" has taken the right side out of the way.

The right arm continues to hug the right side, and . . . the forearm, which to this stage is facing upward, now begins to assume its natural position—this straightening process continuing until after the ball has been hit. The work of the left at this stage of the swing is all-important, and herein lies the secret of a long drive. The torque motion of the right arm has a tendency to overpower the left, and great care and effort must be taken to keep the left arm in front as long as possible traveling outward across the line of flight and fighting the tendency of the right to force the club inward around the left side. Meanwhile the head of the player, which has remained steady on the upward swing, falls back, as the body begins its forward movement, thus holding the center of balance behind the hitting point and bringing the shoulders and back muscles into the stroke.

One must take into consideration the greater necessity of the stout person exaggerating the body movement as compared with the slender person. This exaggeration of the body shift must be made in order to compensate for the lack of the full pivot, which the stout person is generally unable to complete to its full advantage. On the other hand the slender person, being able to complete the full pivot, finds it much easier to execute this "forward shift" of the body. The full pivot, of which I speak, is necessary to place the body in a position from which it can readily be started forward at the commencement of the downswing. This "forward shift" enables the right shoulder to roll under much in the manner of the baseball pitcher throwing an underhand ball, thereby getting the punch into the shot; and it also prevents a premature turning of the body which would cause the arc of the downswing to go outside of the line of flight causing that "nemesis" of all golfers—the slice.

. . . Many golfers have the mistaken idea that a great deal of effort must be made before the ball is reached. This is not so. The real hit in golf is made between the ball and the hole, not between the top of the backswing and the ball. The latter is a common error—the cause of wasted effort and many missed shots.

After the ball has been hit, the great thing to bear in mind is to keep the clubhead traveling toward the hole. That is why I have stressed that great care and effort should be made to keep the left arm in front as long as possible. This will, if applied correctly, assure one of greater distance and accuracy and will also be the beginning of the last and one of the important parts of the swing—the follow-through. Personally, I always try to picture the clubhead going out for the hole. This practically assures me of a straight left arm at the moment of impact and prevents the clubhead from leaving the correct arc of the swing. The finish of the follow-through is almost a duplicate of the top of the backswing—the difference being that at the finish of the swing the left arm is bent with the elbow toward the ground, while the right arm is more or less straight. The correct follow-through not only helps to carry out the fundamentals of the downswing but it adds a certain amount of grace and ease to the finish. . . .

From *Golf Illustrated* (February 1931), by Helen Hicks.

You must not begin the downward swing as if you were anxious to get it over.

ALEXANDER "SANDY" HERD,
EARLY SCOTTISH CHAMPION AND GOLF INSTRUCTOR

The Correct Swing

1933 ✏ ALEX J. MORRISON

In 1910, Alex Morrison landed a job at the Los Angeles Country Club, the perfect fit for a man who favored multi-patterned sweaters and bright argyle socks and had the nervy showmanship to smash golf balls off a man's head. Still, Morrison was a serious instructor, who prided himself on using "impersonal, scientific" principles and state-of-the-art films of famous golfers to demonstrate technique. His clientele included Charlie Chaplin and Douglas Fairbanks—Hope and Crosby frequented his driving range in New York City—and Henry Picard, who would win thirty tournaments. Byron Nelson was Morrison's early model for his left-side-dominant theories, but it was Picard who would pass on his secrets to Ben Hogan and Jack Grout. In this excerpt from his groundbreaking book, Morrison provided the prototype for decades of downswing theology, plus a tip about keeping the chin behind the ball that is often resurrected by golf magazines.

———

Only by winding up the body to its fullest, then releasing the accumulated force in an expanding motion like the uncoiling of a spring, can a golf club be swung easily, naturally, accurately, and with maximum power.

. . . Golf is, in a way, a left-handed game for a right-handed player and a right-handed game for the left-handed player. This is rather an unfortunate way of stating the case, for the statement is inexact. Golf really is a two-handed game; yet it is still a left-handed game for the right-handed man to the extent that muscles on the left side of the body dominate those of the right side in every swing that is correctly made. *In the correct swing conscious use is made of only one small group of muscles on the right side of the body.*

I have studied the anatomy of golf as thoroughly as any layman could. I know the names and understand the action of all the principal muscles, bones, joints, and tendons used in swinging the club. There is no point, though, in airing my knowledge of anatomy in presenting this general description of the swing. Suffice it to say that practical experiment on myself and others, analysis of the swings of leading players by the slow-motion camera, discussion with surgeons and anatomists, and many hours with textbooks on anatomy have plainly proved that only when the swing is made . . . with the muscles of the left side of the body actively dominant during the action, can there be a free, natural, uninterrupted, powerful motion. When the muscles of the right side of the body are permitted to enter actively into the swing, there is conflict, constriction; muscles that should be expanding and unleashing their strength contract and hinder the action. One side of the body is fighting the other. The result? You have only to compare the heavy-handed, muscle-bound lunges of the average player with the easy, "professional" swing of the expert to know.

And so we can trace the force that propels the club as follows: It originates in the muscles of the lower back through body torsion. . . . It is transmitted through those muscles around the *left shoulder* to the *left arm*, through this arm to the *left little finger*, and so through the shaft of the club to the clubhead. In addition, the hinge-like action of the *left* wrist helps to increase the power and speed of the clubhead. When properly carried out, each movement progresses into and harmonizes with the one following, so that the swing truly is made one full, smooth, flowing motion without mental or physical interruption. Furthermore, as I believe . . . the use of the muscles on the left side of the body is perfectly natural, even though generally unfamiliar to most golfers.

The Swing in Slow Motion

. . . The brief overlapping of the backswing and the downswing results in an eccentric motion between the lower part of the body and the upper part, including the shoulders, arms, and hands. The forward shifting of the hips while there is still some winding up in progress brings the torsion of the body to its maximum and causes the unwinding process to begin immediately.

After the lower part of the body has been moved toward the left, the body unwinds in precisely the same order in which it was wound up. Thus the order of movement in the downswing is, first, the hip action, coupled with the action of the shoulders and the downward swinging of the arms and then the hinge-like action of the wrists. It is only through this late action of the wrists in the downswing that the muscles of the left arm and those of the little and third fingers of the left hand can produce a leverage to increase the speed of the clubhead to its maximum as it descends upon the ball.

Starting with the lower back, the force of the downswing is transmitted through the muscles of the left shoulder, through the fully extended left arm, through the left little finger into the shaft of the club and on to the clubhead.

The unleashing of the same muscles that bore the main stress of the wind-up results in whirling the club downward in a motion which, needless to say, requires but a fraction of the time taken for the backswing. As a single example of the length of time in which the downswing is accomplished, the heel of the left foot barely settles into position before the clubhead strikes the ball. In fact, the motion of the club-head toward the ball is entirely too fast for the human eye to follow.

The center of the body, the shoulders, arms, and hands must arrive at a certain point opposite the ball at the same time, and since one member has a greater distance than the other to travel, the various members must move at a speed in proportion to their distance from the hub of the whirling motion.

The Moment of Impact

The spirited reaction of the muscles of the left side to the winding-up process depends entirely upon keeping the chin pointed back of the ball. With the chin under control the correct positions of body, arms, and hands as well as the club are assured at the moment of impact. The proper set of muscles will bring the club down to form a straight line between the left shoulder and the ball and have the clubface meet the ball at right angles to the intended line of flight.

Almost any amount of force can be expressed through this set of muscles without upsetting the timing of the swing—provided the chin is kept properly pointed.

It is mechanically and anatomically impossible for the muscles and joints in the right side of the body to do more than harmonize with and supplement the action of the dominating muscles of the left side if the clubhead is to travel in a true arc at its maximum speed. The moment the muscles of the right side take charge, speed and accuracy are greatly decreased. This invariably happens; there are no "ifs," "ands," or "buts" about it.

The proper set of muscles should dominate the action of the swing until well after the clubhead has struck the ball. There should be *no conscious* lessening of the speed or power of the clubhead until after the moment of impact.

Even though maximum power and speed are being expressed in this stage of the action, even though the temptation to move the chin along in the direction the club is swinging seems almost too strong to be resisted, the chin *must* be kept pointed back of the ball until after the ball is on its way. This is the most valuable contribution you can make toward the general efficiency of your stroke. It helps particularly to effect a clean hit.

AFTER IMPACT

The action that takes place after the ball has been hit is due almost entirely to the momentum of the swing and has no bearing on the flight of the ball.

In the correct swing the path traveled by the clubhead is at all times a curve. No matter how flat the arc, the clubhead still travels in a curve, and, since the ball must fly in approximately a straight line, it follows that the path of the clubhead can coincide with the line of flight only at a single point of inter-section. . . .

For a considerable part of the downswing the right side of the body has been subject to the outward motion of the club. As a result, after hands and arms have both passed well beyond the point where the ball is struck, the right arm is drawn out to its full reach and the momentum of the club causes it to roll over the left arm.

THE FINISH

The mechanics of the swing is completely reversed in its last stages. Instead of the body, arms, and hands moving the club, the momentum of the clubhead moves the hands, arms, body, at last the chin.

Because the action after impact has no effect on the flight of the ball, it is necessary to keep the chin pointed back only until after the ball has been hit. However, as a precautionary measure, it is better to permit the hands, arms, and shoulders to respond to the momentum of the club before allowing the chin to drift forward.

In this manner the entire body comes to a position of rest as the action of the swing finishes.

From *A New Way to Better Golf*, by Alex J. Morrison. William Heinemann, Ltd., London, England.

Maximum Impact Speed, Can Impact Speed Be Increased? *and* The Finish of the Swing

1948 ⚌ T. HENRY COTTON

Henry Cotton's swing was picture perfect from start to high finish. But if there was one area that he concentrated most on, it was the furious, split-second surge of his downswing into the ball. "A strike of awesome authority," as John Jacobs called it in *50 Greatest Golf Lessons of the Century*. Like Ben Hogan, Cotton was not a "natural" talent, and often practiced until his hands bled to improve and improve some more. Again like Hogan, he perpetually searched for the "secret" to golf—as is evident in this excerpt from a book that was written the year Cotton won his third British Open, gave up regular tournament play, and settled with his wife, Toots, in Portugal. Cotton was never fully satisfied with his findings, but at least he was looking in the right place—where the club meets the ball.

———————◆———————

MAXIMUM IMPACT SPEED

"Where is the maximum speed?" This was [a] point I discussed by correspondence with the late Mr. P. A. Vaile, the well-known Chicago golf writer, who sent me a copy of an article written by Bobby Jones in which the following paragraph was quoted: "When I am hitting the ball well I feel no shock at contact because the club is swinging freely. I am making no effort to lash through with the clubhead; I feel that the mass of the club has acquired momentum from the speed I have given it, that this speed has been built to its maximum immediately prior to contact, and then I do nothing to hinder it from carrying on." Vaile added, commenting on this paragraph, "At impact his stroke is considerably slower than its greatest speed during his hit, because he is now swinging on his shoulders with straight arms and un-cocked hands, which means that the hit is done."

I challenged the statement, particularly the one added by Vaile, that Jones's impact was slower than the greatest speed during the hit. I had a very interesting answer forwarded to me by Bobby Jones in which he goes on to explain that when he wrote the lines stated, he was aiming at correcting the mistaken idea held by some players that they can accomplish something by a sudden effort just at impact, or by continuing to work on the ball as long as it is in contact with the club. Usually, this sort of effort does more harm than good, either by yanking the clubhead off its proper path, or by creating forces which impede rather than aid the hit. Attempting to cause the stroke to reach a crescendo precisely at the moment of impact, introduces a requirement of timing which is far too exacting. The ideal which Jones conceives is of building up maximum speed a few inches before contact, and by letting the club swing through without hindrance to maintain this speed undiminished through the ball.

On reading this explanation I agree that it would give the average golfer a better idea of timing the ball; and he explained in another paragraph, which I have not quoted, that it was impossible to define the exact moment at which the club is traveling at its fastest. It is naturally assumed that this maximum speed is at impact, probably before, and is then maintained till the ball is struck. . . .

But while the ideal would be to arrive with the maximum speed on impact, it is safest to have the maximum speed coming before the ball is struck; too late is no good.

Get up to your maximum speed early, and then keep it up for the bit of swing up to the ball. You cannot go wrong on this.

CAN IMPACT SPEED
BE INCREASED?

It has always been a great source of interest to me to try to discover how I could increase the speed of the clubhead at impact without decreasing the weight of the head. Reducing the weight of the head, of course, lessens the momentum available for hitting the ball.

I have tried many ways to acquire more speed at impact—by building up strength in the hands, wrists, and arms, altering the swing itself, and using various types of shaft and different lengths of clubs. . . .

Another conclusion I have arrived at is that every golfer has his own particular speed, and that though this speed may be increased a little it can never be improved very much.

If a player can increase the weight of his clubhead and still swing at the same speed, the ball goes further.

On the different driving machines I have seen in action, the clubhead and the shaft play no part, except to make contact with the ball. The shaft and the head are usually very solid and only the speed is variable.

All of you will have experienced the thrill of trying out a new driver, and noticed that often it inspires a swing that is different from your old one. The impact speed, it may be, is different.

How far a change in weight, either up or down, can be made with the object of increasing the momentum of the blow, there is no guide. However, as a general rule a slow impact speed drives the ball better with a heavier head, and a fast "swishy" swing needs a lighter head to allow it to develop its greatest speed.

As I have always maintained, there are certain combinations of head and shaft, which, when swung in the range of average human speeds, give the best results with the modern ball. That is why I have every confidence in recommending players, unless they have plenty of time and money for experimenting, to keep reasonably near the accepted proportions of first-class clubs. . . .

So we shall go on looking for the ideal club, which will drive the ball better than ever all the year round, an almost fruitless task, we know, but it is fun hunting.

THE FINISH OF THE SWING

A player can be said to have a good style when he has a free, full backswing and a wide, high finish with a good body balance. Sam Snead comes to mind. A controlled three-quarter backswing can produce a fine finish, and the whole swing, in my eyes, is then just as good-looking and often more certain than the always admired, free, slashing swing.

It is not impossible to arrive in a good position at the finish of the drive having done the preceding movements incorrectly—many people are said to have good-looking swings and yet have poor results. This is because, although the movements are correct, they are weak. Thus a player with a fine-looking swing may

not always get perfect results because his wrists are not able to accelerate the clubhead sufficiently to keep up with the rhythm of the rest of the swing.

For example, after watching a good golfer in action, players often get the general rhythm of his swing—which they succeed in imitating, but due to this lack of speed and control at impact, still get poor results. Then they see some of their friends with ugly, unorthodox actions getting excellent results and it occurs to them that, after all, style does not matter.

To watch a field of first-class players drive off anywhere in the world would confirm this, but these players have developed individual styles to suit their physical make-up. I like pupils to develop a good swing—to practice a suitable backswing (this they find by experiment), and then to finish off the swing with a wide, high finish. . . .

I like to feel that I hit the ball hard, but disguise the hit in a swing as much as possible; but many players who would imitate my swing should learn to hit first, as no golf ball was ever sent a long way without a very hard hit. . . .

Those of you who watch big golf can recognize players literally a mile off when you see them swing, as the finishes are so different.

. . . [T]he way a player uses his wrists and shoulders decides the look of the finish. I like to see a high, wide finish where the player has taken a long time to come to a position of rest, rather than a finish where the player has hugged his arms to the body, because I feel that where the finish is wide and high, the player has used the weight of his arms to help the work of the wrists, and following on with his arms and wrists in one piece breeds consistency.

. . . When playing through the green different lies, different stances and different types of shot that are called for—cuts, hooks, high and low trajectories, etc.—all have an effect on the look of the finish, so it is unfair to criticize or compare finishes of players either with other finishes they have done or with those of other players, without knowing the facts.

Some players, too, arrive sooner than others at their position of rest after the shot. George Duncan is the quickest player I have known to finish his swing—not only is he quick to make up his mind to hit the ball, and to hit it, but it is all over quicker than that of any other player. The late William Laidlaw, with his lovely long, wide swing, seemed almost to be doing it at slow-motion speed, because it was so complete and smooth, and he could hit the ball "a mile." It was a great loss to British golf when he was killed in action.

It is not actually a question of speed of action that decides the type and length of finish, but this has something to do with it: The type of wrist-action put into the stroke has quite a bearing on the finish,

and so has the grip. The position of the left hand, governing the opening and shutting of the club in the upswing, sometimes calls in the shoulders to adjust the squaring of the clubface as impact approaches, and this might change the appearance of the finish.

From *This Game of Golf*, by T. Henry Cotton. Country Life Ltd., London, England, and in New York by Charles Scribner's Sons.

In Henry Cotton's book, The History of Golf, *he included the photo on the left of Babe Zaharias finishing her swing.*
He was impressed by the athleticism and power of Zaharias, who began as a long-hitter and developed into a skilled all-around player.

The Art of Hitting with the Hands

1953 ✎ TOMMY ARMOUR

Born in Edinburgh, Tommy Armour emigrated to America to make his fortune playing golf. Boasting a killer instinct, a way with irons, and the ability to play the toughest courses well, the "Silver Scot" won a U.S. Open at Oakmont and a British Open at Carnoustie. Eventually cashing in on twenty-five wins in the '20s and '30s, he became a highly paid instructor. Sitting in a director's chair under a large umbrella, the impeccably groomed Armour dispensed advice in posh venues from New York to Florida. Central to his philosophy was a singular attack on standard orthodoxy of the day—that the left side dominates the swing. He insisted that it is more natural for right-handed golfers to rely on their dominant side, urging them to "whack like hell with the right hand." Controversy over this idea continues to this day—which Armour doubtless would have relished.

The great hitters in golf are those who move their hands faster than those whose distance and precision are inferior. That also is the case in sports other than golf. A fighter accomplishes knockouts by having his fists move with devastating speed. Ruth's home-run record was set during seasons when the liveliness of the ball varied, but because The Babe's hands moved faster than those of any other batter, he was supreme as a long hitter. When Jimmy Thomson was consistently the longest driver in golf, motion pictures showed his hands moving at amazing speed.

To let you in on one of the great secrets of good golf, which really isn't a secret at all, one golfer gets more distance because he uses his hands for power, while the other fellow is trying to get distance by using his body.

The long hitter gets his body in position so his hands can work most effectively.

The science of hitting in golf is a matter of a formula involving velocity and mass. The mass of the clubs varies only very few ounces, but the velocity of the hits differs tremendously among golfers. From the scientific viewpoint, a volume could be written about the physics of golf, but the practical application of such information would be limited since hitting a golf ball is more of an art than a science. It's the human element that makes the performance an art.

What misleads people into thinking that swinging and hitting are different is principally a matter of the player's temperament. Macdonald Smith and Byron Nelson have been generally identified as swingers because of the graceful appearance of their actions. Hagen and Sarazen were labeled hitters because their common characteristic was to wield their clubs with what appeared to be violent and impetuous slashing.

But, all four of them—and every other great player—had the clubhead coming in with all the speed they could command while retaining steady balance of their bodies.

Hitting the ball a long way isn't a matter of size or weight of the player. It depends on effective use of the hands, rather than on trying to throw the weight of the body into the shot or even, within reasonable limits, lengthening the backswing in the belief that a longer backswing will enable one to accelerate clubhead speed more and get the clubhead moving at maximum speed at contact with the ball. . . .

[In short]:

Hold the club firmly with the last three fingers of the left hand . . . , let the left arm and hand act as a guide and whack the hell out of the ball with the right hand.

On your long shots, hit the ball with the right hand just as hard as you can while keeping the body steady, and on the shorter iron shots, hit with the right hand briskly and then, too, keep the body steady.

The reason for keeping the body steady is plain, if you'll stop and think. You can reason it out in the following logical steps:

You know you must have clubhead speed to make the ball move far.

Your hands are holding the club; therefore, your hands are the main elements in making the clubhead move. Your body and arms could remain in fixed positions, yet your hands alone could hit the ball a crisp blow.

The faster your hands move, the faster the clubhead is going to move.

But, if your body is moving ahead, too, the relative speed of your hands will be diminished.

Therefore, to get the greatest speed of the clubhead, you must get the greatest speed in your hands, and that can't be secured unless your body is on a steadily fixed, upright axis.

Your right hand, being the human element closest to the clubhead, is the instrument located to produce the clubhead speed you want.

It all adds up to the swift-moving right hand being the source of the dynamic power.

The false idea that golf is a left-handed game for right-handed players shares with the keep-your-eye-on-the-ball idea, the guilt of wrecking the development of many potentially fairly good golfers.

The left-handed game notion grew out of failure to diagnose an error correctly. The error was in blaming the right hand for overpowering the left, when what really happened was that the left hand was too weak. That error accounted for many mistakes in golf instruction and learning, since it made weakness, rather than strength, the governing factor.

No right-handed player ever has naturally hit a golf ball with the left hand, from the very beginning of the game when some ingenious shepherd took a right-handed whack with his crook at a pebble.

There is offered as proof of the argument that golf is a left-handed game the statement that Hogan and Snead were originally left-handed players. Leaving aside the accident that they fell heirs to discarded left-handed clubs as their beginning implements, consider the logic that their left-handed starts gave them strong left hands which, when they switched to right-handed golf, provided them with firm control of the club. Naturally, then, they'd give the clubhead all the right hand they could get into the shot because they had no worries about the left hand being too weak.

And with Hogan, Snead, and every other star, it is the right-handed smash that accounts for masterly execution of the shots. Don't let anyone tell you otherwise.

Abridged with permission of Simon & Schuster Adult Publishing Group, from *How to Play Your Best Golf All the Time*, by Tommy Armour. Copyright © 1953 by Thomas D. Armour. Copyright renewed © 1981 by John Armour and Benjamin Andrews.

Downswing and the Smash *and* Turning on the Steam

1962 🏌 SAM SNEAD
WITH AL STUMP

It's hardly surprising that Sam Snead would declare "this is the part I like the best" when analyzing the downswing, because no one had a better one. Not only was hitting *into* golf balls fun for Snead, it also was in this phase of the swing where Snead lived and made a considerable chunk of change. In his classic book with Al Stump, Snead was characteristically precise, economical, *and* humorous in writing about a beautiful downswing and finish. They resulted from endless practice—during which he sometimes went barefoot to assure balance and ingrain a dynamic quality—belying the idea that he was simply a "natural" talent. It's apparent that his swing technique has no place in the tedious arguments about which muscle groups need be employed—when Snead hit the ball, everything worked together and was of a piece.

DOWNSWING AND THE SMASH

This is the part I like the best. The left hip, with the right immediately joining it, leads me into the downswing. I want the force which begins building at my feet and then is generated by the whole body to pass through my arms and hands to the ball. So as soon as the unwinding begins, I go into a forward thrust—a drive at the ball—off my right leg. With my right elbow riding toward the right hip, the arm on this side is relaxed until I'm well into the downswing. The left side is taut, guiding the club and dominating things until both hands are below belt level.

During this, my right knee turns in toward the direction I'm hitting, and this action is very important. As the knee comes in fast, it helps release all the hitting muscles of the right side—especially giving me strong hip thrust forward.

At impact, my right heel is coming off the ground and the inside sole is pushing against the resistance of the left leg, which has straightened and braces my thrust, or weight shift. The right foot, digging in, gives me that bit of extra power that means yards of carry. The force thrown against the left foot may cause it to roll over, but with the heel dug in firmly it takes the pressure.

Notice I'm *digging in*—drawing all the help from the ground that I can—all the way down and through the ball. That's one reason why feet make a swing more than any other part of the body.

I get maximum clubhead speed at impact the usual way: by uncocking the wrists as late as possible and turning loose right-hand power. But there is a bit more to it than that. At contact I want both left and right sides of my body fully extended, as well as my arms. Extended, they give me full power both at the ball and during the next split second—when the ball is flattened against the clubface and rides with it. The longer and stronger you can weld clubface and ball together, the farther it'll travel.

If my left-side muscles don't feel "used up" in a flat-out swing—if my left arm isn't straight all the way through—then I'm wasting power. The right side I don't worry about: it hits hell out of the ball naturally.

TURNING ON THE STEAM

As long as a man doesn't take a death grip and lurch off balance, it's not bad practice for him to haul back and swing with most of what he has. Soft swingers don't prosper as much as hard swingers. For one thing, when you prepare to hit with steam, your muscles tune themselves to the coming effort. The golfer who tries holding back goes into too slow and mushy a backswing; then when he realizes that he's in no position to give the ball a ride, he rewinds and begins hitting before he's ready. If he's intent on hitting hard from the word go, that's all he thinks about. All those hot flashes that come with cushioning the blow are removed.

Even better than that, you don't get weak at the knees but go on the offensive. Getting tough is the only attitude that can save the fellow who can swing smoothly in his backyard but chokes up when the ball is teed and money is up.

Many a golf course and many a big gambler would have eaten me up if I hadn't eaten them first by having a mean frame of mind.

From *The Education of a Golfer*, by Sam Snead, with Al Stump. Simon & Schuster, New York, N.Y. Copyright © 1962 by Sam Snead and Al Stump. Reprinted with the permission of Jack Snead.

FINISH WHAT YOU START

Vance Levin, a Stamford, Connecticut, golf pro with E. Gaynor Brennan Golf Club and Sterling Farms Golf Club, uses a drill that ingrains the idea of accelerating through impact. He instructs his clients to assume a normal address position, but to put the clubhead in *front* of the ball and then swing to the finish—never touching the ball. Repeat twenty-five times a day! ❧

Your Through-Swing Will Be a Reflex Action

1972 ✦ JOHN JACOBS
WITH KEN BOWDEN

Englishman John Jacobs was an international star player in the '50s, a Ryder Cup captain in the '70s and '80s, and the driving force behind the formation of the European Tour. A Hall of Fame instructor who probably has helped more golfers than anyone, Jacobs still teaches, writes, and breaks down the swing for his clients. Despite his complex life, Jacobs's approach to golf can be refreshingly simple and direct. His signature philosophy revolves around the physics of the game, and how to apply clear principles of cause and effect to hitting the ball. In this excerpt from *Practical Golf*, he assures golfers that if the backswing has been completed correctly, the downswing will be almost *reflexive*, in effect telling them to trust their swings. However, true to his calling, Jacobs then offers a detailed analysis of how the downswing unfolds, and tells golfers to apply that knowledge during practice.

There's a simple way of knowing whether you are coiling properly during your backswing. Try to hold your top-of-the-swing position for 10 seconds. If you've really coiled the spring, you'll find this, if not impossible, certainly a considerable muscular strain.

You will also find that the need to "unwind" is a *reflex* action. As your shoulders reach the limit of their turn, the opposing force in your resisting legs and hips will already be winning the battle. Almost before your shoulders have reached the limit of their turn in one direction, the lower half of your body will have started to pull in the opposite direction. This is what is meant by "starting the downswing with the legs and hips," a recommendation made by nearly every golf book author and modern teacher of the game.

This natural reflex action, the result of opposing forces acting upon each other irresistibly, is the start of the downswing.

It is an observable fact that in a good golf swing, the downswing begins before the backswing finishes. This change of direction, this victory of one force over an opposing force, is, for most golfers, a crossroads equal in magnitude to starting the club away from the ball. The clash of opposing forces *must* take place if the golfer is to get his maximum power into the shot. But it can only take place if he has wound up properly in the backswing. In the backswing, the top half of the body has been turning, the lower half resisting, as the arms swing up. In the downswing *the lower half turns while the top half resists and the arms swing down.*

As the lower half of the body wins the battle, the bulk of the player's weight shifts to his left foot while his head stays behind the ball. The legs move laterally to the left and the hips begin to turn to face the hole, thereby clearing the way for the arms to swing the club *down and through* the ball. The right knee—which has been flexed throughout—"kicks in" as the left hip pulls the weight back to the left side. The right leg, now "released," adds thrust to the pull of the left side.

As I've stressed, all of this—subject to a proper windup—is largely a reflex action. You can hardly prevent it from happening if you've coiled properly. But the real trick is not in the lower-body action. It lies in the action of the top half, the torso and the head.

Throughout the downswing, the head must remain *back*; pretty much where it was at address and during the backswing, behind the ball. And the upper torso, notably the shoulders, must *resist* the pull of the lower half of the body until the arms have swung down. This is the key to power, the *natural cause* of the "late hit," which so many club golfers have sought so long in vain.

If your top half effectively reverses its backswing role (after resisting the pull and turn of the lower half), the arms and hands, instead of flinging the club from top—altering the swing's arc and plane, and dissipating power—will be pulled down *inside* the target line. The set or cock of the wrists established by the weight of the club at the top of the swing will be retained until—as the big muscles of the legs, hips, and back pull the hands down—the wrists automatically un-cock, whipping the clubhead into the ball as the hands flash past it.

These are all the "mechanics" of the through-swing you ever need to know—and ideally you should not even think consciously of them, except in practice sessions.

From *Practical Golf,* by John Jacobs, with Ken Bowden. Stanley Paul & Co., Ltd., an imprint of the Hutchinson Group. Copyright © 1972 John Jacobs and Ken Bowden. Used by permission of John Jacobs.

Step Five: Move Down to the Ball

1994 ⚊ JIM McLEAN

Although he played in two U.S. Opens and a Masters, Jim McLean soon found that he was more adept at helping others harness their swings than trying to tame his own, which he admits sometimes wilted under pressure. Studying under such diverse instructors as Carl Welty, Ken Venturi (a Hogan protégé), Johnny Revolta, and Jimmy Ballard, McLean emerged with a unique and very successful teaching approach. McLean focuses on eight checkpoints in the golfer's swing motion. But he isn't fanatical about exact positions for each stage in the way Hogan often could be, preferring that the golfer simply stay within acceptable ranges of motion—or what he calls "corridors of success." *The Eight-Step Swing*, a best-selling book and video, encapsulates the approach, and "Step Five" takes the golfer from the top of the backswing to just before the moment of truth at impact.

If there is a secret to employing a good golf swing, it occurs here [after Step Four: 100 Percent of Your Shoulder Turn (Backswing Completed)].

In all of the great swings I have studied, there is no evidence of a "stop" and "start" that together reverse the direction of the club from backswing to downswing. Instead, I see a smooth, flowing transition. The arms, hands, and club respond to the actions of the lower body or lower center of body. In fine golf swings, the last thing to change direction at the top is the clubhead. This, of course, makes perfect sense, because all the centrifugal and centripetal force we apply in the swing is designed to do nothing else but load the clubhead with energy and deliver it down the proper path.

In the transition, your arms and hands are passive. The first move is backward and down. The clubhead sinks lower as your hips start to unwind. Your hands and wrists respond immediately to the reversal of direction. Your right elbow automatically drops into the proper slot by your right side. The Step Five checkpoint position in many ways resembles the Step Three position [the Three-Quarter Backswing Position] on the backswing. From a head-on view, it looks as if the hands and clubshaft were passing back through the same positions they were in at Step Three (*only considerably narrower*). There is a sense that the hands free-fall down to the delivery position.

The right shoulder helps determine the path of the downswing. If, in its first motion, your right shoulder rocks down, all systems are go. Thanks to the shoulder, your right elbow can now drop into its proper slot and align (head-on view) with your right hip. This lowering of the right shoulder is a response to the legs' initiating the forward motion. But if the first motion is initiated by your right shoulder out toward the ball, you've got no chance to attain the correct positions at Step Five. The down tuck of the right shoulder can be overworked, so proceed with caution. You don't want to cause your left shoulder to "over-climb" through impact.

Note: to clear up any possible misconception, I have not said that the first move in the downswing is made by the right shoulder. The downswing starts with the hips or lower body center moving toward the tar-get. The shoulder motion, good or bad, is a responsive motion that ties in with the hips or lower body.

In a model swing, the hands and arms are passive during this step and respond to rather than initiate any action. The right elbow gives the appearance of attaching to, then being glued to, the right side just above the right hip area. The left arm is fully extended from the body—straight. It is here that good players feel pull, but that is only a sensation, not a result of any conscious pull with the hands or arms. With your right elbow glued to your right side and your left arm straight, it is easy to see that Step Five is a very powerful position. Your hands and arms have not "run off" but are simply responding accurately and appropriately to the body motions. The clubshaft is very close to the same position it was in at Step Three—exceptions include ninety degrees of angle or more with the left arm and clubshaft. The downswing is inside (narrower than) the backswing. (This is one of my fundamentals.) Your wrists are in a fully cocked position. The club should not be outside your hands unless you intend to hit a cut. If it is outside the hands, this is a perfect illustration of "casting" (starting the release motion too soon) or exaggerating the initial rotation of the shoulders. The *"delivery position,"* as I call it, will always show you the golfer's impact position. It is a critical spot in the swing that determines all ball flight. It is always a position I carefully analyze in my teaching.

At Step Five, body weight has shifted back noticeably to the left. It has re-centered the body and weight is shifting forward and *diagonally left*.

Your belt buckle as viewed from the front has slid seven to twelve inches toward the target, from Step Four to Step Six [Impact]. This slide is a natural response to the lower body—the feet and legs—initiating the downswing. It happens *automatically* in a sequenced swing. If you monitor the belt buckle on any top players, you'll immediately see this powerful lateral movement.

At Step Five, the shaft should have traveled down along a path that, when viewed down the target line, is between the tip of your shoulder and your right elbow. If the shaft stays in this Corridor of Success with the butt end of the club pointing to an extension of the ball-to-target line, this indicates an on-plane swing and promising solid contact and good trajectory.

Jim McLean stresses the modern power angle to his students.

In viewing the swings of the amateurs I teach, I sometimes see the shaft improperly low—dropped beneath the elbow. In this case, the dotted line from the shaft butt hits the ground at a point well beyond the target line. From this position you will push or hook the ball—if you make solid contact. Often, you will hit behind the ball from this inside, shallow swing arc.

A far more common problem I witness is indicated when the shaft moves downward on a path that takes it above the tip of the shoulder. In this instance, a line drawn from the butt of the club would point to the player's feet. We call this "shaft tip over." From this position at Step Five, you will usually contact the ball with the toe of the clubface and hit a weak slice—Death Position! If you manage to square the clubface, you'll pull the ball. Finally, this move is also characteristic of the shank.

STEP FIVE: FINAL CHECKPOINTS

→ The right knee has kicked forward (toward the ball or target line), and there is a substantial space between your knees.

→ The hips have shifted a few inches, in response to your weight-shifting action, and reached the square position. The shoulders trail the hips.

→ The head has stabilized at, or slightly behind, its address position.

→ The right heel is grounded or, at most, slightly off the ground. At this point in the swing, it should never be extra high.

→ The flexed left knee is forward of your left hip. The left knee is more or less in a straight line with the middle of your left foot. The left leg is still flexed but is in the process of straightening.

→ The body has entered the classic "sit-down" position many players and teachers have long observed.

- The clubshaft is on plane.
- The shoulders are unwinding at a rapid pace, yet still lag your hips in rotation. The golf swing depends heavily on "connection," but in the downswing we also see two instances of *separation*—first, the lower body "leaves" the shoulders, then the hands and arms "separate" from the shoulders. The distance between your hands and right shoulder increases as the club reaches our "delivery position."
- The right arm should be slightly visible under your left starting down.
- Your eyes are fixed on the ball.
- The clubhead is behind your body.
- Many golfers will benefit by *slowing down* the turn back to the target. Sometimes it is useful to slow the upper torso—other times the lower—and sometimes both.
- A big secret to good shotmaking is the clubshaft position at Step Five and the square orientation of the clubface. I call this "the delivery position."
- Supinate the left wrist on the downward move. This happens during Step Five. Sometimes we actually teach this move. That is making the left wrist flat or slightly bowed. If the wrists, hands, and clubhead truly respond to the lower body this flattening should happen with no conscious thought. When it does not happen, we teach it. When you stop the club at Step Five, check your left wrist position. It must not be cupped.

From *The Eight-Step Swing*, by Jim McLean. Copyright © 1994 by Jim McLean. Reprinted by permission of HarperCollins Publishers, Inc.

Impact

2 0 0 0   Johnny Miller

In 1974 and 1975, Johnny Miller won twelve PGA tournaments, including one by fourteen strokes and another by nine. Overall, he won twenty-five titles, including two Majors, before burning out in the late '70s and becoming a golf commentator. On the air, Miller is famous for his blunt, often controversial remarks, so it's not surprising that his ideas about his own golf swing are provocative. In more than a century of golf instruction, few have ventured where Miller does, focusing on that split second when the clubhead meets the ball. His knowledge of impact, he contends, is what elevated him to the top of his profession. In this excerpt from *Breaking 90*, he makes the intriguing claim that he developed muscle memory for the perfect impact position. He describes how to achieve this ideal by what professionals call "covering the ball"—a term related to Hogan's "supination"—which involves maintaining a subtle, downward angle of the right palm.

I got my bachelor's degree in Physical Education from Brigham Young University in 1969. But I got my PhD in impact from twenty-five years of study, trial, and error on the PGA Tour.

From the time I started playing professionally in 1970, I made it my mission to develop a complete sense of swing feedback. I wanted to know exactly what the clubhead was doing at impact and how that affected my shots. To accomplish this, I didn't rely just on feel. I was one of the first pros to invest in stop-action and movie cameras to make pictures and videos of my swing. Just like Tony Gwynn, who has a video record of every baseball swing he's made during his career, I built a huge library of video and sequence pictures of my golf swing. After hours of studying those images and by hitting thousands of balls, I could pinpoint exactly what positions I needed to be in at impact to send the ball where I wanted it to go, with very few mis-hits. I actually developed muscle memory of the perfect impact position.

The result was that I played some stretches of golf that I can hardly believe myself. Everyone remembers the 63 I shot at Oakmont to win the 1973 U.S. Open, but that was only one dream round. For me, 1974 and 1975 were dream years. I won eight tournaments in '74, then three of the first four I played in '75. . . . I can say without bragging that for 16 months, anyway, I could play golf as well as anybody, ever. . . . For that . . . period . . . I was furious if I hit a mid- or short-iron more than five feet off line. I looked at that kind of miss—and we're talking birdie-range if my yardage was right—as a failure. . . .

I'm not saying you're going to develop that level of confidence with your irons. But, if you become a student of impact, not only will you be able to understand why your shots do what they do, but you'll be able to take control and make the ball do what you want it to do. If you deliver the clubhead solidly and precisely to the ball, it doesn't make any difference what the rest of the swing looks like. That's why I am surprised that no instructors talk about impact. They tell you everything you want to know about the full swing, but leave out the most important part—the moment the clubhead connects with the ball. All the ball knows is impact.

Impact—which can be defined as the split second your club comes into contact with the ball to

Johnny Miller's singular focus on impact is now the basis of his popular instructional programs.

about an inch past when the ball leaves the clubhead—is everything in golf. Depending on where your clubhead is at that moment, you will hit a hook or a slice, a draw or a fade, a low runner or a high soft shot. If you can master impact, you can control and shape your shots. However, if you make a tiny mistake and your clubhead is left open as it hits the ball, even just a hair, you could slice the ball twenty yards wide of your target. That's how important impact is. In fact, a small but crucial difference in clubface position at impact is exactly what separates total hackers from the best players in the world. I've heard people say that golf is a game of inches, but when it comes to impact, it is a game of fractions of fractions of inches.

If you're an average amateur player, your sense of feel isn't going to be fine enough to do more than make a rough estimate about what happens at impact. But even at that level, you can learn enough to make some really positive changes in your swing. At the absolute minimum, you need to know that every good professional golfer, from an aggressive swinger like Sergio Garcia to a controlled technician like Annika Sorenstam, reduces the loft on his or her mid- and short-iron shots, just before impact. That's called "covering" the ball. . . . A good golfer's palm faces down at impact, creating that reduced loft angle. If you took the club out of my hands at impact, you'd see that my right palm faces the target and is angled slightly toward the ground. I'm swinging down and through the ball. The shaft of the club is staying vertical long after the clubhead passes my left toe, and my right hand won't turn over until it gets to my left pocket.

Every bad player does the opposite—usually because he or she isn't convinced that the loft on the club is enough to get the ball airborne. Once you try to scoop the shot into the air with the club by rotating that right palm under and up toward the sky, at best you're going to hit a high, weak shot. In fact, most of the worst swing problems beginners have, from reverse pivoting to coming over the top, create more loft. With that right palm upward, not only does the club have more loft, but the face is flared open, causing even more of a left-to-right curve. It is impossible to hit consistently good shots if you add loft. Your only chance would be to hang back and pull one twenty yards left, and that would happen strictly by luck. To take the next step, you need to learn to cover the ball.

Watch an aggressive swinger like Garcia hit his 7- or 8-iron. He'll take a divot the size of a folded dinner napkin, yet his shots are struck cleanly and crisply. You're probably saying to yourself, when I take a divot that size I'm hitting it fat and about twenty feet. If you check out your divot on a fat shot, you'll see that it started before the ball. Once you jam the club into the ground behind the ball, you slow any clubhead speed you generated on the downswing. If the club can plow through all that turf and get to the ball, it usually sends it rolling about twenty or thirty feet. The difference in Garcia's shot is that he's hitting the ball, *then* hitting the turf. In other words, he's hitting the ball just before he gets to the bottom of his swing. He's angling that clubhead toward the ball, with his palm facing down, and striking the ball crisply with a descending blow. That divot is coming from the ground directly in front of the ball, after the ball is gone. He's pinching the ball between the ground and the club, causing the backspin that makes his irons hit the green, then stick like a scared cat.

If you spend enough time on the practice range hitting balls, you'll be able to get impact feedback through your hands and your ears. Just like a home run struck right on the sweet spot, when you hit a pure golf shot, you don't feel a thing—no vibrations. The sound is very distinctive, too. Go out and watch a PGA Tour player hit an iron from the fairway, and you'll know the sound of that pure strike—not the clattering of metal on balata, but a crisp click with a swooshing noise attached.

It's true that those last moves happen very quickly. I can remember playing a practice round with Jack Nicklaus early in 1975, when I was in the middle of that incredible run. We had played a few holes and I hit it to kick-in range on each one. As we got ready to tee off on the next hole, Jack asked me what I worked on in my practice sessions, and I told him about my ongoing quest to know impact. He looked at me like I was crazy. "It happens too fast—how can anybody know what happens at impact?" he said. Maybe that's why so many instructors spend so much time on swing mechanics and basically ignore impact. The swing takes time, so it can be shaped and fiddled with. Once they set you up in the proper position, most teachers think it's just a matter of firing away and letting the ball get in the way of the swing. I say that's leaving too much to chance. Jack hit some of the most solid iron shots I ever saw, so he knew something about impact. Don't sell your brain short. That impact move is very trainable. I've had great results working both with my kids and with average amateurs in just an hour or two on the range. You can easily work on it by yourself in front of a mirror.

In a lot of ways, impact is the most important thing I can teach, because no matter how many other swing fundamentals or positions I talk about, your personal body shape and flexibility level are going to determine to what extent you can imitate what I suggest. Study the swings of the players who have had the most success over the years by watching videos of their swings or looking at swing-sequence photographs. It's easy to see what kinds of backswings and downswings promote that kind of solid impact. But that study also shows that there's more than one way to do it. Even when two swings are as different as, say, mine and Lee Trevino's, if you took a picture of the two clubheads at impact, you wouldn't be able to tell us apart.

If you want to get better at this game, you need to understand impact and what position you'll need to be in to achieve it just right. Then you can craft a swing with the body you've been given that will help you get where you need to be during those crucial split seconds of impact. Even if you understand the general mechanics of the swing, if you don't know impact, you're golfing in the dark.

From *Breaking 90*, by Johnny Miller. Copyright © 2000 by Callaway Editions, Inc. Reprinted with the permission of Callaway Editions, Inc.

HANDS ON

Henry Cotton, one of the great "hands" players, told pupils to hit an old tire with a 7-iron to build up strength in their hands and wrists. The modern equivalent is the "impact bag" —a plastic sack one fills with rags—sold by most golf outlets as a swing training aid. ✍

PART THREE

THE SHORT GAME

THE BEAUTY OF GOLF IS that players who aren't blessed with great power can best their more crowd-pleasing, long-hitting adversaries. They can do it with pinpoint pitches and chips, skilled bunker play, and accurate putting. That's as true today as it was in the late 1800s, although approach shots evolved from being primarily a ground game to more of an aerial assault. As equipment improved and golf moved from the seaside to inland forests and parks, instruction shifted from the low-flying chip—once the staple of links-type play and still a potent tool—to high-flying pitches for clearing bunkers and other hazards. Notions about bunker play also changed. Until Gene Sarazen debuted the sand wedge at the 1932 British Open, some regarded landing "on the beach" as a near calamity. But with this new weapon, instructors preached that escaping with "explosion" and "splash" shots was an easier challenge. Today, the consensus is that landing in a bunker is *preferable* to many other greenside lies. In the early twentieth century, outstanding putters Walter Travis and Jerome Travers developed the now standard reverse-overlap grip and pendulum motion. Later golfers, playing on well-manicured greens, would refine ideas about gauging speed and line, yet recommended combining sophisticated, modern technique with the artistry of early pioneers. Dave Pelz would introduce statistical analysis into putting. Confidence and consistency remain vital to steadying nerves, because as Bobby Jones said, "There is nothing so demoralizing as missing a short putt."

CHIPPING AND PITCHING

GROUND AND AIR ASSAULT

Approaching

1896 ✦ WILLIE PARK, JR.

Willie Park, Jr.'s, bewhiskered father was the first British Open champion in 1860 and fellow Scot Old Tom Morris's archrival for more than a decade. Uncle Mungo also won the Open, and Junior became champion himself in 1887 and 1889. When he played, *The New York Times* said, "He appeared to be encased in a triple armor of philosophical composure." A student of the game, who designed clubs and courses in Europe and North America, Park devoted an entire volume to putting in 1920, but is best remembered for *The Game of Golf*, the first complete instructional book by a professional. In this excerpt, he used terms that modern readers probably won't recognize—such as "wrist strokes" and "hitting off the left or right legs"—but they should realize he's describing how to chip, pitch, and execute tricky cut shots in ways not that different from current methods.

———

The approach is the most difficult, and sometimes the most delicate, stroke in the whole game. . . . In approaching, not only must the ball be hit truly, but the distance to the hole must be calculated and the force employed proportioned thereto, and consideration must be given to the nature of the ground to determine whether the ball is to be lofted or run up. These considerations make the stroke more complex. But in no part of the game is there afforded a greater opportunity for the display of skill, as opposed to force, than in this, and nowhere is skill better repaid. For at every hole the player who can lay his approach near the flag has the chance of saving a stroke off his less skillful adversary, provided he does not, by indifferent putting, throw away the advantage. . . .

Three-quarter and half strokes are to my mind much more difficult to play than full shots. . . . There is always a disposition to jerk the swing, as if to compensate for its being shortened, and this generally results in topping the ball. . . . There cannot be any possible reason for pressing a half or three-quarter stroke, because, if it is desired to drive the ball further, the proper course is to lengthen the swing and take a full shot. Therefore, in playing these strokes, there should not, under any circumstances, be pressing: swing easily. . . .

The position of the ball and stance for playing half-shots is somewhat, though not materially, different from that [for a full shot]. . . . The ball is nearer the player's body, and nearer also to the line of the right foot. The right foot is also further advanced. . . . It need hardly be pointed out that, as the club is not swung far round, the shoulders and body do not move so much as in playing a full stroke. The shoulders must move round, and the body must be eased . . . to a certain extent, it is true, but the less they do so the better, consistently with letting the club go sufficiently round. The left foot will be just raised off the heel and nothing more, the left leg being flexed to ease the swing. It may, in fact, be said that the feet should not, if possible, be moved at all. The elbow of the right arm should be kept in to the body and not allowed to rise, but all the same the arms will be thrown out just as in playing full strokes. The follow-through will take place at the end of the swing; but instead of throwing the club and arms after the ball, they will rise quicker, and continue upward over the left shoulder more than in the direction of the flight of the ball.

Some golfers can drive a very long ball with a half-swing; but the half-swing used in such a case is hardly the half-swing desirable for playing approaches. This half-swing is more of the character of a very long sweep along the ground succeeded by a good follow-through; and although the club may not be taken so far round the shoulders as in a full swing, the distance actually traversed by the clubhead will not be much less, and being a sweep, it gives a great amount of forward propulsion to the ball.

Of wrist strokes there is an infinite variety of gradation—anything less than a half-stroke falls under this definition. No further remarks on this subject require to be made, save that the ball should be nearer the player, and the feet closer together. . . . [B]oth legs are slightly more bent at the knees than is the case in playing a full shot, and the body moves very little; in fact, wrist strokes are almost entirely played with the wrists, assisted to a small extent by the arms. I would only add: Stand firmly, and do not move the feet at all; keep the right elbow well in to the side, and play from the wrists, giving the ball a quick, sharp hit.

In all these strokes the club must be held firmly with both hands, to give more command over it, and to prevent its turning. It will be found of material assistance if the club be grasped further down the shaft; and the shorter the distance of the stroke to be played, the shorter a grip of the club may be taken.

In standing according to the directions above given, it will be found that while the weight of the body is supported on both legs, the right really gives the greatest amount of support. This can be easily tested by trying to lift either foot off the ground. For the above reason, this mode of playing approaches has been termed "off the right leg," and it is the method most usually adopted. Hereafter an alternative method, termed "off the left leg," will be explained.

With the view of making iron approaches fall dead, more especially those played from shorter distances, it has been advocated that they should be played with slice, or cut, as it is more frequently termed in this case. This is done . . . by drawing the arms in toward the body in the act of hitting the ball, and omitting the follow-through. This probably may have the desired effect—and theoretically it is all very well—but practically it is exceedingly difficult to do successfully; and placing the risk of failure against the advantage to be gained, I do not think in the ordinary case it is worth attempting. I therefore recommend that all approaches be played without slice. If, however, the player has sufficient confidence in his ability to put on the cut, and is desirous of trying it, he will have to keep in view that the effect is to make the ball run to the right-hand side, and he must make allowance for this by playing, not straight on the flag, but to the left of it. . . . It is not difficult to put on cut when a ball is teed or dropped on a fine piece of turf, simply for the purpose of illustrating the stroke; but it is quite a different matter to play approaches in this manner from the multifarious lies—good, bad, and indifferent—that occur in actual play. . . .

With wrist shots there is more run on the ball in proportion than with any others, and it may be absolutely necessary to make a wrist shot fall dead, as, for instance, where the hole lies between two bunkers, one in front over which the ball must be pitched, and one behind into which it will certainly roll if there is much run on it. There are other expedients resorted to for this purpose besides putting on cut. One is to lay back the face of the iron. To do this, the player must stand in such a position that the ball will be more in a line with his left foot. But this method is no better than using a club with a very great deal of pitch. . . . There is another method, known as "cutting the feet from it," and this is the most effectual of all, and undoubtedly the proper way of playing the stroke. It is, however, somewhat difficult to play this stroke, and it is still more difficult to describe it. The stance and position are the same as for an ordinary iron approach, and so is the grip. The swing must, however, be much more of an up and down nature than in the ordinary approach, and played sharply. The head of the iron is slipped in between the ball and the turf (not swept over the ground), with the result that a large amount of backspin is imparted to the ball, and in the follow-through the arms are not thrown out

Willie Park, Jr., a short-game artist beyond compare, advised golfers to "cut the feet out" from under the ball when hitting a delicate shot over a hazard.

in the line of play, but are lifted up straighter, with the object of "whipping up" the ball. The essence of the stroke lies in hitting the ball smartly and quickly; and the more quickly the ball is hit, the more backspin is put upon it, therefore the higher will it be lofted, and the shorter distance it will travel. If the face of the iron be looked at after playing, it will be found that the mark made on it is not a round mark . . . it is a sort of oval smear from the bottom toward the top of the blade, as if the face of the iron had forced itself under the ball before the latter had moved. This, I anticipate, is what actually does happen; and hence, as above stated, the more quickly the stroke is played the more backspin is put on the ball. The stroke will be an utter failure unless the clubhead gets well under the ball. On a soft green such a stroke can invariably be played with success; but on a hard green, and out of a bad lie, it is difficult, but not impossible. Such strokes can best be played with a lofting-iron.

The alternative mode of playing approaches is "off the left leg." The best exponent of this style is

Mr. Laidlay, [who sets up with] the weight of [his] body thrown upon the left leg, and the club . . . held toward [his] left side. Mr. Laidlay also prefers to play approaches with an iron that has not a great deal of loft on it, thus getting a comparatively low shot, and allowing the ball to finish with a run after the pitch; but for lofted approaches he invariably uses a mashie. . . .

Regard must always be had to the nature of the ground between the place where the ball lies and the hole, and upon that will depend the club to be used. If a putter be used, the ball will not, of course, rise at all, but will roll along the ground; if a cleek be used, the ball will rise but a few feet, depending upon the length and consequent strength of the stroke, and will roll a good bit after the pitch is exhausted; while using the iron, the stroke will be pitched up to the green and roll a comparatively short distance. On a hard green, running up will be found most successful, because it is difficult to pitch a ball dead off an iron, and should it happen to alight on any irregularity it may shoot forward or may bound off in any direction; hence the superiority of running up, because there is much more forward motion on the ball, and it will not, if it hit some irregularity, be deflected to such an extent as if pitched. There is also this advantage, that, the straighter the face of the club, the less is a ball affected when not quite accurately struck, and it is easier to judge the distance—that is to say, an error in calculating the strength tells less against the stroke.

The more pitch there is on a club the less striking surface is presented to the ball, and the more is any mistake magnified. . . . The iron is undoubtedly the best all-round club for playing approaches, and where the ball requires to be lofted, it, or a similar club, must be used.

On courses where the ground is soft, and possibly the putting greens are surrounded by rough grass, it is not possible to play cleek or putter approaches—the ball will not run; and in these cases it must be pitched on to the green. . . .

In all approach play remember the motto, "Be up," unless there is some reason to the contrary. It is quite possible, and indeed frequently happens, that an approach may be holed out; but unless it is up, this can never occur.

From *The Game of Golf*, by Willie Park, Jr., Longmans, Green & Co., London, England.

The Run-up Approach

1925 ✦ MRS. HURD
(MISS DOROTHY CAMPBELL)

In 1926, Dorothy Campbell Hurd pulled out her faithful mashie, Thomas, while on the fringe of the 18th green at Augusta Country Club, and holed out, thereby breaking Walter Travis's record for fewest putts in a round, 19 to 21, and confirming she could chip as well as putt. While living in her native Scotland, and then Canada and America, this great international player won an estimated seventy-one titles, including three women's championships in each country. In 1909, she was the first to capture the U.S. and British Amateurs in one year. Even better, she emerged from semi-retirement and won her third U.S. Amateur in 1924, a record thirteen years after her second victory. At thirty-five, she became the oldest winner and silenced harsh criticism. Then she wrote this amusing essay which illustrates "freakish" self-taught approaches can be effective—her famously "eccentric" approach shot was essentially a long, running chip. It anticipated by one year her record-making chip.

The saying that an approach is like a log, easier to roll than to pitch, is probably the reason in a nutshell why my best shot has always been one of the running-up variety. Apparently the gods turned their faces from me while serving out ability to play, with any degree of skill, what is known today as a pitch shot.

Being an entirely self-taught golfer, I apparently picked up by chance or by an unconscious imitation a shot which has been the real factor in any success that I may have had, a shot which by reason of the extreme ease of its method has rarely failed to yield a dividend when a match has been in a critical stage.

This shot can be used when the ball is lying at a distance of forty or fifty yards from the hole, if there is no intervening hazard, and is equally effectual from a point that is only a few feet from the green. Even there its sphere of usefulness is not ended; it can be played with deadly effect instead of a very long approach putt on courses where the area of the greens is so great that it precludes the use of an ordinary putting cleek, because of its attendant necessity of hitting the ball so hard that the requisite delicate touch on the club is lost.

To illustrate the fact that my method in making the shot apparently differs somewhat from that of the majority of golfers, I shall relate a more or less amusing little anecdote.

A few years ago I won the North and South Championship at Pinehurst, North Carolina, and was considerably helped thereto by holing two chip shots of about forty yards in the final against Mrs. F. E. Letts, of Chicago. In the gallery was an American lady who came under the categorical definition of "recently fortunate" and who was smitten with a craze for golf. She determined to add my type of stroke to the rest of her lately acquired possessions and characteristically went to the local professional and said, "I want you to teach me Mrs. Hurd's chip shot," to which the Scot with equally characteristic brusqueness and brevity replied, "I'll no; yon's a freak shot."

While being quite ready to allow the professional to make my favorite shot a subject of mirth, I must dissent from the statement that it is freakish in its origin and its execution, for the effect of the contact with the clubhead is exactly the same as that of the "dead ball" brought into usage on the billiard table during the last decade, and played with particular effect by Hosson and his imitators.

No special club need be carried for this shot, it can be played equally well with a mashie-niblick, mashie, or mid-iron, although in the case of the latter the length of the shaft will possibly be considered as somewhat detrimental. In the former the length of the shaft is ideal, but the angle of the clubhead necessitates its being faced down rather sharply, so the average golfer will probably prefer an ordinary mashie. For my own part, I have had much the best results from one of the goose-necked variety, but that is perhaps simply a matter of personal preference, or what my old Scottish nurse would chillingly have termed a "caper."

The stance differs materially from that which is usually adopted for the pitch shot; the weight of the body, instead of being evenly distributed, or somewhat more on the right foot, is almost entirely poised on the left, with the toe pointing slightly toward the hole and the ball in line with the left heel.

The grip is, frankly, both ugly and unorthodox, but in its very heterodoxy lies the secret of one-half of the value of the shot. When the club is taken from the

The chip is the greatest economist in golf.
BOBBY JONES

caddie it should be grasped rather firmly in the palm of the left hand with the thumb around the shaft. The right hand must then be placed quite distinctly *under* the shaft with the greatest amount of contact also in the palm, and with the thumb pointing toward the ground. This is, of course, distinctly divergent from the axiom of Vardon and that the Vs of the hands must be parallel; and it is the fact that the club is forced into the palms by this very divergence that produces the curiously dragging motion on the ball that typifies this particular shot and causes its similarity to the "dead ball" of Hosson.

The swing is an easy one to control, being of the "closed-face" type, caused by the grip in conjunction with the fact that the elbow is not held quite so closely to the side as for a pitch shot. No haste or snatching must be apparent in the timing, and the ball must be hit on the downward journey, taking a fraction of turf just after the moment of impact. At no time must the ball rise more than four feet from the ground, and a golfer of experience will know that, after the first glance at the hole, the maximum of concentration must be given to making the ball land on the spot that will allow it to run the requisite number of yards after it touches the ground.

It is quite remarkable how straight will be the flight of a ball if struck in the manner described and how often it will come to rest at a distance of two or three feet from the hole. . . .

From *The Best of Golf*, edited by Eleanor E. Helme. Chapter by Mrs. Hurd (Miss Dorothy Campbell). Mills & Boone, Ltd., London, England.

Approaching

CIRCA 1928 ⚬ P. A. VAILE

Pembroke Arnold Vaile's long-out-of-print books and old clubs, such as the "P. A. Vaile Stroke Saver," are items at auctions. Only collectors and historians seem to know the Chicago writer who learned golf late in life and then explained it in numerous books. Vaile wrote about international economic relations in *Cosmocracy, the Science of Peace*, and some of his golf books—and tennis books—were, if less high-minded, equally esoteric, bearing such titles as *The Soul of Golf*. Others, such as *Putting Made Easy* and *The Short Game* (originally a booklet in the late '20s) could still be understood by readers who had never held a club. In this excerpt, Vaile told beginners to use a putting grip to chip and keep the body out of the shot, advice that still is golden. He reinforced his once disparaged theories by quoting similar views expressed by Johnny Farrell and Bobby Jones.

The grip for the short approach strokes is almost the same as that for the putt. Approximately the same grip is used for all clubs, with the important difference that in the putt and short approach shots the club lies more uprightly in the hands. . . . This follows naturally as the lie of the club becomes more vertical.

The stance should be open, substantially the same as the half-open stance . . . for the putt, the left heel, however, in the open stance being a trifle farther from the line of flight than the right heel.

Be careful to keep the face of the club at right angles to the intended line of flight. Up to about fifty yards from the pin there is comparatively little knee and body movement, the hands and arms doing most of the work.

The grip must be firm with both hands, and the stroke should be crisp. Keep the left arm straight and the right elbow close to the side. The knees, hips, and shoulders start the downswing, which, even in the short strokes, is not entirely independent hand and arm movement. Keep the head still and guard especially against ducking or lowering it during the stroke. . . .

There must be *absolutely no lateral movement of the hips away from the hole*, or as it is termed, swaying. This unsettles the center, or base, of one's swing in a class of strokes wherein one should confidently strive for as much accuracy as in putting. . . .

It is impossible to exaggerate the importance of this in golf generally and especially in the short game, for it means limiting body movement to the minimum and getting it correctly instead of exaggerating it and moreover doing it incorrectly. It is unnecessary to dilate on the advantage of this to those who are trying to master the golf stroke.

It is interesting to note, in Bob MacDonald's book, *Golf at a Glance*, that he is especially emphatic in stating repeatedly that *there must be no lateral hip shift away from the hole.*

We may, in the circumstances, take it that what I have, practically alone, insisted on as correct golf for over twenty years is *now accepted as sound doctrine.* I put it so emphatically, for this means a blessed relief to a great army of hip-swayers who were ruining or had ruined their game.

Few, if any, expert golfers consistently play from tee to green in par figures for eighteen holes, yet rounds under par are now quite common.

Such under-par rounds must be and are made by pitching and chipping for one putt consistently. The value of approach practice can hardly be overestimated, as the approach shot is unquestionably the biggest factor in a low score. . . .

An article by ex-Open champion of the United States, Johnny Farrell, in *The Amateur Golfer*, is practically a complete lesson in approaching itself. . . . I shall quote only [from] the first two paragraphs here, as follows:

THE CHIP SHOT—A LONG PUTT

"The one point that I would like to impress upon golfers playing the chip shot is the fact *that it is nothing more than a long putt.* If the player will bring himself to realize this really important fact it will simplify the play greatly and create a mental condition that will reduce the tension that seems to be a handicap of the amateur golfer. . . .

"The most common fault that I have observed is that the player stands too far away from the ball and the feet are usually too far apart. This fault makes the result of the stroke very uncertain as control of the wrist is lost. The proper method is for the player to stand as close to the ball as he can with comfort and freedom—without feeling cramped. Both arms should be tucked close to the side; the forearms and wrists only are used in swinging the club. The swing should simulate that of the putt. With the idea of a putt in mind, and by following the principles of the putt, the irritating and annoying habit of stubbing the ground is not likely to occur."

Farrell, indeed, carries this principle into the niblick shots . . .

"Bobby Jones has recently published an interesting article on the run-up shot, from which I shall give a few extracts:

"'Although lack of familiarity with the run-up has caused the majority of players to regard it as a very difficult shot, it is actually far simpler and far less risky than the pitch. That is the greatest virtue of the run-up—it will never finish very far away.

"'The shot ought rarely to be played with any club of more loft than a No. 4 iron. I carry in my bag a cleek *shafted to a little more than putter length* which I use for run-up shots of thirty or forty yards. It is very useful, for it makes of the stroke very little more than a long approach putt.'"

Note this carefully, for it is of great importance to golfers. We here have Bobby Jones's statement that the run-up shot up to forty yards is "very little more than a long approach putt." We are now arriving at simplified golf within forty yards of the pin— and it need not stop at forty yards.

"Carry your putt back into your game as far as you can" has persistently been urged by me for years and to have this instruction now supported by many of the country's most capable players and instructors is valuable corroboration which, combined with the use of proper clubs, must tend to improve the game where most it needs it.

There is now a very strong and general endorsement of my age-old argument in favor of shorter clubs on and around the green and carrying one's putt as far back into one's game as possible. It is basic science, both as regards the game and the construction of golf clubs.

The old slogan used by me more than twenty years ago, "A short putter for short putts," bids fair to be indefinitely extended to "Short clubs and short strokes for the short game." . . .

Johnny Farrell, in one of his articles, recently said: "The chip is primarily a stroke saver"—to which I replied, "Johnny is *nearly* right. It isn't *a* stroke saver. It is *the* stroke saver"—or as Bobby Jones puts it: "The great economist of golf strokes."

You can [now] hardly read an issue of any leading golf magazine without finding much valuable information in support of the short club for short shots, so what possible defense can any golfer have for not equipping himself with suitable clubs for playing the short shots, or admittedly two-thirds of the game, when he carries eight to twelve clubs for the other one-third?

We all know too well that a shaft projecting eight to twelve inches above the grip for approach shots destroys balance, engages one's clothing, prevents one from taking the proper stance and from playing the stroke in good form.

Why do it?

The Approach

1960 ⚌ MARLENE BAUER HAGGE

In 1950, child prodigies Marlene Bauer, almost sixteen, and her sister Alice, twenty-two, turned pro and were among the thirteen charter members of the LPGA. In 1952, the Hall of Fame–bound Marlene became the youngest winner of an LPGA event, her first of twenty-six titles. Her father Dave Bauer boasted that his dainty daughters hit 200-yard drives in his 1951 book *Golf Techniques of the Bauer Sisters*, but Marlene, like Paul Runyan, viewed the short game as the great equalizer. Like her chips and pitches, her writing on the subject is well-reasoned and has teeth. Modernists may quibble with her advice on ball position for pitch shots, but few will disagree with her admonition not to "scoop" the ball or her chipping techniques. Modern wedges and "target golf"—necessitated by hazards near greens, particularly in America—have made the run-up shot she described almost obsolete, but high-handicappers may think it worth considering.

———◆———

With the approach shot—and this term includes the pitch, chip, and run-up—the golfer comes to the heart of the short game. These shots are important to every player, but it is imperative that they be played well by women. And here again, achievement is based, first, on learning the proper fundamentals and then on practicing these until they have truly become second nature.

For the pitch shot, the stance should be a little wide, the left foot drawn slightly back from the intended line of flight and the ball placed approximately off the heel of the right foot. This gives the player a fairly upright position, which she will need to make the downward swing that will connect with the ball first and the turf afterward.

This last point—that the ball be hit a descending blow—is perhaps the most important element in any of the approach shots, for only this motion will give it the backspin that means control, which is an absolute necessity at short distances from the green.

The hands should be placed slightly ahead of the clubhead at address, the weight distributed equally or over to the left. As with every other shot in golf, the approach needs a strong left side to hit into.

On this shot, I use either a 9 or a [pitching wedge]. When the shot is a short one, anywhere from 30 yards in, I prefer the [wedge], but there are some definite don'ts in connection with this club. I've noticed that when a club with a definite loft is involved, most women tend to scoop the ball. This is dangerous anywhere; it can be fatal on the approach shot. Scooping will *not* get the ball into the air, let alone get it into the air for any distance. And another warning: those women who do not try to scoop the ball very often hood, or close, their clubface.

Obviously, this error is just as severe as scooping, since it dissipates the loft intended for that particular club and necessary to the pitch shot. *I usually address the ball with a slightly open clubface,* which helps give the club its proper loft and I keep it slightly open coming through the shot, with a very firm hand action, which means both hands working as a unit.

The golfer must always remember that the approach shot—and here we're specifically talking about the pitch—is one that is hit to the pin with a lot of backspin, so that the ball will bite. Too many golfers take a fairly long backswing and then baby the shot coming through. *The correct way, the only way, is to take a short backswing and remain firm throughout the swing.* To this end, the swing must be initiated with the left shoulder and arm. The club is never picked up—no jerky movement, please—it is always swung, rhythmically. It helps with the approach if the player keeps her right elbow close to her side; in other words, practically stationary. From the start of the backswing, the work should be done almost entirely by the left side, and the wrists are cocked when the clubhead is approximately a foot away from the ball.

It is extremely important *not* to pick up the club with the right hand. If the player is guilty of this seemingly easy out, she will find her hands working against each other. The downswing, too, is work for the left side. That right hand comes into play only at the point of impact. The player's left shoulder and arm actually pull the right elbow and the right hand into position so that the wrists un-cock correctly and are fully un-cocked at the point of impact.

For myself, I find one other thing a help. I usually take the clubhead back a bit on the outside and then hit across the intended line of flight. This gives me a slight cut shot and, consequently, a little extra bite on the ball.

Now for the run-up shot. Most players like it. I do and I know, too, that it can be an easy shot; just give it the proper attention. It's particularly handy if the distance between the edge of the green and the pin is short and the green doesn't hold well. In a case like this, it obviously would be impractical to use a lofted approach. Instead, the player should try hitting the ball into the green so that it will check or stop by the pin, which is what a successful run-up will do.

This approach can be made in either of two ways. The first involves a less-lofted club like the 5-, 6-, or 7-iron and the ball is hit in much the same way as a putt. The ball is approximately centered in the stance, the line of the shoulders to clubhead is straight, and the swing is pendulum-like. Here, the center of the pendulum would be the shoulders, with very little wrist action involved, so that the ball is almost parallel to the ground when in flight. The second method of dealing with the run-up requires a club with a little more loft and, in this instance, it is permissible and even desirable to hood the face slightly. This is the run-up I prefer, since it affords more control. Here I usually use either the 7- or 8-iron.

I place the ball off the heel of my right foot, with my hands slightly ahead of the club at address. I start the club back with the left shoulder and arm and keep the clubhead low and close to the ground. The ball is hit with a descending blow—sharply enough so that I take a small divot. All these elements—the more lofted club, a slight hood to the face, and the descending blow—give a little more spin to the ball. Consequently, the player can pitch the ball farther, with less run on it. I feel that the more I can keep the ball in the air, the less chance I have of being defeated by the natural defects of the course: an unexpected bump, a small patch of rough, or another player's divot. In any case, the air *is* much smoother than the ground, so that the farther the ball travels through the air and the more spin the player can get on her ball, the more successful the run-up shot.

I will say this, however. The golfer's choice of run-up shot must be the one with which she feels more comfortable, the one in which she has more confidence. Confidence is probably ninety percent of a woman's golf game (really, of anyone's golf game), and since this means that golf is mental, it follows that if the player uses the shot she's happiest with, that shot is the one that will come off for her.

The chip—perhaps the most important of the approaches—is used for any shot from one to five feet off the green. It is important to keep the ball low to the ground, and you need to get some run on it. A 7-, 8-, or 9-iron is used, depending on the length the player has to carry over the edge of the green. Normally, I use an 8 for a chip. The stance here is slightly open, with the left foot drawn a little back from the intended line of flight, the ball placed off the heel of the right foot. The player's weight should be on the left side and it remains there throughout the shot. As in the pitch and run-up, all movement—the downswing as well as the backswing—is initiated by that left shoulder and arm.

With the 8-iron, the clubface is hooded slightly at address, while the hands are ahead of the clubhead. The right elbow is kept close to the right side. For the chip shot, I grip the club down quite a bit farther than I do with the other approaches and I bend more at the waist. The grip itself, while firm, particularly at impact, should be an easy one. That is, you're not gripping the club to death. Here again, the ball is hit a descending blow by the hooded face to give it backspin. This extra control makes it easier to judge the distance and that is possibly the most important factor in chipping.

The last important thing the player must remember on the chip shot is the terrain she's playing. If she is going downhill to the hole, the best method is the one I've just described—that is, a slightly hooded 8-iron hit a descending blow. If the chip is uphill to the pin, I would go to a less-lofted club, like the 6 or 7, hooding the face a trifle, but hitting the ball with a more side-powered blow, not quite the descending shot the downhill position requires. This is so that the arc will be a little flatter. And there should still be backspin on the ball.

To generalize on all of the approach shots: keep the shoulders, arms, and hands flexible. Aside from these focal points, there is very little body movement involved. It's a question of control. And to repeat, exercising control requires confidence. Really, a woman's golf game is such a psychological thing that it sometimes defies description. I've played with my husband often enough to know just how psychological it is. I know from the women I play with just how psychological it is. Because approach shots are crucial to her short game, the woman golfer's tension as the green gets closer is worse than the man's. But if a woman lets panic take over on the approach, she is lost.

This short game is the part of golf that women should and must concentrate on, because it is the part of golf in which they can excel. A woman who can keep the ball in play on the other shots, while chipping and putting well, will be up there with the best of them. I should know because I'm a small girl. If it weren't for these areas of my game, I wouldn't have a chance.

From *Golf for Women*, edited by Louise Suggs. Chapter by Marlene Bauer Hagge. Copyright © 1960 by Rutledge Books. Used by permission of Doubleday & Co., a division of Random House, Inc.

The Basic Pitching Stroke

1983 ✤ TOM WATSON
WITH NICK SEITZ

Getting Up and Down was Tom Watson's first instructional book and one of golf's bestsellers for more than a decade. The average hacker should find comfort in what he writes on the pitch shot. Most star players tell their readers how they easily can apply spin to the ball, but forget that for handicap golfers this is a highly advanced technique. Watson reassures the nonprofessional that even he does not complicate things by trying to add much, if any, extra spin. But he does emphasize avoiding the cardinal sin of the short game: decelerating the clubhead through impact. A student himself with a cautionary eye for pitfalls, Watson borrows ideas from golfers he admires: Citing Byron Nelson, he invokes his mentor's famous "rocking chair" image for good weight transfer, and then offers a swing key from Tom Kite, who focuses on equalizing the length of his backswing and through-swing.

In my opinion, learning how to pitch the ball is the most difficult lesson for a golfer. Why? Because you must learn how to hit the ball with an abbreviated or less-than-full swing. You must feel how far to hit the ball, and feel is the most elusive part of golf.

Almost all golfers practice nothing but a full swing. Very few practice the short, 40-yard pitch shot. A full swing is easier to master, since the golfer is usually repeating the same swing for each club to make the ball go the maximum distance with that particular club. But to hit the ball less than maximum distance with a particular club, you must shorten the swing *yet still hit the ball firmly*. This shot causes many golfers to shake with fear and has resulted in the club as well as the ball being launched in disgust.

The two main requisites to good pitching are setting up well and making a firm swing that accelerates through the ball. When you face a less-than-full shot, you have to think in terms of a less-than-full backswing. The common error is taking the club back too far and decelerating through impact, which is like a boxer pulling his punches. It causes all sorts of mishit and misdirected pitch shots.

. . . My philosophy is to play pitches [and chips] with as little spin as possible, because spin is hard to control and predict. Learning to pitch the ball with control and finesse, over hazards and near the pin, is a joyful part of the game and an art form in itself.

THE PROPER ADDRESS POSITION PREVIEWS THE IMPACT POSITION

My setup position [for a pitch] as in all my shots, is very similar to my impact position—a sneak preview.

It's basically the same as my chipping setup. My stance is slightly open, 10 to 20 degrees, since I want my left side to be out of the way or slightly open at impact. The body weight favors the left foot and is centered on the balls of the feet. My knees are slightly flexed, my rear end stuck out so that I can hang my upper body and arms out over the ball. I call my rear end my "ballast." When stuck out properly, it serves as a counterweight to my upper body, which must hang out over the ball so that the arms can swing freely without running into the body on the downswing. I sole the club very lightly.

Two common faulty setup positions are:

→ Standing too tall, which means the upper body doesn't hang over enough. The upper body then must either dip on the backswing or turn too horizontally, forcing the arms and club to swing too flatly around the body. Both of these

Tom Watson wrote that golfers should equalize the backswing and follow-through when hitting pitches.

swings result in poor balance and poor timing, causing inconsistency.

→ The knees are too straight and the body slumps over the ball, forcing too much weight onto the toes. In this position you must rely on perfect hand-eye coordination for consistent shotmaking. With straight, un-flexed knees you cannot transfer the weight properly during the swing.

I Advocate Byron Nelson's "Rocking Chair" Weight Transfer

The pitch shot is made easier and more consistent when the lower body moves in timing with the arms and hands. Lack of movement in the lower body causes an inconsistent path of the club through impact. I jokingly refer to this bad habit as having "cement legs."

Do not stand still and just use your hands and arms. Use your hips and knees in the swing.

How? I picture Byron Nelson, whose short, firm pitching swing was a smooth blend of both upper and lower body movement. Byron teaches a rocking-chair motion that coordinates the upper and lower body action, making possible a consistent hit time after time.

The weight, which starts mostly on the left foot, transfers to the right foot and back to the left foot during the swing. The hit of the ball occurs during the transfer of weight from the right foot to the left foot. Byron couldn't help but hit the ball solidly and straight. His clubface stayed square just prior to and through impact the longest of any player I've ever watched—for nearly a foot; not only pitching but on his full swing as well.

A simple thought that Byron taught me is to return my hips and elbows to their original address

Tossing a ball underhand: a classic drill taught for both pitching and chipping.

position as I'm hitting through the ball. This forces me to synchronize the motion of my arms and lower body.

ACCELERATE THE CLUBHEAD AND DON'T OVER-SWING

Tom Kite, who is an excellent pitcher from 30 to 40 yards with a wedge, makes sure to avoid the common pitfall of decelerating the club through the impact zone. Tom's key thought is to swing the club back only as far as he swings it through.

Many high-handicap players swing with little or no weight transfer. Therefore they have to take the club back too far in the effort to produce the same clubhead speed they could produce with a proper weight transfer and shorter swing. If you have a prob-lem over-swinging, first check your weight transfer. Then try swinging the club back shorter and accelerating it more firmly through the ball.

MAKE AN UNDERHANDED MOTION

Golf is an underhanded game. Since we are swinging down at the ball, we have to use an underhanded motion with the right hand and arm through the impact area. You can get the feeling by throwing a ball, because the underhanded motion we're talking about is similar to a throwing action.

The Pitching Supermodel: Tiger Woods

2000 ✦ JIM McLEAN

Through a series of books and videos, frequent appearances on the Golf Channel, countless essays and lessons in *Golf Magazine* and now *Golf Digest* (for which he serves as an "Instruction Editor"), and his school in Miami, the inexhaustible Jim McLean has established himself as one of the era's most familiar and influential golf theorists. This former PGA Teacher of the Year, who once played on a University of Houston team that featured future Tour stars Bruce Lietzke, Fuzzy Zoeller, and Bill Rodgers, is one of the best at analyzing the techniques, from setup to follow-through, of great golfers past and present. In this essay, he scrupulously breaks down Tiger Woods's 40- to 60-yard pitch shot, as developed under the auspices of his former coach Butch Harmon. Beginners in particular should note the differences he points out between Tiger's approach to driving and his setup and backswing action for the pitch.

I love to see juniors copying a tour player's swing to learn a new shot. I think you do yourself a disservice by not taking a serious look at the pitching action used by Tiger Woods to hit high, soft-landing pitch shots from around 40 to 60 yards out from the green. This shot is magical, because the ball seems to stop the moment it hits the green. It doesn't spin back or take several hops forward. To quote a former golf commentator whose name escapes me, "it sits down like a hound dog in front of a fireplace."

Tiger is a short-game wizard, although most fans know him for his power-driving skills that allow him to drive par-4 holes and reach par-5 holes in two shots, instead of the regulation three. It's no wonder that Tiger won the 1999 PGA, his second major championship, and finished the year off at the top of the PGA Tour's money standing list.

I give Tiger and Butch Harmon, his coach, a heck of a lot of credit for their hard practice and perseverance. There was a time when Tiger was criticized for not being able to control his wedge shots, with Butch taking much of the heat. They both had a plan a couple of years ago, and nobody can doubt it's been executed. Tiger has evolved into such a great wedge player that I consider him a supermodel.

Super Setup

When watching Tiger set up to play a 40- to 60-yard wedge shot under normal conditions of lie and weather I have noticed that he's very careful not to position the ball well back in the stance. This is because he knows that such a position promotes a steep backswing action, sharp descending hit, and a shot that spins back. Tiger's priority is to hit the ball all the way to the hole and have it come down so softly you would think it were attached to a miniature parachute. Therefore, he plays the ball closer to his left heel than to the midpoint of his stance. He sets his hands even with the ball or slightly behind it. Ultimately, Tiger wants to come into impact with the clubface going nicely under the ball, not digging into the turf, so he is careful not to set his hands well ahead of the ball, which takes bounce off the wedge. I have noticed too that quite recently Tiger has widened his pitching stance some to prevent an overly steep swing and those *shooters* he was criticized

for hitting early in his career. Don't get me wrong. Tiger's stance is still narrow, with the distance between his feet measuring about 10 inches.

Tiger's stance is slightly open, too, with the left foot a few inches farther from the target line than the right foot. His hips are also slightly open, pointing slightly left of target. This setup provides Tiger with a heightened sense of freedom. Because the hips are in a cleared, or open, position, he prevents an inside takeaway and too much action on the backswing. The added bonus of setting up this way is that he feels more confident about making square and solid contact with the ball. So will you.

Although Tiger opens his feet and hips, he's very careful to set his shoulders fairly square or just the slightest bit open to the target line.

This pitching setup is much different from the one Tiger uses to launch the long ball on the golf course. When driving, he closes his feet as Ben Hogan did and opens his shoulders as Jack Nicklaus still does. This combination of closed feet, open shoulders

The perfect body angles for a pitch shot.

was used by another great player, Sam Snead, also a super powerful driver of the ball.

When hitting the soft pitch, Tiger is not interested in generating power. He is looking to finesse the ball to the hole. This is why he sets up the way he does and tracks a line from the ball to the target with his eyes. This tracking work helps him sense or feel the distance in his hands. Incidentally, like Jack Nicklaus, Tiger uses an interlock grip rather than the overlap grip used by most PGA Tour players. The interlock grip should be considered simply because it provides you with a sense of unity to the hands. Further, and more important, when hitting this particular shot the way Tiger does, you must keep the clubface open through impact. Gripping like Tiger may help you avoid slippage in the hitting area. It certainly doesn't hurt.

When you feel you are comfortably correct at address, be sure to follow Tiger's other fundamentals to success: taking a nice fluid practice swing that matches the action he intends to employ when actually hitting the shot; and visualizing the perfect shot in his mind's eye before swinging.

Super Backswing

The wonderful thing about Tiger's backswing action is that it's relaxed, with the wrists hinging freely. It's very different from his full-power swing in which he has a late wrist set. There is no effort on his part to make a one-piece takeaway—that is, with the club straight back along the target line, low to the ground, and directed by the triangle formed by the shoulders and arms. Many high handicappers make this mistake, thinking all shots require this type of one-piece action.

Going back, Tiger's arms swing on a much more upright plane than his turning shoulders, while the club moves slightly outside the target line. As for the weight-shifting action, it is more of a mini-shift. I say

that because Tiger leaves much more of his weight on his left foot and leg when hitting this shot than any full shot.

Tiger usually swings the club back to the three-quarter point, for this length shot. This helps him stay relaxed and maintain a certain good personal feel for the clubhead.

Super Downswing

Indeed, Tiger employs perfect shifting and rotating action of the lower body, but the action is far less powerful or forceful. Another reason the shifting and rotating action is not so brisk and full is that Tiger is controlling the pace of his swing with the pace of his rotation.

A lot of speed Tiger generates on the downswing comes from the turn of his body. While he nudges the majority of his weight over to his left side, his upper body stays well behind the ball. As the shifting action continues, Tiger's arms accelerate faster. His arms bring the club through the ball, rather than down into it on a sharp angle, while his wrists unhinge.

Butch Harmon . . . worked with Tiger to maintain a firm pressure in his left hand to keep his left wrist stable in the hitting area. If the left wrist breaks down, the right hand and forearm tend to rotate rapidly in a counterclockwise direction, causing the clubface to close. The result is a low shot that runs upon landing. You want to keep the clubface of the sand wedge or lob wedge open when playing this shot so that you loft the ball nicely into the air and land it super softly onto the green, next to the hole.

From *The Complete Idiot's Guide to Improving Your Short Game,* by Jim McLean. Copyright © 2000 by Jim McLean. Used by Permission of Alpha Books, an imprint of Penguin Group (USA) Inc.

— 9 —

SAND PLAY

TOILING THROUGH
THE BUNKERS
OF REPENTANCE

In Hazards

1912 ✦ HORACE G. HUTCHINSON

Considering that Horace Gordon Hutchinson's many books included ones on war heroes and big-game hunting, he probably considered getting a ball out of a bunker as no worse than an inconvenience. However, he was almost apologetic to his golfing readers when informing them that they surely will experience an annoyance that is less fair than those found in the other leisurely activities he wrote about—fishing, cricket, and bird shooting. In fact, he points out that in those days before Gene Sarazen invented his sand wedge, golfers who landed on the beach often gave up the hole. Yet, even when balls are buried, Hutchinson didn't advocate retreat. Pleading with players to eschew their usual flat swings, he advocated a more modern, upright swing and an early version of the "explosion" shot—though with his usual flourish, he preferred the term "volcanic."

Of any beginner in golf, however eminent he may be in other walks of life, it may be assumed, and that without insulting him, that he will sooner or later get into a bunker. Even if he never make[s] a bad shot, a large assumption, he will, in these days of far-flying balls, occasionally drive his tee-shot so far as to be caught in the bunker that is meant to trap the second shot of weaker vessels. Therefore he will be well advised to learn the art of getting out of it as quickly as possible, and he is to consider that it is an art, and not merely an affair of brute strength and good fortune. Most bad golfers give themselves up for lost when their ball disappears into a bunker; and not without reason, for they are singularly inept in extricating it. Yet to have a reasonable hope of getting out of a reasonably bad bunker in a single shot should not to be too lofty an ambition for any ordinary mortal who will take the trouble to learn to play the stroke properly. . . .

Balls that lie in bunkers . . . may be primarily divided into two classes, those that lie heavy and those that lie clean. The former are taken first because they are the more frequently met with, and also because they alone demand a stroke which may be termed *sui generis*. By a ball lying heavy is meant one that has partially burrowed its way into the sand, that is lying, in fact, more or less cupped, and the great point to remember about such a ball is that the golfer's whole duty is to get it out—a contemptibly short distance maybe, but out. The first thing to do, then, is to take a niblick, a niblick with a very strong stiff shaft and broad heavy head, liberally dowered with loft, and to take it in a firm determined grasp. The shot that has now to be played is unlike any other in the game of golf, in that the one thing to be avoided is the hitting of the ball. The ball is to be removed from the bunker by means of an explosion, and the player merely resembles the gentleman of anarchist proclivities who lights the fuse. The explosion is caused by the club descending forcibly into the sand close behind the ball, and the ensuing commotion hoists the ball more or less straight up into the air, to fall no great distance away, but, let us hope, upon the turf; limp and lifeless, perhaps, but safe. The most important point of all is to keep the eye rigidly upon the particle of sand which it is intended to hit—which is an extremely difficult thing to do—and not, in the course of the stroke, to let the eye glide forward toward the ball itself, which is a fatally easy thing to do. As to exactly how far behind the ball the club is to be plunged into sand, it would perhaps be rash to dogmatise. It may be some two inches, it may conceivably be more, and it may certainly sometimes be less. For one thing a great deal must depend on the nature of the sand, which varies enormously, not only with different courses but with the weather. . . . Wet, hard sand . . . must necessarily require different treatment to sand which is dry and powdery. . . .

[T]he stroke is to be far more of an up and down character than any other; indeed, it is not to be very far removed from the common chop. One of the gravest and commonest forms of original sin is the lifting of the club up too straight, with the almost necessary corollary of bringing it too straight down. Yet, curiously enough, when the golfer is told to give full rein to his sinful proclivities and take up the club almost as straight as he can, he appears incapable of doing so; either he does not in his heart believe what his instructor tells him, or else, having laboriously learnt a flat swing, he cannot suddenly convert it again into an upright one. Whatever the reason, there are hundreds of players who are practically helpless when their ball lies near even a moderately steep face of a bunker; they beat the ball again and again against the wall of its prison, simply because they will not or cannot come down straight enough into the sand to make the ball rise sufficiently vertically. Therefore it is essential to go straight up and come straight down, and let this maneuver be executed with all the freedom and vigor that is consistent with a reasonable measure of control and the keeping of the eyes glued to that particle of sand. This word of warning should be added: the bunkered one must not think that his whole duty has been done when he has brought his club down into the sand. He must not let it remain there,

Horace Hutchinson didn't languish on the beach.

but must take it through to the best of his ability. This following-through is a very important part of niblick play, and, just because it appears so superfluous, we are particularly apt to forget it. The explosion has to take place under the ball and not merely behind it.

I have used the word chop, but I recognize that herein lurks some danger of a misunderstanding, because the art of chopping rather implies that the chopper should stand well over the choppee, as the executioner might stand over his victim. Now, with the niblick experience shows that this will not do. The player must stand well away behind his ball, preferably with rather an open stance and having the ball opposite his left foot; he may also keep the right shoulder down and the left shoulder up, an attitude which seems natural to one about to perform the action of heaving or hoisting.

Little more can usefully be added to this description of the volcanic shot, as it has been called; practice must do the rest. It must not be imagined, however, that this shot is only to be employed when the ball lies more or less heavy. It is generally to be used, however well and cleanly the ball may lie, whenever the cliff of the bunker is so near that any stroke wherein the club hits the ball and not the sand would fail to make it rise sufficiently abruptly. Indeed, whenever the cliff is anything but exceedingly low and there are desperate circumstances to call for desperate measures, it is by far the safest shot for any one, save the expert, to employ. Even if the ball lies clean and the cliff of the bunker is a negligible quantity, this stroke may be infinitely useful. It sometimes happens that a ball lies in a bunker, and yet is but a few yards from the hole, so that the player's object is to make the ball just pitch out of the bunker, and fall as dead as possible on alighting. To hit the ball itself, however cleanly and accurately, will impart a certain amount of run, but the explosive stroke, skillfully played with nice judgment of the amount of sand to be taken, can be made to drop the ball as dead as a stone. . . .

However, all bunkers are not close to the green; more often than not the player would like to hit the ball out [of a fairway bunker] as far as he possibly can, and then a clean-lying ball represents a direct intervention of Providence, to be taken the fullest advantage of. Much must, of course, depend on the proximity and steepness of the face . . . and so for our present purpose it may be assumed that the face will not interfere with a fairly low-flying ball, and the player may take almost any club he has a mind to. Account should be taken of the exact circumstances: it may be wise to take no risks at all, or things may have come to such a desperate pass, that the only hope lies in taking a big risk and the only club that will reach the green. There is just this to be added on this point of tactics; before making his decision the player might well put the question to himself, "Which is more likely, that I should successfully reach the green with the longer club or that, having played short, I should either lay the ball dead with my pitch or hole a long putt?"

. . . [T]he straight-faced or driving-iron is the most ambitious club that he should ever employ in a bunker, however tempting the lie. To hit a long shot out of sand is not an easy thing to do; only a slight inaccuracy will mar the stroke, and much confidence is required; wherefore, if the player is in any real doubt . . . he will do well to take the more lofted [club] since a lofted face is a great begetter of courage. [He should also] apply his mind to swinging easily, and to keeping his eye upon the ball with a greater ferocity than usual. . . .

From *The New Book of Golf,* by Horace G. Hutchinson. Longmans, Green, and Co., London, England.

If your opponent is playing several shots in vain attempts to extricate himself from a bunker, do not stand near him and audibly count his strokes. It would be justifiable homicide if he wound up his pitiable exhibition by applying his niblick to your head.

HARRY VARDON

How to Recover from Bunkers

1924 ✦ CYRIL J. H. TOLLEY

Cyril Tolley, a pipe-smoking, ascot-wearing former P.O.W., was one of Great Britain's top amateurs after World War I, but is best remembered for almost snuffing out Bobby Jones's 1930 Grand Slam bid—extending the Yank to nineteen holes in the British Amateur. Tolley already had won that championship in 1920, the Welsh Championship in 1921 and 1923, and the French Open in 1924. Then he wrote an instructional book boldly called *The Modern Golfer*. Indeed, at times this piece about playing various bunker shots sounds as modern as later ones by Raymond Floyd and Ernie Els, especially concerning "explosion" shots—but with one important difference. Tolley and his compatriots—lacking a sand wedge—employed a "niblick," a club like today's 9-iron, and used a firm grip and little wrist break. The club almost stopped when it struck the sand, curtailing the follow-through—quite a contrast to the high finish today's teachers often recommend.

The common form of trouble all grades of players encounter is bunker trouble. There are many ways of trying to recover, but they all vary in execution, according to the situation of the particular bunker on the course. The bunkers around the green will be the first I shall deal with. I should have said that the texture of the sand will help you in deciding what kind of recovery you should attempt, and another factor will be what kind of lie you are fortunate enough to find in the bunker.

If you are lying badly, you have no option in the matter; the ball must be dug out, and the method employed is called the explosive shot. If the ball is lying well, you can either play an "explosion" or take the ball cleanly. It will be found from experience that the former is the one most generally used, for it is less dangerous, and is also easier.

The theory of an explosive shot is that the ball is not hit by the club at all. The stroke is played by aiming at a mark some distance, anything up to three inches, behind the ball. As the club enters the sand, it displaces a certain amount, which has the effect of heaving out the ball. This displaced sand forms a wall between the clubhead and the ball, and it is this wall which causes the ball to move. As a general principle . . . the shorter the shot required the steeper should be the angle of descent of the club, and the less sand you aim at behind the ball. The longer the shot, the flatter must be the swing of the club, and the club has to enter the sand also but not quite as near the ball. If the sand is very light and loose, you can afford to take plenty of it, and you also can hit your hardest. If it is heavy and wet, there is no need to hit so hard or to take so much sand. To play any of these shots you must remember above all things that the head and body must be kept absolutely motionless; in other words, the body may pivot but must not move laterally.

You stand fairly open, with the ball about opposite the left heel, and you play the stroke as a slice.

That is to say, you aim to the left of the hole, and in taking the club back you take it away from the body. Your forward swing is across your body, and you will finish your stroke with the club well to the left of the line. The divot mark must also point to the left. You address the ball with the face of the club turned out, and the stroke must be played and finished with the face in relatively the same position. . . . The club is taken back by the left hand, but all the hitting force is supplied by the right hand. The wrists must be kept fairly stiff, and the club gripped, if anything, tighter than usual. On account of taking the sand well behind the ball, you will find that it is impossible to take a long follow-through. Try as hard as you like and the clubhead will be found to have only just emerged from the sand. The hands must be kept low after the ball has been struck.

Very often you will find that the utmost you can hope for is to get the ball on the green, and having accomplished this you have to be satisfied. When the shot does not look so fearsome or difficult, you should try to get the ball out on that side of the hole which will give you the easiest putt. So many players do not consider the necessity of doing this, and rush headlong into the hazard, and have a terrific lash at the ball. Sometimes it will come out—generally it won't. Don't forget that golf is a thinking game, and must be treated as such. . . .

If the ball is lying well in the bunker, and not too close to the face, the player can try playing a clean shot; by that I mean you do not attempt to displace more sand than that which lies under and on the far side of the ball. This is a very dangerous type of recovery, for the slightest miscalculation will ruin the stroke, and the ball will probably have moved only a few inches.

The first thing you have to do is to fix your eye most intently on the ball, if possible, at the point nearest under the ball that you can see. Having done that, you must be prepared to stand absolutely stationary in executing the shot. Stand with the feet close together, the heels can touch if you wish, and have the ball opposite the left instep. Now you can either have the face of the club turned out very slightly, or have it square to the line. Personally, I prefer the latter position. The reason why so many players, and good players at that, fail in this delicate little shot is the fact that they do not know what to do with their wrists. Nine-tenths try some kind of flick with their wrists which occasionally will give the very best result, but to succeed only occasionally is no good; you must play the shot so that it is a success every time. . . . Here is the secret of these little delicate chips out of bunkers—*the wrists must not move*. Incline the shaft of the club so that the hands are in front of the clubhead to such an extent that the left arm and shaft are in one straight line. Keep this position all through the stroke, and you will find you cannot bend the wrists at all. Bring the club as near to the ball as possible in the address, for the nearer you get to the ball, the better the result must be, since your backswing will be more nearly a replica of your hitting stroke. Take the club back flat and slowly, and bring it forward smoothly and deliberately, taking care that the sand behind the

FACE UP IN THE SAND

Vijay Singh won nine times in 2004, including the PGA Championship, to vault to the number-one ranking in the world. Although famous for his booming drives and lengthy practice sessions, his short game skills are often overlooked. In *Golf Digest*, he offered a tip for putting more spin on sand shots—to freeze the ball on the green—by holding the club open through impact and well into the finish, leaving the face pointing upward. ⚓

ball is not touched either in taking the club back or before it hits the ball. . . . Do not allow the wrists to bend after the ball is hit, and this will ensure that the head of the club will keep low to the sand, and will prevent the stroke being fluffed. It is extraordinary the amount of check you impart to the ball, which, on pitching on the green, will bite to such an extent that it will run no distance, so you can be bold and hit the ball firmly up to the hole from the bunker, knowing all the time that on hitting the green its pace will be taken off by the spin. . . . Play this shot with a fairly heavy type of niblick with not too much loft, and if there is practically no bank to the bunker you can safely use a mashie niblick.

When you find the ball lying on a downhill lie in the sand, you have a more difficult shot to play, yet in reality all you need to make the shot a success is confidence and courage, combined with an absolutely rigid poise of the body. You must make yourself hit the ball first and then follow-through the ball, taking the sand well after it. You require a lofty niblick for this, and you can have your hands just a trifle in front of the clubhead. Hit the ball just under the center with the bottom of the club, and it will rise sharply with an extraordinary amount of drag, and on striking the green will pull up on its second bounce. It is not possible to get the ball up very high in playing this way, but generally you will have plenty of room to negotiate the bank of the bunker. Should, however, the bank be very near the ball, you must play the explosive shot, even from your hanging lie, making the club come across the back of the ball, and, above all, concentrating on finishing the stroke with all your weight on your right foot. The stroke is to be played with an open stance, and with the ball opposite the left heel. . . .

If you are unfortunate enough to be caught in a [fairway] bunker . . . the type of shot you employ to recover depends firstly on the position of the ball in the bunker. If you are lying well back you have, provided the lie is not a bad one, a reasonable chance of completely recovering the resultant loss of distance caused by your faulty tee shot. Sometimes you can take as strong a club as a light iron, and to play the shot successfully you should play slightly across the back of the ball, but you must allow for the ball to swing to the right near the end of its flight. Take a long, flat swing with the face of the club turned out, and endeavor to strike the sand not more than half an inch behind the ball. If you follow through close to the sand, the loft of the club will get the ball up quickly enough. Take great care not to move your head or body, and concentrate on looking at the sand under the ball. Play the stroke in a similar way to an iron shot. . . . If, on the other hand, you are lying badly, or are too close to the face of the bunker to get any distance, you must first see in what direction you should hit the ball to give you the easiest possible next stroke to put you on the green.

Sometimes you can only just get out of the bunker, and then you must try to get out with the least possible chance of failure. Never try to do too much out of a hazard, for you must not forget you are considerably handicapped in not being allowed to sole your club in the sand. The great thing to remember in bunker play, and in all golf, for that matter, is always to play the easy shot; do not try to play the difficult and spectacular shot; you will only look ridiculous, and your remorse will be ten times greater if you fail to get the ball in play again.

Sometimes when near the green, and your ball is lying in a bunker, owing to the shape of the bunker face the ball can be run out to the green. If you are so favorably placed as this, it will pay you not to take an iron to run the ball out, but to take a putter. . . . Great care, however, must be taken that the ball is hit cleanly, and obviously, the harder the sand the more chance of the shot succeeding.

[Finally,] never take a wooden club out of a [fairway] bunker . . . however easy it appears to be; always make a point of never using a more powerful club than a light iron. It is only to super-confident players that this dangerous kind of recovery should offer any temptation, and only once in ten times will it come off, and the risk is not worth the candle, to put it crudely.

From *The Modern Golfer*, by Cyril J. H. Tolley. W. Collins Sons & Co., Ltd., Glasgow, Scotland. Copyright © 1924 by Alfred A. Knopf, Inc.

Man-Afraid-of-a-Trap

1933 ❧ FRANK CONDON

In his 1926 book *The Duffer's Handbook*, Grantland Rice, the editor of *The American Golfer*, included a hilarious chapter about how a poor golfer can almost set up residence in a bunker. So it's not surprising that a few years later Rice would commission a witty article from journalist and humorist Frank Condon about his inability to escape sand traps. Significantly, Condon wrote this essay after the invention of the sand wedge. In a lamebrain scheme that probably most frustrated golfers of his day contemplated during a long stint in some bunker, Condon tried to duplicate what Gene Sarazen did to become the supreme bunker player, which was to design what he believed to be the perfect club for himself. He confirmed that most things in golf are best left to geniuses, not hackers.

We were discussing shots and shots, and which shot causes the greatest suffering in the mind, both before and after execution, and I told them of my favorite agony shot. I cannot get out of a trap and I will never learn how, if I played golf five thousand years. The trap shot has me whipped, despite my enormous opportunities to learn, as I am always getting into bunkers and fumbling my way out.

This frank confession is no premature outburst prompted by a first frenzy of despair; rather is it a conclusion of finality, born of long years of fruitless and futile struggling, and that too, in spite of the conglomerate advice and suggestions of a legion of instructors, expert and not so expert, whose motives varied all the way from a desire to give voice to their deep wisdom, to candid pity and sheer commiseration.

I have never yet hit a ball in a bunker with any shadow of confidence or security, never with a feeling that I knew where the ball was going, and I have probably blasted and chipped my way out of four million, five hundred and six thousand bunkers in my time, wide, narrow, shallow, deep, wet, and dry. I have purchased and used every club ever invented for escaping from the treacherous sands and not one of them has ever worked, except possibly the good, old sand wedge, invented I believe, by Horton Smith. The sand wedge, with its concave face, seemed to be what the doctor ordered for me, and just about the time I was beginning to feel confident, Tack Ramsey and his merry men invalidated the sand wedge and shoved me right back where I started.

I have carefully watched golf pros play the most beautiful explosion shots, almost carelessly confident, dropping the ball on the green, with a reasonable putt for the can, and then I tried to do it and failed utterly. Everything I think I know about the golf swing instantly departs from me the moment I step into a trap. All I realize is that you have to hit down there somewhere near the ball, and not actually strike it, but sort of ooze up on it, carrying a thin layer of sand on the face of the club, or a thick layer, depending on conditions. If I ever have a successful shot out of sand, and the ball lands near the pin, I know it is an accident. I cannot go back and do it over. And yet, I saw Gene Sarazen hit ball after ball from a trap at Deepdale, and they all went for the flag, as surely as if he were hitting ordinary niblick shots from the fairway.

He invented a club that he liked and learned how to use it and that is the difference between Gene and me—that and a stroke a hole. I, too, invented a sand trap club, but I never learned how to use it, and incidentally, I all but drove a clubmaker plumb daffy in the process of invention. He was a kindly old bozo, with thin, graying locks and a seamed countenance and pale blue eyes that had been looking at golf clubs and golf nuts for thirty years. I breezed into his shop in Hollywood and informed him that I was inventing a club to get out of sand traps.

"I wish you to make a club for me," I directed, "a niblick type club, with the face laid well back and covered with velvet."

He looked at me pretty hard.

"You want a niblick with a velvet face?"

"I do not insist on velvet," said I. "Anything soft and mushy will do. Maybe you can face the club with soft cork, or leather, or felt, or bear-skin—any softish substance that will produce the desired result."

Naturally, the man said to himself: "Here is a guy that is totally insane, but I will humor him."

I explained my theory of getting out of a sand bunker and the old clubmaker listened with quiet attention. I told him that when I struck the ball with my steel-faced niblick, I went entirely too far, flying clear over the green into distant places. Therefore, I desired a soft, gummy kind of face, so that when I hit the ball, it would stagger or wobble up on the green

and remain there. If one could hit a golf ball with an inch of felt, say, or some woozy substance, it could go only a short distance.

Well, the man nodded, I went home and he tackled the job. He first attempted but could not produce a felt-faced club, so he hunted about Hollywood for a soft, yielding piece of leather, like the hide of an unborn doe, and found it. He attached the leather neatly to the face of my old niblick, and when he handed me the finished result, I looked at it and was delighted.

It was a grand job of clubmaking, neat as a pin, and a club the like of which existed neither on land nor sea. I paid him off happily and went out to my golf course, San Gabriel, where I displayed my strange implement to the boys, who made comment in their own rough fashion. Then I went off by myself to a deep bunker that always bothers me and dropped a ball in the sand. I swung on it with my leather golf club and the ball rose in the air and traveled at least five miles due north. I never saw such a long shot out of a trap. It seems that leather sends a ball much further than steel, a scientific fact of which I was unaware.

Trying it over to see if I might have been mistaken, I hit another ball and this one went six miles. So I broke the club over my knee, threw the pieces away and have never given the subject any further thought from that day to this. I am and always will be a citizen who gets into bunkers and cannot get out. . . .

From *The American Golfer* (December 1933), by Frank Condon.

For a right-handed player, the sand shot is executed almost entirely by the right hand slapping or thumping the sand behind the ball.

CLAUDE HARMON

Getting Out of Traps Easily

1949 ✣ JOHNNY REVOLTA
AND CHARLES B. CLEVELAND

In his prime, Johnny Revolta won the 1935 PGA and competed in the Ryder Cup that year and again in 1937. His teammates on the American "Dream Team" that captured the 1935 Cup were Walter Hagen, Gene Sarazen, Horton Smith, Paul Runyan, and Henry Picard, all short-game wizards. Years later, as teachers and writers for *Golf Digest*, Runyan and Revolta became, perhaps, America's leading short-game authorities. If Runyan wrote for students of the game, Revolta wrote for the masses, pitching a system that would have sold well on late-night infomercials. He made everything sound easy, including bunker shots. Sarazen's invention had made such a claim possible. In his 1949 book, which Think And Reach Par recently reissued and turned into a three-part video, Revolta said one needs merely to trust the sand iron and use the "modern" variation of the explosion shot, assuring readers they have a wide margin for error.

———◆———

The sand trap shot is—and should be—the easiest shot in the bag.

There is more room for error in this shot than in any other. You can hit a half inch, an inch, or even two inches behind the ball and still be all right. With other shots, that margin of error would result in a bad shot.

An explosion shot out of a sand trap is easy with a No. 9 iron. With a sand iron this shot is a lead-pipe cinch.

If you don't already own a sand iron, by all means add it to your set. It has a heavy sole (bottom of the clubhead) which prevents its digging into the sand. It is heavy, so it encourages you to swing it and let the club do the work. It has plenty of loft to get the ball into the air . . . [and] it is especially designed for sand shots—[requiring] little more for you to do than to hold on. It is also a handy gadget for approach shots. . . . For lower scores and for licking the sand traps, you can't make a better investment.

Ordinarily sand traps are located in two places—bordering the fairways between the tee and green or right around the putting green. Golfers just taking up the game often don't get into these bunkers because their shots are generally short enough to miss them. As your game gets better you'll find yourself in these traps fairly often. The fellows who lay out golf courses specifically locate these traps so as to catch the better golfer either when his shots go a little off line or when his fairway shots get enough distance to carry to the edge of the green. So don't overlook this phase of your game.

Beginners have a great fear of sand traps. I presume this is due to some mental quirk which ties up traps with the difficulties of the game. They try to roll the ball out with a putter, scoop it out with an iron—anything, in fact, just to get the ball out. And generally they wind up taking several strokes to do it.

There are, of course, all kinds of sand traps. Some are so shallow they are little more than dents in the fairways filled with sand. Others are so deep that you need a ladder to climb in and out of them. And there are those in between.

In some the sand is loose, and in other traps it is packed tight. Especially after a rain the sand is most likely to be packed hard in any trap.

In very loose sand, the ball occasionally will fall in with such force as to become partially buried. Sometimes in demonstrations I take a golf ball and stamp on it so that it is completely buried and then blast it out onto the green. You are not likely to en-counter that tough a problem. But I have found it an effective means of showing what can be done with an explosion shot.

Occasionally—but very rarely—a chip shot or an approach shot [similar to those taken off grass] . . . are feasible out of a sand trap. These few possibilities exist when you have a shallow bunker. Sometimes a professional, gambling, may even use a No. 4 wood out of a shallow bunker for a long shot.

But I can't advise gambling for the average player. The odds are too much against him. In at least 90 percent of the cases, the explosion shot is the surest, safest, and best way out of sand.

And—with the sand iron—the easiest.

Johnny Revolta made sand play look easy.

A very open stance is needed for an explosion shot. The left foot will be drawn back even farther from the line of flight than it [is] in the chip and approach shots.

. . . Take your approach stance; then shift the clubface slightly back and readjust your grip. Rearrange your stance so that the clubface is square to the hole. Then follow with your natural swing. Seemingly you will be aiming to the left of the cup as you swing, but don't worry about it. The maneuver will send the ball straight for the hole. Just follow your normal swing.

Let me encourage you to work on this explosion stance until you have it well in mind. . . .

Sand, as you know, shifts. So it is especially important that you get your feet well anchored. As you take your proper stance, wiggle your feet until you get a good footing.

As in most other shots, you play the explosion off your left instep.

But—and this is an important difference—you aim for a spot just behind the ball instead of aiming to hit the ball itself.

The reason is that you want to hit the sand before the ball. Your clubface hits first the sand and then the ball. The sand acts as a cushion. Actually the force of the blow drives the sand against the ball and the pressure pops it out onto the green.

For this reason don't be afraid to hit it too hard. The sand will deaden most of the force and leave just enough to toss the ball out onto the green.

In getting ready for this shot, take your proper stance for an explosion. Then pick the spot you want to hit in the sand—about a half inch to an inch behind the ball—and aim for it. It is against the rules to ground your club in the sand and mark your spot, so it will take a little practice to adjust your sights.

But remember, you don't have to worry. You have plenty of room to hit and still make a good explosion shot.

Using my system for getting out of traps, you will find it easy whether the sand is fluffy or packed hard—whether your ball is lying on top or buried in the sand. If the ball is buried deeply, just aim a little farther behind and put a little more speed in your swing.

Where does Danny the Duffer go wrong? He makes his error in failing to have confidence in his club. The sand iron is designed to get the ball out of the sand. It has the heavy flange to keep from being buried. It has a big clubface to give you plenty of hitting surface. It has a lot of loft to get the ball into the air. Everything is built into the club.

Danny the Duffer, however, doesn't trust his club. He wants to help get the ball into the air. He scoops at the ball. As a result the club either digs into the sand or he tops the ball. And it is still in the sand trap.

Trust your club to do the job. For yourself, simply concentrate on swinging it properly.

This shot to be effective has to travel through the sand and emerge in the normal fashion, just like any other swing. It can't hit into the sand and stay there. You can't hit down at the ball and have the club stop as it reaches the ball. It has to cut through, spraying sand, and follow on through.

Combined with chip shots, the average player will cut six to eight strokes off his score with good explosion shots. And there isn't anyone who wouldn't give plenty to knock his score down that much.

From *Johnny Revolta's Short Cuts to Better Golf*, by Johnny Revolta and Charles B. Cleveland. Thomas Y. Crowell Company, New York, N.Y. Copyright © 1949 by Johnny Revolta and Charles B. Cleveland. Used by permission of Richard Myers and New South Media, LLC, as publisher of and agent for the re-issued copyrighted book (www.thinkandreachpar.com, 864-675-0038).

The more I practice, the luckier I get.

GARY PLAYER

The Blaster

1962 ✦ GARY PLAYER

Gary Player, golf's eternal optimist and greatest ambassador, never saw a course he didn't like best. And he never saw a bunker he didn't enjoy hitting out of. Johnny Revolta insisted sand was an easy challenge, but Player went further by claiming it was often the preferable lie around the green, and saying bunker shots, while sometimes problematic, were part of the short game, distinguishable from *trouble shots* that can be executed only by advanced players. By 1962, the young, fit, 155-pound, practice-obsessed South African had won three of an eventual nine Majors and joined Arnold Palmer and Jack Nicklaus in the era's "Big Three." He also began writing instructional books, including the nearly forgotten *Play Golf with Player* in which he endorsed the explosion shot, or "blaster." We pay strict attention because, as Jack Nicklaus stated, "The best sand player I have ever seen is, without doubt, Gary Player."

I am not going to start off by telling you that the bunker shot is the easiest to play. It is not, but I do think it is not half as difficult to play as some golfers imagine. With only a little know-how you should always succeed in getting the ball out. It takes a lot of practice to get it close.

Preparation for a bunker shot starts immediately after you walk into the trap, for you must quickly decide whether the sand is hard, wet, or soft, because a slightly different technique is required in each case.

Start by taking a firm stance. You are allowed by the rules to imbed your feet into the sand. If you think it necessary don't hesitate to dig deep—but please, please smooth the sand again when you have completed your shot. A man who leaves his marks in a bunker is one of the worst pests in golf, and if I had my way I would penalize him two shots. There is enough chance in golf without an innocent party having to play out of your footmarks.

For the normal bunker shot, i.e., soft sand, the feet are comfortably close together and the stance is opened fairly wide, the left foot drawn about eight inches back of the right. With the clubface slightly open at address, the club is taken back *outside* the line of flight to the hole. This is one of the few occasions this happens in the swing and will result in you hitting from outside to in, across the ball.

This action would normally cause a slice, but in this case it helps the clubhead cut through the sand. Some left-to-right spin is imparted to the ball however, and this should be allowed for by *aiming left* of the hole, depending of course on slope.

For bunkers close into the green, the club must enter the sand *two inches behind the ball*, so the club is held in that position at address. Do not watch the ball. Watch the spot of impact, which in this case is the sand. In bunkers twenty yards or so from the green, hit one inch behind the ball. Farther out than that you can hit the ball cleanly.

No matter where your ball lies in a bunker, position it opposite the left heel, otherwise the club is inclined to bury itself in the ground. The bunker shot

Gary Player "blasts" his way out of a pot bunker during the 1961 British Open Championship at Royal Birkdale.

does not require strength and before describing the swing you should appreciate that it is not a case of punching down into the sand, but of cutting through the sand.

The most important aspect of the swing is that it must be firm throughout. If you hold back, or quit on the shot as the Americans say, you have little chance of making a good stroke.

The stroke is played mostly with the hands and arms and the natural movement of the knees. The backswing is curtailed, with the wrists cocking naturally, but the follow-through is full. In a bunker you can never follow through too far.

The method just described is for a normal, good lie in a bunker. If the ball should be plugged, or in a foot mark, or if you are prevented from swinging back, play short of the hole, because the ball is going to run farther than it normally would.

Many Americans play this shot with a square face at address, but I still prefer to open the face and concentrate more on hitting deep than following through.

I think the *most difficult lie* in a bunker is when the ball rests in the bunker face. Here the tendency is to sky the ball by hitting too far behind it. In this position hit only one inch behind the ball and apply less force to counteract the height which is bound to result. It is difficult to follow through fully on an up-slope, but try and swing normally.

When the reverse position applies and your ball lies on the down-slope, hit two inches behind and again concentrate on hitting down. This is one time you really must trust the loft of the club to pop the ball out.

Playing from a *side-slope*, or hanging lie, when the ball is higher than the feet, you will be inclined to hook the ball, so grip the club short to enable you to swing more upright and aim right. When the ball lies below your feet, grip the club fully, play normally and aim left.

For a normal bunker shot I grip the club an inch or so short of the top because I get better feel this way.

If sand in a bunker is wet or hard, the clubhead will skid in the first instance and bounce in the second. Play this shot more softly than the others, for the tendency here is to be too strong. It will help if you imagine the pin three yards closer than it really is. Still hit two inches behind the ball.

The only time you hit with all your might in a bunker is when a clod or stone or some similar obstruction lodges between the ball and club. Then you hit hard behind the obstruction—and hope.

Normally in a bunker I am very confident of getting close to the hole. I try my best to hole out every bunker shot. This is not arrogance on my part, only my way of training myself not to funk the shot. It paid off handsomely in the 1959 British Open when I was in twelve traps near the green and only once failed to get down in two.

If I had to back any particular phase of my game against the best in the world I think it would be out of a bunker. . . .

One last word to handicap players. Make sure you get out of the sand at your first attempt, even if you do knock the ball over the back of the green to start with. When you are out at least you might have a chance to chip close to the hole, or even putt. If you stay in the sand, the chances are you will be rattled and will still hit a bad shot at your second attempt anyway.

From *Play Golf with Player*, by Gary Player. Collins, London, England and Glasgow, Scotland. Copyright © 1962 by Gary Player. Reprinted with the permission of Gary Player Group, Inc.

WHAT GOES UP . . .

While riding shotgun for "aviator" Howard Hughes, Gene Sarazen was inspired to create the sand wedge that revolutionized bunker play. After observing that lowering the flaps makes an airplane go up, he added gobs of lead to an old niblick, creating a flange that tilted the leading edge of the face upwards. Thus, when struck downwards, it would slide, or "bounce" through sand, rather than dig in. After using his "secret weapon" to win the 1932 British Open, he likened wielding it to how "you would swing an axe when chopping a tree." ◢

Relax, Here's How to
Master the Sand

1 9 8 9 ⚌ R A Y   F L O Y D
W I T H   L A R R Y   D E N N I S

Raymond Floyd, who joined the Tour in 1963, and Sam Snead are the only individuals to win PGA titles in four decades. Unlike Snead, Floyd won the U.S. Open, as well as a Masters and two PGAs, as his confident short game contributed to his clutch play. Mark O'Meara said Floyd was "the most intimidating player I've ever played against. He plays every shot like it's the last shot of his life. He's like a black leopard, stalking the jungle." Despite this description, Floyd, in this essay from his popular book, instructed readers to *relax* when hitting the relatively easy sand shot. Floyd, whose swing was less steep than Gary Player's, described the splashier *modern* explosion shot, saying the follow-through should match the length of the backswing. He also offered a "flight plan," detailing how far the ball will carry, and then roll—plus instructions on how to apply spin.

I've been named Sand Player of the Year on three occasions by *Golf Magazine*, an honor determined by vote of the Tour players, so I guess I know something about getting out of bunkers. Maybe it's because I get in so many of them. But anybody who plays much golf is going to get in a lot of them, too, so he had better find a way to consistently play the ball out and onto the green, hopefully with a chance for a one-putt. . . .

You need a method to get the ball from sand repetitively and well, and it must be one that incorporates some kind of blast or explosion shot. Picking and putting out of sand usually doesn't work unless the bunker is flat with no lip, and you don't see many of those around.

Let me quickly mention a few different techniques. One technique I call the skimming method, which calls for more of a wide, shallow swing, taking a very shallow cut of sand very close to the back of the ball. Ken Venturi, among other good players, is an advocate of this style. He almost (but not quite) picks the ball off the sand. Kenny has described it as "clipping the ball off a carpet." It's an excellent method from good lies and when the sand is shallow and firm. Properly executed, the shot puts a lot of spin on the ball. But I feel it's rather dangerous for most players, mainly because you must strike the sand so close to the ball.

The opposite method is one in which a steep, V-shaped swing is used, striking down farther behind the ball and making a steep entry into the sand. The club cuts deeply under the ball and throws out a lot of sand. Gary Player, Lee Trevino, and Billy Casper, among others, use this method, which is very good from poor lies and deep, softer sand. Because it lets you strike farther behind the ball, it allows a great margin for error, but because of the steep angle you have to be careful not to leave the club in the sand. I think you have to work too hard with this method, because you are digging out a lot of sand, and I don't use it myself. But the three guys I just mentioned are among the best sand players in history, so who am I to say it's wrong?

I use what I call the explosion method, as do many good players, and I recommend it for you. It is more or less a compromise between the two styles I've just described. I think it's the easiest method with the least chance for error.

You will encounter many different kinds of shots in a bunker. The explosion method, with variations, will handle all of them. I can play any kind of bunker shot I desire. I can play a low, running shot, a low shot that spins, a high lob, [and] a high shot that spins. I can hit 10 inches behind the ball in a footprint and pop it out nicely. I literally can take a 4-wood into the sand and play a pretty decent shot onto the green. . . .

THE NORMAL SAND SHOT

First, let's get rid of your fear. Most amateur players are afraid of the sand for two related reasons: The shot is an unknown, one they don't know how to handle because they don't know the proper technique to use; and they seldom, if ever, practice it, probably because they don't know how to do it in the first place. Let me explain how to do it, which will take care of both problems.

The normal sand shot, one in which the ball is sitting reasonably well on top of the sand and on a reasonably level surface, is really a pretty easy shot. I know you've heard that before, and you probably don't believe it, but it's true. It's one that does not require precise club-to-ball contact, and so allows a considerable margin for error. . . .

All sand shots require that you create an explosion of sand that carries the ball out. Think of having a handful of sand with the ball perched on top, then just making an underhand toss out of the bunker. That same motion removes the ball from the sand with a club, only now the clubface sliding through the sand creates the handful of sand with the ball sitting on top. . . . Open the clubface about 30 or 35 degrees to allow the flange or bounce—remember, that's the bottom portion of the club that on a sand wedge hangs below the leading edge—to work properly. The clubface should be open to your *stance line*, which is pointing to the left of your target, but the face should be pointing at your target, which is the flag or wherever you want the ball to start. Then swing the club back along your stance line, a little to the outside of your target line and on an upright plane. It will come back down across and to the inside of your target line on the follow-through, but because the clubface is aimed at the target, the ball will start there. It's not something you have to worry about. During the swing, keep your eyes focused on [a] point 2 or 3 inches behind the ball. Be a little wristy, letting the hands hinge and unhinge freely, and use your right hand to send the clubhead down and underneath the ball and up again in a slicing action. The impact will force the sand up, carrying the ball with it. . . .

The finish is critically important. Do not let the club stop in the sand, because if you do the ball will

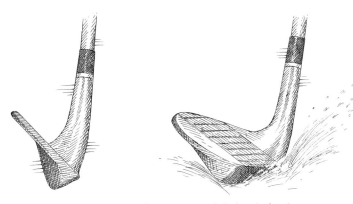

Bounce is what counts in the sand wedge because it prevents the leading edge from digging in.

Ray Floyd wrote that a steep, narrow swing arc produces a high, short shot; and a wide, shallow arc results in a longer, lower shot.

stop there too. A good rule of thumb is to make your follow-through as long as your backswing.

The consistency of the sand—how coarse or fine it is, how soft or firm—has a great effect on the shot. With practice, you will learn how to handle it. In coarser, more firmly packed sand, the ball will come out hotter and travel farther, so you swing easier; soft, fluffy sand tends to deaden the impact, so you must create more speed with a longer swing.

Practice also will help you determine how much swing speed—thus, how long a swing—you need to carry the ball certain distances from sand of certain consistencies.

The arc of your swing—how steep or shallow it is—also determines the height and length of your shot. The ball will come out of the sand at about the same angle that the club enters the sand. To get a higher, shorter shot, make a steeper, more sharply descending entry into the sand. For a lower, longer shot, make a shallower, more sweeping entry.

In general, shots from the sand should carry about three-quarters of the way to the hole and roll the rest of the way. Thus, on a 60-foot shot you should try to carry the ball 45 feet and let it roll 15 feet. That will vary, of course, depending on the slope from which you are playing and the lie of the ball. . . . On certain shots, when you have a good lie on firm sand, you also can make a shallower cut closer to the ball that will apply more spin and stop the ball more quickly.

From *From 60 Yards In—How to Master Golf's Short Game*, by Ray Floyd, with Larry Dennis. Copyright © 1989 by Raymond Floyd Enterprises. Reprinted by permission of HarperCollins Publishers, Inc.

Rotate the face open with your right hand before taking your grip, making sure that the grooves on the face continue to point skyward.

ANNIKA SORENSTAM

The Downhill Bunker Shot
and
The Long Bunker Shot

1989 · NICK FALDO
WITH VIVIEN SAUNDERS

Nick Faldo was inspired to become a golfer watching Jack Nicklaus and Tom Watson on TV. Playing his initial Ryder Cup in 1977, the twenty-year-old Brit and Peter Oosterhuis beat Nicklaus and Raymond Floyd in fourball, and he defeated Watson in singles. In time he'd be a Ryder Cup star and win three British Opens and Masters. During most of his time as the world's best player, he surprised traditionalists by having a female caddie, Fanny Sunesson. A year before hiring her, he broke a literary tradition by writing an instructional book with a woman: golf teacher Vivien Saunders. In this essay about two of the toughest bunker shots, Faldo and Saunders describe how to hit from the devilish downhill lie, and tackle the equally vexing problem of fairway bunkers. On the latter, they offer advice that goes back to Hutchinson, Vardon, and Tolley, cautioning against being too greedy.

———

Perhaps the most difficult of all bunker shots is the one where the ball just runs into the back of the bunker and leaves you with a ball sitting on a down-slope, still with the face of the bunker in front of you to negotiate. . . . [Y]ou are going to get less height to the shot and may be faced with one which is virtually unplayable. Don't expect to get the ball up quickly and even if you do get good height it isn't going to stop easily on the green. The ball is probably going to run as far if not further than it carries. . . .

The difficulty with the downhill lie is that there is in effect no sand directly in front of the ball but lots of sand to negotiate behind it. You need to produce a fairly steep up-and-down action where the clubhead rises well in the backswing, then gets down into the sand behind the ball and very definitely is held down beyond impact as the ball starts on its way.

To play this shot you need to get the wrists cocking early and suddenly to get sufficient steepness in the backswing. I play the shot with a wide stance, the weight well on my left foot and with the right shoulder held high at address. This helps to get the swing moving up and down the slope, with the added feeling of picking the club up sharply. . . . It is well worth having a couple of rehearsals of the backswing. . . .

I keep the clubface open, ensuring that the clubhead goes into the sand about an inch behind the ball.

The last thing you want is to catch too much sand behind the ball. For this reason you should play the ball quite well back in the feet. . . . The swing is now one which goes very much up and down beyond the ball through impact, working hard at maintaining balance as you do this.

THE LONG BUNKER SHOT

The golden rule with long bunker shots is not to be too greedy. . . . [D]on't take risks unnecessarily and . . . choose a sensible route back to safety. . . . In some countries fairway bunkers give you a really good chance for getting length. They hardly have any lip and you can even take a long iron or a wood if the lie permits. But on most championship courses in Britain, and indeed elsewhere, the fairway bunkers are relatively punishing and you have to look carefully at the face of the bunker in front of you to see what loft you need. . . . Look at the bunker shot from the side and really do gauge what height is needed.

Next look at the lie. If the ball sits down at all in the sand you need to produce a contact which is the equivalent of a ball-divot contact on grass. This kind of shot should be played exactly like a normal iron shot, making absolutely certain that there is no question of taking any sand before the ball. You want a clean, but slightly downward attack, taking the ball with a little bit of sand beyond. This time the danger is in a slightly fluffed contact which won't get the length you require. With a lie like this I would always be hesitant about taking a medium iron and certainly a long iron, unless there really is no bank in front of you.

If on the other hand the whole of the ball sits above the sand, you can pick the ball off almost cleanly, but again paying particular attention to the height you need. If the bunker is one of those low traps with nothing to negotiate then you can in effect try to catch the ball slightly cleanly or almost thinly for maximum distance. . . .

The danger here for the really good golfer is in catching a "flyer" which goes a little further than you expect and may run a little more on landing. . . . Long shots from a bunker are always very slightly hit-or-miss even for the very good player, the slightest contact with the sand taking the sting and distance out of the shot.

Sand Play Made Simple

1998 · ERNIE ELS
WITH STEVE NEWELL

Ernie Els, who has won three Majors and a record six World Matchplay titles, reached his position in the pantheon of today's golfers with a flawless all-around game and a laidback temperament—evident during stressful situations—that earned him the nickname "The Big Easy." He's so calm and creative on bunker shots that he recalls fellow South African Gary Player at his peak. In this essay, Els approaches bunker shots with the positive, keep-it-simple attitude of

Player, but provides more specific advice in the characteristic way of modern instruction. And instead of advocating "blasting" the ball free, he concentrates more on the genial "bounce" and "splash" effects. His point is that the sand iron's weight and the momentum of a free swing will give golfers the necessary shallow angle of attack and a smooth, accelerating swing that slides through the sand—*if* they allow the club to do its work.

The first thing I want you to understand is that your sand wedge is designed to help you a lot more than you probably realize. Gene Sarazen, a golfer known as "The Squire," and one of only [five] players to have won all four major championships, invented this club way back in the 1930s. And he did it for a good reason. The wide flange on the sole of the club encourages the clubhead to slide through the sand. And that is the essence of good bunker play. The clubhead slides through the sand, throwing the ball up and out on the green. This is known as the "bounce effect." In many ways, though, it is better to think of it as the "splash effect." The clubhead splashes the ball out on a cushion of sand.

If you have a sharp leading edge, which was the case with the pre-1930s sand wedge and every other iron club in your bag today, the clubhead tends to dig into the sand rather than slide through it. And from a decent lie that's definitely not what you want. That's why Gene Sarazen re-invented the sand wedge. If it weren't for his good thinking, you can be certain that bunker play would be a lot more difficult today. Not a nice thought, is it?

THE STANDARD GREENSIDE BUNKER SHOT

Bunker play becomes 10 times easier if you stick to a few basic principles at address and 100 times more difficult if you ignore them. . . . The bounce effect on your sand wedge works best when the clubface is open—there's absolutely no way that clubface can dig too deep into the sand if it stays open. So that's your first principle of good bunker play, you have to open the clubface at address so that it actually faces right of the flag. It's important that you open the clubface first and then form your grip, which should be a little weaker than normal. If you grip it first and then open the face, it'll return to square at impact and cause you problems with height and accuracy.

Open your stance, too. That means your shoulders, hips, and toes need to be aiming, say, 30 feet left of the target. Spread your weight pretty evenly on both feet and, as you look down at your grip, I want you to check that your hands are level with the ball, maybe even a fraction behind it. Finally, ease the pressure on your grip approximately 20 percent to ensure a nice, sensitive hold on the club. Now you're in good shape.

SWING ALONG YOUR BODY-LINE

The key now is to swing along the line of your toes and body—that's why the angles you establish at address are so important. Using a harmonious blend of body rotation and arm swing, try to make sure the clubhead follows the line of your toes as you swing it smoothly away from the ball. Then hinge your wrists to "set" the club in position at the top. Keep your grip pressure light and, as you change direction into your downswing, you'll sense a little bit of "lag" in your hands and wrists. That's good.

Now focus on an exact spot a couple of inches behind the ball to help regulate your point of entry and swing the clubhead through the sand. Your open stance will ensure that the clubhead travels on the necessary out-to-in path, but it helps if you sense that your hands stay close to your body through impact. The design of your sand wedge will take care of the rest for you. Also . . . my knees stay nice and flexed, stabilizing my swing as the club swings back and forth. The ball sets off a little left of target and then spins to the right, with a little bit of run on landing.

Once you've sorted out your technique, controlling distance will come a lot sooner than you think. . . . Simply alter the distance you want the ball to fly by lengthening or shortening your swing. The actual tempo of your swing and the pace at which you accelerate the clubhead through the sand should feel pretty much the same every time. That's a far more reliable method than trying to hit harder or softer from identical length swings.

HOW TO MAKE THE BALL FLY HIGH AND SIT DOWN

When there isn't much green to work with . . . I adapt my technique slightly to produce a higher, softer trajectory with virtually no run on the ball. I also use my 60-degree, rather than my 56-degree, sand wedge. Maximum loft for maximum height.

The changes you need to make couldn't be easier. Place the ball more central in your stance and feel that your weight favors your left side just a fraction. Then in your swing consciously hinge your wrists a little earlier in the takeaway basically pointing the shaft of the club more at the sky. That establishes the steeper swing plane that you need for this shot.

In the downswing there are two things to bear in mind. Firstly, take a little less sand at impact—aim to hit behind the ball, say, one inch instead of two. Secondly, make a slightly longer swing than you would for a regular bunker shot from the same distance and really "zip" the clubhead through the sand under the ball to help generate the extra carry necessary to get it to the hole.

Take these thoughts into the bunker with you and commit yourself to being 100 percent positive. Remember, with this shot, the ball will have virtually no run on landing so you can afford to pitch it right up to the flag. Get this one right and it's a very satisfying, spectacular-looking shot.

DRILL: RIGHT-HANDED SWINGS KEEP THE CLUBHEAD MOVING

There are two features of good bunker play that are worth mentioning again. First is the necessity to keep the clubhead moving through the sand. This sounds obvious, but I mean keep it moving in a smooth, flowing motion. Sadly, I don't see that too often when amateurs play this shot. Second is the angle of attack. The clubhead needs to swing on a shallow path into the sand, not a steeply descending one. The following exercise gives you the right feeling for both.

Assume good bunker play posture and take your left hand off the grip. Let your left hand hang free or put it in your pocket or behind your back, whatever feels most comfortable. Also, open the clubface. Now using your right hand only, make slow, rhythmical, almost lazy practice swings down and through the sand. Grip mega-lightly and keep the movement very free, almost as though you are letting go of the club.

Notice how the clubhead just slides through the sand? You don't even have to force it. And the clubhead doesn't bury itself, either. Simply the weight of the club and the momentum of a free swing give you the two key ingredients I was talking about—a shallow angle of attack and a smoothly accelerating swing. Introduce the sensations from this practice drill into your proper swing and you've cracked it. You'll have a better technique in no time at all.

From *The Complete Short Game,* by Ernie Els, with Steve Newell. Collins Willow, London, England. Copyright © 1998 by Tee-2-Green Enterprises. Reprinted by permission of HarperCollins Publishers, Ltd.

— 10 —

PUTTING

THE GAME WITHIN
THE GAME

Holing the Ball

1 9 0 1 ✦ WALTER J. TRAVIS

Walter Travis, who came from Australia to America as a child, was called "The Old Man" because he first played golf at age thirty-four. Four years later he won his first championship, the U.S. Amateur, and defended the title in 1901 using the revolutionary rubber-cored ball patented in 1899 by Coburn Haskell. Playing with a dangling black cigar, he'd win another U.S. championship and shock the British by taking their title in 1904. Called "a deep thinker," Travis founded and edited *The American Golfer,* and wrote books to popularize the sport, emphasizing putting, at which he replaced Willie Park, Jr., as the world's best. In his historic *Practical Golf,* he was among the first to promote the now standard reverse-overlap putting grip—which he taught Bobby Jones—and discourage overuse of the wrists. He also furthered the concepts of "straight-line putting"—taking the putter straight back and through—and picking an intermediate target.

Once the golfer has managed, more or less successfully, to get on the green, the serious business of getting the ball into the hole in one or two strokes presents itself. And mighty serious business it is too. Putting, that is consistently good putting, is perhaps the most difficult part of the game . . . [and] calls for the highest degree of skill and the nicest kind of judgment both as regards accuracy and strength. By accuracy is meant the passage of the ball over an imaginary line between it and the hole. You may possibly be able to keep your ball along this line, but if it is hit too hard it will probably jump the cup, while if the necessary strength is lacking it certainly cannot go in. It all seems easy enough, especially to the man who has never tried it, and who is not saddled with recollections of innumerable misses in the past, sins of commission and omission. . . .

ACCURACY IN PUTTING

Let us examine into the character of the stroke in reference to accuracy more particularly, dismissing, for the time being, the question of strength. If one can succeed in getting the ball to run true, more than half of the terrors of putting are gotten rid of at the outset, and the mind may then be concentrated on the important matter of strength.

In respect to accuracy, it is imperative that you should act upon some well-defined principles. Proceed first by taking a glance back of the ball toward the hole, and trace the line over which it must pass, noting for subsequent guidance a particular blade of grass on this imaginary line. Take your stance and square the face of the putter at perfect right angles to the blade of grass you have picked out by resting it immediately in front of the ball. By resting the club in this way in front of the ball it is easier to get the correct base-line, and, furthermore, it assists in going through the ball properly when the stroke is made.

Now withdraw the club and let it rest gently on the turf close up behind the ball, taking care to preserve the correct angle. Let the eye run quickly over the imaginary line to the hole, so as to determine the requisite force to be applied, and then make the stroke.

If the club presents a perfect right angle in reference to the line of play during the period of contact with the ball, and no irregularities of surface or obstructions interfere, the ball will almost certainly run straight, and assuming that the right amount of strength has been employed it will stand a much better chance of finding the hole than if the player simply trusted to luck, and with each new putt changed his method according to the whim of the moment. . . .

Regarding the Grip

The . . . grip affected by [this] writer [is different from the conventional one]. It is not contended that [my grip] is in any way better than the orthodox grip for the general run of players, but exhaustive tests—and under fire—have demonstrated conclusively that it serves its purpose somewhat better than does the prevailing style. It will be observed that both thumbs are laid down the shaft, and that the index-finger of the right hand touches it also at the tip, toward the back of the shaft. Grasping the club in this way, with the fingers, one seems to *feel* it better and to be able more accurately to determine the proper degree of strength to be applied to the stroke. Then, too, it lessens one's innate tendency to pull the ball, a tendency which the orthodox grip rather encourages. Close observation of all missed putts discloses the interesting fact that by far the large majority go to the left of the hole, thereby indicating the presence of a pull, due to the arms being slightly drawn in just after striking, instead of following through on the line to the hole. Throwing the burden of the work on the right forefinger seems to counteract any such fault, and not only is the club guided better, but greater delicacy of touch is apparent, and, consequently, the matter of strength is better controlled and regulated.

It will be found, generally speaking, that better results follow by gripping the club pretty firmly, with the fingers—firmly but not tightly. A very light grip is usually at the sacrifice of delicacy. A firm grip insures the ball keeping its line more accurately and not being deflected by irregularities of any land. The rougher the green the more is this essential. The hands should be kept as close together as possible, the grip of the right rather predominating.

Putt the Ball; Don't Hit It

The club should be taken away from and brought back to and follow through the ball with a smooth, even movement, free from any jerk. A choppy kind of stroke, a tap, or a hit is not recommended. Putts may, of course, be holed by each and all of these methods, but not, I think, with the same degree of consistency. Endeavor to take the club back and let it follow after the ball on the correct line of the putt. Aim to strike the ball exactly in the center, and don't be in any hurry to look up after the stroke. As a general thing, the center of the club is the best part to strike with, but a great deal of course depends upon the balance. With certain clubs better results are obtained by striking somewhat off the toe.

In addressing the ball do not allow the club to weigh heavily on the turf; rather let the touch be very delicate. Whatever the distance may be, always go for the hole; in other words, be up. In this way a certain proportion of long putts will be brought off. Aim to be just a shade *over* the hole, but not so far beyond as to make at all uncertain the holing out of the next, in case of missing. . . .

Keep the Body Immovable

In putting, it is of prime importance that the body should be kept immovable, the hands, wrists, arms, and to a certain extent, the shoulders only entering into the stroke. If the body be allowed to participate in the work an element is introduced that only complicates the situation, and makes this part of the game altogether uncertain. It is difficult enough, in all conscience, to control the strength of the stroke by simply using the other members; add the weight of the body, however little, and you will get such additional run on the ball as will carry it away over the hole and prove utterly demoralizing to the player. Neither should the wrists alone play any undue part. The less they are employed the better, for uniformity. They should act in perfect harmony with the other factors, the whole so blending and merging into each other as to produce a rhythmical unison, and leave the player wholly unconscious of any particular element being present. There should be more or less of an air of stiffness about the stroke, free, however, from any rigidity born of tautened muscles.

KEEP THE EYE FIXED ON THE BALL

The head, of course, must be kept absolutely still. At the moment of striking, the eyes—particularly the left—should be intently fastened, not only on the ball, but on the dead center of the ball toward the back, where you intend hitting it. It has been suggested that the left eye more especially should be directed at the ball. This will involve a slight turn of the head away from the hole. In this attitude less encouragement is given to pull the ball—and, as I have previously remarked, this matter of pulling is one of the greatest of all putting sins. As a further aid, it is advisable to get both elbows in line, parallel with the line of the putt. This will necessitate the turning of the left elbow away from the body, the right being somewhat tucked in toward the thigh, but not being allowed to rest on it. By letting the club swing in the manner described it will be noticed that it meets and goes through the ball with the face at a perfect right angle with reference to the line to the hole, and that is the whole essence of good putting. There is no mystery at all about it. The laws of motion are unchangeable, and given that the ball be hit truly on scientific principles, such as I have endeavored to outline, it will assuredly run straight on a smooth and true green, and be far more liable to keep a straight line on an indifferent one than if hit "in any old way."

From *Practical Golf*, by Walter J. Travis. Harper & Brothers Publishers, New York, N.Y.

Putting, a Test of Nerve

1913   JEROME D. TRAVERS

At age seventeen, American Jerry Travers upset Walter Travis by switching to the controversial center-shafted "Schenectady" putter Travis had just used to win the 1904 British Amateur. At age twenty, Travers won his first of four U.S. Amateur titles, although Travis had the top qualifying round; in winning the following year, he knocked out Travis, again the top qualifier, in the semifinals. In 1915, Travis got revenge in their last match, winning with a 30-foot putt. If Travers, an icy, enigmatic player, wasn't as phenomenal with a putter as his archrival, it was, according to Grantland Rice, only because Travis was also a whiz with the club off the green and even in some bunkers. On the green itself, they were equals. In his 1913 book, Travers established the concept of the putting stroke as a pendulum-like motion, and stressed the importance of having confidence in one's technique and choice of putter.

Although putting appears to be the simplest thing in golf to the beginner, after a little experience he will find out that it is not only the most important but also the most difficult part of the game. As the address, or aim, must be absolutely correct as well as the estimate of the distance and the amount of power needed for the stroke, the putt demands a greater degree of skill than any other shot.

Furthermore, in order to be a good, consistent putter the player *must* have confidence. Good putting is half confidence. The only way to secure confidence is by practice. There is no reason why every golfer should not be a good putter, provided he gives the correct amount of study and practice to this department of the game. Although over half a million people are playing golf in America today, there are comparatively few really great putters. The reason for this is lack of confidence.

It is on the putting green that most of the matches are lost and won. It is on the putting green that you have your last chance of winning the match, or of making up for the shot you missed through the green, and many a hard-fought contest has been decided by a single clever putt. The greatest test of a golfer's nerve in a close match is on the putting green, and there are situations in which the strain calls for every bit of steadiness and self-control the golfer possesses. . . .

Learn how to putt well, so that you will possess confidence. Devote as much of your spare time as possible to this part of the game. A golfer has the nightmare when he dreams he is taking three putts on every green. Don't have golfer's nightmare! Practice putting for an hour at a time. As there are many different kinds of putters, the beginner will have to find out from experience which putter suits his game best. . . .

After you have taken your stance and placed your putter at right angles to the hole, back off the ball, allow your eyes to pass over an imaginary line from the ball to the hole. When you have judged the distance, or the amount of strength required to send the ball the distance between you and the hole, allow your eye to pass back along this imaginary line from the hole to the ball. Take plenty of time to make up your mind about the shot, but once having arrived at a definite decision, do not wait any longer but putt the ball. The longer you wait and fuss over the putt, the less chance you have of holing the ball. If there is any noise or movement nearby, wait until it ceases, because the slightest distraction at the instant you hit the ball is apt to cause disaster. . . .

The hands, wrists, and arms are the only parts of the body that enter into the putting stroke. In long, or approach putts, the shoulders enter the stroke slightly. The body should be kept absolutely immovable. In short, two of the most important things to remember are to keep the head and body still.

In addressing the ball do not allow the club to rest with its full weight on the ground in back of the ball, but let it touch the ground lightly. The club should be taken back straight from the ball along the ground with the wrists and arms. Keep your left eye on the back center of the ball and do not lift your head until you see the club strike that place. If you take your eye off the ball a fraction of a second too soon you will unconsciously check the stroke and the ball will go to the right of the hole.

Remember that the wrists and arms should work in unison. The true putting stroke is best described as a pendulum movement in which neither the wrists nor arms predominate. Do not tap the ball, but take the club back in the manner I have already outlined and follow-through. I know a number of very good putters who merely tap the ball, but if you wish to be consistent you will have to adopt the pendulum swing and follow-through. . . .

If you should lose all confidence in your putting, a change in stance or putters will sometimes be of great assistance. I first used a putting cleek, but . . . I now use the Schenectady putter, the shaft of which rises from near the center of the head. This club is barred in Great Britain, but may be used in the United States. The putter I use has been my property for eight years and is my most prized club. When I am playing for a championship I feel like taking it to bed with me at night for fear it may be lost or stolen. I have used it in every match since the day I first had its aid in defeating [Walter] Travis at Nassau in 1904. I believe the center-shafted putter is built on the right principle and that it will improve one's game because it has a tendency to make one follow-through.

My Angle of Putting

1929 ✧ WALTER HAGEN

Walter Hagen, the king of gamesmanship, employed it to best effect on the green. His modus operandi in match play was to concede putts early in the round and then surprise his opponent by forcing him to make an even shorter key putt later on—unprepared, out-of-practice, and with the gallery watching, he often blew it. Hagen understood that nerves most betray putters during the heat of battle. A brilliant putter, he attributed his success, as this piece attests, to his ability to be comfortable over the ball. The relaxed player, he said, held the club lightly and was more apt to make a smooth stroke and maintain "feel." Hagen used a wide stance—the opposite of earlier theorists such as Travis—with the ball forward and most of his weight on the left foot, allowing him to add topspin and avoid a sway that would pull the putt off line.

It is surprising how many golfers seem to think that putting is all a set pattern where everything is grooved and the body must be held as stiff as a post so that nothing can move but the wrists.

Sometimes I doubt if anyone ever hits two putts in succession exactly alike. I know I don't. Putting is too much a matter of feel and touch to be treated that way. And while the body must be kept out of the swing, it is a mistake to keep the body stiff and rigid.

My first thought in putting is to get comfortable in taking my stance. If you don't feel comfortable you will tighten your hands and wrists and start jabbing the ball. All I try to think about once I have taken a comfortable stance is to be sure I have a smooth swing, more of a stroking motion than a hit. Yet I often putt just the way I happen to feel that day, sometimes even cutting the ball slightly.

Putting is much more a mental proposition than it is a physical matter. Let me try to explain what I mean by this. At the last amateur championship I stood by the edge of the eighth green and watched the field come by. This green was quite keen, with some unusual slopes and grades. I saw golfer after golfer come up to his ball and apparently study the line of the putt. But you could see from the expressions of most of them that, under the strain, they were not thinking about anything but getting the putt over. Few of them had any sharp, clear idea of what the right line was. Many of them would putt directly for the cup and then watch the ball slip well off to the right below the hole. They thought they were concentrating in the right way or actually thinking out and solving the problem of the right line, but they were not. They looked to be in a trance. At least many of them did. Or else they were still guessing as they hit the ball nervously, often lifting their heads to see whether or not they had guessed correctly, and the result was disappointing.

Then later on I saw Bobby Jones and George Voigt come by. They were different. Both lined up the approach putt and you could see from their expressions that each one was doing some clear, un-muddled thinking. They made up their minds in advance and then stroked the putt in the right way and the difference was marked.

The first thing needed for good putting is mental balance. This means mental and nerve control—coolness, lack of worry, a feeling of ease, and decision that isn't half guessing. Make some decision on the line and the speed of the greens and then play it that way—right or wrong. You are almost sure to be wrong, if you are still guessing as you hit the ball.

Have you ever noticed how often you hole a five- or six-foot putt with one hand when you are out of the hole? That means that with the strain lifted you are relaxed and you let the head of the putter have its way without checking it or hurrying it. When golfers begin to miss short putts of two, three, and four feet it is usually because they are gripping too tightly, the sign of too much tension. Loosen the grip a little, try to pick out a more comfortable stance and keep the swing smooth. This will often help a lot.

I keep my weight largely on my left foot, but such fine putters as Bobby Jones and Jerry Travers keep their weight almost evenly balanced. The matter of weight and stance doesn't matter so much, so long as you feel comfortable and natural, anything to cut down tension and the feeling of stiffness and tightness. Keep your body out of all short putts or fairly short ones, but that doesn't mean to turn your body into a stone post. There can be no feel when you are that way, all tightened up. I've seen a lot of good putters use a lot of different methods, but I never saw a good putter who looked stiff and uncomfortable. They simply don't go together.

From *The American Golfer* (May 1929), by Walter Hagen.

Putting

1931   JOYCE WETHERED

In the neglected British gem *The Game of Golf*, Joyce Wethered; her brother Roger; golf architect and designer Thomas Simpson; and the sport's greatest chroniclers, Horace Hutchinson and Bernard Darwin (Charles's grandson), discussed almost every feature of the game. Among Joyce's tasks was to cover one of her great skills, putting, which she regarded as both an art and a science, although the evolution of the game was by then giving more of a nod to the latter. She said that golfers no longer needed to worry about using spin to avoid weeds, worms, or mushrooms as they did when Travis, Travers, and Park, Jr., wrote on the subject, but could concentrate on clean striking. She, too, advocated a pendulum motion, urging a "happy medium" between the wrists and arms, while urging golfers to combine inspiration with sound mechanics to both improve their putting and build their confidence level.

Most golfing strokes, it used to be said, could be cultivated, but putting was an inspiration. There was evidently some hope of improving the one, but no right or wrong way with the other. No doubt the subtlety of the distinction conveyed an element of truth at the time it was uttered. At the present day, the same inference would scarcely carry much weight. The feeling with us now is that the use of the putter demands every bit as much scientific, let alone artistic, skill as any other club in the game, and that it carries, in addition, peculiar difficulties of its own to grapple with. Mr. John Low, a great exponent of the art, expressed the opinion that putting was the most important factor in modern golf. . . . If the statement is correct, it proves beyond dispute that anything which has to be done on the green cannot, at any rate, be left to the dim chances of inspiration. Putting must be founded on method. . . .

A natural question to ask is, why such an apparently simple affair as putting, should, after all, be found so difficult. At first glance the question is not too easy to answer. . . . [But experience readily demonstrates that a] player has many difficulties to contend with. He is neither on the same level as the ball, nor behind it, but above and at a peculiarly awkward angle for getting a clear view of the line. These details add very considerably to the difficulty of aiming or striking correctly. Also, the ball must be induced to travel often along doubtful contours and over deceptive surfaces. Instead of being a simple, easy, or inspirational branch of the game, it obviously demands the highest scientific skill, and can scarcely be regarded in any other light than as demanding the closest technical study.

The art, too, of putting has changed within recent years, in sympathy with every other department of the game. . . . We need only remind ourselves of the scrupulous order in which greens are kept nowadays, mown probably more days in the week than they used to be cut in a month, or, possibly in some instances, during the course of a year. The surface presents few of the difficulties with which the older players were faced. In Willie Park's *Art of Putting*, it is a significant fact that one important section of the book begins with the words—"When the ball is lying cupped on the Green." We [now] scarcely expect to be faced with problems of quite such a drastic nature. . . . Even the worms are extirpated, and weeds are not supposed to exist. The story of Ben Sayers confronted with mushrooms on the greens of St. Andrews may be familiar as a matter of history, but it's very unlikely to find a modern day parallel. . . .

With a surface [on modern greens] rivaling a billiard cloth, the ball can [now] be rolled up to the hole with every confidence that it will be treated with a fair share of justice. . . . [So] the present aim is to arrive at the greatest possible mechanical perfection. The old masters had every manner of device at their fingertips to counteract declivities or inequalities; they applied a variety of spins which would be quite unnecessary today. . . . Perfect cleanness of striking is now sought after before any other consideration. The ball perfectly hit so that it rolls without any sideway spin will, with remarkable regularity, disappear from view. . . .

The object that should be aimed at in striking the ball is to hit it in such a way that it runs toward the hole on a vertical axis and is free from any sideway spin. [But] "rolling" the ball quite smoothly in putting—to turn it, as it were, on an even keel—is not

The big trick in putting is not method—
the secret of putting is domination of the nerves.
HENRY COTTON

quite as simple a matter as it looks, because there is an insidious tendency to turn the club . . . and to give it the slight side-spin which is known as "cutting" the ball. The influence may be almost microscopic, but it is the microscopic on the green that generally counts in the long run. Naturally, if the clubhead is dragged across the line of the putt as well, the spin is vastly accentuated. . . . [Many golfers now] realize that a very slight upward and outward motion of the head of the putter just as it meets the ball—while keeping the blade at right angles to the line of the putt throughout the stroke—is necessary to turn the ball over on its vertical axis. Then, and then only, will the ball run perfectly truly.

The majority of the technical discussions regarding putting center round the question of the path which the clubhead takes. The older players . . . as a rule . . . struck the ball rather than stroked it. . . . It was considered, and probably considered rightly, the hallmark of good putting to bring the ball either into the center of the hole or from the right side, never from the left. The older putters, too, were almost to a man purely wrist putters, and the path of the clubhead tended to be somewhat concave. . . .

The question of stance must be decided with a view, firstly, to finding the best position in which the balance of the body can be controlled. On the whole, it is preferable to keep the weight back on the right foot, and well back on the heels, in order to prevent the dangerous practice of swaying forward during the stroke. . . . [T]he hold of the feet on the ground determines the steadiness of the body—a very necessary form of support when such a very delicate action as putting is being carried out. . . . [T]he stance should [also] be such as to assist the feeling that it is comparatively easy and comfortable to keep the clubhead running in its true line to the hole. An open stance should be avoided if the natural inclination is to bring the club inward across the line—and this is the commonest fault of all. It seems to be natural for some people—of whom Mr. Bobby Jones appears to be an example—to use a two-eyed stance and putt away from the body. This probably has the advantage of being the most natural and most effective way of seeing the line to the hole.

As to grip, there is again a liberty of choice. The ordinary overlapping grip serves very well, with the variation from that used for the other shots of keeping the back of the left hand facing toward the hole rather than showing on top of the shaft—the back of the right hand at the same time being kept well behind the shaft. With the hands set against each other in this manner, the left hand is in an excellent position to resist the right and still keep the clubhead moving in the path which is visualized. Many good putters overlap the forefinger of the left hand over the little finger of the right.

We now come to the stroke itself, and it might be remarked in passing that the supreme difficulty in putting is to preserve the straight line from the moment of impact till the stroke is finished. . . . Both wrists and arms should take part in the stroke. If the wrists alone do the work, the clubhead is lifted too high in the backswing and in the finish of the stroke. . . . The arms are brought into play just sufficiently to allow the clubhead to keep low. The whole action should be a happy medium between too much wrist work and too stiff a movement of the arms. The stroke is made slowly and deliberately, in order to give full time for the completion of the shot.

The tendency in recent years, with the finer surfaces available, has been toward keeping a straight path with the face square to the line. This has led in extreme cases to an almost complete arm movement, with the wrists locked and kept out of independent action, the elbows being spread-eagled away from the body in a position as nearly parallel to the line as possible. . . . In expert hands a pendulum arm movement of this kind possesses the one undoubted advantage that, whatever the length of the swing, the angle of the clubface never varies. . . .

The putting styles of Mr. Bobby Jones and [Walter] Hagen, to take two examples, are quite distinct, but they seem to sum up the principles which are admirable both in point of results and as models for imitation. . . . These players seem not only to be mechanically perfect, but to rely on perfection of mechanism. The swing of the putter is visualized according to a plan in which the nature and strength of the stroke is calculated to a minute fraction. The head of the putter is then directed from one definite point to another, with the ball, as it were, resting at a point between. There is no looseness of control, the distance and direction of the backswing is known, and the stroke is carried through to the definite finishing-point which has been visualized from the beginning. . . . The face of the blade is kept scrupulously square to the line of direction, and along it, or if anything, outside it. There are differences in the stance between these players, but with both the hand or forearm receives support from the body. The principle underlying such a formulated swing as this is that, if the swing is perfectly executed, only one result can follow. Make the right gesture, as it were, and the ball will obey. . . .

[T]here is the greatest care taken in the matter of looking up. . . . The danger of looking up too soon lies in the shifting of the shoulders, and shifting the shoulders produces a dragging across of the clubhead which at once causes side-spin and loss of direction. . . .

It seems a pity to disparage inspiration as an ally on the putting green and to urge in its stead processes that seem to be purely mechanical. But they are not as mechanical as they seem. It needs the hand and brain of an artist to putt beautifully; and most people would very likely add that it also needs confidence, by which is probably meant that an easy, assured way of hitting the ball with a positive feeling of certainty that it will fall into the hole is the greatest asset that any player can possess on the green. But there may be reasons for disagreement from, or at least qualifications of, a view which in reality associates confidence with inspiration. The supreme artist does not leave matters to chances such as these more than he can help. Yet although it may be the gravest error to imagine that confidence alone makes for good putting, there is little reason to doubt that good putting makes for the right kind of confidence.

From *The Game of Golf*, by Joyce and Roger Wethered, Bernard Darwin, Horace Hutchinson, and T. C. Simpson. Chapter by Joyce Wethered. The Lonsdale Library, Volume IX. Seeley, Service & Co., Ltd.; London, England.

Four Main Factors in Putting

1948 ⚬ MILDRED DIDRIKSON ZAHARIAS

The daughter of Norwegian immigrants, gregarious Texan "Babe" Didrikson Zaharias may have been the greatest athlete ever. After winning two golds at the 1932 Olympics, she competed in almost every sport, from bowling, boxing, baseball, and basketball to diving, tennis, and shooting. Then she became serious about golf. Evolving from a long hitter to a fabulous all-around player, she dominated both the amateur game—winning seventeen of eighteen tournaments in 1946–47—and later the professional ranks, until her early death in 1956. An LPGA co-founder, she is credited with forty-one professional wins and ten Majors. In this deceptively simple excerpt from her book, *Championship Golf*, Zaharias wrote about the twists and turns that golfers encounter on the greens of championship courses, giving a quick brief on how to study those breaks for the proper line and read the grain to gauge speed. Like Hagen, she advised to *hit* with topspin.

You read a golf green like you read a book. When you learn to do this, you are on the way toward getting those all-important last shots in the cup.

There are four important factors in putting, aside from grip and stance, [and] if these are followed closely you *will* get results:

- ✦ Contour of the green.
- ✦ Texture or grain.
- ✦ Lining up the putt.
- ✦ Swinging the clubhead to get over-spin on the ball.

In studying the surface of the green you look for rises and depressions to determine the borrow to compensate for rolls to the right or left. Obviously, if the green slopes from right to left, you would not attempt to putt on a true line, which would cause the ball to roll past the cup on the left side.

You will learn to adjust your putts to the contour with experience, which is the only way this factor can be learned.

The same goes for learning to govern the speed of your putt by the grain of the green, whether you are putting with, against, or across the grain, which is the equivalent of the surface on a rug.

In lining up the putt, you take into consideration the contour and the grain and with a couple of easy practice swings determine how hard you should strike the ball to get a true putt into the cup. Remember to be up to the cup on putts.

It is advisable to look the putt over at least from behind and from one side before hitting it. And take your time. An old saying on the greens is "miss 'em quick." It is better to take a little more time and sink them, but don't delay needlessly to the point where you are tied in knots. Some people may be born putters, but serious, thoughtful practice will go a long way toward improving any golfer's play on the greens.

Remember to determine the speed of the green and the other factors before you stroke the ball, and concentrate solely on the stroke finally.

My putting grip is the conventional reverse overlapping grip with both thumbs on the very center of the top of the club handle.

By reverse overlapping grip is meant that the forefinger of the left hand overlaps the little finger of the right hand, which is the opposite of the grip used on the other clubs.

My hands work together on a putt, but I have the feeling that the forefinger and the thumb of my right hand are doing most of the work. They serve as the guide to the stroke. This is a matter of individuality.

My feet are fairly close together—about eight inches apart. Weight should be fairly evenly distributed between the two feet, with just slightly more of the weight on the left foot. You lean forward so as to be looking down on the ball. Whether you putt with a slight bend in your knees or with your legs straight is a matter of choice. I putt with a slight knee-bend. I hit the ball from a point exactly opposite the left toe.

My right elbow rests against my lower side and my left elbow points toward the cup.

I hit short putts and stroke the long ones.

Whatever you decide upon as your putting style, always remember:

- ✦ Check on the contour, or break of the green.
- ✦ Determine the speed of the green by the grain.
- ✦ Check your grip and your stance.

Line up the clubhead behind the ball so that it is square to the hole. Take the clubhead back slowly and bring it into the ball close to the ground in a free, smooth motion which catches the ball on a slight upswing to impart over-spin. This helps to keep the ball on a true line.

After the putting blade has made contact with the ball, follow through and gradually turn your head with the stroke *without* lifting your head.

Don't try to putt with a jerky, indecisive stroke.

Make your putts with confidence.

A trick I employ in lining up a putt may be helpful to you. Pick a blade of grass or some other similar mark a foot or so in front of the ball and in line with the hole and use it as a guide. This will help you to avoid pushing or pulling your putts offline.

From *Championship Golf*, by Mildred Didrikson Zaharias. A. S. Barnes and Company, New York, N.Y. Reprinted with the permission of the Babe Didrikson Zaharias Foundation.

My Putting Grip
and
My Method of Putting

1954   BOBBY LOCKE

Four-time British Open champion Arthur D'Arcy "Bobby" Locke, prompted by Walter Hagen, left his native South Africa and spent several years playing in America. The World War II bomber pilot had instant success, winning six times in thirteen tournaments in 1947. The media disliked him for charging money for instructional questions and resentful American pros criticized his slow play and unorthodox style, including a hook on putts that recalled Willie Park, Jr. In this essay, he states how he, probably the best putter of his day, emulated Hagen by keeping the clubface square despite taking the putter back to the "inside," using the classic pendulum motion that takes the wrists out of the stroke, and achieving topspin. His most compelling idea was that putts can be holed from the front or from two side "doors." Fittingly, it was golf's most painstaking putter who first said, "You drive for show, but putt for dough."

MY PUTTING GRIP

Among golfers the putter is usually known as the pay-off club, and how right that is! Putting, in fact, is a game by itself. . . . From early in my career I realized that there was far more in putting than actually striking the ball, and I do not think any prominent golfer has devoted more time and thought and practice to this side of the game as I have.

. . . I change my grip for putting. . . . First of all I grip the club in the left hand, and the grip is normal except that I position my thumb down the center of the shaft. The art of putting lies in the tips of the fingers. If you have a delicate touch, you are lucky. It helps a great deal. But remember you must not grip tightly. You must grip loosely and do everything possible to acquire a delicate touch. The shaft of my putter is much longer than the standard men's length. I find that this gives me what I call "better head feel." By that I mean I can feel more clearly the weight of the clubhead as I swing. I grip my putter at the very end of the shaft and I use the same grip for all putts.

. . . [I complete my grip by adding my right hand with] the thumb . . . down the center of the shaft. Having [both] thumbs in this position enables me to follow the clubhead through dead in line to the hole, and also helps to put topspin on the ball. It is so necessary to put topspin on the ball when putting, as it makes the ball run through on the line to the hole.

MY METHOD OF PUTTING

Most putts are missed not because they are mishit but because they have been started on the wrong line and at the wrong speed. I examine the line of the putt, concentrating particularly on a radius of about three feet around the hole. This is where the ball completes its run, and what happens here is going to make or mar the putt. During this quick inspection I remove any obstacles which might deflect the run of the ball, but, more important, I check the pace of the green, determine how closely the grass has been cut and whether the green is fast, slow, or medium-paced. Also I check the lie of the turf around the hole to see whether the ball will be going slightly uphill or downhill or dead level as it approaches the hole. It is at this stage that I determine how hard I am going to hit the ball, always, of course, taking into consideration the length of the putt.

I work to the rule that if the green appears to be fast, I will aim my putt at an imaginary hole six to twelve inches short of the hole. If the green appears to be slow, and particularly if during the last two or three feet to the hole the ground is uphill, I hit it firmly for the back of the hole.

Having made up my mind how hard I am going to hit the putt, I now get behind the ball to examine the contour of the part of the green my ball will have to cross. Chiefly I am concerned with slopes and any hills or hollows. According to the slope, I make up my mind on the direction of the putt, whether it shall be dead straight or whether I should aim for the right or left side of the hole. Once I have made up my mind as to the line of the putt and how hard I am going to hit it, I never change my mind. It is fatal to let second or third thoughts intrude as you are putting. . . .

Now for the actual putt. In the first place, the weight is evenly distributed on both feet. I place the

South African Bobby Locke insisted that golfers could use three "doors" to the hole.

feet about four inches apart, with the right foot three inches behind the left in relation to a straight line from the hole to the left toe. This is known as a closed stance, and I adopt this to prevent myself from cutting across the ball and imparting any side-spin. I position the ball directly opposite the left toe. This enables me to hit the ball slightly on the upswing, whereas if the ball were farther back toward the right foot, there might be a tendency to chop or jab it. . . . I begin the address with the ball opposite the toe of the putter but actually strike the ball with the center of the blade. I do this to avoid cutting the putt. If one addresses the ball with the center of the putter blade, there is a tendency to swing outside the line on the backswing resulting in a cut and the ball not running true. By addressing the ball near the toe of the putter blade it is easier to take the putter back "inside" the line of the putt, and in this way one is able to impart topspin at impact. Never hit a putt with the heel of the club. That puts check on the ball and it will not run as far as you expect.

[I start] the backswing, [by] keeping the putter very low to the ground, almost brushing the turf. I am careful to take the putter back to the "inside," and . . . there is no wrist-work at all. Throughout the swing, the putter blade stays square to the hole. I want to emphasize that the blade *does* stay square to the hole. There are people who say it is impossible to take a club back "inside" without opening the face. With a putter it is not impossible, and this is how I putt. I learned the method largely from Walter Hagen in 1937. The term he used for taking the club back and still keeping it square was that you "hooded" the face. He proved to me that this backswing applies true topspin to the ball and is in fact the only type of backswing with the putter that will apply topspin. Hagen in his heyday was probably the world's greatest putter and I was happy to learn from him. It is essential . . . that there should be no wrist-work. Wrist-work results in inconsistency—and missed putts.

[At the] completion of the backswing, the putter[,] left hand and left arm to the elbow, are in one piece. To make sure that the clubface does not open, the back of my left hand keeps pointing to the grass. I have now reached the "hooded" position. By "hooding" I mean keeping the putterface dead square, or if anything slightly closed, in the backswing. This will make sure of getting true topspin on the ball, provided the putter returns to the ball on the same line.

[A]t impact . . . I keep the left wrist firm in relation to the forearm; the position of the left hand in relation to my putter is exactly the same. This means that the putter blade is kept square to the hole. My head is being kept well down until the ball has been struck.

[Just past impact there is] still no wrist-work in the accepted sense. I am concentrating all the time on keeping the clubhead square to the hole and on keeping my head well down. It is only necessary to follow through as far as the club went back in the backswing.

. . . My method of swinging the putter is the same as the swing of a clock pendulum. The club goes as far through in the follow-through as it goes back in the backswing. [Al]though the head is turned to watch what is happening to the ball, it is still in the same position in relation to the body. It cannot be too much emphasized that the putting action must be slow and smooth, and above all the grip must be loose to maintain the most sensitive touch.

My putting is based on the fact that if a ball has true topspin, there are three entrances into the hole, three chances, providing the speed is right. There is the front door and there are the two side doors. Obviously it is safest to use the front door, but with my method, if the ball catches the left side of the hole it will fall, and if it catches the right side it will also fall. By thinking of these three entrances, I always feel that I have three chances of sinking every putt.

From *Bobby Locke on Golf*, by Bobby Locke. Copyright © 1953, 1954 by Country Life, Ltd.

Borrow and Break

1961 ⚒ HORTON SMITH
AND DAWSON TAYLOR

Horton Smith broke onto the professional tour with a start that anticipated Tiger Woods. At age twenty-one, he won eight titles in 1929, beginning a career that would include thirty-two victories. The lanky Missourian had an all-around game—he even preceded Gene Sarazen by using a specially designed club for sand play (a concave-faced model that would be banned)—but he's still known for his brilliant putting. His most famous victory, by one stroke in the inaugural Masters in 1934, was the result of an 18-foot birdie putt on the 71st hole. He won a second single-stroke Masters title in 1936. Twenty-five years later, the retired PGA president covered every aspect of putting in *The Secret of Holing Putts!*, reissued as *The Secret of Perfect Putting!* Especially helpful is this thorough piece on how to master breaking putts and on why playing for the "pro side of the cup" is so important.

"How much should I borrow?" "How far do you think this putt will break?" You will hear these expressions time and again as golfers seek advice from their partners or their caddies. So let's explain them with a few illustrations.

Think of steel balls in a pinball machine rolling up one slope and then down one side or the other. Or think of the banked corners around the Indianapolis Speedway, where the racers go high up into the corners and then come down into the straightaway. Or think of the way a boomerang sails out on a cushion of air and curves back so gracefully to the arms of the thrower: These are three illustrations of the same principle that makes a golf ball "borrow" and "break."

As you know already or will soon discover as you play golf and learn putting, many golf course greens are "banked." Consequently, you will have to allow for the curving roll of the golf ball as it travels over their slopes. How much should you allow? Obviously, the more the "bank" or "tilt" of the green, the more the allowance for the alteration in the roll of the ball from a true, normal, straight path. As you play, experience will be your teacher. You will also find that for a long while you will tend to underestimate the amount of effect a banked slope will have on your ball.

Suppose you are contemplating a 20-foot putt on a green that is banked higher on the right than on the left. Obviously, you would have to hit this putt off to the right of a straight line between the ball and the cup. The degree to which you hit the ball to the right is the "borrow" from the right. The tendency of the ball to curve to the left is called its "break."

You "borrow" so many inches from the slope, but your putt "breaks" so many inches from the slope toward the cup. A green banked from right-to-left would naturally work in exactly the opposite fashion. That is, you would be "borrowing" from the slope on the left and your putt would be "breaking" to the right. I hope you are not confused, but that is the language of golf.

TOLERANCE FOR ERROR

It is my firm conviction, based on years of my own experience, and on watching thousands of golfers attempt putts on a "borrowed" line, that 90 percent are missed on the "low" side of the cup. . . .

Perhaps you have never seen a greens-keeper cut a fresh cup on your course. Well, he uses a tool that might be likened to a huge cookie-cutter to slice a circular cut into the ground, in order to remove a cylinder of turf about 10 inches long. He must necessarily pull this section out of the ground from directly above so as to have a perfectly level cup. Very rarely does the greens-keeper, much as he might try or wish to do so, actually remove the cut turf straight up. The result is, even on a supposedly level area, a cup with one side higher than the other.

When the cup has been cut from an area with slight or even great slope in it, you will nearly always find the "high" side of that cup on the side toward the slope. This is very important for you to know, understand, and act upon. For when the ball is slowing down and is near the "high" side of the cup, it acts as though a magnet is there to draw it into the cup. I have seen this happen many times when it might appear that the ball is at least half an inch away from the line of the cup and cannot possibly be expected to fall.

Now, let us go back to my first statement that 90 percent of "borrowed" putts are missed on the low side of the cup. Suppose you are surveying a 10-foot putt with a right-to-left break or "borrow" of six inches. . . . [T]he normal track of this putt necessary to hole the ball [is] in the exact center of the cup. But knowing two things about this situation changes your strategy for sinking this putt. First, your eye has informed you that the right side of the cup is the high side (this is also called "the pro side of the cup," for the obvious reason that the pros play for it all the time), and therefore, this is the side you will aim for.

Horton Smith preached hitting to the high, or "pro," side of the hole to go low.

Second, since you and probably most golfers, are inclined to underestimate the amount of roll on a "borrowed" putt, I suggest that you add an arbitrary 25 percent to your original estimate of the required degree of "borrow." This gives you what I call "tolerance for error," or margin for error. By allowing this margin, you can take advantage of the chance to enter the cup from the "high" side.

Remember, too, that the "dying ball" is much more affected by the contour of the green than a ball that is still moving from the power supplied by the putter. So why not make sure that the "dying ball" curves into the cup? Don't take my suggestion of a 25 percent compensation too literally. It may be that your eye consistently overestimates the necessary roll or break. Only you can be the judge of that. In general, however, golfers tend to underestimate, so 25 percent is generally sound.

When you are putting on the practice green you should experiment with various amounts of roll in the following fashion: Put down a ball 10 feet from the cup and arbitrarily try to figure the break. You might, for example, figure the putt to break four inches right to left. Then place a tee four inches to the right of the cup and putt for the tee. Watch most carefully to be sure you are putting on the line four inches right of the cup. By experimenting with this system you will have a graphic illustration of the points I have been trying to

Known as the "Joplin Ghost," Smith won two Masters with his flat-stick and was adept at making putts of all distances "die" in the hole.

make. After a while you can discard the tee and simply imagine the point toward which you are putting.

Another way to approach this problem is to decide that on right-to-left putts of lengths from six feet and up, you will arbitrarily open the blade a little bit more than your eye tells you to, and, in the opposite fashion, on left-to-right putts of the same distance, close your blade slightly more than your eye tells you.

Whichever method works best you should adopt as a general rule and work at strenuously on the practice green until you have established your exact formula or percentage of over-allowance. It is entirely possible that you will even wish to try this system on shorter putts.

You should also experiment with the ball position on borrowed putts. I find it more effective to have the ball slightly back toward the center of my stance on left-to-right putts and slightly in front of normal position on right-to-left putts. I feel that these variations in ball position are merely individual "margins for error" which help me to hit the ball on the line more often. Perhaps this method will help you too.

Putting Overview

2 0 0 0 *DAVE PELZ*

When Phil Mickelson hired Dave Pelz to help him win his first Major, it underlined the status of the Texas instructor and *Golf Magazine*'s Technical and Short Game Consultant as today's leading putting guru. Pelz's 1991 book *Putt Like the Pros*, was straightforward nuts-and-bolts mixed with scientific analysis of his putting experiments. It is primitive compared to the bestselling *Dave Pelz's Putting Bible* (a companion to *Dave Pelz's Short Game Bible*), which the former NASA research scientist filled with graphs and statistics to support his recommendations for approaching every kind of putt. Much of his data-backed theory is, perhaps, too remote for beginners, but this excerpt, culled from three chapters, can be useful to all golfers. There is no instruction and no charts, but readers can better understand the odds of making putts of various lengths, and learn how to use that knowledge both to focus their practices and make better judgments when they play.

Golfers are always looking for a cause-and-effect relationship. It's human nature to want an explanation or reasons why things happen, especially when you are trying to enjoy yourself but you keep seeing putts miss the hole. In golf, as in other areas of life, the phrase "the easy way out" comes into play. Many golfers chose to hope or spend money in an attempt to buy improvement, rather than have to read, practice, or learn how to improve. But putting does not succumb to such desires or offers of cash. Rather, just to make things interesting, the game throws in a number of unknown and unknowable factors that make success a statistical uncertainty.

The statistical nature of putting is one of its charms. . . . [T]he world's best putters (the golfers on the PGA Tour) make only about half of all their putts from six feet away; however, if they were on perfect and known surfaces, their strokes are so good that they would hole approximately 90 percent of these same putts.

How Well Can You Putt?

Something . . . you need to think about before actually beginning to work on your stroke are the answers to a few questions. They are important questions, but only if you want to know just how good your putting can get: 1) How good are the world's best putters? 2) How well do you putt now? 3) How good can one get at putting? 4) How good will your putting be in the future?

Let me answer these as best I can:

I believe the best putters in the world are playing on the PGA Tour. My proof is the results of the first two World Putting Championships, where the Tour pros were seriously challenged by some Senior Tour players, several LPGA Tour players, and a number of amateurs, both young and old. However, the PGA Tour players placed higher as a group than any other.

Also, my data on the percentage of putts holed from different distances shows that the PGA Tour players lead all other groups. Don't think that you can look at the statistics quoted in the newspapers and find this information, because the numbers that the papers publish (provided by the Tour) simply show how many putts the players average on greens hit in regulation, which is affected by the quality of their iron shots (the better the iron play, the shorter the putts). And these are the new putting stats. Years ago, the Tour's statistics measured putts taken per green, which was influenced by how many greens players missed and how consistently they chipped close to the hole (again, leaving them shorter putts). Neither of these statistics measures the quality of a player's putting, because both are strongly influenced by the quality of different shots (approaches and chips).

The true measure of the Tour pros' putting is indicated by the percentage of putts they make ("convert") based solely on the length of putts. . . .

If you want an answer to question 2—"How well do you putt?"—you must measure your percentage of putts holed from each distance. You can do this, but it will take some effort. You have to record the distance of each putt on your scorecard as you move around the course, and indicate those you hole. After 10 to 15 rounds (and at least 5 to 10 putts from each distance), you'll begin to be able to plot your own conversion chart and compare it to those of the pros.

As for question 3—"How good can one get at putting?"—the answer depends on a number of things: the quality of the greens, how well a player reads those greens, and the quality of the player's stroke and touch. Although none of these questions can be answered definitively in this book, I assure you that all of the above are getting better all the time. As greens improve, putting strokes improve, and golfers learn to read greens better, a higher percentage of putts from every distance will be made in the future.

Finally, "How good will your putting be in the future?" That depends on your ability to learn the mechanics of a better putting stroke, your ability to learn better putting feel and touch, your ability to learn to read greens better, and your ability to produce the right stroke at the right time. Depending on your lifestyle, your determination and intensity, your focus, your self-discipline and practice habits, and your ability to learn, only you can provide this answer.

Stop Three-Putting

For most golfers to improve their scores, it is often easier to reduce their number of three-putts than it is to increase their number of one-putts. This is generally true for golfers with handicaps greater than 20, although it is even true for some very fine, lower-handicap players. . . . [T]he length of the most frequent first putt on greens hit from outside 60 yards is 38 feet. (This distance varies a little with the handicap of the players measured, but, obviously, there are many more long first putts than short ones.) . . . [T]he most frequent first putt to follow shots hit from inside 60 yards is an 18-footer.

. . . This means that you shouldn't practice only short putts; the long ones are also important. And you must stop three-putting those long ones if you want to be a good putter. . . .

SIMPLER IS BETTER

There are many different ways for golfers to putt. Having said that, it does not mean that I'm advocating all, or any of these methods. But it's important that you are aware of the choices a golfer has, and even a few he doesn't, unless he doesn't care about the Rules of Golf (which I think you must if you're going to be serious about this game).

The old adage "different strokes for different folks" is very meaningful, because some putting strokes work better than others for certain players, while no one stroke works perfectly for everyone. While no strokes, even perfect ones, make all their putts, some really awful strokes do make some putts. And sometimes the difference between good and bad strokes are very difficult to measure or see. But believe me, the differences are there.

. . . [L]et me pass on to you the one thought, the one axiom that governs all my theories on putting. It is this: Simple is better. You'll find research test results in many different disciplines that validate this conclusion. It is certainly true in almost all of sports. Why? Because regardless of your level of talent, the less you give yourself to do (and still get the job done), the more consistently you can learn to do it. Whereas the more compensations that must be made in your putting stroke, the more difficult it will be to repeat in such a way that it actually makes your putts. The more complex a putting stroke (that is, the more compensations that must be made to make it effective), the more uncertain (or inconsistent) its results by any golfer regardless of skill level.

All this may sound routine, and you may have heard it many times before, but that doesn't mean it isn't true. And more important, that doesn't mean it shouldn't be taken seriously. So there's no question about it: In putting, simpler is better. The simpler and easier the stroke is to execute, the more precisely and repetitively you'll be able to learn to execute it, especially under pressure. And that's why all my teaching begins with that principle.

BETWEEN THE EYES

In *Amy Alcott's Guide to Women's Golf*, the former LPGA star and Hall of Famer recommended positioning the body so the eyes are right over the ball or just inside the target line when putting. If the eyes are outside the target line, the golfer will pull putts to the left. To check, she counseled, put a ball down, take a putting stance, and then drop another ball from the bridge of the nose—or from right between the eyes—onto the ball below. The golfer also can use a putter to do this, putting the tip of the grip handle between the eyes and then sighting down the shaft. ॐ

How to Square Your Putterface and Hole More Putts

2003 / TIGER WOODS
WITH PETE McDANIEL

During Tiger Woods's long reign as golf's top-ranked player, he was the most consistent clutch putter on the PGA Tour. Woods attributed his success to his pre-putt routine, a ritual that provides a few moments of needed serenity. What precisely goes through his mind before he pulls the trigger is his secret, but when it comes to the mechanics, Tiger is a pure traditionalist. He commits to line and speed—which he says is the most important element in putting—aims at where the putt will break, and keeps his head down to avoid yanking putts off line. In this brief piece for *Golf Digest*, Woods wrote about another essential to good putting—keeping the clubface square to the target line. When he writes to practice putting along a string to make squaring the clubface automatic, it carries weight because he claims he has used this classic drill himself.

Good, consistent putting involves several factors, not the least of which is the ability to visualize the line and get the ball started on that line. You can get the ball rolling properly if you can square the putterface to the target line at impact without having to manipulate the putterhead.

I recommend using a string or chalk line to help you practice squaring the putter. You can buy a ready-made string-drill training aid or make your own by tying a piece of string to two small stakes—a couple of pencils will do. Stretch the string taut on level ground, high enough so your putter can travel under it.

I used the string drill during my rehab from knee surgery, before I could make full swings. The extra work on my short game paid off my first tournament back, the Buick Invitational. I struggled with the pace of the greens early because of rainy conditions, but my alignment was sharp, which contributed to a lot of par-saving putts. To win right out the blocks felt pretty good, too.

GETTING A LINE ON SQUARE CONTACT

The string drill gives you great feedback on the path of your stroke, the angle of the putterface and the target line. Here's what I do:

On putts of five feet or less, I swing the putter straight back and through. I use the string to practice keeping the putterface square, or perpendicular, to the string throughout the stroke.

On longer putts . . . where you make more of a shoulder turn to take the putter farther back, the putterhead tends to move to the inside a little. It also moves a little inside on the through stroke. The key is the putterface stays square *to the swing path* throughout the stroke. This should happen naturally.

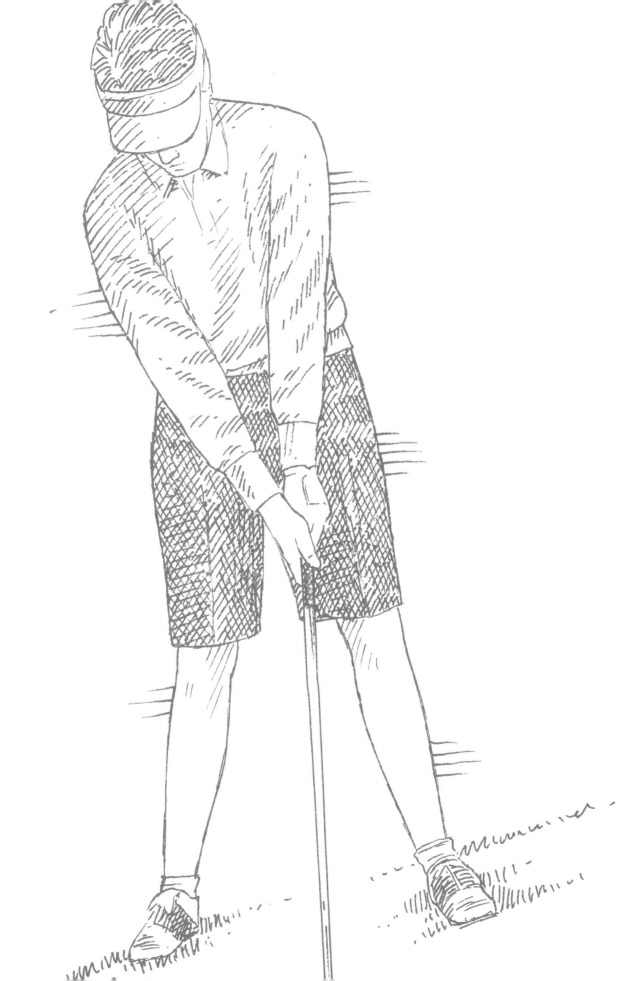

PART FOUR

SHOTMAKING

WALTER HAGEN FAMOUSLY MAINTAINED that golf was a game of managed imperfection, and modern golfers would do well to accept that to err is human and only the divine can hope to consistently split the fairway. Since Harry Vardon's time, golf books have included chapters on "faults and cures," but it was Vardon's great rival, J. H. Taylor, who earlier set the tone for future discussions on such problems as slicing, hooking, topping, and shanking. Dismissing those who would rely on "natural" methodology, Taylor advised the golfer to learn precise technique from the ground up. Decades later, John Jacobs would reverse that concept—while still embracing the core lesson—when he suggested first watching the flight of the ball, and then working back to cure the fundamentals. Alongside such advice inevitably comes an examination of how to deal with "trouble" when the anticipated error does occur. Since the 1880s, instructors have advised how to cope with a multitude of bad lies as well as the vagaries of the weather. Early instructors were often folksy and less thorough, while modern instructors, such as Chi Chi Rodriguez, offer ideas that mix flair, cold-blooded analysis, and recuperative drills. In complement to such teachings, golf writers consistently evolved theories on that most exquisite phase of the game: employing advanced techniques. From early twentieth century champions to Tiger Woods came methods for mastering intentional slices and hooks that can steer players *over, under,* and *around* obstacles, and manufacturing shots that laugh at the wind and nullify slick greens.

— *11* —

FAULTS
AND CURES

PRESCRIPTIONS
FOR THE
AILING SWING

Mashie Play

1904 · G. W. BELDAM
AND J. H. TAYLOR

When Horace Hutchinson came home from Oxford on holiday, one of his parents' servants caddied for him at the famous Westward Ho! links nearby. The caddy, also a greens-keeper, was J. H. Taylor, and within a few years, Hutchinson was writing about the former houseboy beating the Scots at their own game. The first of the Triumvirate to win a British Open title—he'd win five overall between 1894 and 1913—Taylor was the superior putter, and was renowned for his approach shots with his favorite club, the versatile, mid-iron mashie. In this excerpt from their book of articles that appeared in *C. B. Fry's Magazine*, Taylor and pioneer golf-and-cricket action photographer George Beldam, set the precedent for instruction on faults and cures. Refuting those who contended golf is a "natural" sport, Taylor offered "stern and unsympathetic detail" about correct technique and how to stop hitting fat shots and shanking the ball.

I have heard it said many times—and even by golfers whose experience should have taught them better—that the easiest way—viz., the way which comes naturally to each player—is the only right way for him to adopt. In my experience I can count many golfing failures entirely due to the too ready acceptance of this fallacious theory. I go so far as to state that this so-called natural way is generally the wrong way, and often violates the fundamental principles of the game. I quite sympathize with anyone who is lured on to play the game in this "natural" way; but to yield to the temptation is not to his best interests, as he may discover in after years, when it is too late. A little perseverance, application, and determination to master the difficulties at the outset will bring a full and certain reward.

To come to stern and unsympathetic detail, which in such practice is met with by all, strong and flexible wrists are undoubtedly necessary, but these will be of no avail if other requisites are neglected. The head *must* be kept perfectly steady during the upward stroke, and until after the ball has fairly started on its way; this to obviate the prevalent fault of looking up too soon. The eyes, during the upward stroke, *must* be riveted on the ground, at a point immediately behind and almost underneath the ball, but still *on the ground*. If this is really done, there will be fewer half-topped balls. Further—and still very important—the player *must feel* that the wrists are controlling the club in taking it back; indeed, care must be exercised that the wrists do not rise beyond a certain point, or control and power will be lost. What is that point of control? I answer—where the player *feels* he is losing *leverage* from the wrists. Assuming that the wrists are working in the correct manner, it will be found that the right elbow moves naturally round, and close to the side. I mention this because some people are apt to make too great a point of the position of my elbow with regard to my body. Of course, if the swing be upright, the right elbow will be more liable to leave the side; but as I understand the golfing swing, it should be round the body rather than up and down the line of flight. . . .

Supposing the club has arrived at the top of the swing for the full mashie in the manner described, and the leverage which I spoke about has not been lost through over-swinging, the responsibility of starting the club on its downward course will remain with the wrists. But if this leverage is lost, the task of starting the club is thrown on to the arms and shoulders, and this will cause a hurried, jerky movement. The result of this will be most disastrous; for control, accuracy, timing, power, and everything will be sacrificed. I think I need say no more, for if the upward swing has been worked out satisfactorily, it is a sure index of effectiveness throughout the downward swing. The most important thing of all is, what takes place at the moment of impact.

[Hitting fat or behind the ball is] one of the most general of faults indulged in not only by novices but also by golfers of more mature experience. . . . The fault consists in the over-anxiety of the player to "get down" to the ball. To do this he bends the right knee too soon, and this causes the right shoulder to drop, with the probable result that the ground in front of the ball is struck first. The knuckling in of the right knee tends to throw the hands forward just before the moment of impact, and this is one of the most frequent causes of socketing [or shanking] that I know. If, however, the ball be struck with the face of the club, and not off the socket, it will most probably be pushed out, and fly, sooner or later, to the right of the intended flight. The left arm has left the side, and therefore power also has been lost. It then follows that the right forearm must be in the ascendant, over-powering the left. Indeed, in most pushed out shots the right hand obtains the mastery. . . .

[Many golfers try to help the ball into the air by drawing the club] across the ball . . . [then] pulling the arms in close to the side directly [after] the ball has been struck. Some players do this to put "cut" on the ball, and that they accomplish this I readily admit, but I consider it must be at the expense of accuracy and command of the ball. With this system too much cut, at the expense of propelling power, is obtained. This finish would be all right if distance were no object, and the ball were required to leave the club in a perpendicular manner to clear some steep obstacle. If I were to finish my pitching strokes of, say, about 60 yards in [such a] manner, I should be "cutting the legs from under the ball," and be short. As the ball ought to go well up into the air, it has to travel considerably more than 60 yards in its flight. It will therefore be seen that, to get this distance with cut, it is essential neither to pull the arms nor the club across the ball.

. . . [In] the correct finish of a pitching stroke with cut . . . the arms are carried through much more than [in the above example.] . . . The position of the clubhead [would have] the face looking upward [with] the left forearm controlling the club. . . . Combined with [an open] stance, [this] produces natural cut; and . . . distance is more accurately gauged when the stroke is played in this straightforward manner. From questions I have been asked it seems to me that some players imagine the difficulties in this stroke which do not exist. With the exception that the stance is as if I were playing to the left of the hole, and that the clubhead is turned slightly outward *before* the club is gripped, the stroke is played in the same manner as if no cut had been intended.

From *Golf Faults Illustrated*, by G. W. Beldam and J. H. Taylor. George Newnes, Ltd., Southhampton Street, London, England.

It's a strange thing that we know just how to do a thing at golf, and yet cannot do it.
BERNARD DARWIN

Common Faults and How to Cure Them

1927 ✦ A B E   M I T C H E L L

Abe Mitchell, who hit balls almost 300 yards with a hickory-shafted driver, was Britain's best golfer between the Triumvirate and Henry Cotton. Cotton wrote, "No golf balls have ever been struck harder and truer than those struck by Abe Mitchell . . . from about 1910 to 1933." Cotton also believed Mitchell was too nice to close out big matches, the reason he'd be known as the best golfer not to win the British Open. He was a superb match player, however, and the star of three Ryder Cup teams. Hired by multi-millionaire seed merchant Samuel Ryder for private tutoring, Mitchell became the model for the golfer atop the Ryder Cup trophy. In this essay from Mitchell's 1927 book, he offered still-relevant instruction on how to cure slicing, pulling, and topping the ball. Note his remedies for a reverse pivot and his advice on how to check for grip and posture problems.

———◆———

The faults dealt with in this chapter are the commonest in golf. Everyone may be said to pull and slice occasionally in every round; some commit one or other of these faults at almost every hole. If they are only slight deviations from the straight line, there is little wrong and the errors will right themselves. Once the player starts altering his stance or grip or swing, the change produced is almost certain to do more than correct the error; a slice will probably give place to a wicked hook, a hook to a depressing slice, and so on, the remedy proving much worse than the disease.

But many players have spells of one particular form or other of these golfing maladies, and obviously some remedy is necessary in their case. It is for these unfortunate people that his chapter has been written. . . .

It does not follow that the advice in these pages is wrong; in all probability it has not actually been followed. It is not enough merely to endeavor to carry out these instructions when playing a round. The player must have it out with himself on a quiet part of the course. At first he will probably exaggerate everything he is advised to do, and so substitute one fault for another, a pull, say, for a slice. This is highly desirable, for it will convince him of the efficacy of the cure. Soon he will be playing well if he is an intelligent player and thinking keenly. . . .

SLICING

Cause 1: Wrong grip.

This may be contributory to the slicing habit but is unlikely to be the root cause. See that the grip is normal for the shot. For an ordinary drive two knuckles

Long-hitting Briton Abe Mitchell, who was enshrined atop the Ryder Cup, counseled the wealthy on curing their golf faults.

of the left hand should be visible and if the back of that hand is too much in front of the shaft, it should be slightly altered, but very slightly.

The right hand grip should . . . not be allowed to creep farther over the shaft.

CAUSE 2: TOO MUCH WEIGHT ON THE LEFT FOOT IN THE ADDRESS.

In the backswing the club is brought too soon round the body; in fact the left foot may be said to be the center of rotation. As a result the player is cramped at the top; the elbows are bent and the body is bent well forward throwing extra weight on the left foot. In the downswing the player corrects this forward movement of the body by going back on to his right foot. Consequently, at impact, the club is cutting across the ball through inability of the hands to go through.

CAUSE 3: SHOULDERS TOO LEVEL IN THE ADDRESS.

This indicates that already the right is gripping unduly and has taken control. In the backswing, the right lifts and the body leans forward on to the left foot. . . .

CAUSE 4: A STIFF UPRIGHT STANCE.

This is a common fault among lady players. There is scarcely any pivot and both sections of the swing are largely arm movements. The first movement in the swing is usually a backward sway of both the trunk and the head accompanied by a lift of the hands.

The hips appear to be locked in the address and to remain so, thus preventing either a hip swing or a shoulder movement. This is really the root of the trouble.

Similarly in the downswing, the absence of body twist prevents the hands from going through and thus the clubhead is brought inward across the ball.

CAUSE 5: STANCE TOO OPEN.

The remedy in every case is the same, viz. get more width in the backswing. Decide in the address that the backswing is to be a dragging back as far as possible of the clubhead along the line of flight, until the right hip has gone back to its braced position. If this movement has been consciously prepared for, or been actively in the mind, the faults of stance and grip [already] mentioned will remedy themselves.

In the downswing, and especially at impact, the grip with both hands must be firm.

On no account start altering the grip so as to encourage a pull, that is, by putting the left hand more on top of the shaft and the right more under it.

. . . This may be a palliative but does not eradicate the disease. In this connection, as in any other, two wrongs do not make a right.

Tackle this disease firmly and do not pander to it by playing toward the left of the fairway. This practice only makes matters worse, for as the player does not intend the ball to go into the rough on the left, he instinctively, if not deliberately, cuts across it to get the slice necessary to finish on the fairway.

If there is difficulty in getting extra width, the player should, for a time, stand more square, for this will facilitate a wider backswing. Also, at impact, he should be thinking keenly of his clubhead and should have courage to roll his right forearm in the follow-through. He may pull horribly for a time, but the slice will disappear and a much longer ball will result. Firm up the grip, keep the head down and have courage.

PULLING

CAUSE 1: A WRONG GRIP.

The grip is frequently contributory to the pulling habit, more so than to the slice. It is more natural for the right hand to get under the shaft than over the top and, usually, the players who grip habitually with the right in this way are right-handed players, that is, the blow is delivered largely by the right. With the hand in this position, the knuckling over at impact or just before is apt to be exaggerated, especially if the grip with that hand throughout the swing be very tight, as it is apt to be. The puller's grip, then, must be altered to the normal grip. . . .

CAUSE 2: THE RIGHT SIDE IS BRACED IN THE ADDRESS.

This throws undue weight on the right foot. The first movement is a draw away of the whole body along the line of flight, the right hand lifting but keeping the clubhead shut.

The right hand is in control, but unlike the slicing positions, the right elbow is away from the body. . . . From this position it is difficult to get the elbow down to . . . the proper position for a normal swing. Instead, it describes a circular outward arc, and the clubhead comes on to the ball with shut face and the result is a pull from the very commencement of the flight.

REMEDY.

See that the grip is normal and that the left hand has control. Let the grip with the right be slack in the address. Get width in the backswing and keep the right elbow well in to the side. It ought to be noted in connection with pulling and slicing that the method of grounding the club in the address may have a distinct influence on the backswing. Thus, if the clubface be open in the address there is a tendency to swing at once round the feet; thus width is lost, the left elbow bends, and a slice results. On the other hand, if the face be too shut, a pull may ensue.

It is best, in the long run, to address the ball with the clubface fairly shut, that is, with the toe well forward. This mode of address invariably tends to a wider backswing and fuller pivot.

TOPPING, BALLOONING, DIPPING RIGHT SHOULDER, ETC.

CAUSE:

These are all symptoms of the same faulty backswing already dealt with. . . . The right hip has not moved laterally, the right hand has had control and the club has been lifted rather than slung.

At the top, the player feels mewed up. Both elbows are spread-eagled, and as there has been little pivoting the player is conscious that the body is now cut out and that the downswing is largely dependent on the arms and wrists. Consequently, the downswing becomes a snatchy movement, as the arms are not actuated from a braced trunk.

Anything may happen. The clubhead may hit the ground behind, and the caddie or partner on being appealed to will probably tell the player that he is dropping his right shoulder in the downswing, as it is the most obvious thing to say. The real fault, of course, occurred in the backswing and escaped notice.

From *Essentials of Golf* by Abe Mitchell. Edited and arranged by J. Martin (Verulum Golf Club of St. Albans). Hodder and Stoughton Ltd., London, England, and George H. Doran Company, New York, N.Y. Reproduced by permission of Hodder and Stoughton, Ltd.

Curing Golf Ailments

1951 ✦ JOHNNY FARRELL

Stylish Johnny Farrell—who twice was selected America's best-dressed golfer—is arguably the best player not in the World Golf Hall of Fame. He won twenty-two tournaments—including seven in 1927—and played on the first three Ryder Cup teams. Because of family obligations, he retired and became the head pro at Baltusrol for thirty-eight years. And this son of poor Irish immigrants gave lessons to presidents, British royalty, the social set, and celebrities. Perhaps his biggest admirer was Bobby Jones, whom Farrell upset by sinking an 8-footer in a 36-hole playoff in the 1928 Open. In his introduction to Farrell's book, Jones called him a "great golfer and a fine teacher." In this excerpt, Farrell took a different approach than Abe Mitchell to "prescribe medicine" to cure slicing, hooking, shanking, topping, and skying the ball. His process was to scrutinize the stance, timing, and swing path.

Nobody needs a professional to tell him what's *good* with his game. The weekend golfer probably likes to hear that he has got good hand action in his swing, or that he is all in one piece coming back, but as soon as you comment on it, he invariably eyes you sourly and says: "A devil of a lot of good that did me today, I was slicing the ball all over the place!"

So I'm going to tell you about slicing—as well as some of the other common ailments that creep into any man's game on occasion—and try to prescribe some medicine. . . .

THE SLICE. There are many reasons for a slice but there's only one way *how* it's done, and that's by bringing the clubhead across the ball—outside in— and giving it a right-way spin.

Of the ways *to* slice, the number one enemy is getting the right side into the shot too quickly. You generally do this because you *sway* on the backswing,

rather than *pivoting* around on your hip.

An inside arc going back that becomes an outside downswing is another fatal slice producer, and usually is caused by losing control of the shaft at the top of the backswing.

A slice can also come from a left arm that isn't firm, and because it isn't firm, the *right* elbow strays. Tuck that right arm in, and when you unwind your left hip it will follow the inside arc naturally.

But both the loss of hand control and the straying elbow are generally the result of (a) rushing the backswing and (b) not waiting for the downswing. Hand in glove with a rushed swing is a tendency to lunge at the ball—to drive it fifteen miles. This causes you to leave your hips out of the shot entirely, so that it is the arms, and not the clubhead, that are swinging at the ball. My advice, then, is to practice coming back extra-slow—all in one piece . . . then unwind, keeping the right shoulder behind the shot, and let the clubhead come through the ball.

Many golfers slice, too, because they *die on the shot*, as the expression goes. They come back in one piece, wait, come back down again, and then quit completely as the clubhead strikes the ball. This failure to stay with a good swing oftentimes can be traced to the club the golfer is using. It may be too heavy to continue on through naturally, or so light that it cannot withstand the speed and power of the uncoiling pivot.

An open stance with a wood or a long iron will also produce a slice. This is usually due to the fact that the hitter is not aware he stands that way, but believes his feet are square with the direction of the shot and the ball. Line up the shot carefully. . . .

In any event, never get saddled with a slice and begin . . . facing off to the left to compensate for the curve the ball is going to take to the right. If anything, face *into* the slice—and by doing this you'll be squaring your stance.

Finally, a slice may be traced to your grip. Be certain that your left hand is around the shaft and not slipping to the left so that the palm is facing up. Check, always that the V of the forefinger and thumb points over the left shoulder. Don't waste the power of that all-important left arm, hand, and wrist. The right hand—thanks to the overlapping grip—is meant to be nothing more than a guide for the swing. And be sure that you are holding the clubshaft in the fingers of your right hand and not palming it. You must, at all times, have *live hands* that can feel the whip in the shaft and control the swing.

THE HOOK. It has been my observation that the beginners do most of the slicing—it takes an experienced golfer to develop a bad hook. It's true. During the first five years that a man plays golf he tries so many things to rid himself of a slice that he suddenly finds he is faced with the problem of losing a disastrous hook. But "Hookitis" is not confined to any one group of golfers, for the simple reason that a hook is most often the result of timing that has gone bad. And when the expert golfer hooks a drive or a long iron it is generally spectacular because he *trusts* his swing. He bends back and lets go—and if his timing is off, however slightly—the hook that follows is sometimes unbelievable.

But the expert knows what to do about his hook. The weekend golfer sometimes does not even realize that his timing is at fault and can be corrected without the use of drugs or yoga.

First of all, keep your left foot in contact with the ground throughout the swing. In practice, do it consciously and make yourself aware that you are pivoting all at one time and all in one piece. . . .

Your timing may also be off at the top of the backswing. You may be failing to *wait* for the shift of power to the left side and allowing your hands to come down far ahead of the hip. This gets the clubhead out *ahead* of the hands and the ball takes an impact that curves it to the left after it has left the tee. Failure to wait also causes the ball to be *pulled*—which is a straight flying ball that veers sharply to the left when hit.

A *smothered hook* results from a swing that is too flat, and this can be corrected at the stance. Stand tall and swing tall should be your reminder, with knees relaxed and slightly bent. If your back is straight, without being stiff, the arc of your backswing will be bigger. Don't crouch over the ball or you will find that you're getting too much of your caboose into the shot.

Check, too, that your left hand is not over too far on the shaft. Beware the creeping left hand! Don't let it swing to the right—as opposed to palming it for the slice—and be sure that you can see no more than the first three knuckles after you've taken your grip. If you have been hooking then you had the recent company of Ben Hogan, who told me that he corrected his by allowing only *two* knuckles of the left hand to show on the grip. Other experts favor a somewhat tighter grip with the left hand to correct a spell of hooking.

A hook may also be caused by a clubface that is closed at point of impact, or toed in as the backswing starts. Hold the face of the club upright and square with the ball.

Also, a closed stance, with the left foot up, will pull a ball sharply to the left and even give it a spinning hook. With woods and long irons, play a square stance.

SKYING THE BALL. A common complaint, especially from the tees or with the woods, is that the ball is popped high in the air. It comes from hitting too hard from the top of the swing, which causes the right shoulder to drop and the ball to be scooped skyward by the downward force of the clubhead. You correct this by slowing down on your downswing and not *pressing* the shot. If you really want to hit the ball a long way, let the *clubhead* do the work. Never rush a shot.

TOPPING THE BALL. On the fairway, many golfers have a tendency to try and *lift* the ball into the air, and in doing so, they lift their body on the downswing as though their arms were going to pick the ball up and send it away. But the only way to get a ball in the air is to *hit down into it*. The loft of the club, plus the down-and-through motion of the downswing, gets the ball in the air and makes it impossible to top it.

SHANKING. The question always is: Do you *shank* a shot with an open or closed face? I believe it is the result of coming down at the ball from the outside-in with a closing clubface. To correct a shank, come back straight from the ball and stay in that same inside arc on the downswing. Have the feeling that the ball must get over a high tree and you will stay back on your heels and not lunge forward on the shot and hit it from the outside.

Shanking usually develops from hooking the ball. To avoid going to the left, you come too much from the inside of the line and push your hands through to avoid hooking. This causes the locking of the wrists at impact. Take the club straight back and have more action with your wrists at impact of the ball.

But always remember this: There is nothing wrong with your golf game that a good swing can't cure. Keep your head steady, control the club with your hands, and come back and down again in a one-piece swing.

This Is My Secret

1955   BEN HOGAN

In 1947, Ben Hogan stunned the golf world, announcing that he'd found "the secret." Typically, he then went mum. Hogan went on to win eight Majors, intensifying speculation over whether he really had discovered something, or was just goading his competitors. Finally, in 1955, for the then-tidy sum of $25,000, Hogan told all to *Life* magazine. In this legendary essay, Hogan described how he turned his ruinous hook into a high fade—the shot that became his trademark—with a series of complex maneuvers that are not for the fainthearted. First, Hogan weakened his grip. Then he employed an old Scottish trick (pronation) to fan the clubhead open on his backswing. And finally, he turned his wrist inward (or "cupped" it) at the top. Hogan's clubface was thus immunized from closing down at impact, but the method, as he warned, could bring "ruin" to the average golfer's swing.

The better swing you have and the better player you become—as far as hitting the ball, that is—the more definitely you become a hooker. The mechanics of a good swing demands a hook. To get distance the hands roll into the ball just before the point of impact and after it is hit the wrists roll over the top of the shaft. When hit this way—the way the best tournament players hit it—there is nothing for the ball to do but take off low and hard. It curls from right to left at the end of its flight. It comes into a green or fairway hot, like a fighter plane landing. It is very hard to control, or at least I found it so.

Most of the top players on tour today are fighting a hook. They fight it on almost every shot they make. When they miss a shot you will find them missing the green on the left. A hook is hard to judge. Maybe one week you will be able to judge it adequately, but then the next week you aim a little farther over to the right to compensate. Sometimes a hook gets so exaggerated that you don't know where to aim, or have room to aim it. I was in this predicament in 1946, although it was more of a crisis than a predicament. I was having trouble getting the ball in the air. I had a low, ducking, agonizing hook, the kind you can hang your coat on. When it caught the rough, it was the terror of the field mice. I tried all the conventional cures—opening the stance, altering the grip, using more left arm, and cutting the ball. They all worked, but in the process they cut down my distance by five to 10 yards. Five yards is a long way. You can't give anybody five yards. You can't correct a fault with a fault.

I was finishing in the money and occasionally winning a tournament, even with a terrible game. But the handwriting was on the wall. If I was going to stay and make a living, something had to be done. I left the tour and went home to Fort Worth about as desperate as a man can be. I sat and thought for three or four days. I did not pick up a golf club, although I wanted to in the worst way. One night while laying awake in bed I began thinking about a technique for hitting a golf ball that was so old it was almost new.

It had been recommended by the Scottish pros who came to this country to teach golf long ago. Called pronation, it flourished for a while and was then discarded as antiquated and unsound. It is a movement which commences the moment a player begins his backswing. The hands roll gradually to the right until the back of the left hand is facing almost straight up at the top of the backswing and the back of the right hand almost straight down. The face of the club opens with this roll of the hands. On the downswing the face of the club gradually closes again until it is theoretically in its original position as it meets the ball. In itself pronation is no cure for a hook. If anything, it helps promote one. But for me it was the basis for a new experiment, and before the night was over I had added two adjustments, which on paper made pronation hook-proof without any loss of distance.

I was so eager to get out to the practice tee the next morning that I don't think I slept the rest of the night. The first ball I hit behaved in spectacular fashion. It had a nice, high, straight flight. Instead of hooking at the very end it had a slight fade to the right. It came down light as a feather. The harder I hit the better it worked. There was no loss of distance.

I practiced six or eight hours and couldn't wait to come back the next day. It worked even better then and for a week after that. But I had to put it to a test. Sometimes things tried in practice fall apart when tension is put on. I went to Chicago for the Tam O'Shanter and it worked under all the stresses. I won the tournament. It was like learning to play golf all over again.

The two adjustments had transformed pronation into a bonanza for me. They were so delicate that no one would ever think of looking for them—and I certainly was not going to tell anybody where to look. The first was in the grip. I moved my left hand one-eighth to one-fourth inch to the left so that the thumb was almost directly on top of the shaft. The second adjustment, which is the real meat of the "secret," was nothing more than a twist or a cocking of the left wrist.

I cupped the wrist gradually backward and inward on the backswing so that the wrist formed a slight V at the top of the swing. The angle was not more than four or six degrees, almost invisible to the human eye. This simple maneuver, in addition to the pronation, had the effect of opening the face of the club to the widest practical extreme at the top of the swing.

At this point the swing had been made hook-proof. No matter how much wrist I put into the downswing, no matter how hard I swung or how hard I tried to roll into and through the ball, the face of the club could not close fast enough to become absolutely square at the moment of impact. The result was that lovely, long-fading ball which is a highly effective weapon on any golf course.

Since stumbling onto this magic device 10 years ago, I have not seen it used by any touring pro. I was certain that it would take at least one stroke a round off a score and since we were competing, I withheld my discovery. It took more than one stroke a round off my score. I found that I did not have to work as hard because I had a ball that was easier to control. I did not have the worry and fright of getting the ball away. I was more secure in my game and did not have to practice as long or as hard as before.

In normal tournament play I used the secret approximately 90 percent of the time. Whenever I did there was nothing automatic about it. I was very conscious of cupping the left wrist. In fact, it was the only thing I concentrated on, the rest of my swing operating on muscle memory. I did not use it every time. If a shot required a hook, I simply eliminated the twist of the wrist and got it.

In this year's U.S. Open, I could use my secret only about 60 percent of the time. At the Olympic Club in San Francisco most of the doglegs to the right had a wind from left to right so that the ball had to be hooked to hold a straight line. The 10th hole, as well as the 11th and 12th, required a hook or your ball would find the rough to the right every time. This is not an alibi because I can hook a golf ball about as well as anybody. I was such an expert at it once that it almost put me out of business.

Now that I am through with serious competition—and I worked harder getting ready for this last Open than any tournament in my life—I don't mind letting the world in on my secret. The technique of hitting a golf ball is improving all the time and I hope this will prove a refinement when golfers get to a certain point. I doubt if it will be worth a doggone to the weekend duffer and it will ruin a bad golfer. With the club so wide open at the top of the backswing anybody who fails to close it properly on the way down will push the ball off to the right—or worse yet, shank it off to the right at a horrible right angle. But it will be a blessing to the good golfer. I hope it helps some distinguished but frustrated hooker get to next year's U.S. Open at Rochester, N.Y., who might not have got there otherwise.

I expect to be there to see if anything new has been added.

The Major Faults

1972 ⚑ JOHN JACOBS
WITH KEN BOWDEN

A half century after John Henry Taylor first offered cures for awkward mashie play, fellow Englishman John Jacobs revolutionized the study of faulty swings simply by looking up. Jacobs concluded that it was more *practical* to diagnose a problem by watching ball flight, then working to correct fundamentals. In effect, where the ball went told Jacobs what the golfer was doing at impact, a revelation that led to his theory of cause and effect. Jack Nicklaus endorsed the idea, a flock of studies examining the physics of hitting a golf ball confirmed it, and eventually the concept was expanded by Dr. Gary Wiren and enshrined in *The PGA Teaching Manual* under the banner "Ball Flight Laws." In this excerpt from *Practical Golf*, Jacobs wrote about specific faults, such as slices, hooks, tops, and fat shots, from his unique perspective, and offered detailed solutions every golfer can take immediately to the range.

YOU CAN STOP SLICING FOREVER IN FIVE MINUTES

I'm writing this chapter hot—and hot under the collar—from some marathon teaching sessions at my Golf Centers. Never before have I realized quite so emphatically how major a problem the slice in golf is. It really is the golfer's curse! I'm sure that at least 80 percent of the people I've seen in these sessions have sliced ever since they started trying to play the game. But the really devastating thing is their ignorance of why they slice. Not one in 50 really knows what causes his ball time and again to start left and dribble away weakly to the right.

"Why do you slice?" I ask, and usually I get the same answer: "Because I hit across the ball." This is a *contributory* factor in a slice, but it is not the basic cause. Hitting across the ball may produce a pull, or, if the clubface is shut, a quick hook. The *basic* cause of a slice—the common factor in every shot started left that bends right toward the end of its flight—is *a clubface that is open to the swing line at impact.*

You slice because the clubface is open—pointing right of the direction in which your club is traveling—as you hit the ball. Please, *please* get that fact implanted in your golfing consciousness if you really want to eradicate this disastrous shot.

The slice, like so many other faults, stems basically from the grip. Golf is such a difficult and frustrating game for so many people because they can never be bothered to develop an effective grip. Indeed, the very last thing the average golfer wants to be told by a pro is to change his grip. It's too much bother, it's too uncomfortable, it couldn't possibly make that much difference, and anyway, he's sure his faults are in his backswing, or his downswing, or his follow-through. Because he has never thought out the simple ballistics of the game, he doesn't appreciate the fundamental and very simple fact that *everything* in golf stems from the way the clubface meets the ball.

The habitual slicers are the worst in this way. They go on playing with a hold on the club that brings the clubface to the ball in an open position. Then, because with this grip if they stand square to the target line their shots go straight out to the right, subconsciously they angle themselves around until they are facing miles left of the target. The effect of this shoulder alignment is actually to increase the slice potential of their grip. Then, of course, they swing out-to-in across the ball—the only way they can swing with such a setup. With the clubface now very open to this line of swing, nothing but a sliced shot can *possibly* result.

I will repeat once again what I must have said ten thousand times: You must find a grip that returns the clubface square to your line of swing at impact. If you will not or cannot do this, your golf will always be inconsistent and, in most cases, downright lousy.

In teaching I am often able to stop a lot of golfers slicing inside five minutes. I do it simply by persuading—sometimes forcing!—them to aim the clubface at the target, with the right shoulder pulled well around—probably six or eight inches back from the position it has been in. This in itself immediately improves their grip, because it pulls the hands at address away from the left side and brings them more toward the center of the body. From this address position, I then ask the pupil to have the feeling in the takeaway that he is closing the clubface. This is essential in the early cure of a slicer, because, in his previous action, with his very open body setup and hands well forward, he is almost certain to have been rolling the clubface open with his hands and wrists in the takeaway—the only way he can get the club away from the ball on what seems to be the right path when his body is aligned miles to the left of his intended target.

The first essential, then, for the consistent slicer is to square his shoulders to the target line at address. Often this will give him the feeling that he is closed—aiming right of target. But it is *imperative* that he gets his shoulders square, and he will usually only do this if, at first, he feels closed in his upper-body alignment.

The golfer now has made room for his arms to swing up—and consequently down—on the inside. He no longer feels the need to make the pronounced rotary movement of his body to get the club back on the inside that was necessary from his open-shouldered address position—a movement that produced a reciprocal rotary body swivel on the downswing that threw the club outside the target line. It is easy for him now to develop the feeling of swinging his arms *up on the inside* in the backswing. From here they will surely swing *down on the inside*, causing his right shoulder to trail his arms instead of leading them.

I guarantee that anyone who can master this setup and arm-swing will stop slicing in five minutes. I also guarantee that he or she will be staggered and delighted by the feeling of solid striking that results. Indeed, many golfers realize after a few dozen shots like this that, for the first time in their lives, they are playing golf in a way that enables them to apply the clubhead fast and solidly into *the back* of the ball. It is a whole new experience for most.

The next stage, of course, is to modify the action according to the flight of the ball, by experimenting with the grip and shoulder alignment. If the ball hooks, the shoulders may be a little too closed at address. If it is pushed straight out to the right, the grip may be a little weak, and the hands can be moved slightly more to the right. Trial and error is necessary to consistently produce straight shots—but it must, for the congenital slicer, be within the framework of a square or slightly closed shoulder position at address and no independent action of the hands and wrists in the takeaway of the club, instead of a swivel of the body and roll of the wrists.

Another vital factor for the inveterate slicer is head position at address. Most slicers set their heads too far to the left—over or even in front of the ball—

which forces them into the open-shouldered, open-bladed setup that guarantees a slice. They should observe how the very good golfer *always* sets his head behind the ball, and looks into the back of it—the bit he wants to hit.

If you stand so that you must look at the front (or even the top) of the ball, not only are you setup for an across-the-ball swing, but your whole left side is almost certainly going to collapse as you start down. Looking at the back of the ball from behind it establishes a strong left side. Remember, when your game goes bad, that the set of the head affects the shoulder alignment and that the alignment of the shoulders has a big effect on the type of shots you will hit.

We cannot get away from the fact that golf is basically a matter of grip and setup. If you set yourself so that you must swing across the ball with an open clubface, you are doomed to slice—no other shot is possible. And the problem is that golfers who don't understand how important the setup is aggravate their faults by purely instinctive movements.

The slicer, indeed, is the supreme example. The ball goes to the right, and the more it does, the more he sets himself to the left—shoulders open, head in front of the ball, and, worst of all, a slicer's weak grip. Eventually, poor soul, he gets to the stage where the only thing he can possibly do is produce feeble banana shots from far left to far right.

Thus, the slicer's first task must *always* be to get himself into a square address position—shoulders, hips, knees, and feet parallel to the target line, or even slightly "inside" it. This will enable him to grip the club in a way that will let him swing the clubface through the ball looking at the target.

HELP FOR HOOKERS—AND PULLERS WHO THINK THEY'RE HOOKERS

The fact that there are fewer "natural" hookers in golf than slicers is very little consolation to the player whose every other shot darts sharply off to the left. True, he is likely to be a better golfer than his opposite number, but at times he will be in such a mess as to be virtually a non-starter. A genuine hook—a hard-hit ball swinging violently left—is a shot ranking in the disaster quotient with the shank.

The slicer, although a weak striker and short hitter, can usually at least remain in the park, because a "cut" ball flies, lands, and rolls more softly than a hooked ball. It is for this reason that so many professionals and first-class amateurs favor a slight fade, and why at the highest levels of the game one hears so much about "blocking" shots. To the good player, especially if he hits the ball a long way, a hook is a constant threat.

Even though a hooker usually has some knowledge of golf, like the slicer his problem stems from lack of basic analysis of cause and effect. He may have thought hard and long about his swing, but he hasn't taken the problem to its root, which is the direction in which the clubhead approaches the ball and the alignment of its face at impact.

I have proof of this daily. Good players come to me and say they are hooking. I ask them to do so. They hit a few shots, and, true enough, the ball goes to the left. But in many cases it does not "bend" to the left. It flies straight to the left, or starts left and then goes more left. These shots are not hooks. They are pulls and pulled hooks. And the important thing is that they do not stem from the sort of action that produces a genuine hook. They stem, indeed, from the very opposite, from a slicer's action, an out-to-in swing. All they lack is the slicer's open clubface at impact. If these self-described "hookers" were to hit the ball with an open clubface, they would in fact slice. If they were just to swing the club through the ball in the right direction, all would be well.

In golf, it really does help to know what you are actually doing before you try to alter it!

The genuinely hooked shot starts to the *right* of the target, then swings away to the left. If its turn is gentle, the shot is described as being "drawn"—perhaps the most useful "shape" for the average player, in that the kind of spin imparted to the ball increases both carry and run. If the turn is violent, the shot is disastrous at any level of the game. In both instances, and in every variation in between, the shot is made by the club coming to the ball from inside the target line with the face at impact closed to the line of swing.

(I might add here, for the benefit of people who hit the ball straight to the right and think they slice, that in fact they have a hooker's action, except that the clubface is square to their inside-out swing.)

It should be clear by now that the hooker hooks because something in his action brings his club to the ball on an "inside" path with the face closed to that path. What is that something, and how does he adjust to it?

We must go back, as always, to the clubface. If it comes into the ball closed, an in-to-out swing will naturally follow, due to the golfer instinctively trying to swing the club to the right to counteract the "bend" in his shots. The hooker's first job, then, is simple: to square his clubface, which will make the ball fly straight along its starting path—in the same direction as he is swinging. This usually requires nothing more than some intelligent grip adjustment.

If you are a true hooker it is more than likely that you close the clubface at impact because your grip is too "strong"—your left hand is too much on top and your right too much underneath the shaft. Move both hands bit by bit to the left. It will feel uncomfortable for a while, but it will be worth the effort in the long run. A loose grip with the left hand very often closes the clubface, too, so make sure your hands work as a unit during the swing.

Persevering like this, you will eventually find that the ball, instead of starting right and turning left, starts right and continues that way. You have now swapped your hook for a push. Don't be disappointed. You have made the first of two adjustments, and are now ready to tackle the second.

If the ball now flies straight, your hands must be returning the clubface square to the line of your swing. It follows, therefore, that if the ball is not going where you think you are aiming, either your aim or your direction of swing is wrong. In this case you are pushing the ball straight to the right of your intended target. What does that mean? Simply that you are aiming to the right of the target when you set up to the shot, in order to allow for your old hook, and thus are swinging the club along that line of aim—i.e., too much from inside to outside the proper ball-to-target line.

Your second task, therefore, is simple: Aim and set yourself correctly. Arrange your feet, knees, hips, and shoulders—especially shoulders—parallel to the target line with your clubface looking squarely at the target. As a hooker, you may feel as though you are now aiming miles left. You can check your feet by lining up with a club on the ground. Get someone to check your shoulders by laying a club across them after you've taken your stance.

IF YOU TOP SHOTS,
YOUR SWING IS TOO "STEEP"

Ask golfers what causes a topped shot and most will immediately say "head up." You hear it time and again on golf courses all over the world. One member of a fourball scuttles a shot along the ground. "Head up!" exclaim the other three. They haven't actually seen their chum lift his head—indeed, they may not even have been watching him swing. But that doesn't matter. It has to be "head up."

Usually they are wrong. Lifting the head can cause the body to lift also, and when this happens it is true that the ball may be topped. But only a small proportion of thinly hit shots stem from such a movement. Even if you anchored their heads in cement, a great many poor players would still manage to top the ball quite effectively—because the fault is not in their superstructure, it is built into their games by faulty swing patterns.

There are two basic causes of topping, they are closely allied to each other, and they emanate from a particular kind of swing geometry.

To achieve flush contact with the back of the ball the clubhead must be square and also travel through the impact zone on a reasonably shallow arc, moving from inside the target line, to straight along it, to inside again.

The chronic slicer never achieves this shallow arc at impact or an inside-straight-through-inside clubhead path. For various reasons, usually arising from his setup, he brings the club to the ball from well outside the target line—across the ball. Even the most elementary knowledge of geometrical principles indicates that this must severely steepen, or narrow, the arc described by the clubhead as it approaches the ball.

It can easily be understood that, even if the shot is reasonably effective—and 70 percent of golfers play all their lives like this—the club has not hit the ball squarely in the back. To a greater or lesser degree, impact has been made on the top farside corner of the ball as the golfer sees it at address. Now, imagine what happens if the downswing becomes just a little more across the target line from out to in, and thus even steeper. The angle of attack becomes so acute that the clubhead cannot connect even with two-thirds of the ball, as happens in the normal slice. Its approach is so steep that it can contact, if anything, only the top

half of the ball, or perhaps even only the top quarter of an inch. Result: a top—usually a top along the ground to the left.

From this, it should be clear that topping has little to do with your head, but is really the ultimate expression of a steep out-to-in, slicing-and-pulling swing pattern. That, in fact, is why the fault is so common among long and middle-handicap golfers, and so rare among good players.

The cure is equally obvious. To stop topping, you must stop slicing! You must, in fact, set yourself in such a position at address, and use the club in such a way, that you can swing into the back of the ball from behind and inside it, not over and down on it.

The second cause of topping is very much allied to the foregoing. Again, it is largely a poor player's fault, but it also sometimes afflicts the competent golfer, because it can happen even when the setup, swing arc, and plane are good.

At address on every golf shot, the radius of the swing—the measurement from player to ball—is established by the unit of the left arm and the club, held in a more-or-less straight line. In the early part of the backswing this radius is maintained by the "one-piece" (no independent movements) combination of arm swing and shoulder turn. But at some point in the action, where we cock our wrists, the radius obviously decreases. If, then, in hitting the ball, the wrists do not un-cock sufficiently to re-establish the radius of the swing at impact—re-establishing the left arm and club as a straight-line unit—the ball is likely to be topped, or at least hit "thin." Among fairly competent players this is the commonest cause of topping.

In the simplest terms, what basically causes both these "tops"—and also most thin or "bladed" shots—is too little use of the arms, hands, and clubhead in the downswing. The inveterate slicer should understand that this problem is built into his game because of his steep downswing, which in turn emanates from his open clubface and out-to-in swing path. In the case of the better player, such lack of arm and wrist action arises usually from a deliberate attempt to "hit late." He would benefit from thinking of the downswing as a "re-measuring"—of getting his left arm and club back to the full radius of the address position before impact.

"FAT" SHOTS AT ADDRESS

Fluffing is hitting the ground behind the ball, or hitting shots "fat." There are two common causes of this depressing disease.

Among both good and indifferent golfers alike, it can often be caused by nothing more complicated than bad posture at address, leading to loss of balance during the swing. The golfer stands to the ball in such a way—usually crouching or reaching for it—that his weight is pulled forward onto his toes. Inevitably the momentum of the downswing throws him even farther forward, with the result that he either "falls into" the shot, or is forced to dip his head and shoulders to get the clubhead to meet the ball. To avoid such a destructive fault is just one more reason why we must always start the swing from the correct setup, remembering particularly in this case that the back must be reasonably straight.

The most common cause of fluffing among reasonably accomplished golfers is poor coordination of body and hand action in the downswing. It is the opposite of a topper's problem—a tendency to hit *too early* with the hands and wrists, before the hips have cleared a way for them to swing past the body and out toward the target.

As most slicers are prone to topping, so most hookers are liable to fluff occasional shots. What happens is that the fluffer lengthens his swing radius by letting the clubhead catch up with and pass his hands before they have arrived back at the ball. In other words, the arc the clubhead is describing as it approaches impact is too wide—the hit is too "early" with the hands and arms. It is, indeed, to avoid catching the ground that ladies—most of whom must hit "early" to get the clubhead moving at maximum speed by impact—instinctively rise on their toes during the downswing.

For men golfers, however, the cure for this fault is definitely not to be found in ballet dancing. The fluffer's basic problem is to better coordinate his downswing leg-hip movement with his arm and hand action—even to the point, for a time, of deliberately restricting his wrist action—deliberately hitting "later" with the hands and wrists.

From *Practical Golf*, by John Jacobs, with Ken Bowden. Stanley Paul & Co., Ltd., an imprint of the Hutchinson Group. Copyright © 1972 John Jacobs and Ken Bowden. Used with the permission of John Jacobs.

READ THE DIVOTS

In the British magazine *Today's Golfer*, former Masters champion Ian Woosnam said that a golfer can "read his divots" to determine if swing path is correct. If a divot mark is pointing left, the Welshman said, the golfer is hitting the ball from outside to in and cutting across it, which signals a slice or pull. If the divot is pointing to the right, it means the golfer is hitting too much from in to out, which produces a hook or push. ❧

What'd I Do Wrong, Coach?

2000 — Kellie Stenzel

"I assume that the reader knows nothing about the game," Kellie Stenzel wrote in her first book, *The Women's Guide to Golf: A Handbook for Beginners*. Since then, Stenzel, a popular instructor at the exclusive Atlantic Club in Bridgehampton, New York, has been named a Top 50 Teacher by *Golf for Women* magazine and broadened her target audience by writing more instructional volumes. Beginners still flock to her, but, significantly, even with more advanced readers and students, she caters to the insecure novice that lurks inside *all* golfers. In this excerpt from her first book, Stenzel plays coach to the proverbial duffer, providing a highly evolved, beautifully organized, and very welcome mode of instructional writing that details how to cure errors such as shanking, topping, and hitting fat. Stenzel identifies several possible causes for each fault, and then offers advice for corrections that involve checking various fundamentals, or performing specifically tailored drills.

By now in your golf career, you may have concluded that there are unlimited ways of hitting the ball badly, simply by combining your bad shots. So when your teaching professional asks you at your next lesson what your predominant shotmaking error is, you don't have to respond with a puzzled look. Your capability to describe your most prevalent shotmaking error guides your teaching professional to the most direct route to your error. . . .

Shank

A shank is definitely not a fun miss. In the resulting shot, not a pretty one, the ball often travels directly right and low.

Once the manager at Atlantic [the club in Bridgehampton, New York, where I teach] was out playing golf with the manager from another club on Long Island and since they were playing quicker than my foursome we waved them to play through. The visiting manager had a brutal case of the shanks. He just kept shanking the golf ball in a circle right around the green. Eventually he just picked up his golf ball. It was painful to watch him circle around the green, shanking the golf ball, ending up farther away from the pin after each shot.

- *Cause:* The clubhead getting outside the ball, so that the ball is contacted in the neck or hosel of the club.
- *Correction:* Obtain a headcover or a towel from off your golf bag. Lay it down about three or four inches away from your golf ball, on the side of the ball farther away from you and on your intended line of flight. Then swing the club without contacting the headcover or towel. If your club crosses outside the ball, the ball will probably hit the heel. Practice

with the headcover or towel until you stop hitting the box, and your shanks should disappear. In my opinion, you do not want to place anything solid on the outside of the ball; if you shank the ball, you *do* get your club outside the ball. Place something soft, so that when you do make this incorrect motion you will be aware of your mistake, but you will not run the risk of injuring yourself. I have seen people practicing this with wooden boards. It does not seem worth the risk to me. So if this is your problem, please use something soft.

→ *Cause:* Not properly squaring the clubface at impact, which will leave the face of the club open, exposing the hosel of the club to the ball.
→ *Correction:* Practice making half-swings. Hold your finish to check to see if the toe of your club is up or skyward, rather than having the face of the club skyward. If your clubface is pointing to the sky so that you could serve a drink on your clubface you have not allowed the club to naturally rotate through with your body.

→ *Cause:* Addressing the ball in the hosel at setup.
→ *Correction:* Address the ball in the center of the clubface. It may appear more out toward the toe of the club from the player's perspective.

→ *Cause:* Left hand grip rotated too far to the left.
→ *Correction:* Hold grip in fingers, so that the palm faces toward your body and you can see two to three knuckles.

Players who shank their shots will not like their irons. They will tend to prefer the woods, simply because the woods do not have a hosel and the irons do. You can spot shankers by their golf bags. They will have a lot of woods, and their irons will have dimple marks in the heels of the clubs. When they first start to understand the reason that they do not like their irons, because they are contacting the ball in the hosel, they are on the road to being able to correct the problem. You must first understand what you are doing incorrectly, and then you must understand what you need to change to make that correction.

TOPPED BALL

A topped ball, though very common, can be very frustrating to a new golfer. You will hit some tops. It is just part of your initiation process into the game of golf. Over time your percentage of tops should decrease, but expect some of this in the first couple of years. The suggestions here are to help you minimize your tops.

When I arrived at Furman University with approximately a 4 handicap, I would top my fairway woods once in a while. I was so embarrassed I would wait to practice them when the range was nearly

Contemporary teaching pro Kellie Stenzel, here displaying a flawless swing, specializes in curing the swing faults of others.

empty. If a 4 handicap can top the ball, it is OK for you. I forced myself to practice the fairway woods. Working on the weak points of your game is not as much fun as practicing what you are good at, but it will help you improve.

I was giving a playing lesson when one of my students, Carole, topped the golf ball off the tee of a par 3. I quickly picked up the golf ball and placed it back onto her tee to try again. She then proceeded to knock the golf ball into the hole. It was quite an impressive par!

→ *Cause:* If you have a great deal of tension in your arms, this will cause the muscles in your arms to contract, which in turn causes your arms to pull in toward you.
→ *Correction:* Relax adequately so that you can feel the clubhead swinging freely.

→ *Cause:* Terraphobia, fear of hitting the ground.
→ *Correction:* Place a tee in the ground in front of your golf ball, and allow the clubhead to stay very low to the ground in front of the ball, which will allow you to use the loft of the club properly. Many women fear hitting the ground for two reasons: it will hurt or it will make a mess. It should not hurt unless you are "death-gripping" the club, and it is OK to make a mess, also known as a divot.

→ *Cause:* A lack of understanding of how the ball gets into the air.
→ *Correction:* Understand that the lower side of the club must be allowed to swing down to the ground to get the ball into the air. There is a phrase in golf "let the clubhead do the work." The true meaning is "permit the loft of the club to lift the ball into the air for you." Our tennis players must specifically watch this. In tennis you must swing up to get the ball into the air, because the tennis racket has no loft. In golf we must get the club down to the ground to get the ball into the air. So in other words, we are hitting the ball as the club travels on a descending path.

→ *Cause:* Standing too far away from the golf ball.
→ *Correction:* Check your setup to make sure that there is only one hand's distance between the end of the grip of the club and your body.

→ *Cause:* Your weight is too much back toward your heels.
→ *Correction:* Bend forward from your hip joint, so that your chest is over your toes.

→ *Cause:* Loss of spine angle, also known as "standing up."
→ *Correction:* Maintain posture throughout the swing until contact with the ball.

"Fat" Shot

A fat shot occurs when you hit the ground before the golf ball. The ball will travel significantly shorter than anticipated.

→ *Cause:* Standing too close to the ball.
→ *Correction:* Back away from the ball adequately, so that you have approximately a hand's width, fingers outstretched, between the end of the golf club and your legs.

→ *Cause:* Tilting, rather than turning on your swing.
→ *Correction:* If your shoulders dip, rather than turning around your spine, when your right shoulder drops on the forward swing the ground will often be contacted before the ball. Cross your arms across your chest and practice turning around your spine, so that your sternum turns away from the target, rather than the shoulders' teeter-tottering.

→ *Cause:* Staying too flat-footed on your forward swing.
→ *Correction:* As you make a natural underhand throwing motion on your forward swing you should allow your body to turn to face the target so that your right foot comes up to the toe in reaction to the body turning to face the target. The turning of the body toward the target will pull the club to swing through toward the target.

TOED SHOT

This is a shot hit off the toe or tip of the club. It usually goes 90 degrees to the right and is potentially lethal. Do not allow anyone to stand directly to the right of you when you are practicing if you tend to toe your shots. Or place something like your golf bag to the right of the ball, to stop the ball from advancing too far to the right.

I was giving a lesson in New York right next to two other lessons. My student proceeded to toe the ball excessively off the end of the wood. The ball ever so softly lofted right over the instructor and the student directly to our right and landed like a marshmallow on the chest of the instructor two doors down. It landed so softly it was unbelievable. Nobody was hurt, but it was amazing to see the golf ball go so high, so right, and so short.

> ✷ *Cause:* Standing too far away from the ball.
> ✷ *Correction:* Determine if you have only one hand's distance (fingers extended) between the end of the club and your legs.

> ✷ *Cause:* Arms pulling in on forward swing.
> ✷ *Correction:* Work on swinging wide on the forward swing. Place a tee several inches ahead of your ball, along your flight line. Try to hit that tee as you swing through the ball. You will also want to check hand position in your grip. If your grip is too weak or, in other words, your hands rotated too far to the left, you will often try to pull across the ball to square the clubface, causing you to pull in and toe the ball.

> ✷ *Cause:* Loss of spine angle.
> ✷ *Correction:* Maintain posture throughout the swing, as opposed to standing up. Your weight should maintain its position on the balls of your feet and not throw back to your heels at any point in the swing.

SKIED SHOT

A skied shot or a pop-up with your teed woods is a ball that travels excessively high and not very far.

> ✷ *Cause:* Incorrect ball position.
> ✷ *Correction:* Make sure that your ball position for your teed woods is left in your stance, in line with the inside of your left foot.

> ✷ *Cause:* Too steep an angle of attack. The angle at which the clubhead comes into the golf ball is the angle at which the ball will come off the clubhead.
> ✷ *Correction:* Feel that your swing is more circular, rather than resembling the letter V. Take practice swings where your club sweeps an extended patch of grass, rather than digging into the ground. You should not take a divot with a teed wood.

Bad advice that is often given to the beginner who is popping the golf ball up is to tee the ball lower. What you actually want to do is tee the ball higher. When the ball is teed too low, the student feels the necessity to go down to get the golf ball and dives, producing too steep an angle of approach. So tee the ball higher and practice not hitting the ground by sweeping the golf ball off the high tee. . . .

KEEP A NOTEBOOK FOR PROGRESS

We all tend to repeat our mistakes, so keep a small notebook of your problems with your golf and what you and your professional do to correct the particular problem. If that particular problem resurfaces, you can refer back to your notebook and correct your problems quicker. If we learn from our mistakes, they are worth making!

— *12* —

TROUBLE
SHOTS

HOW TO
GET OUT OF JAIL

Hazards and General Remarks

1904 ⚒ GENEVIEVE HECKER
(MRS. CHARLES T. STOUT)

Modern golfers will recognize a timeless piece of advice in this passage from America's first instructional book by a woman for women. Lady champion Genevieve Hecker wrote that if you can let the club—which has natural loft—do the work, you will escape hazards. As any current pro will say, getting the ball up and out of trouble, such as from a lie in long grass, sometimes demands a swing similar to that used in a bunker. Hecker recommended: Open the blade, trust your swing, and hit down and through the ball, rather than try to lift it. Unfortunately, if casual observation during a typical day on the golf course is any indication, Hecker's simple, sound formula has been ignored by many high-handicap female—and male—golfers for more than a century.

———————

When the ball is in long grass the same principles should be employed as when it is in a bunker—that is, the straightest possible swing should be used, and the ground struck a few inches back of the ball instead of the ball itself. The reason for this is that if the rounder and longer swing is used, the grass is apt to catch it and break its force, and even if the force is not broken, to deflect it from its course. Another point to remember for use in an emergency . . . is that by turning the face of the club the ball can be made to fly at an angle, even when played with a straight swing, and this knowledge is often handy when there are trees or fences or other obstructions which make it impossible to play a full stroke in the direction in which it is wished to send the ball.

Another point which most beginners seem to find impossible to comprehend is that the loft which its maker gave to a mashie or niblick is quite sufficient to loft the ball when it is struck with an ordinary stroke. Why this is such a difficult matter to understand I cannot imagine, but it is a fact that nine out of every ten players make the mistake. That it is one, a moment's reflection will show, for if the club's face were not made as it is for just this purpose, why should it be changed from the straight face of a cleek?

Under no circumstances, therefore, try to make a swing which will aid the ball to rise—all that you need to do is to play the stroke correctly and see that you hit the ball.

Of course if you [need to create extra loft to clear a high object in front of you] it is advisable to turn the club in your hand so as to lay back its face a little, and to stand a little further behind the ball than usual, but under ordinary circumstances the club's face will do all that is required, provided you hit the ball squarely.

From *Golf for Women*, by Genevieve Hecker (Mrs. Charles T. Stout). The Baker & Taylor Company, New York, N.Y.

Recovering From the Rough and Playing From Difficulties

1924 ✣ CECIL LEITCH

Charlotte Cecilia (Cecil) Pitcairn Leitch grew up on the windy, hilly links of Silloth—a championship course in northern England—playing with the boys and imitating their swings. She emerged with an aggressive style that set a new tone for British women golfers prior to World War I and into the '20s. She won twelve national titles, including the British Women's Amateur Championship a record four times, while engaging in a ferocious rivalry with Joyce Wethered. She beat Wethered in 1921, but lost to her in 1922 and 1925. In this excerpt from her book, *Golf Simplified*, Leitch offered timeless advice on coping with the difficulties free-wheeling players such as she inevitably encounter. She included an engaging description of how despite wearing the restrictive, long skirts of the period, she managed to scramble, straddle, and improvise shots from a variety of sloping lies, and creatively bend the ball in howling winds.

———◆———

There are many lady players who are as good as the best so long as they keep down the middle and on the fairway, but when they are called upon to recover from the rough, or play from difficulties, their weaknesses are disclosed. Then, again, the majority of lady players are very poor performers in a wind. I shall try, therefore, to make these difficulties appear less terrifying by explaining the methods of play which I have found to be the most satisfactory under these varying conditions.

When the ball is lying in the rough the player is inclined to overestimate the difficulty of the shot. Instead of trying to get as far as possible many players are quite content to find the fairway. This may be a wise precaution under certain circumstances, but playing for safety does not tend to improve one's form. It must be admitted, however, that it is almost impossible to get any length from the thick juicy grass, which is a difficulty to be feared by every player on an inland course during the summer. This type of grass has an unpleasant habit of winding itself round the shaft of the club and taking the sting out of the shot. To recover from a lie of this kind the niblick must be used and gripped very firmly, the player must stand well over the ball, and the swing must be of an upright nature. A point about an inch behind the ball should be aimed at and the action should be more of a chop than a sweep. It might be truthfully described as a stab with a full swing. From difficulties of this kind the player must apply all the force at her command, and in order to do so she will have to use a well-controlled full backward swing. No mere half or three-quarter swing will remove the ball. . . .

The ordinary wiry grass of a seaside links or that to be found on an inland course during the winter is not really so trying. . . . The player must use her discretion as to which club is the right one, but here I should like to point out the value of a spoon for use in the rough. . . . Unless the ball is cupped in the rough, I invariably take my spoon, and standing well over the ball, use a swing similar to that employed in the push shot.

For a more cupped lie a mashie iron, a mashie, or niblick should be taken and the ball stabbed out. It is utterly useless to try to get a ball out of the rough with the ordinary sweep and hit of a full drive or brassy shot.

When playing a ball that is teed up in the rough, it is essential that the player address it with the club off the ground. She who puts the clubhead on the ground in such circumstances, instead of keeping it on a level with the ball, not only runs the risk of causing the ball to move, but will be almost certain to cut right under it.

Heather should be treated in the same way as grass, but here again I must refer to the versatile qualities of the spoon. Having been brought up on a links where heather abounds, there are few things I do not know about it. From thick heather the player must be content to regain the fairway by methods similar to those employed when in the thick grass of an inland course, but when the ball is lying even reasonably well the spoon is by far the best club to use. It is strange, but nevertheless true, that heather has far less effect upon a spoon or even a brassy than it has upon an iron club. In some strange way a spoon seems to glide over the heather and meet the ball truly, but the player must assist it to do so by putting a little bit of "push" into the stroke.

The Hanging Lie

We have been in the rough long enough; we must now deal with difficult lies on the fairway, of which the "hanging lie" is the one most feared by lady players. When called upon to play in this position many players use a lofted iron club and play for safety, but there are many occasions that make a brassy or spoon the more effective club. Provided there is not a sharp rise immediately ahead the player need not lose very much distance from a clean hanging lie. There are two methods which can be adopted, but the easier, to my mind, is as follows. Use the ordinary grip and

take up a stance rather behind the ball, putting most of the weight on the right foot. Address the ball about an inch behind and use a full easy swing and follow-through, similar to an ordinary brassy shot allowing the clubhead to travel along the slope of the ground in the direction of the hole. Many players are inclined to dig at a ball lying in this position, but this is quite unnecessary and every player would be well advised to depend upon the loft of the club to raise the ball. It will do so naturally if this smooth sweeping action and hit are employed.

The other method of playing from a downward slope with a wooden club is to use an open stance, stand behind the ball, placing most of the weight on the right foot, and draw the face of the club across the ball by means of the swing which imparts a slice or cut. In this swing the clubhead is taken back in a line outside the ball and is brought down sharply by bending the right knee at the moment of impact. This is the more difficult method of playing the shot as the player has to allow for the slice, but I must admit there are times when it is the only one to play. Risks have to be taken sometimes and when rising ground has to be avoided and the ball has to be played from a hanging lie on to a green which can only be reached with a brassy or spoon, this shot must be attempted, as it gets the ball up sharply.

The Uphill Lie

The "uphill" lie is a very simple one from which to play, and a brassy, spoon, or iron can be used according to the length of shot required. Throughout the playing of the stroke the right leg is used to support the body and in order to do so it must be stiff. The head must be kept still, as there is always a tendency to fall back from the ball. The right shoulder should be dropped slightly in the address in order to bring it and the left shoulder parallel to the slope of the ground. Provided these points are observed the player can play the stroke in the same manner as she would if the ball were lying on level ground, in that the clubhead must be allowed to follow the slope of the ground.

It is as well to add that when playing to the green from an uphill lie the player should always use a club one higher in power than she would were the ball on the level. The upward slope causes the ball to be thrown high in the air and so takes from the distance.

Cecil Leitch urged aggressive play when hitting from the inevitable "bad patch."

Above and Below the Ball

The variety of lies and stances to be found, especially on a seaside links, compels me to mention those in which the player is standing above or below the ball.

For the former the players must grip the club as near the end of the leather as possible. Playing a great deal of golf on undulating links, I find it advisable to have my brassy an inch longer than my driver, in order to be prepared for this type of lie and stance. The player is obliged to adopt a rather stooping position, but if she keeps her head still the shot should not present any further difficulties and can be played as an ordinary brassy or spoon shot. Of course, should an iron club be used, it will be played in the usual manner.

When standing above the ball there is a tendency to slice with a wooden club, but this is due to the player's failure to follow through. It is wise to allow for a slice by playing to the left of the direct line. The majority of players will probably agree that it is easier to play a shot when standing above the ball than when standing below it. The latter is an unpleasant position, as one feels unable to get any power into the stroke. When length is required I find my spoon a most accommodating implement. The rounded sole does not object to being dropped at the heel as would that of an iron or brassy. I have often played satisfactory shots with this club when the ball has been lying on a level with my waist. A still head, a shortened firm grip, and a stance slightly behind the ball are the chief essentials. This alteration in stance is the simplest way to overcome the inevitable pull from such a lie and stance. . . .

Playing in the Wind

Lucky is the golfer who started to play the game on a windy seaside links. There is no finer nor fairer hazard than a stiff breeze or young gale, and she who can play well in a wind will find all other conditions simple.

There is no doubt that any successes with which I have met are largely the result of the experience I gained as child on the Silloth links, where the wind blows hard and often.

Let me, therefore, try to help those who have not been so fortunate, by handing on certain points which I have discovered and found effective when playing in a wind.

When playing against a wind a low ball is essential and the well-hit ball will not be seriously affected. In order to hit a low ball I have found the following method the best and safest.

With a driver, brassy, or spoon, I shorten my grip, hold the club very firmly and stand rather nearer the ball with my feet gripping the ground, the weight rather more on the left foot and my knees stiff. My backward swing is flat, slow, and not as full as usual. The forward swing is well controlled and finishes with a low follow-through. Pressing and snatching must be avoided at all costs, and the player must endeavor to make the clubhead follow along the line of play for a few inches after it has met the ball, in order to avoid the tendency to fall back onto the right leg at the moment of impact.

The "push" shot should be used with all iron clubs when playing against the wind. The ball that is hit in the more ordinary floppy manner is absolutely at the mercy of the wind, and can be blown hither and thither like a feather, but the ball that is hit with a punch will cut through the wind like a bullet.

Approaching against a wind is a comparatively simple matter, so there is no need to dwell upon the subject.

Playing downwind is also a simple business, but I should warn the player against the tendency to stand too far behind the ball. It is correct to have the weight rather more on the right leg than usual, but I have seen players overdo this action sufficiently often to know that a warning is necessary. The result of this is a topped ball, as the clubhead hits the ball on the up-ward sweep of the follow-through. After playing against the wind for a number of holes the first drive downwind is invariably topped on account of the player's anxiety to get behind the ball and so hit it up for the wind to assist it on its way.

I always consider the iron shot downwind onto the green with a bunker just short as one of the most difficult shots. This is one of the few occasions when the "floppy" iron shot is preferable to the "push" shot. The latter will race over the green, but the former will drop in a tired manner if hit high. When approaching with the wind behind it is advisable to keep the ball as low as possible. The pitch and run will generally give the best results.

As I am here writing for those who have passed the elementary stage, it is almost superfluous to add that the player should always try to place her ball in such a position that she is approaching or putting against the wind rather than with it. The difficulties of playing against the wind or downwind are nothing compared to those to be encountered when a strong wind is sweeping across the course.

On uphill lies, Leitch put her weight on her right leg and set her shoulders parallel to the ground, employing techniques still taught by today's pros.

Ladies are at a greater disadvantage than men under these conditions as skirts are a handicap, and there is nothing so tiring nor so trying as endeavoring to keep one's balance, when the wind is blowing on one's back or face. A firm stance and a still head are terribly difficult to retain under these conditions, but they are essential.

Some players make use of the wind by playing for a slice when it is blowing from left-to-right, and for a pull when it is blowing from right-to-left. Personally I do not recommend such tactics, and I always try to hit the ball through the wind. It is surprising how little the flight of a well-hit ball is affected by a crosswind. Once a player begins to tamper with her game by trying to use the wind she will find herself in all kinds of trouble. It is all very well for first-class amateurs and professionals to play advanced golf of this kind, but I am convinced I am right in saying that every lady player should try to hit the ball down the middle of the fairway with a short, well-controlled swing recommended by driving and brassy and spoon shots against the wind. It is true that when the wind is blowing from right-to-left the pulled ball will travel farther, but bunkers and rough await the errant shot, and the rubber-cored ball is exceedingly difficult to control when topspin is applied. . . .

When playing in a right-to-left wind I prefer slicing my wooden-club shots rather than pulling them. A sliced shot may not go so far, but it is invariably kept on the fairway with the help of the wind, and to be on the fairway is the main thing after all.

One of the worst gales I ever played in was that which prevailed on a certain Open Meeting day held by the Guildford Ladies' Golf Club. It was bad in the morning, but it was ghastly in the afternoon, and many of the competitors retired with wrecked umbrellas and soaking wet clothes. Personally, I quite enjoyed the experience, as the weather conditions and the very hilly exposed course called for the playing of unusual shots. Anything but a firmly hit ball with a low trajectory was carried away by the gale, and when playing with the wind blowing from left-to-right one had to lean against it to avoid being blown onto the ball.

My partner and I were rewarded for our perseverance . . . by winning prizes which took the very appropriate form of umbrellas; but the experience we gained during that round would have been quite sufficient reward.

The wind is a wonderful teacher, and every player should seize the opportunities offered to her of becoming acquainted with its tricks. It will emphasize one's faults, it will point out one's weaknesses, but, at the same time, it will show its appreciation of one's real skill and it will at all times treat everyone with fairness.

From *Golf Simplified*, by Cecil Leitch. Thornton Butterworth, Ltd., London, England.

HOLD TIGHT

Lee Trevino offered classic advice for playing out of the rough, the only shot in golf where gripping the club tightly is a good idea. "The deeper the grass, the tighter the grip," Trevino said in the August 1985 edition of *Golf Digest*. Golfers as far back as Cecil Leitch offered the same counsel because a tight grip keeps the club from twisting and closing in the cabbage. ❧

In Difficulties

1940 ◆ RICHARD BURTON

Dick Burton holds one record that will probably never be broken—he was the defending British Open Champion for seven years. A club pro from Cheshire, Burton won in 1939 at St. Andrews, and then spent his prime golfing years in the army during World War II while the championship was suspended. Sam Snead won the next Open in 1946 with Bobby Locke the runner-up, while Burton faded to 12th. In this essay from the man who Dan Jenkins listed among the worst golfers to ever win a major, Burton showed what he *was* best at: breezy instructional writing that holds up exceedingly well even today. Focusing on both the strategy and execution of shots from the rough, he advised golfers to assess their lies and then determine the options, suggesting that sometimes it is more prudent to lay up than attempt "miraculous" recovery shots.

Practice! I seem intent on keeping the student's nose to the grindstone, but I am loathe to make golf an irksome duty, even if I gave you the credit of resisting the lure of the round itself while you are seeking the path to efficiency.

Let us then, as an antidote to boredom, even if it is only a subterfuge to coat the pill, play a few holes. I cannot hope that you have sufficiently imbibed the principles I have laid down to carry yourself untroubled from tee to green, and it is impossible for me to expunge from your play the human element, those errors and omissions which seem to endow the ball with a will of its own, so that it finds the rough which [has] been placed there to receive it. While [such] checks to good scoring can be annoying, they are also part of the charm of the game, and a very successful recovery shot can give as much pleasure as any other, signifying as it does a triumph over adversity.

But trouble too often means a troubled mind to the player. As he walks into the rough . . . his assurance is at low ebb, and too often he feels that he must pay for his previous bad shot, which may not have been so bad after all but only slightly off line. In this frame of mind he usually pays, because he has not determined that recovery is not only possible, but probable if he tackles it in the right way. At some time in the round he is going to need his resource and determination to escape the consequences of a loose shot, and it is necessary for him to be equipped with the means of getting out of trouble. . . .

A tendency exists in golf to exaggerate our difficulties, not because of the difficulties themselves, though they in all conscience can exercise our minds, but because of their relation to the task we have to undertake. Ideal golf, I suppose, is a drive down the fairway, a shot to the green, and two putts; anything that tends to deviate from that standard does not become a simple difficulty in itself, but grows in relation to what is still left to achieve in getting that par four. Thus, a drive that has found the rough off the fairway 200 yards from the green leaves us, in our minds, with a shot of 200 yards to be made from the rough. To get out of it at all respectably may in itself be a difficulty; it becomes emphasized when we have to think also of hitting the ball 200 yards in order to reach the green, take our regulation two putts, and so preserve our four.

Thus our approach to the shot from the rough is wrong. We are in no frame of mind to deal with the next shot as it demands, that is, to consider it purely on its own merits; the nature of the rough and whether the ball is lying well or ill in it. This should be our first consideration, and all else for the moment should be shut out of our minds. Only in that way are we in a position to deal adequately with the shot itself. By deciding our shot on the position as we find it we give ourselves the best chance of recovering, and if only we could rigidly adhere to that policy we should save ourselves from repeating over and over again our mistakes in shots from the rough. Usually we walk up to the ball conscious that we have to hit it 200 yards, and somehow we have to give ourselves the chance to do it. At first sight our common sense tells us to take a No. 7 and be content to get back on the fairway. Yet what are we prone to do? We take out our spoon, say: "I'll have a go at it," and swing distractedly at the ball with the foreknowledge that we are doomed to failure. Even if we recognize that an iron is suitable to the occasion we use a No. 3 instead of a No. 5 in the hope, too often in vain, that we can at least make an appreciable inroad on the distance that lies before us. The result is likely to be that neither the spoon nor the No. 3, if they do succeed in clearing the rough, send the ball as far as the No. 5 would have done, and we are left with another desperate shot if we are to rescue our par figure.

To be fair to ourselves we should acknowledge that rough has been left to grow off the fairway to exact a penalty for a wayward shot, and that to ignore that penalty is to invite disaster. Golfers, being but mortal, cannot suddenly take on superhuman qualities and escape impossibly from the consequences of having strayed from the fairway. If we recognize this we give ourselves the greatest possible chance of circumventing the implied penalty. First-class golfers will appear to play miraculous recovery shots from the rough, but that is because they have undertaken what is unquestionably within their control. They are naturally better equipped, because of their skill and strength, to deal with awkward situa-

tions, but they, too, have to admit their limits or suffer the consequences. Like all golfers, they, too, are sometimes tempted to undertake the impossible when the green is still a long way off. Occasionally they succumb—I, alas, am no less guilty than the rest—and a bad shot is the result.

So, in tackling a shot from the rough, do no more than is within your compass. Right, in these circumstances, is might. Let us suppose in going on with our round—an eventful one!—that we have hooked our second drive. We may find the ball lying well and in that case we can be thankful and take out the spoon for that 200-yard shot. The rough may be of the short, thick type, and it is only necessary in playing the shot to feel that we are swinging the ball away to the green; the danger exists if we reach down for it, of carrying the club under the ball and so spooning it into the air with the top of the club. The spoon is undoubtedly our best weapon because it will cut through the slight resistance offered by this type of rough and prevent the slowing down of the club's action. My advice is to shorten the shaft by a lower grip to give a greater feeling of control and to induce a more upright swing which will meet with less resistance from the rough.

It is imperative, however, that you should make up your mind immediately [when] you get to the ball, and be guided solely by what you see. If you believe that only a No. 7 is possible, take the club and aim to get the ball out to a position that gives you the greatest chance to play for the pin with your next shot. You cannot expect a spoon to turn into a magic wand; it wasn't made in fairyland. Nor is there some special stroke which can be communicated to you by lessons which will by itself achieve more than the position promises. I am not saying that the desperate shot does not occasionally come off, but for each one there are many, many failures. Never for a moment should you throw away your control; by it you can give your third shot a chance of looking for the pin and still may save your four, without it you may be left burrowing in the rough with nothing better to hope for than a dismal six. An uncontrolled shot, even if it does rise from the rough, may be anywhere and leave you little better off.

If you are fortunate enough to have the green within distance of the club you use, remember to guard against forcing or a downward chop of the club induced by the feeling that you are not going to get the ball up. You must keep a firm grip of the club to prevent it from turning in the hands by the resistance that will be offered by the rough before the club reaches the ball, while this firm grip is just as important after the ball has been struck in order to carry the clubhead through. There must be no relaxation at any time in the swing, and if you concentrate on this necessity you are all the more likely to concentrate on the shot first and the result after. Another point to keep in mind as an aid to getting the ball firmly away is to take up a stance that will bring it nearer to the right foot than the left. This will serve the double purpose of presenting the clubhead to the ball just before the end of the downswing, when it can be most effective in making the ball rise sharply, and, in conjunction with the shortened grip, of cutting down to a minimum the club's contact with the rough before it reaches the ball. This is not over-stressed detail. The shot itself will be difficult enough to play with any degree of accuracy, and any consideration that will aid that accuracy must be deemed important. Remember, but do not be awed by, what depends on the shot.

Do not forget also that you can seldom get "stop" on the ball from the rough. For this reason, when the green is, say, a No. 5 shot away take a No. 6 to do the work. The extra loft will make the ball rise still more quickly, and when it falls it will have sufficient run on it to complete the distance which a No. 5 normally covers from the fairway.

But above all else, take to heart the lesson that in rough, first impressions are the real guide to the shot to be played. The twenty-to-one chance is not worthwhile; nineteen times out of twenty you will be beaten by the favorite—par.

From *Length with Discretion*, by Richard Burton. Hutchinson & Co. (Publishers) Ltd., London, England, and Melbourne, Australia.

HIT LEFTY

n the July 1991 issue of *Today's Golfer*, two-time Masters champion Jose Maria Olazabal wrote that when the ball ends up against a tree, wall, or fence, right-handers should play the shot left-handed (or vice versa for left-handed players). Take a 7- or 8-iron, turn it upside down so the toe is pointing at the ground, aim a bit left, reverse the position of the hands on the club (left below right grip) and take a short, controlled swing, the objective being to get out of jail rather than hit it long and to save the penalty stroke for an unplayable lie. Harry Vardon used to carry one left-handed club in his bag for just such rescue shots, but modern golfers will want to carry an extra wedge, which they are more likely to need on today's courses.

Unplayable Lies, Unusual Situations, *and* Conserving Strokes in Windy Weather

1960 BYRON NELSON

After retiring to the Texas ranch he worked so hard for—grinding out the game's unassailable record of eleven straight wins in 1945—Byron Nelson settled comfortably into the role of "greatest golfer emeritus." From that lofty perch, he has dominated as a significant swing mentor, television's first golf analyst, and host of his own tournament. Nelson also wrote two books, *Winning Golf* (1946), which, strangely, provoked little lasting interest, and the more detailed *Shape Your Swing the Modern Way* (1976), which is the primary source for Nelson scholars. This excerpt, however, comes from a little-known pamphlet that *Golf Digest* licensed to clients as a promotional giveaway. Like Richard Burton, Nelson spoke directly to his audience, offering sage counsel on how to negotiate a variety of troubling golf situations—at times benefiting from knowledge of the rules—and how to deal with winds from all four points of the compass.

———————

If there's one thing I've learned on this tournament tour," commented an itinerant pro recently, "it is that I know now I *can* hit the ball where I can't play it."

What the man was saying was that he had finally pounded it into his sun-baked cranium that it is possible for a golfer to knock a ball into a position from which no mortal can extricate it in less than six to 10 strokes, if at all. In short, it would be unplayable. . . .

> It is important to know whether you can hit a ball out of a difficult spot. . . . How can you tell if a ball is unplayable? First, you must determine if you can negotiate a backswing. The rules allow you a trial backswing, if you don't disturb the foliage. If you can't swing, you're dead. If you can take a backswing, the next question pertains to the ball. Can you get at it? . . . You can use as a rule of thumb the stipulation that you must have at least eight inches of clear ground around the ball in order to get it out. I wouldn't advise trying a shot from a more restricted area.

> Play the ball from more to the right in your stance when you hit out of a divot hole. This is a difficult maneuver for the best of them. If you are using a spoon, play the ball three or four inches inside your left heel. It is vital you hit down on a shot like this. To help in this venture, cock your wrists a bit from the beginning of the

backswing. Then continue with your ordinary swing.

The subconscious desire to scoop the ball is the bugaboo here. Using enough loft in the beginning may help. If you have never shaken hands with that real friend of the duffer, the No. 5 wood, ask your pro for an introduction.

→ *When you hit into a water hazard which crosses the fairway, you may drop your ball anywhere on the line on which the ball went into the water, choosing a level lie as far back as you desire. . . .* This is a case when not knowing the rules can cost you strokes.

→ *It isn't a bad idea to use a 3- or a 4-iron on short chips. . . .* You no doubt have become acquainted with two-level or built-up greens (where the apron is lower than the putting surface). There are two choices for an approach to one of these greens: If the pin is far enough back you can get the job done with a high pitch; if the pin is fairly close your best bet is a run-up.

The run-up is a most valuable shot, one least often recognized by the average player. Play the shot just as you would a long chip shot—half back, wrist break from the start of the backswing, and a firm, crisp downswing.

→ *It is best to putt or chip the ball off a wet and/or hard sand trap. . . .* The wedge is designed with a large flange to bounce a bit in soft sand. It bounces too much off wet sand.

If you can't putt out because of a lip, and the bank is not too formidable, you might be able to chip out with a 5-iron. When chipping out of sand, try to avoid hitting the sand before contacting the ball. Play the ball a bit to the right of stance center and swing as you would for a fairway chip, stressing an early wrist break. This is no easy shot, but it's almost impossible to pull it off with a sand wedge.

→ *You should change clubs to play from an uphill or downhill lie.* Step down one number to a straighter-faced club for an uphill lie (two numbers if the hill is steep). Step up one number to a more lofty clubface for downhill lies. An uphill lie will produce a higher shot and less distance while a downhill lie will cause a lower shot.

The ball should be played opposite the uphill foot on both uphill and downhill lies. This will permit the lowest part of the swing arc—in relation to the hill—to be at the position of the ball. On uphill and downhill lies follow the slope of the hill on both the backswing and follow-through.

CONSERVING STROKES IN WINDY WEATHER

Sages of the fairways say you see the Texas tagline on tournament winners so frequently because they have learned to play in a variety of weather conditions here—all bad.

That is true. Furthermore, Texas has an abundance of everything except water. We kids who grew up with the game learned to play shots off turf that looks more like a stretch of U.S. 80 than something out of the USGA's turf management book.

Add it all up and you find yourself playing a 50-yard pitch to a green that is hard as a jawbreaker, with a 30-mile wind at your back, and nothing under your ball but adobe. You must have shotmaking savvy in this situation or you won't last long in the nickel Nassaus.

The day Joe Neil came out for a playing lesson at the club it was one of these Texas days. The wind was whooping it up at 30 or 35 mph. Joe said, "Let's skip it." I said, "Let's go learn to play in it." We did.

We played nine holes, but I will tell about only three of them. The first is a short Par 4, downwind. Then we put our heads down and came back into the wind on a Par 5 which is tough even on a calm day. The next one is a Par 3, and we caught a strong crosswind on that one. Joe had to learn to cope with the three problems—all very different.

The tournament player is able to make a lot of swing compensations in the wind that the average player cannot make. I don't recommend this for the once-a-week golfer. The three top hints I will pass along to you if you are an 8 or 10 handicapper—and up—are these:

→ *Make only changes in ball position and subsequent changes in clubface position to outsmart the breeze.*

→ *Be smart in club selection when you are playing in the wind.*

→ *Change your target rather than trying to fade or draw the ball into a crosswind.*

Watch Joe Neil play this downward hole.

WITH THE WIND

The first suggestion I gave him was to take advantage of the wind on this hole, because he is going to be bucking the same wind on the next one. The wind can help you get more distance, naturally. But you have to get the ball into the air.

Joe has a tendency to hit his driver low, like many high-handicappers. So I suggested that he do one of two things:

→ *Either tee the ball higher and play it more to the left, or forward, in his stance or—*

→ *Hit a spoon or a brassy.*

The choice of a driver or a high-lofted wood on a downwind shot depends upon how hard the fairways are. If Joe knows the turf is heavy, he will be better teeing his ball high and hitting with the driver. By high, I mean just about a half-inch higher than usual. Then he will play it a couple of inches farther to the left than usual. Moving the ball to the left means there is another adjustment: He must make sure the clubface is square to the hole. There is a tendency to let the face close when the ball is played to the left.

Following these suggestions, Joe got off a respectable tee shot. It stopped rolling at a spot about 20 yards past the small tree he had spotted as his personal "landmark." From this tree he knows he can get home with a 7-iron on a calm day. But now comes the calculation.

"I'm 20 yards past the tree. That would mean on a calm day I would be hitting a full 9-iron to get home," he said.

"Right," I answered. "But you have that breeze behind you, and the wind is going to do more than add distance. It has been blowing this way since last night and that means the greens are very likely to be dried out. Furthermore, the wind is going to take backspin off your shot, and besides that pin is close to the front edge of the green."

"Can't hold it," Joe said, with a hint of moroseness.

"Nope, can't be done," I replied. "Now you'll have to start playing like a Texan."

"How's that?" asked Joe.

I told him. There are several situations in which Joe and any player—pro or rank amateur—should run the ball to the green. Here they are:

→ *Downwind, when there is no trouble in front of the green.*

→ *From a bad lie.*

→ *To hard greens, when there is no chance of holding a pitch.*

→ *When the pin is close to the front edge.*

So rather than pull his 9-iron out of the bag, Joe grabbed a 7-iron and hit a half-shot with it. The ball landed about 20 yards short, scooted forward and finally coasted to a stop 15 feet past the hole. He could never have done it with a 9-iron.

The only advice I gave Joe about putting in the wind was to widen his stance for more stability. The wind has to be mighty husky to affect the ball on the green.

INTO THE WIND

Then we faced the tough one—into the wind. This Par 5 is not easy at any time. I reminded Joe of the idea I had given him previously, about imagining a Par 5 as a series of three or four Par 3 holes, to pick a target for each shot and try to forget that the hole is over a quarter-of-a-mile long.

"Today," I told him, "you'll do all right against the boys if you play this as a Par 6. Figure it will take you four to get home."

Most players figure that there is a reserve of brute strength they can call on to out-power the wind. There isn't. Any shot error you tend to make ordinarily probably will be exaggerated by the wind, especially if you press. So I had Joe pick out a target for his first shot about 30 yards short of his usual target. I had him play the ball a little farther to the right in his stance than usual. And I had him square up the clubface to make up for this. I didn't tell him to make any changes in his swing.

Joe hit a beauty, about 10 yards past the target he had picked. The same thing applied to his next two spoon shots. He hit one of them real well, then half-topped the next one, but it didn't make too much difference with the wind against him. This left him about 25 yards short of the green, and left me with the obligation to explain the situations in which you pitch the ball in preference to running it. They are:

→ *Into the wind.*

→ *Into soft greens.*

→ *Into elevated greens.*

- *From a good lie.*
- *When the pin is far back on the green.*

Joe tested the wind by throwing a little grass into the air. The grass told him what he already knew—he was dead into it. That meant he had to throw that 9-iron pitch at an imaginary target about 10 or 15 feet past the pin. There wasn't any danger of its not stopping: the wind would take care of that.

CROSSWIND

The next hole at our club is a fine Par 3. But it is a fooler on a windy day, because the tee is well-protected by a grove of trees. I let Joe hit his first shot without giving him any advice, just to see how he would handle it. Just as I thought, he figured the wind as it felt to him on the tee. The wind was blowing strong at the green, which is unprotected, and it caught his slight fade and carried it over to the right of the right hand trap.

"Now, look," I told him. "Look at the flag on the green for one thing. It will tell you a lot about weather conditions yonder. But better yet, look at the tall tree about 30 yards behind the green. See how those upper branches are bent? That will tell you how strong that wind is up there where your ball is going."

So Joe took another shot. This time he started it for the far corner of the left hand trap. It drifted in just right and came down on line and about 30-feet short.

"Another thing you have to remember," I cautioned him, "is that a crosswind can knock off about one club's worth of distance for you, just like a headwind. Use one club more."

When we finished the round, and Joe was summarizing his new Texas know-how on playing the wind, I added a final cliché:

"The best thing to remember about the wind," I told him, "is that you can't fight it. You have to join it."

You can bet Joe Neil will join it next time on a breezy day.

From *How to Score Better Than You Swing*, by Byron Nelson. Golf Digest, Trumball, CT. Reprinted by permission of Byron Nelson, individually, and Byron Nelson, Trustee, of the Byron Nelson Revocable Trust.

I'd like to see the fairways more narrow. Then everybody would have to play from the rough, not just me.

SEVE BALLESTEROS

Rainy Day Play

1960 · DOUG FORD

If golf writers bother to discuss playing in rainy conditions, the advice is usually terse and basic, much like a mother might say: Bundle up, keep your grips dry, and try to grin and bear it. But in this brief, but original piece, Doug Ford, a star during the 1950s—he won a Masters and a PGA— and a much-respected instructional writer, presented strategies for how to actually *play* in the rain, and even relates certain advantages that soggy conditions afford. Most noteworthy is that Ford insisted that club selection should be much different in the rain, and explained why golfers should adjust their short game techniques in order to handle different conditions on the greens. So next time you play during or after a downpour, you'd be advised to take along Ford's recommendations, wrap them in clear plastic, and tape them to the underside of your umbrella.

Your pattern of play should change considerably in wet weather, yet so few average golfers seem to appreciate this fact that I feel a brief word on playing in the rain can help the club golfer considerably.

The choice of clubs, particularly on long shots, changes a great deal in rainy weather. It should be dictated by the lie, the ground to be covered ahead, and the condition of the turf underfoot. Bear in mind that a golf ball will fly, or float higher in the air, when hit off wet turf. This happens because the ball sits up more, and a wet face gives the ball more up-spin. Because of this it is bound to carry much further in the air from soft ground. This is important to remember, because in such going, a club with more loft than would be used from a dry lie should be used. Bear in mind, too, this applies to the long clubs.

In rain or dampness, I think the 4-wood becomes the most essential club in your bag. Many of the circuit stars will leave their 2- or 3-irons in the clubhouse when the weather gets heavy.

The important thing is to make sure to keep the ball air-bound. With turf conditions aiding you, you can get as much distance with the more lofted 4 as with a 2 in dry weather. And a 6-iron will fly the ball as far as a 5-iron from un-soaked turf.

Also keep in mind, however, that the absolute reverse is true in the use of the deep-faced, pitching clubs when the turf is wet. As an example, let's take a pitch with an 8-iron from just off the green. Normally, the division on such a shot should be to pitch about one-third of the distance to the pin, with a roll the remaining two-thirds.

When the rains come, and the grass is saturated, you don't get the bounce and roll, so therefore you must be bolder and hit the ball more firmly. Now you should pitch two-thirds of the distance and expect the roll to be about one-third.

To me, playing in the rain offers a big bonus, particularly on the greens. I know the ball will roll much better and truer, though certainly slower. Wet greens call for firmness, and a firm putt is always the best.

Uneven Lies, Playing From the Rough, *and* Playing Out of Divots

1989 / BEVERLY LEWIS

Beverly Lewis's *Golf for Women* has sold well throughout the world; been translated into several languages; had an impact on female golfers; and not surprisingly, as Lewis has pointed out with pride, been purchased "by a lot of men as well." In this excerpt by the much-respected teacher, broadcaster, and captain of the British PGA, Lewis goes back over some of the same terrain covered seventy years before by Cecil Leitch. But she does so in a characteristically modern way, giving specific solutions for hitting off various sloping lies, and even offering alternative strategies for coping with every gradation of play from the rough. Then, in clear language, Lewis offers astute advice on one of the trickiest shots in golf—hitting out of a divot—that both the novice and experienced golfer can put into practice.

UNEVEN LIES

It is only on the tee that you can be assured of a level stance and a good lie, so it is important to know how to play shots from uneven parts of the course, and from less than perfect lies. So often in golf, if you know how the ball is likely to react, then you can allow for it, and the result can be quite satisfying. But if you don't know how to tackle a severe downhill lie for instance, then you'll end up frittering shots away.

UPHILL LIE

With an uphill lie from the fairway, you need to set your spine at right angles to the slope, just as it would be at right angles to the ground on a level surface. This means putting extra weight on your right foot, with your right shoulder lower than usual. This setup will add effective loft to your club; depending on the severity of the slope, a 5-iron could have the loft of a 6 or 7, so you need to use a less lofted club. Position the ball a little nearer your left foot, which will help sweep the ball away.

When playing uphill shots around the green, you should lean into the slope, with more weight on your left leg, so that your spine is more at right angles to the horizontal. This will encourage you to hit into the slope causing the clubhead to come to an abrupt halt. On gentle slopes the better player may be able to play this shot leaning away from the slope, producing a higher, softer shot.

During the swing, the clubhead should follow the contour of the slope as much as possible, so there is almost a feeling of hitting up through impact. It is difficult to use your legs as well as usual, therefore the hands are likely to become more active, closing the clubhead through impact. The ball will probably finish to the left of where you aim, so allow for this by aiming right of your target.

DOWNHILL LIE

For a downhill lie you have to set your spine at right angles to the slope of the ground by putting more weight on your left leg, with your left shoulder very much lower than usual, and the ball well back in your stance. This setup will deduct effective loft from the club so, depending on the severity of the slope, a 5-iron could have the same loft of a 3 or 4. You should therefore select a club with more loft.

You can also use this setup for many shots around the green, but where the slope is severe you will have to play the shot differently. To maintain your balance set your spine at right angles to the horizontal, but still play the ball back in your stance. In extreme circumstances you may find yourself playing the ball outside the right foot, and gripping the club right down on the shaft.

The swing is made primarily with the hands and arms, with little body turn or weight transference. You must swing the clubhead along the contour of the slope, which, if the ground rises steeply behind the ball, means swinging your arms up with an early wrist break. It is essential that you then swing the clubhead down the slope, resisting all temptation to try to help the ball into the air. Keep the right knee moving toward the target. The ball is likely to fade or be pushed to the right, so allow for this when you take aim.

To help you get the correct adjustments for fairway shots from uphill and downhill lies, remember it this way: weight to the low foot, and ball to the high. If you have trouble remembering that, low and weight both have a "W."

SIDEHILL LIE . . . BALL ABOVE THE FEET

Up and downhill lies require altered weight distribution, but for sidehill shots you will need to change your posture.

Setup on an uphill lie from the fairway.

When the ball is above your feet, you do not bend forward so much from the hips. So keeping your spine more upright, more weight toward your heels, choke down a little on the club, and position the ball more centrally in your stance. This setup will cause you to swing on a flatter plane, resulting in a drawn shot, so aim to the right to allow for it. If the lie is not too severe, you can easily play a fairway wood when you need distance.

For shots around the green, make similar adjustments, allowing for the shot to pull to the left.

SIDEHILL LIE . . . BALL BELOW THE FEET

Playing the ball from below your feet is one of the most disliked shots in the game. Keeping your balance is key, once you have made the setup adjustments. The ball is lower than normal, so stand a little closer, bend more from the hips, increase your knee flex, and be sure to grip at the end of the club. You will have more weight toward your toes than usual, but keep sufficient on your heels to maintain balance.

This setup results in an upright three-quarter hand and arm swing only with little body turn, which

The clubhead follows the contour of the land.

On an uphill lie near the green, lean into the slope.

creates an out-to-in swing path. This causes the ball to fade, and thus lose distance, so you should take a less lofted club than normal, and aim left of target. However, on severe slopes, especially where distance is needed, it would be unwise to take a very straight-faced club; instead be content with keeping the ball in play. As a rough guide, higher handicap ladies and beginners would be better using nothing more than a 5-iron. Try to stay down through the shot, and feel that you punch the ball away with your hands and arms. Do *not* try to hit the ball hard. The main danger with this shot is falling forward and shanking the ball, so it is crucial to remain balanced.

Similar adjustments are needed for shots around the green, aiming left to allow for the ball drifting to the right.

With all shots from hilly lies, keeping your balance is one of the main keys, so always have a practice swing to test the feel of the shot as well as to check your balance. More often than not a three-quarter swing will prove successful, although occasionally from a gentle sidehill lie with the ball above your feet, you can swing more aggressively.

PLAYING FROM THE ROUGH

It has to be admitted that strength is involved in hitting from the rough, but you can get round this to a great extent if you know how to play the shot correctly. I think your first criterion must be to get the ball back onto the fairway in one shot, even if that means taking a more lofted club; in other words, don't be greedy by trying to make up for your mistakes. So often I see players wading into quite deep rough with a 3-wood, simply because there is still a long way to the hole. This is bad planning, since they are likely to take two or three shots to get back to the fairway. There are two methods of playing from the rough, depending on the situation.

METHOD 1
Position the ball well back in your stance. Place more weight on your left leg, and keep your hands ahead of the ball, so that the shaft slopes toward the target. The reason for setting up in this manner is to encourage a steep angle of attack. Because there is a lot of grass behind the ball, you need to swing the club up steeply,

Setup on a downhill lie from the fairway.

The swing is made primarily with the hands and arms.

or else it will get caught up. Likewise on the down-swing, if the clubhead approaches from its normal path, too much grass will intervene between it and the ball. So from your setup think mainly of swinging the clubhead up steeply away from the ball, then hit down as hard as you can. The setup reduces the effec-tive loft on the club, and because the intervening grass prevents backspin, the ball will come out lower than usual and run on landing. One more tip: Grip more firmly to offset the extra resistance of the grass.

METHOD 2

Position the ball centrally in your stance, but open the clubface and aim your feet and shoulders just slightly left of the target. This setup will promote a steep out-to-in swing path, with an open clubface. The club will not impact much sidespin because of the intervening grass, but the ball should come out quite high on a line between swing path and clubface. Again grip firmly and try to keep the left hand in control throughout.

CHOICE OF CLUB

Choice of club is governed by the lie, and the situa-tion. Obviously from light rough the shot is not too difficult, although distance and accuracy may be impaired.

- → If you wish to play a shot that comes out low and runs, choose method 1.
- → If you wish to play a higher shot that does not run too much, choose method 2.
- → Clubs to avoid are the long irons; instead, if you need distance, use a high-numbered wood, perhaps choking down on it for extra control.
- → In rough that is about 2 inches deep, where the whole of the ball is below the top of the grass, use a short iron.
- → In deeper rough use the sand iron and be con-tent at getting back onto the fairway. The extra weight in this club will help you to cut through the rough.

On a severe downhill lie, choke down on the club.

THE VERY GOOD LIE IN THE ROUGH

You may be lucky enough to find your ball sitting up in the rough, on top of the grass, almost as though it were on a tee. The one problem to recognize is that the clubhead could go completely under the ball, in which case contact is made only with the top edge of the club, and the result is poor. To overcome this, at address keep the clubhead level with the ball, and do not nestle it into the grass as you could dislodge it and incur a penalty. Your setup should be the same as for a fairway shot, but you could put a little more weight on the right foot for exceptionally good lies. Swing the club a little flatter than normal, sweeping the ball off the grass. If the lie is very good, you could use a 3- or 4-wood and cash in on your luck!

PLAYING OUT OF DIVOTS

When the ball lies in a divot you have to make a more upright swing than normal. If the clubhead approaches from its usual angle, you will not make contact with the bottom of the ball, and the shot will be topped or thinned. Play the shot as described in Method 1 . . . punching down firmly into the back of the ball, with little follow-through. Because of the setup, the club will have less effective loft, so the ball will fly lower than usual. If the ball is sitting at the back of the divot it is almost impossible to get a lot of height on it, so consider this when planning the shot. If the ball is sitting at the front of the divot, you should be able to hit it a little higher, but the direction may be affected if it is deflected by the edge of the divot. Middle and short irons, *not* long irons, are best for these shots, but the stronger player may find a lofted fairway wood is good from a shallow divot, when length is needed.

In golf when we hit a foul ball,
we go out and play it.

SAM SNEAD

Six Super Shots

1 9 9 0 ✎ C H I C H I R O D R I G U E Z
W I T H J O H N A N D R I S A N I

Chi Chi Rodriguez's hardscrabble life started in the sugarcane fields of Puerto Rico, where he fashioned his first golf club from the branch of a guava tree. Whacking tin cans when he couldn't find balls, Rodriguez envisioned an escape route. His break came when he was caddying at a local resort and his game caught the eye of Laurence Rockefeller, who staked him to $12,000 for a fling at the pros. A half century later, Chi Chi is in the Hall of Fame after a solid career on the PGA Tour, and a stellar one on the Champions Tour, where he has twenty-two victories, including a record four straight. In this excerpt, golf's flamboyant master of adversity—whose foundation helps poor, at-risk kids—details how to overcome the toughest lies in golf from leaves, pine needles, hardpan, heather, and even "off the knees," and how to do it with "pizzazz."

THE OFF-THE-LEAF LIFT

The trickiest part of playing this shot takes place at the address. Avoid moving a ball that sits on a leaf, otherwise be prepared to accept a one-stroke penalty for violating *The Rules of Golf*. Fearing this penalty, I never rest my club behind the ball in this situation; I let it hover slightly above the ground, just behind the ball.

Since good balance is key to playing this shot well, I flex my knees quite deeply and distribute my weight evenly between the ball and heel of each foot.

Because the ball must be *picked* off the leaf as cleanly as possible, good hand action is also critical. A light grip will greatly help you liven your hand action.

Pick the club up quickly in the backswing to set yourself up for a nice firm downswing hit. Keep the entire backswing action compact.

Drive both knees toward the target, and pull the club down and through the ball, making sure your hands lead the way.

THE SOFT TOUCH

Wiry Bermuda rough reminds me of steel wool. It's very hard to spin a ball that lodges itself in this dense grass that lines the fairways of many southern courses in the United States. Nevertheless, you can get the ball to sit down on the green pretty quickly if you switch from your normal technique to a highly unorthodox, yet easily workable swing.

To hit this shot, I address the ball with my feet, knees, hips, and shoulders aligned precisely parallel to the target line. Then rather than balancing my weight evenly on each foot I put 65 percent of it on my left foot. This manner of distributing my weight helps me propel the club on an upright arc. That arc, in turn, promotes a down-and-through hit rather than an upward sweep with the clubface at impact. Trying to sweep the ball with the clubface at impact will not work for this type of lie. You must hit down and across the ball to get it to land softly on the green.

The key to setting up a reciprocal across-the-ball downward hit is swinging the club outside the target line on the backswing.

On the downswing, keep your head behind the ball, and pull the club down very hard with both hands. Again, because you swung the club outside the imaginary ball-target line, you'll automatically swing down and across when you're coming through.

Due to the out-to-in shape of your swing path, enough cut-spin will be placed on the ball to make it land softly on the putting surface.

THE OFF-THE-KNEES HIT

The average golfer sometimes takes a penalty drop when he shouldn't. Most often he does this whenever his ball lies under a bush or small tree. Granted, dropping clear of trouble and taking a one-stroke penalty is often the smartest solution. Nevertheless, don't be so quick to drop a ball until you have first carefully examined the situation and stretched your imagination, looking as hard for a shot as a lawyer does for a legal loophole.

Actually, it upsets me to see a golfer take a drop from under a tree, if I know he could have hit the ball pretty solidly and accurately by playing off his knees. Kneeling down can give you ample room to swing the club so that you'll be able to at least hit the ball down the fairway. That's better than losing a shot and then still playing from the rough.

In setting up, spread your knees wide apart, as if to build a solid and balanced foundation for swinging the club back, down, and through mostly with your arms. Let both arms stretch out, since this extension keeps your hands and wrists quiet during the action, and prevents the club from catching the ground well before contact is made with the ball. Quite a portion of the clubhead's sole will be off the ground as you jockey yourself into

position. So to guarantee that you'll trap the ball at impact and make solid contact, close the face of the club a bit.

Lock your hips and swing the club back on a flat arc, being careful to let the arms control the action. Rotate your shoulders in a counterclockwise fashion while swinging your arms freely through to sweep the ball cleanly off the light rough grass.

THE PIZZAZZ PLAY
OFF PINE NEEDLES

Whenever your ball lands on pine needles you must exercise extreme care. Not only is the ball sitting in a precarious position, but also your footing is usually unstable.

If you intend to move any loose impediments near the ball—twigs, leaves, etc.—proceed with caution. One false move could set off a chain reaction that will dislodge the ball, costing you a penalty stroke. For an identical reason, don't ever ground your clubhead when you address a ball resting on pine needles. Hold it just above the needles and be certain to grip down on the club's handle to increase your control over the shot.

To play a solid shot off pine needles, *good footing* is very important; therefore, set up firmly and carefully, in a square stance. Also, since pine needles are very slippery you must take a slightly wider stance than normal.

Make a wide flowing backswing with minimal wrist cock. This type of action will dissuade you from flicking the club through the ball and hitting a fat shot. What you want to do is pull the club down squarely into the back of the ball, with as little interference from the needles as is possible; so stay steady and wait for impact.

THE HARDPAN HANDLER

Patches of worn-down ground, or hardpan, are often found off the lush fairways of golf courses. The uneducated player who hits a shot haphazardly off hardpan gets a big surprise watching his ball shoot far to the right, often into bigger trouble.

After the club has swung from inside the target line on the backswing, hardpan prevents the clubface from squaring itself to the ball. At the moment of impact the clubface is open to the target—looking right of it. Consequently, you have two choices at the address: to set up open to the target to allow for the ball's inevitable left-to-right flight (more open if the club you're hitting with features a low degree of loft), and to setup square, with the clubface toed in a few degrees, so that it faces left of the target when it's set behind the ball as a means of offsetting the blade's tendency to open at impact.

In my youth, when I experimented even more than I do today with different swings and shots, I tried to discover a way to get a solid hit on a ball lying on hardpan. When I tried to pick it cleanly off the hardpan by exaggerating the sweeping motion of the clubhead through impact, I usually topped it. This happened because the clubhead actually bounced off the hardpan into the ball.

I got my best results, and so will you, from employing a very upright backswing, which makes for a very crisp downward hit. Don't misunderstand me. You'll never feel as if you're hitting the ball as solidly as you do from fairway grass. At least with this type of swing, however, you will avoid hitting the hardpan behind the ball.

The most critical thing you must do in setting up is to set your hands two inches in front of the ball. Make a very short upright swing, being sure not to sway off the ball. On the downswing, encourage a full, free, fast swing, and a *whip* of the club through the hitting area, by trying to straighten your right arm.

THE SURE OUT FROM HEATHER

Chances are you're a golf nut, which means that one day you'll probably play St. Andrews, in Scotland, the most historic course in the world, where the game is believed to have begun over five hundred years ago. Whether you play that famous course, or any other links, be prepared to tackle heather, a wiry purple-flowered plant that will grab the neck of a golf club and close its face as surely as a Venus flytrap catches flies.

A ball that lands in heather rarely perches high on the plant's upper branches; therefore, you'll usually face a tough lie that requires you to hit a pitching wedge shot back to the fairway. Don't mess with this stuff by gambling foolishly or you'll quickly chalk up strokes. Get the ball back to safety and try to make a great par or a good bogey.

In setting up for this shot, assume an open alignment and put 65 percent of your weight on your left foot. Let the clubhead hover *above* the springy-textured heather with its face open, because the gentlest touch will move the ball out of position, costing you a penalty stroke.

In swinging back, pull the club almost straight up in the air.

Lead the clubhead down into the ball with your hands.

From *101 Super Shots—Every Golfer's Guide to Lower Scores*, by Chi Chi Rodriguez, with John Andrisani. Harper & Row Publishers, New York, N.Y. Copyright © 1990 by Chi Chi Rodriguez, with John Andrisani. Reprinted with permission from Chi Chi Rodriguez Management Group, Inc.

13

ADVANCED TECHNIQUES

MASTER CLASS
FOR THE
PRECOCIOUS GOLFER

Pulled and Sliced Shots

1914 ❧ ARNAUD MASSY

Arnaud Massy remains the only Frenchman to win the British Open. His two-stroke victory over J. H. Taylor in 1907 was no fluke, as he also won four French Opens and two Spanish national titles, and narrowly missed bagging a second British Open in 1910 when Harry Vardon defeated him in a playoff. An outstanding putter and superb wind player, Massy had, like all French champions, élan both on and off the links. In fact, he was known for his stylish wardrobe while serving as a club pro in southern France, working for the LaCoste family. In this excerpt from *Golf*, readers will recognize basic principles that have evolved into modern techniques for advanced shotmaking. Of special note, Massy described how to satisfy "ardent desires" by maneuvering the ball around obstacles with intentional pulls (hooks) and slices, and offers directions for adjusting the grip, stance, and ball position for those shots.

——◆——

It is difficult to give an adequate definition of *pull* and *slice*. In the pulled shot the ball, after starting at first in a straight line, describes a more or less pronounced curve to the left, occasionally resuming its original line of flight, but more often flying off from it at a greater or less angle.

During its flight the ball is affected by a rotary motion or spin from rear to front, the result of which is that, on striking the ground, it rebounds forward, in the normal direction of its flight.

In the sliced shot, on the contrary, the ball describes a curve to the right, making with its normal direction an angle that is generally more or less pronounced. More than this, during its flight it is affected by a rotary motion *backward*, that is from front to rear, the effect being that, on striking the ground, it almost always has a tendency to rebound to its rear, as if it would come back toward the striker.

Pulled or sliced shots constitute at one time a hindrance, at another an advantage, according as they are unintentional or intentional.

Very often accomplished players purposely execute pulled or sliced shots in order to get round some obstacle in the path the ball has to follow to reach the hole. But such players hardly stand in need of my advice, the fact of their attempting so difficult a stroke being proof enough that they already possess a wide experience of the game and are sufficiently familiar with the management of their clubs to know how to set about it to obtain the desired result. The novice is in a different case and he would be doing very foolishly to risk the consequences of an utterly futile stroke.

We should not forget the old axiom of geometry that says: *A straight line is the shortest way from any one point to any other*. We might add that it is also the surest, at any rate in golf.

The pulled shot is extremely difficult to make successfully, and it is hard to bring any great precision to bear. To make the stroke, the position of the hands is slightly different from that in the drive; the right hand is turned a great deal more outward, and the nails in consequence lie entirely uppermost.

Just the reverse has to be done for the sliced shot, that is to say the right hand must be drawn much more over the left and turned inward.

As to stance, the right foot must be thrown forward in such a way that the ball lies more in line with the left heel than in an ordinary drive.

When a tendency exists to make pulled or sliced shots constantly and unintentionally, the first thing to be done is to discover the initial cause of the evil; it is generally to be found in a faulty stance when striking off, a thing the professional will easily set right.

. . . "What is the prettiest stroke in golf?" Harry Vardon asks the question. Is it the drive, which brings every muscle into play and sends the ball flying two hundred [yards] or more? No, for there are thousands of golfers up and down the world who can perform such-like feats with no apparent effort.

Is it the brassy shot, as fine as the finest of drives, that speeds the ball right down the course, lands it safe and sound close up to the putting-green and saves the playing of a long approach shot? No, certainly not.

Then what *is* the prettiest stroke in golf?

Well, I maintain it is when the ball is purposely sliced or pulled with the object of bringing off a shot utterly impracticable otherwise. Curious too that this shot, which, in his early days, is the novice's despair and constitutes a fault he is certain to fall into, should later on become the object of his most ardent ambition, for it is one he will only rarely succeed in even with the most persevering care.

I therefore hold that this is the prettiest stroke in golf, because to bring it off successfully demands in the player the absolute control of his club, the faultless muscular and nervous mastery of his equilibrium, together with that fine audacity of the true sportsman which no difficulty discourages and which is ready to face all dangers.

I will offer sundry pieces of advice then to golfers who may desire to attempt these masterstrokes. *But*, unless they are already able to execute faultlessly the usual series of shots, if it is still their fate occasionally to slice or pull their balls through want of skill,

Arnaud Massy's classic setup for the purposeful slice.

then let them not read this chapter; it is not for them and could only do them harm. So much premised, I proceed.

When a long brassy shot has to be made toward the green and the way is barred by an obstacle halfway, the only plan to reach the hole is to play round the said obstacle, either to left or right. This is managed by pulling or slicing the ball.

Of the two, the sliced ball is the easier shot, and this is the alternative we should choose when possible—albeit the pulled ball has the longer flight. The fact is the "slice" does not act so quickly and suddenly as the "pull" and does not call for quite the same delicate, masterly manipulation. So we will commence with the former.

[For the intentional slice] I stand much more behind my ball than when I am making an ordinary stroke; now it is the backward stance that is at the bottom of all slice and pull in the ball. . . . The toe of the left foot is [on a line that runs perpendicular to the ball], while the right foot is (say) 25 and a half inches from the same line, whereas in an ordinary shot it is only 19 inches.

The right foot at the same time is pretty close to [a line parallel to the target line], while the left foot is a good deal farther away from it.

The effect of this change of stance is to veer the body round slightly to the left.

There is nothing mysterious about the way a ball is sliced. You will reach the desired result quite simply by drawing the face of the club across the ball at the moment of impact; in fact this is just what happened when in your early attempts you used to slice your balls, when there was no sort of need for doing so.

In addressing the ball you will lean the least trifle more than usual on the right leg, but be sure not to exaggerate this. In fact you ought hardly to notice that you are doing so at all.

The grip is the same as usual, but there is an important difference in the upper part of the swing. At this point of its course the clubhead swings much further outward—by this I mean it turns less round the body and travels more in a straight line. The reason is plain. It follows from the rule which declares that the club in coming down again occupies in succession all the positions it passed through in going up; so, after striking the ball, it will naturally go on pursuing the same oblique course.

The result is that at the moment of impact, and for the space perhaps of a quarter of a second, the face of the club, driver or brassy as may be, will shave across the ball, as if it were going to cut a slice off it.

This brief instant will suffice to impart to the ball a curious rotary motion, not unlike in many respects that which affects the boomerang, and which will make itself felt in a longer or shorter time after the ball has begun its flight.

To fix the distance at which we wish this rotary movement or spin to begin, you have only to fall back upon the same principles that govern the ordinary stroke.

I mean by a ball sliced at distance, a ball that is only intended to deviate from the straight line at a point fairly far removed from that where it was struck, because the tree or other obstacle it has to circumvent lies halfway or sometimes even nearer to the hole to be reached.

This is undoubtedly the most difficult shot to play, inasmuch as the ball has to travel in a straight line as far as the obstacle, and on reaching it, wind round it as if it were endowed with a mind of its own. To manage this, you will make your shot much more deliberately than when you wish to see the effect of your stroke occur immediately.

When the tree or thicket that blocks your way stands twenty yards or so only in front of you, do not hesitate a moment, it is a short slice you must play.

I will take as an instance a case that is likely enough to occur anywhere; you have to play a long hole, and for your second shot, after a bad drive, you find, some thirty yards away, between you and the hole, a clump of tall trees. Of course you might try with a powerful swipe to fly the obstacle, but you would have to send the ball such a height in the air that you would find it impossible to get a long carry as well, and you would land after covering an insignificant distance.

Two courses are open to you. Either you will make up your mind to play to the hole in two strokes instead of one, but if your opponent is a formidable one, these tactics will be perilous; or you will adopt a slice.

Put slice on your ball then, give it such carry as the circumstances demand, and you will have the satisfaction of winning a hole that seemed, to say the least of it, very doubtful.

Now look at the cut figuring the course of a ball sliced so as to deviate quickly and suddenly. I will do my best to tell you how this may be done, but simple as you may think it, I repeat it will take long and painful hours of practice before success comes to crown your efforts.

Now listen. Instead of striking the ball with the middle of the clubface, as you did for the slice at long distance, hit it more with the heel of the club. As for the upward and downward swings, these are carried out in the same way as for a slice at a distance.

By so striking with the heel, the slice will take effect more violently and sooner; only you must take good care the stroke be made with absolutely mathematical precision, under the penalty of drawing down appalling disaster on your devoted head.

It is no easy stroke certainly, but it is such a pretty one that the player who has once attained a certain knack and a certain confidence in himself, will be tempted to use it every time opportunity offers.

Not only will he find himself classed among the great players, players whose doughty deeds will be "told by the fireside long years hence," but this accomplishment will gain him many a match, even in cases when all hope seemed gone.

And now to go on to the "pulled" ball.

Despite all the beauties and attractions belonging to the sliced ball, there are still occasions when it will be better to play a pulled ball.

Indeed you must remember that the pulled ball as compared with the sliced ball is what the range of a rifle is to that of a musket, in other words that it has infinitely longer trajectory. So much so in fact that a great many players, even when they are not in any way constrained by emergencies, always drive pulled balls, taking care however to allow for the obliquity.

. . . [In the case of the pulled ball], we have reversed our stance with reference to the ball; our *right* heel is on [a line perpendicular to the ball] . . . [and the left foot is closer to a line running parallel to the target line].

The effect of this new stance is that the shaft of the club will be in front of the ball. The general difference is further accentuated by the fact that the hand will be held more forward still than for an ordinary stroke. The grip will be correspondingly modified.

Indeed it is indispensable, if the stroke is to be successfully made, for the right hand to do more of the work than the left, and accordingly the club must be grasped less tightly by the left hand than by the right. If this is done, the latter will then automatically perform the extra work we call upon it to supply.

In the upward swing, let your club follow the same course it should pursue in an ordinary stroke. The effect of all this, and in particular of the same share in the work taken by the left hand as compared

Arnaud Massy's classic setup for a purposeful hook.

with the right, is that, in its downward swing, the club will have a tendency to strike the ball with a slight bias from the true.

And this slight bias is precisely what we want to arrive at, for as a matter of fact the right hand *must*, at the moment of impact, turn in this way for the stroke to come off. Then, at the finish of the stroke, the right hand, having done its work, ought now to lie quite distinctively above the left.

From *Golf*, by Arnaud Massy. Methuen & Co., Ltd., London, England.

All golfers, men and women, professional and amateur, are united by one thing: their desire to improve.
JUDY RANKIN

The Crafty Art of Slicing

1926 / GRANTLAND RICE

Grantland Rice covered the gamut of sporting competition, memorably immortalizing Notre Dame's "Four Horsemen," and contributing other brilliant verse: "He marks not that you won or lost . . . " But he had a particular fondness for golf, and was the editor of *The American Golfer* during its golden years, even rewriting his dear friend Bobby Jones. In this piece, from *The Duffer's Handbook*, Rice deployed the necessary full understanding of the game and its never-changing foibles to mercilessly lampoon those who try to conquer it. As with such chapters as "How to Play a Hole in 9," Rice expected readers to do the exact opposite of what he suggested for bad play in order to play well. Ironically, one can slice either by doing various things wrong, like Rice, or by using correct technique—just remember to slice, intentionally, only when that shot is dictated by doglegs, trees, or the wind.

———

There are twenty-five or thirty ways of developing a slice if one happens to be in the mood. There are just as many ways of slicing if one doesn't happen to be in the mood. With so many different methods at hand, slicing is one of the simplest of all golfing arts. Almost any duffer can do it. Almost any duffer does.

You must be sure of course to drag the clubhead across the ball at the moment of impact to have the perfect slice that spirals away into the woods, out of bounds, or the rough. Or possibly a pond, lake or bunker. Perhaps back of a tree.

If you have an uncomfortable desire to slice, the surest method is to start the clubhead back on a line outside the ball, outside the line of flight. Also, bring the clubhead down on this same outside line. Don't start the clubhead back on an inside arc, swinging through from the inside out. This may cause a hook or a straight ball. Another sound slicing method is to aim to the left of the course, allowing for a slice, and then let the hands and body get well in front of a clubhead at the moment of impact. This method rarely fails. Gripping tightly with the right hand on the backswing and lifting the clubhead abruptly is one of the surest of the slicing aids. It rarely fails one time out of ten.

A fairly sure way of slicing is to stand too far away from the ball so you will have to fall or lean forward to hit it. Which you will do with the heel of the club. There is still another simple method of meeting this problem. Sway to the right and throw all the weight on the right foot and right leg. Then start for the deep rough or the thicket on the right side of the course; for that is where the ball will be.

From *The Duffer's Handbook* by Grantland Rice. MacMillan Publishing Co., New York. N.Y.

The Niblick, the Cut Shot, and How to Apply Backspin

CIRCA 1928 ✎ P. A. VAILE

Modern golfers may be surprised to learn this: A century before Phil Mickelson thrilled galleries with shots that land softly on greens, and then roll back 10 feet—as if yanked by an invisible chain—the grand old men of golf could do the same. In this excerpt, the writer P. A. Vaile described how Johnny Farrell hit highly effective "cut" shots with a rudimentary niblick. Using a "lazy" swing and a "crisp" hit, Farrell could freeze the rubbery balls of the time—manufactured in Cleveland, of all places—dead on the tracks of gnarly greens throughout the country. The technique, which contemporary golfers might wish to try after reading this delightful piece of archaism, also pays homage to J. H. Taylor, the first genius of "cut-spin." Vaile insisted somewhat audaciously that if golfers can hit a slice—which most certainly can—they also can hit the delicate cut shot.

———————

The niblick, in its ordinary construction, that is with the full-length shaft for full strokes, is admittedly a treacherous club. It requires considerable practice to master it, but for many shots it is indispensable.

With most players this club is used for pitching over and out of obstructions such as bunkers. It is seldom used for full strokes, and being used for shots just around the greens, twenty-five to fifty yards or nearer, should be played with the nearest possible approximation to the putting stroke. . . .

The construction of [a] special short niblick [with a shorter shaft] allows the golfer to play an extraordinarily delicate shot with a very short swing back, which naturally tends to much greater accuracy in strokes where grounding of the club is prohibited.

Substantially endorsing my emphatic advice to golfers to carry the putt and its principles back into their game as far as they can, Johnny Farrell, Open Champion of the United States in 1928, tells how to play a niblick shot over a mound or hazard and hold the green with backspin.

He says, "A great number of golfers have asked me what particular chip shot I use in pitching over mounds, hazards, and rough spots. I do not advise any particular club for these shots, because each condition calls for a different club to obtain the best results. Sometimes, for example, it is necessary to chip over a mound or hazard and hold the green. This requires a shot with sufficient backspin to cause the ball to remain near the hole. In such a case I use a niblick, standing close to the ball, and have the face of the club open—well laid back. A slow backswing is taken and the ball should be hit through smoothly with the right hand. This is called the 'float' shot and must be played with a 'lazy,' slow swing with a rather sharp or crisp hit at the moment of impact. This shot is ideal for all short pitches over an object from five yards to fifty yards—an elevated putt, if you will." . . .

I understand Farrell's expression, "A lazy, slow swing with a rather sharp or crisp hit at the moment of impact," to mean putting the hand-action, commonly called "the wrists," into the stroke only when very close to the ball. . . .

Instead of being difficult to acquire, "cut" is so easy to get that it seems to come naturally to most people. Nobody ever heard anyone saying that it is difficult to slice. Well, a cut mashie or niblick shot is merely another variety of slice. . . . A few words will suffice to explain how easily this extremely valuable golf stroke may be acquired.

Place the ball on the turf at, say, twenty yards from the hole. Address it with an open stance. Swing your club . . . mashie or niblick . . . backward across the line to the hole and away from you.

Come down on the ball with the clubhead swinging inwardly across the line toward you.

At first bring the club in toward you at about a right angle to the line of run or flight so that it merely "brushes" the ball and scarcely moves it from its base. It is, of course, obvious that this can be done.

When you have satisfied yourself of this it will be clear to anyone of much less acute mentality than yourself that the amount of cut and distance that you will get on your ball will depend on how much and how fast you send your brushing motion *through the ball*: in other words, on how you decrease the angle at which the face of the club moves across the intended line of flight and how fast you strike the ball. The stroke is really very easy to acquire with any club and there is no excuse for anyone with a handicap of eighteen or better to be without it. After all, it is the shot that was mainly responsible for J. H. Taylor's wonderful position in the world of golf, for his cut mashie approaches to the pin are still regarded as the last word in this invaluable and not too well understood branch of the game.

When one has acquired the simple art of cutting, or playing across the line of flight, one can go "all out" at the ball, get a tremendous amount of spin, and yet merely propel the ball a few yards. Perhaps the extreme illustration of this may be seen in the well-known trick of cutting clean under a ball with the niblick, sending it vertically into the air and catching it in the hand as it comes down.

This stroke produces more of what is commonly called backspin than cut, and comparatively little of that, for it is in effect an illustration of the first step in my lesson on how to cut. It shows how hard one can hit *across a ball* and at the same time move it forward very little.

From *The Short Game.* Copyright © 1928, 1929, Beckley-Ralston Co., Chicago, Illinois. Reissued in 1936 by Duckworth, London, England.

THE FLOP SHOT

Lefty Phil Mickelson is a short game artist who uses a variety of sophisticated shots around the green to recover from his sometimes errant ways, one of the most famous being his "flop" shot. When the ball is sitting in high grass and the pin is cut close, Mickelson explained in *Golf Digest*, he opens the blade on his lob wedge, aims for a spot a few inches behind the ball, and makes a very handsy swing. The ball comes out high and lands softly. Walter Hagen used a similar method decades ago, letting the weight of the clubhead drop naturally under the ball, while current British champion Laura Davies said in *Today's Golfer* that she can stop her ball on a "sixpence" using the same technique. ࢯ

Stopping the Ball

1957 ✍ CARY MIDDLECOFF

As a teenage sensation, Cary Middlecoff already was playing in big tournaments, but he opted for college over golf, earned a dentistry degree, and then filled several thousand teeth in the Army before returning to civilian life as a pro golfer, and, until 1948, a part-time dentist. A slow player with a distinct pause at the top of his backswing, he had the skill to earn forty PGA wins between 1945 and 1961, including two U.S. Opens and a Masters victory that included an 82-foot eagle putt in the final round. In this excerpt from his first book *Advanced Golf*—he would write *The Golf Swing* after his retirement—the "Doc" conducted a master class on specialty shots around the green, including an updated version of the high cut that was described by P. A. Vaile. Of special note is his advice on how to add deadly backspin.

———◆———

Consider . . . a shot from about twenty yards out, under these conditions: The green is guarded by a deep trap that makes it impracticable, if not impossible, to get your ball on the green in any other way than making it land there on the fly; the pin is positioned about fifteen feet from the edge of the green nearest you; and the green slopes slightly away from your side.

A tough situation, surely, and the only way you can get close to the hole is to strike the ball in such a way that it will land on the green and stop quickly after it hits. What I am leading up to, then, is my answer to the often asked question: How do I get backspin on the ball?

The first consideration is to have a deeply lofted club. . . . The scoring [or, grooves] should be entirely free of all foreign matter—dirt, grass, sand, and the like—when you make the shot. A wooden tee can be used to clean the grooves before the shot.

The maximum under-spin (or backspin) on a golf ball is obtained in much the same way as the max-

imum reverse English on a billiard ball is obtained—by a downward blow that first comes in contact with the ball at the lowest practicable point. . . .

To go back to our shot, and to the original proposition of stopping the ball quickly after it hits, we will find another factor besides under-spin is involved—loft, or the angle of descent. A pitching wedge or a sand wedge (the pitching wedge is preferable if the lie is a close one in grass, because the bigger flange on the sand club may hinder it getting under the ball) will provide the needed loft in nearly all instances. Some extra loft may be obtained by opening the clubface and positioning the ball about even with the left toe. . . .

Take a slightly open stance with feet close together, a slightly choked grip, a relaxed and fairly erect posture permitting full extension of the arms, and fix your eyes on the ball, which should be positioned a little forward of the left heel. Concentrate on bringing the clubhead into contact with the underside of the ball. The swing characteristics advocated for the chip shot . . . are applicable here—the firmness, crispness, smoothness. . . .

All golf shots from whatever position call for a firm and definite decision in advance as to what, exactly, will be attempted; but on none—unless it be the putt—is this factor as important as on this delicate pitch over intervening trouble where stopping the ball quickly is paramount. . . .

Two other possibilities exist for those shots from around the green where a high pitch would normally be indicated, but is out of the question by reason of a too-close lie, a green of such character that stopping the ball on a pitch shot is patently impossible, or perhaps because of overhanging limbs or other obstruction that must be gone under. You can either roll or bounce the ball over the intervening terrain and up the bank, or you can play a "bump shot," in which you deliberately line the ball into the bank of the green with sufficient force to make it pop up into the air and still have enough forward momentum to carry it on to the green.

The possibilities of this bounce and roll shot were forcibly brought home to me on the 77th hole of the 1952 Motor City Open in Detroit. Lloyd Mangrum and I were tied for first place at the end of the regulation 72 holes, and were engaged in a sudden-death playoff. . . .

On the fifth extra hole, a Par 4, Mangrum's second shot had sailed over the high-banked green and was in the rough about 30 feet from the bank of the green. My second shot was nicely on and I felt assured of a Par 4. When I reached the green and saw Mangrum's position, I also felt assured that I was the winner of the hole and the tournament. The flag was on the back of the green. The green sloped downward and away from Mangrum's position, and any pitch shot he hit would have to roll at least thirty feet past the hole. [In addition] there was heavy grass between his ball and the bank of the green, [so] a run-up shot [also] looked . . . impossible. I well know Mangrum to be a fine, bold, and resourceful player, but I couldn't see him—or anybody else—making this shot stop close to the hole.

He did, however, and implicit in the way he went about doing it is a lesson for all of us. First he looked along the line between his ball and the bank of the green. Then he looked at the bank itself. You could almost see the gears meshing in his brain. . . . "If I hit it so hard and so high it will hit here first . . . then it will bounce into the bank . . . and the next bounce could take it just over the top of the bank . . . and it could trickle down fairly close." What happened was that the ball did just what he figured it might do, and stopped about six inches from the cup. We halved the hole. (We also halved the next four holes and called the tournament a tie, splitting first and second prize money.)

The lesson, as I got it, is that almost no shot in golf is impossible provided you have the room to swing at the ball, and that imagination plus the willingness to keep trying as long as even the slimmest chance remains, will often pay handsome dividends. . . .

The shot just described was played into a bank that had some slope to it, enabling the ball to bounce forward as well as up, even though the ball hadn't a great deal of momentum when it hit into the bank. Some banks, however, are so nearly perpendicular that a considerable amount of momentum will be required to make the ball "climb" up and over. For this type of shot, your 2-, 3-, or 4-iron usually will be best. Position the ball near your right foot, address so as to emphasize the downward character of the blow and thus minimize the chance of having the ball get too much height and clear the bank of the green on the fly.

Pick a spot on the bank of the green for the ball to hit, and simply line the ball at the spot. Ideally, the ball will bounce rather high and be carried a few feet forward by its momentum, stopping after a fairly short roll. But some luck is needed. At times the ball may bounce back despite your wisest choice of a place for it to hit on the bank. At times the bank will be softer than you figured, and the ball will not bounce at all. But as we said, this is a shot to use only when no other reasonable possibilities exist.

Reprinted with the permission of Simon & Schuster Adult Publishing Group, from *Advanced Golf*, by Cary Middlecoff. Copyright © 1957 by Prentice-Hall, Inc.

Shotmaking: The Fun Begins

1987 ❦ NANCY LOPEZ
WITH DON WADE

In 1978, Nancy Lopez, from Roswell, New Mexico, burst on the LPGA scene at age twenty-one by winning five straight tournaments and nine overall titles. That she had charisma to match her talent was the major reason that the gate at ladies' events instantly tripled. And to prove she was no one-year wonder, the future Hall of Famer won eight times in 1979. The title of this excerpt from *Nancy Lopez's The Complete Golfer* seems appropriate because the tough shots that might drive other golfers up the wall actually contributed to Lopez's sunny disposition. She offered clear, usable advice, making advanced shots like the intentional draw or fade less intimidating. She concluded with a lesson on the "knockdown," or punch shot, a useful but often neglected approach that flies low and stops quickly on the green.

I've always enjoyed learning to hit a wide variety of golf shots, and I really admire players who fit the shot they want to play to the shape of the hole and the playing conditions. Once you've mastered the fundamentals of the golf swing, this is an area where you can really improve if you are willing to put in some hard work. It's also an area that can help you save strokes when you are faced with difficult playing conditions such as strong winds or tricky pin positions. . . .

The key to this sort of versatility is understanding some fundamentals about the swing and about what makes balls fly the way they do when hit in a certain manner. Experienced players do this almost by instinct. It's almost as though their eyes see a certain situation, their brain programs the proper shot, and their muscles produce the shot.

In this chapter, I want to give you the fundamentals of shotmaking that will allow your muscles to hit the shots the course and playing conditions require. When you can do that, you'll have taken a giant step closer to becoming a complete golfer.

DRAW VERSUS FADE: WHICH IS BEST FOR YOU?

I like to draw the ball, or hit it slightly from the right-to-left, for the majority of the shots I play. I think the draw is a stronger, more aggressive shot, and it's the swing and the ball flight I feel most comfortable with.

There are times, however, when I need to fade the ball, or hit it slightly from left-to-right. For one thing, a fade will not run as far as a draw because it doesn't have as much over-spin. This makes it a better shot if you are trying to drive the ball into a narrow fairway landing area. It's also a better shot to hit to a tight pin placement because it will stop more quickly on the green. . . .

To draw the ball, or hit it from right-to-left, I want to make sure that I hit the ball with the clubhead moving from inside the target line, to square at impact, to back inside the target line.

The best way I know to ensure this inside swing-path is to address the ball with a slightly closed stance. I address the ball with [a] square stance . . . and then simply drop my right foot back off the target line. In other words, if you drew a line from my right toe to my left toe, that line would point to the right of the target if I was playing from a closed stance. By doing this, I make it possible to strike the ball from the inside, and give it a right-to-left spin. . . .

[F]eel is a very important factor in playing golf, and that's especially true when it comes to shotmaking.

To put a right-to-left spin on the ball, you want the toe of the clubhead to come into the ball ahead of the heel. In other words, you want to have the clubface closing down at impact. To do this, your right hand must pass over the left at impact. The more the clubface closes down at impact, the more spin you'll be able to put on the ball and the more the shot will fly from right-to-left. To get this kind of hand action in the swing, it helps if you think of being very "wristy" at address. As you waggle the clubhead at address, let your hands and wrists feel very loose and make sure you have a nice light grip pressure on the club.

In terms of actually hitting the shot, you want to try to take the clubhead away from the ball farther inside the target line than you would for a normal shot. Don't hurry the swing, which is a natural tendency, but let your hands release fully at impact. Again, you want them to feel very loose. It will also help if you look at a spot on the back left-hand quarter of the ball and try to hit the ball on that spot. In fact, if you are hitting a tee shot or are on the practice tee, you might try putting the trademark in that position and then try hitting the ball squarely on the trademark. This will help you swing into the ball from the inside.

As in all shots, it helps if you visualize the flight of the ball as you address the shot. Burn the image into your mind, and when you make your practice swing, get a feel for how the swing you need to make will feel—and for a draw or hook, it should feel very loose and relaxed.

One final thought: A ball hit from right-to-left will run, and the more spin you put on it, the farther it will run. Take that into account when you study the shot. It doesn't help to crack a big draw off the tee, only to watch it bound through the fairway and into trouble. It will also fly somewhat lower, which makes it a good shot when you need to drive the ball into the wind.

HITTING A FADE

Occasionally logic and common sense really do come into play in golf, and this is one of those times. To fade or slice the ball, you do just the opposite of what you do to bring it from right-to-left. Let's run through the important points one by one, comparing them to the previous section on hitting a draw or hook.

STANCE. Again, this is the most important alteration I make when I hit the ball from left-to-right. I play this shot from an open stance. My feet, knees, and shoulders are all aligned to a point well left of my target. This allows me to strike the ball with an outside, to on-the-line, to inside swing-path. This path sets the clubface open at impact and produces a left-to-right spin on the ball.

GRIP. While I don't change my grip, I do alter my grip pressure slightly. I grip the club a little more tightly in my left hand. This will keep my left hand from breaking down at impact and will help keep the clubface slightly open at impact. The more open the clubface is at impact, the greater the amount of spin put on the ball.

BALL POSITION. To hit a fade, I move the ball slightly forward in my stance. . . . [J]ust as in other shots, you have to experiment to find out which position works best for your swing.

THE SWING. As I've said, the key to this shot is keeping the clubface open at impact. To do this, I take the club away from the ball, trying to move it outside the target line. This will cause me actually to swing on a slightly more upright plane and will help me cut across the ball with an open clubface at impact. You must consciously keep a firm grip with your left hand, not letting the right hand cross over the left until well after impact.

If you are having difficulty visualizing how this swing should look, my suggestion is to watch Lee Trevino play sometime. Actually, he doesn't fade the ball as much as people think, but his swing is designed to fade the ball at will. He takes the club back outside the line, then drives down and through the ball while keeping a firm left wrist. The ball comes out nice and high and lands softly. The beauty of his game is that he takes virtually all the trouble on the left side out of any hole he plays. That's a big edge.

Keep in mind that a fade or slice will fly higher than other shots and will run less. That's important to remember when planning a shot, because you may need to take one more club to reach your target if you plan to hit a fade.

HITTING IT LOW:
THE "KNOCKDOWN" SHOT

There are a lot of times in the course of a round when being able to knock the ball down is a valuable shot to have. It's good in the wind, because the ball will drive lower and be less influenced by it. When you study players from Texas or the British Isles, where the wind is a big factor in the game, you quickly see that they are all good at hitting the ball low and out of the wind.

It's also a good shot if you've hit the ball into trouble and have to hit a low shot under branches and limbs. And it's the shot to play if you find your ball sitting in a divot mark. . . .

The ball should be positioned back in your stance, at least to the middle of your stance and possibly even more than that. Keep in mind, however, that the more you move the ball back in your stance, the more you de-loft the club you plan to hit.

With the ball back in your stance, you will . . . find that your hands are set well ahead of the ball. This is where you want them to be at impact as well, and you'll find this is an easier shot to hit if you have a slightly firmer grip pressure, since it's essentially a "hit and hold" shot.

Take the club back straight away from the ball and remember that this is a three-quarter swing. You just want to set the club at the top of your back"— and then drive down on the ball with a descending blow, with your hands leading the clubhead into the hitting area. All you are doing is "punching" down on the ball. Your left wrist doesn't collapse, and your hands don't release. Just punch down on the ball and hold your follow-through.

The mistake most people make with this shot is trying to hit it too hard. Remember that the harder you hit the shot, the more spin you'll put on the ball, and you'll actually cause the ball to fly higher than you want. It's a three-quarter shot, played with a three-quarter swing at three-quarter speed—and it will run, so make sure to take that into account when you plan the shot.

TIP THE BUCKET

To show pupils how to hit a fade or draw, famed instructor Chuck Cook teaches a variation on Harvey Penick's image of swinging a bucket full of water. (The earliest version is from a turn-of-the-century British magazine that suggested a bucket of coal!) To draw the ball, the right hand must turn over the left in the through-swing, and the golfer is told to imagine twisting the bucket to spill the water to the left. The opposite applies to the fade, where the right hand rolls under the left, and the water is spilled to the right. ॐ

The Finesse Game

1989 · NICK FALDO
WITH VIVIEN SAUNDERS

Nick Faldo, writing with the versatile Vivien Saunders, demystified the "finesse" game in this excerpt from the book they coauthored when the Englishman was at the pinnacle of his career. This is true insider information that acknowledges what professionals *actually do*, but usually don't share in standard instruction books. Advancing the lessons of both Arnaud Massy and Nancy Lopez, Faldo offered his own spin on how the pros bend the ball with precision to attack tight pins and handle treacherous doglegs during a competitive round. And, in an era when "big muscle" theory was the rage, Faldo and Saunders revealed the pro's real secret: how to expertly manipulate the hands to produce both cut shots and hook spin. Also, they described how the pros' thought processes dictate the stance and how to aim the clubface.

MOVING THE BALL FROM LEFT TO RIGHT

The good player needs to be able to move a ball in both directions. Tournament professionals usually like to hit certain greens with a slightly fading action, producing an iron shot which bends perhaps a couple of feet in the air but then lands softly with plenty of stop as it touches down. For the top-class player all it needs is a simple feeling of holding the clubface very fractionally open through impact. . . . The palm of the right hand should give you plenty of control to do this. All the tournament player is aiming to do is to hit what is in effect a straight shot but with a suspicion of cut-spin.

But once you want to move the ball with what is a perceptible bend, you start having to do a bit more. Suppose you want to bend the ball round some trees at the corner of a dogleg. Now you have to ask yourself two questions. Where do I want the ball to start and where do I want it to finish? You choose the direction in which you want to start the ball and very definitely make sure you aim your stance parallel to that direction if not fractionally left of it. You can then set the clubface slightly open, in other words to the right, of that direction, and to where you want the ball to finish.

. . . [E]nsure that the right hand is well up behind the club in the grip or if anything in a slightly weaker position more on top of the club. The right wrist is going to hinge back early in the backswing in exactly the same way as normal but will now very definitely approach impact in a slower, firmer manner so that the clubface is held open through the ball, starting the ball in the direction of the stance and swing and then bending it away to the right. The shot will probably take off with slightly extra height and for this reason you may need one more club than the distance would normally dictate.

BENDING THE BALL RIGHT TO LEFT

Most tournament golfers start out life hitting the ball with a right-to-left draw. This is a powerful type of action which initially gives a lot of length. But although most tournament players can bend the ball well from right-to-left, they don't necessarily have the degree of control over the shot that they do with one which moves from left-to-right.

The method I have described [in the previous section] should give the player the feeling of being able to work the ball very slightly from right-to-left if he wishes, just tweaking the clubface through into a very fractionally closed position through impact . . . which to the player gives a feeling of a very slightly right-to-left spin. To get this feeling, the attack on the ball must always be in a circular path, attacking the ball naturally from the inside. . . .

Now let's look at the way of bending the ball round an obstacle or really hooking into a crosswind. Once you want to get the ball moving from right-to-left so that the bend is apparent, you need to determine carefully where you want the ball to start and where you want it to finish. The stance and swing must be aimed in that initial direction, with the feeling of working the clubface through so that a definite sidespin is put on the ball.

What you are trying to do is to set the clubface and swing at odds with each other so that the clubface is closed in relation to the direction of the swing. The feeling you will probably need here is of attacking the ball with a more in-to-out direction of attack, playing the ball further back in the stance to encourage this. Then have a feeling of closing the clubface through impact, and very definitely letting the left arm fold away beyond impact so that the arms rotate into a more round-the-body action. In other words you are producing a more circular attack on the ball, letting the right hand turn the clubface in a slightly closing action where the right hand very clearly comes through into a palm-down position in the through-swing. . . .

One of the disadvantages of a hook as a shot into the green is that the ball can also kick quite severely left on landing. The additional bounce away to the left can take the ball out of control. . . .

If you are one of those players who find a right-to-left bend difficult to achieve, you may also need to adopt a stronger grip, right hand more beneath the club. I would also suggest that you look clearly at the way in which your legs work from the top of the backswing. It is very easy to attack a ball in an out-to-in direction and comparatively *difficult* to attack it in an in-to-out direction. From the top of the backswing, if you have any feeling of unwinding your legs prematurely, the right hip will come forward and almost be in the way of the direction in which your arms should be swinging. To draw or certainly to hook the ball, you will probably have to have the feeling of turning more in the backswing, of sitting back on the right foot and heel a little longer, very definitely starting the swing down with the arms, and then letting the clubhead pull your right foot through onto the toes so that the leg action feels a little more delayed than normal.

From *Golf—The Winning Formula*, by Nick Faldo, with Vivien Saunders. Stanley Paul & Co., Copyright © 1989 by Nick Faldo. Reprinted by permission of the Random House Group, Ltd.

No matter what kind of stroke you play or what sort of club you use, you need to make only minute adjustments for shotmaking.

GREG NORMAN

Cut It Out—Here's How Ben Hogan Taught Me the All-Important Cut Shot

1991 ⚊ KEN VENTURI

Silver-haired Ken Venturi recently retired from CBS Sports after thirty-five years as a distinguished golf commentator and frequent contributor of instruction tips. Before that he was a top-ranked professional, who lost two Masters at the tape and won the 1964 U.S. Open at Congressional in one of the game's most dramatic finals. Playing in temperatures over 100 degrees, and suffering from heat prostration, Venturi staggered to the finish accompanied by his caddy *and* a doctor. In this piece from *Golf Magazine*, he described a nifty, more modern and practical version of the cut shot Vaile relished. Having learned the technique from his frequent practice partner Ben Hogan, Venturi insisted that even hackers can master it with a minimum of practice time. Plus they can execute it under pressure because they will swing with the arms, rather than relying on the more twitchy-prone hands.

The short cut—a high shot that flies slightly from left-to-right and lands softly on the green—is one of the most versatile shots in golf. I use it often: to hit over a trap to a tight pin placement; over a bank to a hole cut on the top tier of a green; from a grass bunker; or from deep fringe to a quick or downhill putting surface.

Some golfers play the cut by manipulating the club on an outside-to-inside path with their hands controlling the action. There's nothing wrong with this technique provided you have exceptional feel and hours to practice. Years ago, the great Ben Hogan taught me an easier and more consistent way to swing from out-to-in and cut across the ball. This technique uses the arms more than the hands, which gives you more control.

Check out this simple method from the master and play a greenside shot that's a "cut" above the rest.

OPEN THE SETUP

To promote the proper outside-to-inside swing motion, stand open with your feet, hips, knees, and shoulders aiming left of the target. For most shots, play the ball a little forward in your stance with your hands in line with it. If you need extra height, set your hands slightly behind to help you slide the clubface under the ball.

OPEN THE FACE

Use your pitching wedge or, if the lie allows, your sand

wedge. (There must be enough cushion beneath the ball that you can slip the deep flange of the sand wedge underneath it.) Always open the face for a cut shot: This creates the high trajectory and causes the left-to-right flight.

THE GRIP AND SWING

Hogan's secret to a soft cut shot is an extremely weak right-hand grip. Exaggerate the turn of your right hand on top of the club so that the V formed by the thumb and forefinger points at your chin.

A weak grip forces your right arm to extend and rise slightly above the left arm at address. From this position, the only natural motion is an abbreviated out-to-in, upright backswing. Once you start the motion, shift your weight to the right foot; on the downswing, the weight should move back to your left side.

A weak grip also encourages keeping the left hand and wrist firm in the hitting area. Note [that] the clubface points to the sky after impact. This is essential for maintaining the high trajectory of the shot.

From *Golf Magazine* (October 1991), by Ken Venturi. Copyright © 1991–2005, Time4Media, Inc. Reprinted with permission of *Golf Magazine*.

How to Control and Work the Ball
and
How to Play the Bump-and-Run

1993 / TOM WATSON
WITH NICK SEITZ

Tom Watson's mastery of British Open courses and his conquest of the Pebble Beach links in 1982—when he snatched the U.S. Open from Jack Nicklaus on the 71st hole—are testaments to his extraordinary ability to both "work" the ball and play that most un-American of shots, the "bump-and-run." The latter, usually associated with British and European stars—since most Yanks play "target" golf—has been a potent tool for Watson throughout his marvelous career. In this excerpt from *Tom Watson's Strategic Golf*, an often overlooked but highly valuable book, Watson provided a thorough examination of the bump-and-run from the American perspective, and offered lucid instruction on how to shape a variety of shots high, low, and around obstacles with hook and slice spin. Watson is hacker-friendly because he doesn't believe in overly sophisticated techniques—even when hitting truly masterful shots.

HOW TO CONTROL AND
WORK THE BALL

Good strategy demands good control of the ball.

Different players and teachers use different methods for maneuvering the ball. My basic method is based on simplicity.

You don't have to be a low handicapper to hit a low hook or a high slice. I'll ask you to make no adjustments in your swing. I rarely make them myself. I don't change my grip except for exaggerated instances.

The benefits of knowing how to shape your shots are several. . . . You can avoid an obstacle like a tree; you can play a dogleg hole the way the architect designed it; you can get the ball closer to a tight pin position.

. . . I try to make every shot fall left or fall right— a straight shot's an accident. . . .

To curve the ball, I align my body well away from the target, aim the clubface at the target, and make a normal swing along my stance line. I align my body before I aim the clubface. Once my body is aligned away from the target, I rest the club on the ground (assuming I'm not in a hazard), square the clubface to the target, and take a normal grip. Your ball position should be normal, even though changing your stance may make it appear to change. The ball starts out along the stance line and then curves to the target.

HOW TO SLICE—ON PURPOSE

Most of you slice and don't want to, but at least this will help you understand why. To cut the ball, I align my body left of target and aim the clubface at the target, then swing to the left, along my stance line.

The face, in effect, is open and cuts across the ball to impart slice spin. Do not let the toe of the club pass the heel through impact.

HOW TO HOOK

You pretty much can infer from the above slicing segment how I hook the ball. I align my body—shoulders, hips, knees, feet—to the right of the target, aim the clubface at the target, and swing out to the right.

I make a normal swing along my stance line and control the shape of the shot through the angle of the clubface. The face comes into the ball in a closed position and delivers a hook spin.

If you're a chronic slicer, you may have to align your body farther to the right than you think to hit a hook. And you may have to aim at the left rough off the tee to get the ball in the fairway with your slice until you master this approach.

It also can help the chronic slicer to position the hands more ahead of the ball at address and think about making the toe of the club pass the heel through the impact area.

HOW TO HIT IT LOW

Hitting the ball low is primarily a matter of ball position. I move the ball back in my stance.

Moving the ball back reduces the effective loft of the club. Be aware that when you move the ball back you must square your clubface to the target, because your normal clubface position would now be open. I don't consciously adjust my weight distribution. This follows from the ball position.

For a low shot I try to finish my swing low.

A key point: Play the ball an inch or so closer to your body on low and high shots or you'll hit the ball on the toe of the club. The correct path of the club comes from inside the target line to along the line to back inside, and when you move the ball forward or backward, the center of the clubface swings into the ball inside the line unless you adjust.

HOW TO HIT HIGH

I move the ball forward in my stance, adding loft to the clubface, to hit it higher. As with the low shot, I make sure I square the clubface to the target.

Moving the ball upward toward your front foot encourages a higher swing finish, and I strive to finish high with my arms. I also want to stay back with my upper body on the downswing.

Hitting the ball high, I select one more club than usual—a 6-iron instead of a 7-iron, for example—and more than that into the wind, because I'll lose distance. Of course, I still make sure I can clear any obstacle in my path.

Play the ball an inch closer to your body. . . .

HOOK IT LOW

This is a comparatively easy shot. Just smother-hook it. Put the ball back in your stance, align your body to the right and your clubface at the target, and swing normally along your stance line.

Let the club release, making the toe of the club pass the heel through impact. Finish low.

Be sure you select a club with enough loft to get the ball airborne.

HOOK IT HIGH

This one's tougher. You really have to release the club and finish high.

Put the ball forward in your stance, align your body to the right, aim the clubface at the target, and swing out to the right. Keep your head behind the ball on the downswing and feel that you are releasing the clubhead out and up.

An important aid to that kind of release and follow-through is to take the clubhead away from the ball quite low.

SLICE IT LOW

Another true tester. The difficulty is keeping the ball down. I'll put the ball back a bit in my stance to keep from hitting it too high. Gripping down on the club also helps.

Align your body left, aim the clubface at the target, and swing along your stance line. I "block it" hard with my hands—retaining the wrist break on the downswing and making sure the toe of the club does not—repeat, not—pass the heel through the ball.

Finish your swing very low and left, pulling your arms across your body and shutting off your follow-through.

SLICE IT HIGH

Most golfers would prefer to be rid of this shot, and maybe you already know too much about it. Just be sure to keep the clubface open going through the ball.

Position the ball forward and an inch closer to you than normal, with the same body and clubface

Tom Watson has counseled golfers to keep it simple, even when hitting low or high.

position as for the low slice. Keep your head back. Finish high and left.

CHANGE YOUR GRIP
FOR TROUBLE SHOTS

When I face a trouble shot where I have to slice or hook the ball a lot, I will change my grip. Actually it's probably the easiest way for most players to stop slicing and start to hook the ball. And changing your grip in practice is an excellent way to learn about spin and train yourself in trouble shots.

To hit a major slice, rotate your hands counterclockwise on the grip. To hit a large hook, rotate your hands clockwise. Do *not* rotate the clubhead as you rotate your hands. Many people will strengthen their grips to hit a hook—and set the club down behind the ball with the face rotated open. They defeat their purpose. Leave the club aimed where it was, then just relax your hands and rotate them the way you want to.

The position of the left thumb is central here. If you want to slice the ball, your left thumb should be straight down the top of the club or even a little left of that, in a weak grip. To hook the ball, set your left thumb well over to the right and more under the club. That's an extra strong grip.

Make some swings both ways. It will probably feel terribly awkward. But try to make contact and see what the ball does. When your hands are in a very weak position, the ball will go short, high, and to the right. When your hands are in a very strong position, the ball will go lower, longer, and left. This happens almost regardless of your swing path. (Normally I'd rather see most of you use a fairly strong grip than a weak one.) . . .

HOW TO PLAY
THE BUMP-AND-RUN

I love the British Open for the bump-and-run shots you play. . . . Chipping and running the ball is a style of play I didn't like at first, because I thought too much luck was involved, but I've come to consider it the ultimate.

On our tour we play soft courses that force you to fly the ball onto the green. In Britain they play firmer courses that call for more inventive shotmaking into and around the green, which often is open in front. The ground is hard and you want to bounce and roll the ball onto the green in many cases.

Bump-and-run golf is often the way you should play when the weather is poor. For example, downwind with the pin cut close to the front of an open green behind a mound, you probably can't get the ball close unless you run it. . . .

Americans rely far too little on the bump-and-run. On dry courses with a lot of rough, the average weekend player would improve his up-and-down percentage by trying more ground shots and fewer finesse wedges. I will play a bump-and-run shot any time I have the opening and don't think I have enough room to land the ball on the green and stop it within 25 feet of the hole. . . .

AVOID LANDING ON SLOPES

Slope is a major factor playing the bump-and-run. I always prefer to land the ball on a flat area for greater control. I avoid side-slopes like wild animals, because you never can be sure how the ball will kick.

Up-slopes and down-slopes you can handle more easily. Take a less lofted club into an up-slope, a more lofted club into a down-slope. Wind is another factor. You may well need less club than you think going downwind and more club upwind.

The big key to the bump-and-run: Pick the spot where you want to land the ball and then pick the club that will carry it to that spot and bounce and run it to your target.

Don't try a bump-and-run shot through lush, long grass. But under dry, firm conditions, the bump-and-run often is your smartest choice.

This is the most common bump-and-run situation. I'm short of the green and the pin is near the front edge. I want to bounce and roll the ball over a mound and be able to stop it near the hole. Using a basic chipping stroke, I land the ball in a flat "valley" so the ball will have the forward momentum to get up the slope. Usually I try to bounce the ball twice before it gets to the green. The first bounce takes the steam off the shot, the second bounce gets the ball rolling. I want the ball rolling smoothly down the slope like a putt.

Reprinted with the permission of Pocket Books, an imprint of Simon & Schuster Adult Publishing Group, from *Tom Watson's Strategic Golf*, by Tom Watson, with Nick Seitz. Copyright © 1993 by Tom Watson.

I Dare You: Try My Killer 2-Iron

2000 · TIGER WOODS
WITH PETE McDANIEL

After taking the 1997 Masters by a record twelve strokes for his first Major title, Tiger Woods refused to coast. Under the tutelage of Butch Harmon, he retooled his swing and added new shots to his arsenal, eyeing what lay ahead in 2000—coping with the windy, tight links of Pebble Beach and St. Andrews, the sites of the U.S. and British Opens, respectively. By the end of that year, Woods had become only the fifth man—and the youngest—to capture a career Grand Slam. In this short piece from *Golf Digest,* Woods described one of the new shots he rode to victory—the knockdown 2-iron, a "wind-cheater" first made famous 100 years before by J. H. Taylor. As Tiger said, the shot takes both finesse and very strong hands, but for the advanced golfer, he offered the formula for giving it a go.

———◆———

This knockdown 2-iron off the tee is a shot I've developed in the past two years with my coach, Butch Harmon. I use it to keep the ball in play when I'm facing a tight fairway, especially down the stretch in a tournament or in the wind. I used it a lot this year when I won the Mercedes Championships in Kapalua, Hawaii. A low shot, it carries about 220 yards, about 30 yards shorter than my full-release 2-iron. It's designed for accuracy, not length, though on a hard fairway it can run up to 80 yards.

What's different about this shot is that I have very quiet feet, a bowed left wrist at impact, and an abbreviated follow-through. I've done a lot of strength training in the last two years just for this type of shot. I had to be stronger to hit the ball with a bowed wrist and to hold my follow-through like this. If my feet were more active or my arms weaker, I'd be forced to release the club, and the ball would go higher.

To hit the knockdown 2-iron, I tee the ball low and play it back in my stance, with my hands ahead of it. I also sit a little lower in my setup to get my center of gravity down, and I make a full backswing turn. Average players often try to hit this shot too hard; they end up rushing, restricting their backswing, and coming down too steep, so the ball spins too much and balloons. I'm still working to perfect this shot. I want to be able to hit it the exact same trajectory every time—which means, of course, I can never really perfect it.

PART FIVE

HEAD GAMES

IN HIS 1927 BOOK *Down the Fairway*, Bobby Jones described the moment when he realized that his flawless swing would take him only so far and that golf demands both physical *and* mental dexterity. Watching Harry Vardon, Jones observed: "Harry seemed to be playing against something or someone not in the match at all." That "something" was what Jones dubbed "Old Man Par," and that "someone" Vardon was competing with was *himself.* Jones learned how to conquer both the course and his inner demons, and the balancing act led to his "Grand Slam." For the past 150 years, champion golfers and writers have developed a multitude of theories on how to think their way around a course, deciding when to attack and when to play conservatively in a land-scape booby-trapped by the designer to fool the eye, mind, and spirit. They also addressed how to handle an annoying opponent—or how to goad a competitor into making mistakes. Several ideas evolved into what now sound almost like modern, though highly useful, clichés. Victorian writers counseled, "Play within yourself." Early pros talked about "muscle memory," "fear of failure," and "mental hazards." Stars from the 1930s onward discussed "concentration," "imagination," and even utilizing the "inner" being. Modern sports psychologists filled in the last piece of the mind puzzle, offering strategies for how both the pro and hacker can momentarily stop obsessing about fundamentals, and revert to what comes naturally—or, as Harvey Penick instructed, "take dead aim."

14

COURSE
STRATEGY
AND SCORING

BEATING THE HOUSE
AND YOUR OPPONENT

Of Match and Medal Play

1 8 8 7 / S I R   W A L T E R   G .   S I M P S O N

In his timeless classic, Walter Simpson didn't merely expound theory. He also wrote about what Bernard Darwin would term the "reveries" of playing the splendid outdoor game in a manner duplicated by only Darwin, Arnold Haultain, Henry Longhurst, Herbert Warren Wind, Peter Dobereiner, and a few other twentieth-century writers. Additionally, he was the first to write that golf can be silly when golfers take it too seriously. In this brilliant, amusing excerpt, Simpson mocked troubled nineteenth-century golfers, contending that the idiotic and the unimaginative have an advantage over deep thinkers. But he sympathetically added: Bad play is common, meltdowns can be predicted, and your opponent may be annoyingly perfect; but if you relax, feel content in a bunker, avoid horrible pitfalls, and sink key putts, you may learn firsthand why winning is so much better than losing a competition.

———◆———

There is no such thing for the properly balanced mind as an uninteresting match at golf. Some greedy and ill-conditioned persons will not play in what they call "duffers' foursomes"—matches in which the real flukes are the clean-hit shots, and the winning side that which has the luck to make the greatest number of these. On the other hand, there are dull fellows who will not stake their reputation on a serious match in which defeat means sorrow and victory joy, which classifies them as golfers, or decides the ownership of a £5 note. The wise golfer who wishes his game to flourish will supply it with a judicious mixture of the two kinds—the friendly and the big match.

A friendly match is the earnest golfer's holiday, and his opportunity for practicing as well. It gives him time to listen to the singing of the birds, and to observe the natural non-golfing beauties of the links. It is also his time for trying new clubs, modifications of style, or fancy shots which have been clamoring for recognition, more pleasantly, than in an hour's solitary practice . . . [and] without his partner knowing that his half-crown is being trifled with. But to play too many friendly matches is a great mistake. It is the direct road to a bad style and careless putting. The tone of mind during most games one plays ought to be an earnest . . . desire for victory, which alone will fix a man down to the great monotonous essential of hitting the ball true, and distract him from the will-o'-the-wisp of style. . . .

It has already been remarked that excessive golfing dwarfs the intellect. Nor is this to be wondered at when we consider that the more fatuously vacant the mind is, the better for play. It has been observed that absolute idiots, ignorant whether they are playing two more or one off two, play steadiest. An uphill game does not make them press, nor victory within their grasp render them careless. Alas! We cannot all be idiots. Next to the idiotic, the dull unimaginative mind is the best for golf. In a professional competition I would prefer to back the sallow, dull-eyed fellow with a "quid" in his cheek, rather than any more eager-looking champion. The poetic temperament is the worst for golf. It dreams of brilliant drives, iron shots laid dead, and long putts held, while in real golf success waits for him who takes care of the foozles and leaves the fine shots to take care of themselves. . . .

Everybody knows that to press a drive will not add to its length; but it is not equally acknowledged that extra mental pressure for an approach or a putt is worse than useless. The supposed necessity for pressing is born of too much respect for the enemy. Because they have got the best of you for the moment, and played the hole perfectly up to a certain point, they are credited with being infallible, and you see no chance of their going into a bunker or taking four to hole off an iron. It is scarcely ever politic to count the enemy's chickens before they are hatched. Cases constantly occur of holes being lost because it seems absolutely necessary in order to save them to get home from a bad lie. Your forcing shot sends the ball from bad to worse, and what might have been won in five is lost in seven. A secret disbelief in the enemy's play is very useful in match play.

This contempt must, however, be largely seasoned with respect. It does not do lightly to lose the first two holes, or any hole. When one is down it is natural to hunger for holes, but even with five up play greedily for more—play a yard putt as if the match depended on it. Likely enough it will turn out that it did. With five up express, as is polite, regret at laying a stimy, but rejoice in your heart.

It is a great thing in a match to be one or two up, and to keep the lead. An advantage maintained for seven or eight holes almost certainly breaks down the enemy and wins the match. Yet everyone is inclined to be carelessly confident when they are ahead, and when they have lost their lead and some more, partly by their own fault, to apply themselves with undue and fatal earnestness. If golfers would but humbly acknowledge to themselves (which is true) that they lose heart and have bad luck when they are down, they would be more careful to husband their advantages. How men "funk" is comically noticeable at the close finish of a big match. With all even and three to play, the side which can finish in fair figures is almost certain to win. But in these circumstances even first-class players generally give an exhibition of lamentable bungling all round.

Some particularly tender-hearted golfers play better in foursomes than in singles, because in the latter they are apt to have their bowels of compassion moved and their game made loose by the grumbling and lamentation of the adversary whom they have got well in hand. Playing a foursome will not lessen his dread of the other side when down, but it will prevent the merciful man from being moved by pity. The wailing, the discontent about the odds . . . the harping on the flukiness of long putts held, his good luck, their bad luck, will not melt his heart and soften his muscle. Between him and them is one nearer and dearer—his partner. It is not selfish to crush the enemy; it is duty—duty to the partner. What are the tears of two enemies to the joy of one friend?

. . . What is the ideal partner? He should be of a Laodicean disposition—neither too hot nor too cold, ready to utter one hearty groan over any gross mistake he happens to make, and then to say no more about it. At yours, he should show disappointment in so far as they affect the game, letting you believe at the same time that they were simply failures, not the results of vainglorious attempts—of selfish attempts—to do something brilliant. When you have bad luck he should sympathize; but fulsome falsehoods about the badness of the lie are loathsome to an upright-minded man. Gross hypocrisy on his part is only politic when you miss a short putt. . . . There are grave circumstances in life which make lies moral. This is one of them. A short putt missed may bring on a holing-out paralysis unless it is promptly treated.

The perfect partner, without letting you know it, looks upon himself as the backbone of the game, on you as the flesh which may err. He plods on whilst you miss—plods on still when you are brilliant. If you are efficient, he lauds you; if variable, he says nothing; if hopeless, he smiles and says, "It can't be helped." . . .

The perfect partner never volunteers information as to why you are playing badly, never suggests that you are taking the wrong club, although certain you cannot get up with it. He knows that although you accept a correction civilly, or even with hypocritical gratitude, you would not be human if you were careful to prove yourself wrong by making a good shot. . . .

A perfect partner is what one desires. A perfect adversary on the other hand is to be avoided. To be regularly beaten is—Well! It is not golf, and it is politic to avoid or watch carefully those adversaries who have a knack of getting the best of it in every match they make. The two most dangerous types are the grumbler and the flatterer. The former begins by huckstering for more odds than he ultimately intends to accept, asserts that he is best in a foursome if a single is proposed, reminds you that you out-drive him, speaks about his liver, has a sore hand, or a sprained wrist—can't play in wind if it is blowing, in hot weather if it is fine, in bad weather if it rains. If you are wise, make a match irrespective of these things, or let him go home to bed. But the wariest are apt to be caught after winning the first match and lunching. They are apt to lose the next two by carelessness, believing what he says about being out of form. It is so difficult to judge of an adversary's play. Unless one is getting beaten off the green, there is a predisposition to believe that the grumbling enemy is not as good as ourselves, and that (if he is winning) he is winning by luck. If we are some up, and he harps on his bad shots, walks with his head bowed, only raising it to wail, there is a risk of his being treated as nought, and perhaps pulling off the match in consequence.

Flattery is still more dangerous than grumbling. Under its influence, a level match for shillings may be followed by a round for pounds, giving odds. Out of the hundred shots more or less you have made in a round, the flatterer easily finds five good ones with which to turn your head. With putts especially he will succeed. A very straight or a very long drive may be used against you; but a few good putts are still more dangerous in the mouth of a match-maker. The drives—unless utterly given over to vanity—you know to be exceptional. But putts! Who doubts that on his day his putting is remarkable?

. . . Judged by his apparent merits, the most dangerous man is he who is exceptionally good within the hundred-yard radius. To estimate the comparative efficiency of men's driving is easy, but near the hole casual observation is quite deceptive. . . . If you are puzzled at So-and-so constantly winning, the key to the enigma will probably be found in the inconspicuous regularity with which he performs the apparently simple duty of holing in three off his iron. His approaches are not brilliant perhaps. It may even be that many of them are scuffed along the ground; but a close observation will show that they are invariably straight. Nobody is oftener past the hole than short, but the deadly player will have a good average of approaches finishing on the far side. In short, an adversary who does not seem to be playing his short game at all well, may be winning every hole because each approach is laid within fifteen yards and each long putt within fifteen inches—a very simple matter, which rouses no astonishment, but is perfect play nevertheless.

In match play, as a rule, it is the finish, in medal play the start, which is most exciting. In the latter, one feels how dismal it would be to drag round the links with an incubus of ten or twelve strokes too many

Each hole is a miniature golf game,
an individual challenge, an individual
chance to 'feel' the pitfalls of the course
and attempt to beat the odds.

Louise Suggs

for the first three holes. . . . Successful medal play, however, calls for more nerve and patience than match play. So long as our card remains good, each shot is as important as the first and as we near home with a good record the excitement becomes intense. Even from the last tee a carefully compiled and credible card may be driven to the winds.

Some men give a very good account of themselves on medal days by playing a bold, gambling game, which either comes off, or requires three figures to record it. For him who is always there or thereabout, the medal round is too trying to be pleasant. Each shot is a solemn and difficult interview, on which depend the momentous issues. After each there is a moment for thanksgiving, a moment of relaxation, a short walk, and to business again—to the business at hand. There should be no thought of anything else. The good medal-player is no Lot's wife, ever adding up his card to see what is behind him. When he has to drive, he drives. Approaching, he does not see himself in the bottom of the hole in three; he only sees the ball which has to be struck. Visions of the calamities of missing do not flicker along the line of his putt. . . .

Some golfers advise great caution in medal play. They advise to drive gently, to play round bunkers, to play putts for dead. It is not likely that the cautious medal player will have to tear up his card, or that there will be any double figures on it, but he may easily have a worse total than if there were one or two, while anything better than a moderate score is improbable. An easy shot is as uncertain as a pressed one. . . . To play round a bunker is to give yourself leave to top—a permission likely to be taken advantage of, for the golfer's body hates to hit and loves to foozle. . . . Besides, a bunker is not necessarily a very terrible place when you are in it. The player in one is as likely to win the hole as his adversary thirty yards further back on the grass. Especially when the bunker

is within forty yards of the hole is caution folly. A cupped ball on the grass is as likely a contingency as a very bad one in the bunker. The bunkered ball will likely be got out, while the same pusillanimous spirit which played the other shot may likely put it in. Besides, why should the bold player get in? To hit clean with a driver is not more difficult than to do so with an iron. In short, the bold game saves a shot if successful, and does not necessarily lose one if too daring. That timid play is a mistake will be made apparent on a moment's reflection to anyone who has ever entered for a scoring competition. He will remember having thought, "If I go in there I am done for,"—how he has gone in, got out, and only at most lost a shot. Of course this argument only applies to ordinary bunkers. On every green there are some terrible ones—unfair ones, in which the punishment does not fit the crime. These must be avoided.

It is in putting, more than in any other part of the game, that the would-be medal winners, and those who enter to see what they will do, are apt to fail on medal days. Bad driving, with a turn of luck, may lose you little or nothing; but bad putting runs up a score that you will only reveal to inquiring friends after one or two askings and some explanation as to what bad luck you had. . . . [I]n putting, all formulae but make us more erratic. Any kind of reflection seems to put the delicate machinery out of gear. Resolve to be up, and you are too far past; to be dead, and you are short; to be in, and you are out of holing. Good putting grows like the lilies. In match play it is vigorous when the sun is shining, and fades a little as the prospect grows dark. But the atmosphere of medal play is either too hot for it or too cold. . . . To putt well on a medal day, one must be careless—advice easily given, but difficult to follow until our card is hopelessly beyond the reach of human aid.

From *The Art of Golf*, by Sir Walter G. Simpson. David Douglas, Edinburgh, Scotland.

Training and Tournament Play

1897 ✦ H. J. WHIGHAM

In the late nineteenth century, when golfers were formulating both theories on how best to play golf and notions on the etiquette of the game, two-time American amateur champion H. J. Whigham answered those who attacked golfers who smoked or drank. Perhaps because he was also an old-school journalist—covering one of his own victories for the *Chicago Tribune*—he stated that if the two habits didn't harm the golfer off the course, then they would have no negative effect on it, and even could help him relax and play better. Whigham also advised on diet and exercise, probably raising eyebrows even then. The former college professor, and Highland refugee, excused his fellow Scottish golfers who often braced for the cold with a dram. When it came to home-town athletes, however, he acknowledged that America's "almost tropical" climate called for more prudence at the training table.

There was a time when golf was played as a recreation. In those days anyone would have ridiculed a definite system of training for the big events. But now that the game has become the main business of our lives, any course of exercise or rule of diet which may bring enhanced opportunities for victory must be taken into the most serious consideration. And yet in matters of training golf is unlike any of the other great games which we pursue with short intervals for business. No one can consume an unlimited amount of tobacco and still row in a college race with any chance of success. The captain of a football team would be foolish if he did not discourage pastry and strong drink. Even the devotees of the polo field must refrain from Pommery at every meal. With golf it is quite another matter. Some of our best players are tobacco fiends. One can hardly picture Mr. F. G. Tait without his pipe, or Mr. Hilton shorn of his cigarette. Our best scores are often made after nights of whist and Scotch whiskey; indeed, there are those who believe that the true secret of success is somehow bound up with liberal ideas upon the subject of the national drink of Caledonia. This view of the question impresses itself with startling emphasis upon athletes in this country who have been accustomed to look upon the traditions of the training table as upon the unalterable laws of the Medes and Persians. And they are apt to feel very indignant when in spite of careful diet they are defeated by less scrupulous opponents who, by all the rules of retribution, ought to be incapable of hitting the ball at all.

As a general rule, training is simply a matter of habit. Most American oarsmen would be rather surprised if they could see the members of the college eight, at Oxford, supposed to be in strict training, drinking liberal potations of home-brewed ale during dinner, and washing it down with a glass or two of the richest port that the common room can supply. And I imagine that the captain of an American football or baseball team would be scandalized to hear that in the case of the varsity cricket elevens and football fifteens, in England, such a thing as training in any shape or form is practically unknown. Possibly, the great English universities err rather in the direction of liberality. But after all, a game ought to be played for the sake of recreation, and not studied like a profession. Moreover, I doubt very much whether the winning capacity of any football team is greatly increased by any close restrictions in the matter of diet. One understands, of course, that smoking should be prohibited among college eights, because the consumption of tobacco, particularly on the part of young men, is apt to injure the wind. But in games where there is no continued strain upon the lungs, the question of smoking is totally irrelevant. However that may be, it is perfectly natural that golf, being a game of recent importation into America, has not yet become a subject for any strict laws upon the subject of training.

Believing firmly, as I do, that in every sport latitude in diet and habits of life is strongly to be recommended, both because such a course is consistent with success, and because it is not reasonable to regard any game or sport in too serious a light, I have no intention of writing any prescriptions for use before tournaments. Even if such advice were desirable in dealing with rowing or football, the circumstances which surround the game of golf would rob it of all its value. The players in this case are generally men of mature years and settled habits, who could not change their methods of life without serious discomfort. Moreover, it must always be remembered that the mental condition is of far greater importance than physical fitness. You cannot play golf if you are worried in mind, and therefore my first exhortation to anyone about to enter a tournament or play an important match is that he should divest himself entirely of all thoughts bearing upon any subject except the matter immediately in hand. Concentration of purpose is quite as necessary as strength of arm.

Let no one suppose, however, that a sound physical condition is not of supreme importance. A blind man, a cripple, or a habitual drunkard is not likely to win many trophies on the links.

Whoever is looking for advice upon the playing of tournaments is at least a person of some athletic sense. He knows that the better his health is, the greater are his chances of success; he knows also that practice makes perfect, if he has read his copybook. These are truisms which are granted at the outset. But I desire chiefly to point out that the average man who leads an upright and sober life would act very foolishly to change any of his ordinary habits before a tournament. If he is a smoker, he should on no account discard tobacco; if he is accustomed to stimulants, he should drink just as much as, and no more than, he does on ordinary occasions.

Possibly someone may confront me with the argument that both smoking and drinking are injurious to the health. If anyone thinks so he would be wise to abjure them both, but he should abjure them *qua* man and not *qua* golfer. If, on the other hand, these pleasant habits are not found to hurt the system in other departments of life, it is impossible to see why they should interfere with the game of golf. In fact, I would even go a step further and say that they are positively conducive to good play. Take, for instance, a man who smokes a certain amount of tobacco every day; when he comes to a tournament, or to a close match, he will find a great deal of help and consolation in his pipe or cigarette, as the case may be. Another player, perhaps, is accustomed during a hard day's golf to fortify himself in various ways at luncheon or at dinner, when the game is over. To such a person I would never say, Omit your whiskey and soda during a tournament. I should be much more inclined to admonish him to take two where before he took one. The mental strain of a tournament increases the ordinary fatigue of playing at least one hundred percent, and therefore those accustomed to stimulant of any sort should increase rather than diminish the dose. As for diet, there is hardly anything which a man who is playing 36 holes a day cannot and may not eat with safety. Good food, and plenty of it, is the watchword for every golfer. . . .

Some years ago, when first-class players were not so plentiful, and record breaking was not a matter of everyday occurrence, Mr. Leslie Balfour-Melville, in playing for the medal of the Royal and Ancient Golf Club, at St. Andrews, broke the existing record for medal play, by completing the 18 holes in 85 strokes. It was hardly expected that such a score could be beaten. Mr. Alexander Stuart, however, had not started when

y

300 〽 HEAD GAMES

Mr. Balfour-Melville's card was handed in. With excellent discretion he ordered himself a steak and a pint of champagne, which he discussed at leisure, and thereafter surprised everyone by returning a score of 83, breaking by two strokes the record which had been established only two hours before. . . .

In reality, it is mainly a question of climate. In the cold air of Scotland, no harm can come of seeking adventitious aid from [a glass of champagne] . . . or even the more democratic Glenlivet. In America we are accustomed to play golf in almost tropical weather, and under such circumstances stimulants should be administered after, rather than before, the contest. Anyone who is in the habit of playing games is aware that on a hot day, and especially after taking exercise, the smallest modicum of alcohol is apt to affect the eye, and therefore it by no means follows that what may be done with success in Scotland can be ventured upon with impunity in America. In hot weather it is well to be rather careful between rounds, and when an important match has to be played in the afternoon, a light luncheon is particularly advisable. In other respects, however, care in training may be greatly overdone. . . .

From *How to Play Golf*, by H .J. Whigham. Herbert S. Stone & Co., Chicago, copyright © 1897/1902.

Left-Handed Golf Courses: Our Greatest Need

1924 ✎ RUBE GOLDBERG

Rube Goldberg (1883–1970) graduated from Berkeley with an engineering degree but after a brief time with the City of San Francisco Water and Sewers Department left to become a Pulitzer Prize–winning cartoonist, sculptor, and author. He is still remembered for his "Inventions" cartoons in which convoluted contraptions, with all kinds of extensions, did simple tasks. He was mystified by man's capacity for exerting maximum effort to accomplish minimal results, as well as his willingness to choose the hardest rather than the easiest way to do things. This certainly applied to golf, where things were tough for him because course designers neglected the needs of left-handers. He contended he had the same swing as Gene Sarazen, but, logically, the courses were to blame for his not getting the same results. Beneath the hilarity, he made the valid point that lefties truly are hampered by having to play courses designed for righties.

I have been trying to play golf for the last seven years and have been reading about the game for twice as long. I get no comfort out of the continuous flow of golf reform literature that bellows and splashes against the shores of duffer island. Those who are suggesting new improvements are tackling the game from the wrong end.

When I read that the new rules prohibit the use of corrugated club ends it has as much effect on me as if I had just heard that the Gaekwar of Baroda had issued a decree calling for purple tassels on all elephant saddles on Mondays and Fridays. The only good my backspin mashie ever did me was to use it as an onion grater when we were fortunate enough to have caviar sandwiches on picnics.

Some people think the new metal shafts are a great improvement over the old wooden ones. I have tried both and I would do just as well with rhubarb or asparagus. Every time they bring out a new ball called "The Purple Flash" or "The Comet's Tale" or "The Galloping Dandruff" I laugh so loud I wake up my caddie. I made the best drive of my whole golfing career with a meatball I had picked up by mistake from a passing lunch wagon.

Another thing that seems to take up a lot of time and energy among those who are sincerely but unwisely seeking new antidotes for the duffer's poisonous mistakes is wearing apparel. I have actually gone out on the links carrying eighteen sweaters—one for every hole. Each one of the sweaters, according to the ad, was built to give the player a particular advantage in playing certain shots. Some were fashioned to keep the neck rigid, others were made to keep the elbows dry when playing chip shots out of the ocean, and still others were designed with special cartridge belts for carrying square pencils with which to write down extra large scores. The sweaters were all different, but my shots all remained the same.

I even went and purchased a pair of those terrible-looking English knickers that are baggy enough to hold a radio set, and stop somewhere between the knee and the ankle. They don't look like short pants and they don't look like long pants. They are a first cousin to balloon tires but don't give you near the mileage. I played one round in the pair that I bought and my caddie said to me just before he left, "Gee, your old man must be a pretty big guy, if you can wear his pants cut down and they're still too big for you." I gave the pants to my wife's sister who was having a garden party at her place in the country. She used them for Chinese lanterns.

As I said before, the reformers are trying to reform the game from the wrong end. The thing that needs changing is not the golf ball or the golf club or the golf trousers. It is the golf course. I am surprised that nobody has ever thought of suggesting the left-handed golf course. The left-handed golf course is bound to come if the game is to survive. It is an absolute necessity—for me at least.

I forgot to mention that I am left-handed—and there must be thousands of other unfortunates in this country like myself. I have been advised to switch to right-handed. But why should I? I have been eating soup for forty years with my left and I am not boasting when I say that my shirt front is as clean as the average man's. In the ordinary course of things it is no handicap to be left-handed. No woman ever refused to bow to me when I tipped my hat with my left hand—that is, no woman who knew me. I never made a waiter sore by handing him a tip with my left hand.

When I take a practice swing at home people look in through the window and say, "Good morning, Mister Sarazen." But when I go out on the golf course and take the same identical swing the ball doesn't seem to go anywhere. So I know it must be the fault of the course. Logic is logic.

Here are a few of the handicaps I suffer when I play on the regulation course:

When the average player shoots he stands facing the other people on the tee. Being left-handed I must stand with my back to the crowd. Besides wondering whether or not they are giving me the raspberry, I must try to be a gentleman and say each time I step up to the ball, "Excuse my back." And you know that any talking during a shot throws a man off his stance—even if it be his own voice.

In standard golf courses most of the out-of-bounds limits are on the left side of the fairway. A sliced shot always puts me out-of-bounds. So I naturally stand well around to the right on every tee to play safe, so my drive will slice back into the fairway. Then for some reason or other I don't slice at all. My shot goes straight and I hit the president of the club, who is playing three fairways to the right. This puts me in continual bad standing, besides giving all the club members the extra trouble of finding a new president.

Another thing. When I make a beautiful shot right on the green next to the pin I invariably find that I have played for the wrong green. My left-handed vision has given me a cock-eyed idea of the course.

My greatest handicap is in the traps, where I must admit I spend a good part of my weekends. It takes an experienced miner to go down into a hole with nothing but the blue sky as his only area of vision and still keep his sense of direction. After the seventh shot, my left-handed leanings force me around in an angle of ninety degrees without realizing that I have turned at all. Then elated with the wonderful "out" I have finally negotiated, I rise to the surface only to find that I have shot right back through the foursome behind me and lost about sixty yards. I once had a series of these mishaps and spent an hour and a half on one hole continually losing ground. There was an insane asylum across the road from the course and it took my friends quite a while to convince an attendant who happened to see me that I was not an escaped inmate.

There are many other disadvantages that we left-handers must suffer, including the fact that they're building suburban homes closer and closer to the golf courses. The left-hander, when he dubs a shot, always lands in somebody's backyard and this isn't very pleasant when they're cooking codfish.

I think I have made my case clear. What golf really needs is a course where left-handers can be segregated like smallpox patients. It would be simple to lay out one of these courses. A golf architect can take a plan of any well-known course and build it backwards. He may run into a few snags in the locker room. It will be quite a feat of engineering to get the attendant to mix cocktails standing on this head, and the water to run uphill in the shower baths. But trifling difficulties have never stopped the march of progress. Did snags and prejudices stop Lysander J. Lentil when he started to construct the first portable sink, now socially known as the finger-bowl?

From *The American Golfer* (July 12, 1924), by Rube Goldberg.

For both left- and right-handed golfers, the storied St. Andrews requires brilliant course management for a low score. Here Payne Stewart teed off on the finishing hole.

Brains and Imagination in Golf

1929 Robert Tyre (Bobby) Jones, Jr.

Walter Simpson had written, perhaps with tongue in cheek, that wise golfers were at a disadvantage, but Bobby Jones thought the opposite. To lower scores and beat better players, the greatest weapon, wrote the legendary player in his newspaper column, is the mind—and using the head is easier than swinging like Harry Vardon or Johnny Farrell (or Jones). The player who uses all his resources and makes sound judgments on club and shot selection, wrote Jones, has an advantage over players of equal talent who rely only on their mechanical skills. "Knowing what to do and when to do it," he contended, are a necessary adjunct to talent, and is what separates winners from losers at all levels. Judgment on shot selection should improve automatically with experience, and help especially when trying to manage unfamiliar courses and save strokes. Jones conceded that imagination can result in trouble, but he said it is what distinguishes good golfers from mediocre ones.

The ambition of every man who plays golf, whether his average game be 72 or 95, is to take strokes off his score. That is the aim of Walter Hagen as much as of the rankest duffer in any club. The great difference is that Hagen, aside from any improvement in his mechanical ability, knows that he can save stroke after stroke by simply using his head.

The businessman golfer takes lessons. He reads books. He imitates good players. He buys new clubs. He does everything he can to improve his swing, his shotmaking ability. But he overlooks one important feature. He doesn't ask himself if he is scoring as well as he ought to with his present ability.

In every club there is always at least one man who has the reputation of "making a poor game go a long way," the man who seems always to beat a player a bit better than himself. He doesn't do it by any divine inspiration, nor yet by any trick of fate. He simply uses his head, analyzing each situation as it confronts him, always keeping in view his own limitations and powers. That is what we call judgment, and it is a lot easier to use good judgment than it is to learn to swing a club like Harry Vardon.

Let a person post himself at any particular point on the course during the progress of . . . any really first-class tournament and watch the entire field of 150 players or more go by. Of that number he will, of course, be impressed by the Farrells, Hagens, Armours, and the others who bear illustrious names. But I am sure he will be surprised at the number of fine shots played by men of whom he has never heard. And if he is an intelligent observer, he will appreciate that these fine shots are not mere accidents. What then is the difference between those who finish always at the top, and those who sometimes finish not at all?

The answer is, I think, in what I have mentioned above—the ability to use one's head. The successful man carries a resourcefulness and character of judgment, the lack of which dooms the other fellow, despite his mechanical skill, to a permanent place among the "also-rans." Knowing what to do, and when to do it, is the necessary complement to mechanical skill which maintains a few men at the head of the procession with many others clutching closely, but vainly, for their coattails.

The faculty, which the first-class player possesses, of quickly sizing up the requirements of a shot on a strange course, choosing the club, and the method of playing it, is what I mean by resourcefulness and judgment. On a course that is well-known such decisions are made automatically, and it is then that skill alone is required. But to conquer an unfamiliar layout, considerable work must be done by that which lies between the ears.

Fortunately, sound judgment can be acquired in golf in much easier fashion than can mechanical skill. Experience over various courses and under varied conditions will teach a lot to any man. If he can play the shots, the rest can be learned by proper thought and application.

The average golfer may ask what this has to do with him! Really a good deal, for by training himself to visualize and plan each shot before he makes it and by giving careful thought to his method of attack, he can improve his game even more certainly than by spending hours on a practice tee. Some men, for one reason or another, can never learn to swing a golf club correctly, but everyone can improve the matter of selecting the shot to be played.

The importance of good judgment is undiminished by the fact that the average player has fewer shots at his command than the skillful professional. The problem is nevertheless the same—how best for the particular individual to play the particular shot. Good judgment must take into account the personal equation as well as the slope and conditions of the ground, and the locations of bunkers and hazards.

Here is one example showing how a man can waste strokes and lose holes uselessly. I played a while ago in a fourball match with my father, who plays a fairly good game, in the 80s as a rule. He was playing a match against another member of our party with whom he was about evenly matched. On the 17th hole, Dad hit under his ball on the drive, dropping in the road just over the lake. His opponent topped into the water and played three from the bank.

I particularly noted how Dad's ball was lying in the road. It actually invited a full shot with a straight-faced iron. But there was a 5-foot embankment 10 yards ahead. The green was so far distant that the longest shot would still leave 70 yards or more to go. The other man was in the rough in three. The best he could be expected to do was to play on in four, leaving two putts for a six.

Dad needed, in that situation, only to play conservatively up the fairway with a mashie, another mashie shot to the green, take two putts for a five, and win the hole. He could not hope to do better even if his long iron came off, for the green was a full three hundred yards away. But he didn't stop to think it all out! Bent upon hitting the ball as far as possible, he took the long iron, half-topped the shot, and the ball, striking into the bank, barely hopped up into the fairway.

Having wasted a stroke, he was little better off than before. Now, he could not carry the bunker twenty yards from the green. He played short of it with an iron, pitched on the green in four, and holed out in two putts for a six. His opponent, as it turned out, messed up his iron shot, but chipped to the edge of the hole and secured a half.

Those are the things that not one golfer in a hundred will trouble himself to think about. To take chances is perfectly proper—when there is something to be gained and when there is a reasonable possibility that the shot can be made. But where is there even an excuse for taking a risk when in no conceivable way can benefit result?

I believe that if a person will approach every shot with a cool head, if he will look carefully to what lies before him and think two or three shots ahead, he can improve his average score by from four strokes upward. If you are in trouble, you know you can get out with one club in a certain way, and you think you might get out with another club in another way. Before you try that other club in the other way, think whether or not you will gain anything if it works—not merely whether you may send your ball a few yards farther down the fairway, but whether you will thereby gain any measurable advantage.

IMAGINATION AN ASSET

Imagination, it has been said, is something that a golfer should not possess. To a certain extent, that is true. It is certainly a bad thing to have too clearly in mind, when hitting the ball, all the many kinds of disasters which may befall the stroke. Then, if ever, is the time to have a single-track mind which can hold only the immediate objective in view.

But the golfer who is devoid of imagination of any kind will certainly never rise far above mediocrity. In the main, the shots from the tee and through the fairway, have become stereotyped and require no originality. But every so often there arises a situation which is novel and puzzling. Behind a tree, or on the down-slope of a bunker, the player needs imagination and resourcefulness as well as mechanical accuracy.

At St. Andrews, the people are still talking about a shot made by Francis Ouimet on the 17th, the famous Road Hole. The road back of this green is one of the terrors of the St. Andrews links, and to be in it is regarded as absolutely fatal, for the green is very small, and a terrible bunker awaits the approach which is too strong.

Ouimet's ball, on this occasion, went not only into the road, but across it and on to within three or four inches of a stone wall seven or eight yards beyond the road itself. His opponent was safely on in three so that Francis appeared to have lost the hole, although he had played only two, for he seemingly must play away from the wall with his third, pitch on—if he could—in four, and take two putts for a six.

Francis approached the ball, looked it over for a moment and drew a niblick from his bag. Instead of playing the obvious shot to safety, he squared himself to the ball as though intending to drive it through the stonewall. Then, to the amazement of everyone, he banged the ball into the wall with the lofted club, and it came back like a shot, cleared the road, pitched onto the green and stayed there—a shot brilliantly executed, it is true, but far more brilliantly conceived. . . .

PREVENT WASTE OF STROKES

Situations like these break up the monotony which there undoubtedly is in golf. For hole after hole the shots go along smoothly enough, causing very little mental disturbance. But sooner or later something happens and a brand new situation comes up.

Very likely, it is something like . . . I have mentioned, something outside the realm of past experience, calling for a shot never tried before. Then is the time we need imagination, and a lot of it!

Years of practice and instruction are needed to round out a sound, workable method of hitting a golf ball. For a great many men, it is impossible to give to the game more than enough time to become ordinarily proficient at making the shots. Most of them never will be able to drive like Johnny Farrell, nor to play an iron like Tommy Armour, nor to putt like Walter Hagen. But by using their heads they can learn very quickly to prevent the useless waste of strokes.

From *Bobby Jones on Golf,* by Robert Tyre (Bobby) Jones, Jr. One Time Publications, Inc. Copyright © 1929–1930 by Bell Syndicate, Inc. Revised in 1997 by Sidney L. Matthew, Sleeping Bear Press, Chelsea, Michigan. Reprinted by permission of Sidney L. Matthew, published by IQ Press. Copyright © 1997.

GAME PLAY

Horace Hutchinson likened golf to billiards and others used the image of chess to convey the idea that good course management calls for seeing the next shot and mentally setting up favorable angles and positions ahead of time. ❧

Tee and Fairway Tactics I Use

1962 ✎ SAM SNEAD
WITH AL STUMP

Nobody plays perfect golf all the time, and even Sam Snead readily admitted that he sometimes had to overcome uncertain play with smart thinking. When his body became rigid as he visualized bad shots, he concentrated solely on striking the ball, as did Patty Berg. He thought only about duplicating his perfect practice swing, thinking *with* his swing rather than *ahead* of it, concentrating on "performance, not results." To relax and keep his mind from wandering, he spoke to the ball, long before Mark Fidrych gained fame by talking to the baseball before pitching it. As Snead wrote, if a struggling golfer can think his way back to an automatic swing, he then can think of not just hitting the ball but of sensible course management. In the concluding part of this excerpt, he recalls how he did just that, managing a one-stroke win over Arnold Palmer in a big match.

Earlier in this chapter, I told of "going into a sort of pleasant daydream" when I had the tee jitters. . . . There is a real payoff idea behind this.

The practice swing of most ordinary players almost always carries most of the main ingredients. The fundamentals are there. But when they are in a match, the difference is terrific. The feet are no longer easily set. There is a cramped body turn. Hands and wrists are rigid. When this happened to me, I began thinking in terms of *performance*, not *results*. By this I mean I had no thought beyond the ball—of traps, ponds, rough, or out of bounds. All I did was to go back to my good practice swing, on which I could count, and then to think *with* my swing—not *ahead* of my swing. This takes will power, but it isn't so hard to let your mind relax and say to yourself, "Here goes my practice swing—and I don't care where the ball lights or lands. If I can't play like a good golfer in actual play, at least I can go back to my practice swing and let nature take its course."

Call on your will power to "let the rest of the world go by," and dust that thing with the form you have when nobody is watching—and watch your score go down. Climb inside your old, regular personality, not the one that wants to take you over when the pressure is on.

I BELIEVE IN GIVING THE BALL SOME SWEET TALK

I believe in giving the ball some sweet talk on the tee. Driving is about 75 percent mental, and if your state of mind is out of kilter, ten thousand lessons and a team of mules won't help you. The idea is to have an even, automatic swing, the kind you don't have to think about. If your swing varies considerably from day to day, you'll try to even things up by thinking, and at that point you're more juggler than golfer. To remind yourself of six or seven things you "must do" will mess you up. So I take a firm grip on myself and hold my thinking to never more than one idea when I address the ball.

Sam Snead believed in giving the golf ball a little sweet talk.

There's at least two ways to make the mind behave:

TALK TO THE BALL

"This isn't going to hurt a bit," I tell the ball under my breath. "Sambo is just going to give you a nice little ride." Or I might say, "Hello, dimples, I see you're sitting up fat and ready; let's us have some fun." Under heavy pressure, I've told a ball, "Let's win this hole for Jackie." (Jackie is my teenage son.) By acting as if the ball's human, I distract myself—leaving no time for thoughts of this and that. Sometimes the ball looks back at me and seems to say, "OK, Sam, but treat me gentle." That's a ball that's friendly, the kind that will go for you.

GIVE YOURSELF A SINGLE "KEY"

The power of suggestion (that you'll fail) also can be beaten if you form one mental picture of what you want to do, [and] forget the rest. Johnny Farrell thought only of his feet: of getting a smooth pivot started. Arnold Palmer thinks only of hitting along the line he's picked to the hole, drawing the line with his eye. Byron Nelson tried to see the clubhead flatten out at impact. My own keys depend upon how I'm going.

If I'm hooking, my only thought is to lock my left shoulder along the line to the flag. When I'm not hooking, my key is swinging within myself, at about 85 percent power.

TEE AND FAIRWAY TACTICS I USE

In a big match with Arnold Palmer at Providence, Rhode Island, in 1960, it was a seesaw battle to the fifteenth hole, where I was one-up. Right there, a pair of fairway shots decided the match.

The hole is 510 yards, 5 par, with a slightly elevated green trapped right, left, and rearward. The doorway to the green wouldn't accommodate two skinny men abreast.

Our second shots were long 3-irons. It looked to me like only a close-to-perfect shot would reach that green, and you don't get that kind more than once out of three tries. Also, since Palmer trailed, I figured he might gamble. With a 3-iron it's easy to push the shot right—and this hole sprouted heavy rough and trees to the right. That gave me three reasons just to lay it up there to the doorway, short, which I did. Palmer went for the flag and flew right, leaving himself an impossible angle to the green. In the end, that settled the match in my favor, 67 shots to Palmer's 68.

On tight fairways, 40 or 50 yards wide, you don't shoot down them, you work them. Hitting straightaway, you have only half a fairway, 20 or 25 yards, as a margin of error between you and the trouble that's usually waiting both right and left. If the worst trouble is right, I'll aim down the safer left side, fading the ball back toward the center. If the trouble is left, the draw is the thing. Either way, you've left yourself the full width of the fairway for working the ball.

The draw shot has won big for me, since it fits my natural tendency to hook and is a great weapon on sharp right-to-left dogleg holes and into the wind. A ball purposely drawn from right to left will hold its line until late in flight and bores into the wind, while a fade may go yards off-course and lacks distance. Drawing, I also swing easier—and relaxing is everything.

A single draw in the rich Goodall Round Robin at Wykagyl Country Club helped me to the winner's portion of a $15,000 pot. The 14th hole doglegs left sharp enough to break your back. I put side-spin on the ball by first closing my stance—right foot withdrawn—a good four inches. I aimed down the right-hand fairway. . . .

The shot followed the contours of the hole perfectly, setting up a chip and birdie putt that won the prize.

If all that isn't enough to steer the average golfer away from experimenting with intentional draws and fades or other manufactured shots, I'll say this:

Don't try them. Hit hard and with no tricks, until you are master of the ball.

From *The Education of a Golfer*, by Sam Snead, with Al Stump. Simon & Schuster, New York, N.Y. Copyright © 1962 by Sam Snead and Al Stump. Reprinted with the permission of Jack Snead.

Conquering the Course:
An Overview

1973 ✦ ARNOLD PALMER
WITH WILLIAM BARRY FURLONG

One of the most indelible television images of the 1950s and '60s was "Arnie's Army" marching with their hero down fairways as he made his late "charges." Palmer won sixty-two PGA titles, including seven Majors, and many were of the come-from-behind variety. His thrilling, risk-taking rallies, which gave golf a boost in popularity worldwide, weren't just the result of how well the King played the final holes. Everything he did beforehand paved the way for his finishes—each shot and each hole led to the next. He stated in his most famous book, in perhaps the best instruction he ever wrote, that it pays off to understand all eighteen holes, and prevailing conditions, before playing the first hole. His wise advice was to map out the course, planning both shortcuts and detours around trouble, and deciding which holes you should play conservatively and when you should go for broke.

I've never been bored by the thought of going out on a course, even one that I've played hundreds and hundreds of times. For every day it is a new course with a new subtlety—the weather changes, the rough changes, the pin placements change, the consistency of the sand changes, and the grass is a little longer or, if it's been cut, a little shorter. And of course my own ability changes.

So whenever I step out onto a course, it is with a vast expectancy. On any given day, I want it to tell *me* what it has in mind.

Is it going to be a course for boldness or caution?

Is it a course that offers mental delights as well as scenic ones?

Will it reward the good, or great, golf shot and penalize the clumsy or sloppy one?

How can I plot to conquer this course?

Knowing what I know about the grass, the climate, the design, and the deceits of the weather—now how do I go about attacking the course?

The first step is quite simple: Don't believe anything you've heard about it until you've gone out and personally examined it. For the golfer must never be neutralized, or paralyzed, by the reputation of a golf course. . . .

What you *should* go onto a golf course with . . . is an overview of the course and its potential. For a great many pros, gaining this overview is as reflexive as blinking. But an amateur rarely appreciates how useful it is simply to take a long, studied look at the course he's playing—even one that he's played often—to understand how best to use his skills on it and against it.

In short, he doesn't know how to "think" his way around the golf course, rather than just lobbing the ball around.

The first thing I'd suggest is to get a scorecard and a drawing of how the course is laid out. From the scorecard anyone can learn the obvious, such as how long the course is and what par is. . . . You can also see how many Par 3s and Par 5s there are: I'd be sure to note if there are as many of one as the other—four of one and four of the other is the customary proportion. Then I'd check how long they are: Do the Par 5s run so long that not even a pro has a chance to reach them in two and go for the birdie, or possibly the eagle? (What other use *is* there for a Par 5?) Are

the Par 3s long-yardage—240 yards and up—or short? I'm against these long, lazy Par 3s that demand nothing more of the golfer than that he hit a long tee shot. I'd rather see a shorter Par 3 that's got some challenge to it—that asks the golfer to hit well and precisely with his irons instead of just muscling his way onto the green with his driver. But if the Par 3s do demand more muscle than finesse, it's something you must learn before you set foot on the tee.

Then take a look at the diagrammatic sketch of the course to see what it tells you. For example, is the basic route of the holes clockwise or counterclockwise? . . .

What use is all this?

It tells you:

What kind of golfer the designer laid out the course for.

What kind of out-of-bounds directions he considered to be more serious. If you know that, you'll be better able to gauge how and where to place the emphasis on your bolder shots.

History is a little weak on this point, but my guess is that around the turn of the century, the golf course designers laid the holes out counterclockwise to accommodate the members. Most country club members were figured to be right-handed. And they figured the members to have played golf enough to get rid of the slice and acquire a hook. (Only truly dedicated duffers could afford to belong to a country club in those days; the rest never got enough experience to get rid of their slice.)

The golf course designer also had to be concerned about what was around the golf course . . . [such as fences, roads, walking paths, and so forth].

So if the course was built clockwise—which is a natural kind of design and movement—the right-handed hook-hitter was likely to keep hitting the ball out of bounds on the left, out into the road or street. Even more so if he duck-hooked the ball. This was inconvenient for him: Climbing fences was not in the dignity of the times. It was costly to him. The out-of-bounds rule, with its penalty strokes, was devised in the 1890s at a course whose architect saw the problems of over-the-fence-and-out. And it was a threat not only to him and his sanity but the people who happened to come along the road or street.

By turning the golfer around and getting him to go around the course counterclockwise, the designer didn't cure his duck hook. And he didn't keep him out of the rough. But he did keep him on the golf course—the most wild and erratic duck-hooked shots would not fly out into the street but merely onto another part of the golf course. Into a playable if not pleasant lie. (It's simply more convenient to play back from the next fairway than to try to play out of a run in the trolley lines.) What about the right-handed slice-hitters? Theoretically, they could go off the course on the right, of course. But there weren't so many of them. And none of them could duck-hook one. So the odds that they'd hit into the street were not nearly so great.

Once a trend like that gets set, it endures. For thirty or forty years, golf courses tended to fit into the same pattern. If there were roads around, the hole pattern was counterclockwise; if there weren't the designer could get more creative.

So if you're a right-handed golfer who hits a draw or hook, you know that the counterclockwise course was designed to forgive your own worst faults. . . . That may or may not give you a vast sense of security, but at least you know how the designer felt about the relative threats of the rough to the right as compared to the left. And you can examine them with a critical eye as to how they'll affect a bold philosophy of play.

(In recent years, it should be noted, golf courses have been built much farther from the city than in the past—cars can get out farther in an hour than a horse and buggy could get in a day. So the new courses do not suffer from old disciplines. . . . For my part, I encourage and applaud the trend to a more creative design; I think it will lead to far more thoughtful and challenging golf courses.)

This is a trend—a useful hint—you can get as to how a particular golf course was conceived. And how it might be played.

But you can also learn, by a close look at the overview of the course, whether it otherwise favors the draw or the fade.

Augusta National, for example, is very much a course that plays to a draw. There are, doubtlessly, certain spots on which you'd rather go down the right side than the left side to a particular hole. But in general, the vast reaches and best positions on each hole

Arnold Palmer strategically planned each assault on a golf course, but not every putt fell.

come into play to the golfer who plays the draw rather than one who plays the fade.

To be sure, some of this is apparent only when you play the course. But by looking at a diagram of the course, you can see—as at Augusta—that the pronounced doglegs are to the left. Which is to say that they yield most to golfers who play a draw. There are, in fact, only one or two holes that bend to the right—and . . . the bend is all but imperceptible. So here's a course that determines your strategy of play—a draw, not a fade—without really altering your philosophy of play.

You can also use the diagram fruitfully to see what holes have a sharp dogleg and what the yardage is on those holes. From this, you can determine on what doglegs it's rewarding to be bold in trying to cut the dogleg. Part of the decision is in distance; part of it is in what lies beyond the blind shot if you make the shortcut over the inner angle of the dogleg.

If the total length of a dogleg hole is, say, 350 to 440 yards or so, a Par 4 with a narrow fairway, it would not always be worthwhile to shoot blindly over the trees—over the corner of the dogleg—to shorten your second shot. You can reach the green and make the Par 4 anyway, just by shooting down the fairway to the corner, and turning the corner with your second shot.

But if the dogleg hole is a Par 5, let's say 500 yards or more, and if you're looking for a birdie on the hole, then it may well be worthwhile cutting the corner . . . [b]ecause you may cut an entire stroke off.

What else should you determine from the diagrammatic sketch?

Look for the holes that run parallel to each other. You can learn quite a bit by watching what's happening on a parallel hole that you're soon to play. On the first tee at Augusta, for instance, you can see the action on the ninth green—the two holes are parallel. Similarly on the second tee, you can see the eighth green. At Firestone [in Akron, Ohio], you can seize an even more immediate bit of intelligence: On the second tee you can see the third green, on the third tee you can observe the fourth green; you can not only

check the pin placement and the wind trends, but watch a player putt to see how fast the green is. . . .

In all of this, my point is to suggest that you can learn as much about the course as you can—*before* you set a spike onto the course. It's like going on a trip: You usually buy a road map, choose your routes, know where the shortcuts are, know whether going off the expressway is going to be rewarding in some way, and so on. You just don't start driving aimlessly on a road in order to get from New York to Chicago. Similarly with a golf course: You just don't start hitting a ball aimlessly around it. You look at its "map" and you see what it has to offer: where the birdies are, where the dangers are, how one hole is related to another, where the shortcuts are and whether they are as rewarding as some other way around the course, what you can do to make the course bend to your own philosophy. After all, the course was carefully designed—if not by a rational man, at least by a purposeful one. And you can learn something of that purpose—and how you can deal with it—by studying the overview in advance.

From *Go For Broke, My Philosophy of Winning Golf*, by Arnold Palmer, with William Barry Furlong. Simon & Schuster, New York, N.Y. Copyright © 1973 by Arnold Palmer (with William Barry Furlong). Reprinted with the permission of Arnold Palmer Enterprises.

Every shot in golf should be played as a shot at some clearly defined target. All players realize this when they are playing a shot to the green. But what many of them forget is that the shot off the tee should also be aimed at some target down the fairway.

CRAIG WOOD

How to Psych-Out Your Opponent

1978 / LEE TREVINO

Lee Trevino grew up in Dallas, in a house that had neither electricity nor plumbing, and left school in the eighth grade to work on a par-3 course. When he returned from the Marines, he again worked on a course, but he made more money betting he could hit accurate shots with the fat end of a taped-up soda bottle. As one of the Tour's most popular and successful players from 1968 to 1984—during which he won twenty-nine titles, including six Majors—"Super Mex" remained a scrambler and hustler. To relax, he talked endlessly to the gallery, his caddie, and himself. In this article, he boasted that talking was an effective weapon, particularly when he allowed opponents to overhear him saying "untruths" to his caddie that would mess with their minds and cause them to miscalculate their next shots.

———————

Before I start telling you how to put the clamps on your opponent by messing up his brain waves, I want to clear up a big fallacy. A lot of so-called experts say that the ability to "psych-out" is a subtle art requiring the mind of a near genius. Well, I'm here to tell you that it's not. All it amounts to is common sense, and that's something I pride myself in having a bundle of—at least on the golf course.

Psyching-out, or gamesmanship, revolves around one key phrase—"the power of suggestion." The minute you plant the tiniest seed of doubt or fear in your opponent's head, you might as well figure the trophy is yours. The very best golfers are only human, and therefore even they can fall prey to the wrong thing said at the wrong time.

I've always been able to rely solely on my talent to win, but I've been playing this game a long time and I've picked up a ton of what you might politely call the "finer points," which, since I really don't need them, I'll pass along to you. Hey listen, I'm no saint. I've used a lot of gamesmanship in my day—mostly when I was an amateur—but when you're trying to make a living on the Tour, you'd better be damn sure your skill speaks for itself, or you'll wind up missing the cut at the taco stand.

There are plenty of perfectly legal ways to beat your opponent, aside from simply out-shooting him. The most surefire way I know of is to think out loud to your caddie or the good Lord. It's a great means by which to feed false information to the guy you're playing against, and at the same time it's legal because you're not talking directly to him. I come by this method naturally, simply because I don't have to make a concerted effort to think out loud.

A par-3 hole is a great setup for this kind of *modus operandi*, as my Latin buddies would say. If you're hitting first, you can look upon your opponent as a guinea pig. You see, very few players have ironclad confidence in their clubs, nor do they know the layout that well. So you should take advantage of the other guy's insecurity here.

More likely than not, your opponent will look in your bag to see what you're going to hit, so what you do is fool him by putting something on a club or taking some off. In other words, if it's a perfect 5-iron to the green don't use it. Hit a soft 4 or a hard 6. The next thing you know, your opponent will end up knocking hell out of the wrong club or winding up way short.

But you've got to talk some to set the stage for this kind of confusion.

Here's an example of an effective psych-out conversation between a player and his caddie:

Golfer: "What do ya think? Wind's blowin' right to left."

Caddie: "Yeah."

Golfer: "Do you think we can get this 5 there?"

Caddie: "Man you'd have to kill it."

Golfer: "Really? Well, I'd better hit a 4."

Of course, the two of them know that it's only a smooth 5. But the player goes ahead and hits an easy 4-iron. That'll get to your opponent every time. He'll get up there and jump on a 3- or 4-iron and the ball will fly one-way, non-stop to Pittsburgh. You're sittin' pretty and he's in a heap of trouble.

The same routine applies when you and your opponent are in the fairway getting ready to hit your second or third shot, and the two of you are only a few yards apart.

On the green, if you putt first and should happen to put a weak stroke on it and end up way short, shake your head in utter disbelief and say something like, "This is the slowest damn green I've ever been on!" Chances are that he'll send his into the bunker on the other side of the green.

The secret to success here is to be a hell of an actor. You've got to really pour it on. You have to speak your lines with great realism and sincerity.

Let's say you're a hole down in match play, you're standing on the 18th fairway and you blow your second shot to the green. The only way you're going to tie up the game is to pull a miracle out of your bag. If you're hitting first and your opponent's ball is only five or ten yards in front, you can really pull a Sir Laurence Olivier number on him. The minute you know you've botched your shot, drop your club in

Lee Trevino (right), pictured with Jack Nicklaus, has said that the real secret to his many wins has been skill, but he also admits to occasionally having used gamesmanship.

disgust, kick your bag, and stomp away yelling to yourself words to this effect: "You dumb bleepin' so-and-so! That was only a 6-iron and you're trying to hit a hard 5! Damn, you're 180 yards away, you stupid ----!"

Now if your opponent hasn't checked your bag, you could have just fed him a pile of garbage about what you hit. Your little diatribe might get him to thinking and fretting about what to use. And there's a slim chance he'll make a disastrous choice. At least you've set the groundwork in motion.

An excellent way to instill a little fear in your opponent is to keep complimenting him on something he's doing well. He might start worrying about losing the touch, and if he does, he will. After about the fourth hole, for example, tell the guy he's hitting his driver awfully straight: "Man, you're hitting that driver good. You haven't missed a fairway." Repeat the compliment on several holes, as if you truly are in awe of him. And pretty soon he'll probably self-destruct. . . .

Successful gamesmanship depends largely on knowing your opponent. What makes him tick? What are his prejudices, weaknesses, strengths?

If he's a teetotaler, stroll onto the first tee with a can of beer. If he's an insomniac, talk about how crucial it is to get plenty of sleep the night before a match and he'll toss and turn and show up exhausted. If he's the nervous, Don Knotts type, keep telling him how important the match is and how uptight you are about it, and he'll no doubt end up with a vibrating putter and shaky driver. There are millions of ways to ruffle your opponent, but, again, you have to *know* him.

Without sounding like a Boy Scout working toward his honest badge, I want to stress that the most brilliant way to psych-out your opponent is through skill. Ain't nothin' going to foul up a golfer's game faster than the other guy hitting it stiff to the pin and slam-dunking ten footers.

From *Golf Magazine* (October 1978), by Lee Trevino. Copyright © 1978–2005, Time4Media, Inc. Reprinted with permission of *Golf Magazine*.

The Playing Field

1993 / ROBERT TRENT JONES, JR.

From after World War II through the 1980s, Robert Trent Jones, Sr., was golf's preeminent course architect, designing or reworking 500 courses around the world. His sons, Robert and Rees, followed in his footsteps. Robert "Bobby" Trent Jones, Jr., who was born in 1939, has designed over 200 courses himself, adhering to his father's philosophy for a hole—"Hard par, easy bogey," meaning that it will take great shots to earn good scores. From the point of view of golfers, this chapter from Jones's first book, in which he said he gets ideas from other sports and games, is enthralling because it reveals how a great, creative designer thinks when laying out a course. The quasi-obstacle courses Jones designed challenged golfers to think their way through a round in order to avoid hazards and be in position for good approaches. Smart course management is the only way to play a Jones course.

Among the games that require a formal playing field, golf offers an unusual combination of rigid specifications mixed with sometimes wild and unpredictable irregularities of nature. In other words, no two courses or rounds are ever so alike that you can attack them with exactly the same game plan. For me, the constantly changing conditions and the infinite variety of holes define the essence of the game.

To perform successfully on such a playing field demands a mindset that can quickly analyze the features of a course, including changeable elements like weather and wind, and that can then decide what challenge the architect poses. In every case, there is a risk-reward factor. The course forces you to evaluate each shot in terms of nerve and skill. The more decisive your shot selection and thought process, the greater your chances of mastering the course.

One way to understand how a designer envisions a course is to look at other sporting activities. For example, when I design a course, I have in mind chess, pool, auto racing, and certain target sports.

Chess

Chess is intrinsically a game of attack and defend. Like chess, golf is a silent battle—give or take a few eruptions—in which the architect assumes the role of defender against the golfer attacking the course. Imagine a well-defended golf hole as a giant chessboard where the designer has created a system of defenses. They can be as obvious as a waste bunker or as subtle as a mound or a contour in a putting surface. The designer not only places obstacles on a hole but also may camouflage them. A good rule for playing golf, then, is to start each hole aware that there may be subtle, mysterious, or even hidden elements waiting to sabotage your game.

Your attack on a hole involves land and air strikes. From a land perspective, visualize yourself threading a path through the defenses in search of the best landing and takeoff areas, much the way ground troops move from position to position when assaulting an enemy fortification.

Obviously, attacking a hole by air is a major weapon in your arsenal. Be aware also that designers employ illusions, prevailing wind currents, and land-scape to challenge your attack. Simply getting the ball into the air isn't enough if it lands in the wrong place.

Thinking about golf as a giant chess game played between the designer and golfer will help you understand the need for long- and short-range strategies. Chess masters are great because they have a custom-made strategy for each opponent. You need the same for each hole and each course. . . .

Pool

Golf is colloquially referred to as a "pasture pool." Pool proficiency requires mastery of spins and angles and skill in organizing a sequence of shots. Winning depends heavily on sound, strategic thinking. Champion pool players such as Minnesota Fats or Steve Mizerak, know how to manipulate the cue ball with spin. Their wizardry includes almost perfect control of all angles on a pool table.

Golf is also a game of spins and angles. Pros talk of "working" the ball. Technically, this means imparting various spins so that the while the ball is airborne it moves toward the chosen target and rolls advantageously when it lands. Working includes the skills of fading, drawing, stopping the ball, and making shots bounce forward.

While a well-made pool table is a perfectly planed surface, a golf hole can be seen as a field of hundreds of angled planes, which can deflect the ball in various directions. Visualize a hole as a series of planes without grass, trees, and water. That's the designer's view when he lays out a hole.

Like pool, golf is primarily a game of position. The professional pool player never takes one shot at a time. He organizes a series of shots in his mind in order to sink all the balls on the table. The key is to get a good "leave," or an ideal position for the next shot.

Ask yourself how often you look at a hole in terms of the best leaves for subsequent shots. The value of such positioning is that you begin to tailor your shotmaking abilities to the course. You mentally take control of the design. This strategy is not restricted to tee shots. Playing approach shots to the "fat," or safe, side of greens instead of at the flag may reduce your score dramatically. Designers try to tempt you into hitting risky shots. Smart players know their limits and avoid trouble.

For example, consider the 437-yard Par 4 18th hole at Doral Country Club in Miami, designed by Dick Wilson and nicknamed the Blue Monster. Because of its configuration, low-handicap players normally will choose a route off the tee that is close to the water, significantly shortening the hole. Mid-handicappers and high-handicappers should play away from the water on their tee shots. For their approach, mid-handicappers may attempt to reach the green's right-hand side while less skilled players may elect to lay up short of the water fronting the green. . . .

AUTO RACING

Golf is also similar to auto racing in several ways. All the top drivers have heroic courage and a special talent for shifting gears to match the racecourse. Indianapolis 500 winner Danny Sullivan, an avid golfer, noted the parallels. . . . "I look for the curves and banks on a golf course the way I do when I drive a race car," he said. "If you aren't aware of them, they can ruin your day."

A golf hole starts out like a straightaway, with the golfer flooring it (swinging aggressively) on most par 4s and par 5s for distance. Then he downshifts (approach shot), eases up on the accelerator for a hairpin turn (chip), and guides the car (ball) across the finish line (into the hole). It's an ongoing adventure to get the most from your car or clubs without pushing too hard.

If players are not mentally conditioned, they will fail to master the course. [Major championship] venues . . . are the ultimate test of patience and perseverance. When Tony Jacklin won the 1970 U.S. Open at Hazeltine National in Minnesota, friends taped the word TEMPO on his locker before the final round. Despite slick greens, thick rough, and windy conditions, Jacklin was able to adjust his game and maintain composure throughout the five-hour ordeal. All pros know that rhythm and positive thinking are essential to winning. Just ask their sports psychologists.

On certain holes, a designer may attempt to upset a golfer's balance and mindset. He tempts you to push too hard or take unnecessary chances. I often say, "Lost ball, lost stroke, lost confidence."

TARGET SPORTS

A final comparison can be made with target sports. To understand target golf, we must examine the evolution of shotmaking. Golf started as a knockabout affair in which players advanced the ball with a stick toward an endpoint, the early game being played mostly on the ground. Technical advances in ball construction, club making, and swing mechanics produced a higher shot trajectory, and the game moved from a land campaign to an aerial assault.

The consequences have been twofold. First, golfers today watch pros shoot "darts" from great distances and often believe that is the only way to play the game. Second, on many modern courses, targeted areas have been designed and maintained to receive high-trajectory shots. . . .

One way to view a golf course is as a series of defined target areas. [For instance, consider] the 520-yard par 5 second hole at Wailea's Gold Course on Maui, Hawaii. . . . With your tee shot you can aim for a reasonably large landing area, say 20 to 30 yards in diameter, whereas hitting into the green from 100 yards, you should be trying for an area 20 to 30 feet in diameter.

I encourage every golfer to consider separating some holes into a series of par 3s to better visualize the hole as a group of distinct targets. [Then on a 390-yard] par 4 hole, Player A [might see] a 250-yard par 3 and a 140-yard par 3, while Player B [might see] a 200-yard par 3 and a 190-yard par 3. Each player proceeds with a specific target in mind on each stroke, and the prudent golfer will avoid trouble and play within his ability level.

From *Golf by Design: How to Lower Your Scores by Reading the Features of a Course*, by Robert Trent Jones, Jr. Copyright © 1993 Robert Trent Jones, Jr. Reprinted by permission of Little, Brown & Co., Inc.

Course Management

2000 / ANNIKA SORENSTAM

Some sports fans were first introduced to Annika Sorenstam at the Colonial in 2003, when she became the first female to play a PGA event since 1945. They hadn't watched the Swedish superstar earn that distinction by thoroughly dominating the LPGA Tour since joining in 1994, habitually winning Rolex Player of the Year awards, setting numerous records (including shooting a 59), and quickly amassing enough victories to qualify for the Hall of Fame. What followers of women's golf admired about Sorenstam was not just her matchless talent but her machine-like consistency, hole after hole, tournament after tournament. Her secret is preparation: As this essay confirms, she learns each course before she plays it, devises and sticks to an overall game plan for a low score, approaches each hole with a strategy, and focuses on her own game. Surely, no LPGA golfer has better exemplified the benefits of savvy course management.

———

Course management has to do with developing an overall game strategy. To be successful, you must have a plan for tackling each hole and a strategy for choosing the best routes to the green. . . .

It is important to become familiar with the characteristics of the course before the start of a game or tournament. While some of the specific shot strategy is reserved until actual play, it is still essential to begin with an overall plan. . . . I try to get a feel for what kind of shots I need to play, figure out what places I want to hit the ball and places where I don't want to hit the ball, and see if there are any particular shots that are important around that course. For example, on some courses, it is very important to drive the ball well, so I would work on that before the tournament started. On other courses, it may help to work on some chip shots where there are really tricky greens with big undulations. When I play the course,

I'm just trying to get used to the course and figure out what kind of shots I need.

If you're playing a recreational round, many facilities have a detailed scorecard or yardage book that thoroughly describes course yardage, terrain, hole placement, and even where the flagsticks are placed. . . .

During the game you must . . . come up with a strategy for playing each hole. The first step is recognizing your own strengths and limitations when it comes to executing certain shots. The second step involves carefully scoping out the hole and noting any potential trouble areas, like sand or water, high rough, etc. From this you can designate certain areas as "safe" places to land the ball. By comparing your strengths and weaknesses to the layout of the hole, you can decide the best path to the green and the club you should use to get there.

For example, my ultimate goal in the tee shot is to place it well. To do this, I look at the hole in the opposite way—from green to tee. By measuring the shot this way, I can see where I need to be in the fairway to hit the best shot to the green. Sometimes the driver might not be the best club choice. It could be that the driver would carry the shot too far or that it would put the ball at an angle where it couldn't get to the flag. I always plan at least one shot ahead.

From the fairway, if I can't reach the green in two on a par 5, I always lay up to my favorite distance, which is 80 yards. My caddie counts back how far I have to hit the ball to leave it 80 yards from the flag. To get there on a par 5, most often my second shot is a 7- or 5-wood. From 80 yards, I usually hit a lob wedge, depending on the conditions. This is a strategy that you could also adopt, according to the distance that works best for you.

Club selection varies when the distance is between clubs. It depends so much on where the flagstick is. For example, if the pin is toward the front of the green and I'm in-between clubs, I like to get the ball on the green. So in that case, I would put the ball past the pin. If the pin is in the back of the green and I'm in-between, I'd rather be short just to make sure the ball gets on the green.

In general, I'm a fast player, and I don't like slow play. I think a lot of golfers tend to take too much time reading putts, figuring out the wind, and calculating the yardage. I personally think that once you calculate the yardage, there are not that many shots to choose from. Try to make it simple. Try to hit a good shot and always try to curve it less—the less time you have to think about what kind of shot to hit, the better your shot will most likely be. . . .

To avoid feeling pressured by the play of others, it's very important to play your own game. By this I mean you must hit your shots and the shots that you know how to hit. Hit one shot at a time and focus on your game only. I don't really look at other players when they swing or putt, so I don't get any images of something that could interrupt my focus or composure. I just want to try to remember my good shots and focus on my game, not somebody else's.

Reprinted by permission from Annika Sorenstam, 2000, from *LPGA's Guide to Every Shot*, edited by the Ladies Professional Golfers Association (Champaign, Illinois: Human Kinetics). Chapter by Annika Sorenstam.

AIM AWAY

German star Bernhard Langer won two Masters because he knows how to play courses with tight fairways and shape his shots to avoid trouble on either side. Tee the ball up on the same side as the trouble ahead, he says, and aim in the opposite direction. ◆

— 15 —

THE MENTAL GAME

STRESS MANAGEMENT

Match Playing

1857 ✦ "A Keen Hand" (H. B. Farnie)

Curiously, the person who wrote history's first instructional golf book didn't seek recognition. H. B. Farnie published his slim volume—"under the special patronage of the Royal and Ancient Golf Club of St. Andrews"—using a nom de plume that only the British could love. Ninety years later, in his introduction to a 750-copy reissue, Bernard Darwin confirmed that Farnie's anonymity still existed, writing, ". . . we feel sure that he was a sturdy and cheerful partner . . . and, in the best meaning of the words, a good golfer." Impressive for its time, Farnie's book has probably been undervalued. Though often naïve on technique, Farnie, exhibiting wit and charm, was prescient in discussing topics like faults, the swing plane, and, in this excerpt, golf's "mental game," urging players to remain "cool" and confident when bad things happen. Sounding surprisingly modern, he advised golfers not to "press"—in effect telling them to play within themselves. Interestingly, he presented golf as a competition, not a leisure sport.

When the beginner has played some little time, and has acquired a slight acquaintance with the various clubs, along with the facility in handling them, he turns his thoughts to conquest, and burns to match his powers with an antagonist. . . .

[But we must advise that] the great stumbling block in the way of all players, veterans, and recruits, is excitement. This proceeds from various causes. Sometimes it is generated by heavy stakes being bet on the result. The only remedy we can suggest for this malady is, not to bet at all; or at least to stake such an amount as will not influence the player's nerves by its prospective loss. Sometimes again, a golfer finds himself playing very badly, and losing every hole. Knowing he can do better, and much irritated at his ill-success, he generally takes the very plan to make it worse, if possible, by causing strength to take the place of science, or in some other equally objection-able mode. Sometimes, a player driving beautifully, more so, it may be, than his wont, is inoculated with an intense purpose of accomplishing still greater shots; and, as in the last instance, breaks the charm and his play at the same time. Lastly, excitement is occasionally super-induced upon golfers of nervous temperament by the exceeding closeness of the match. This often causes mistakes to be made even by the finest players. . . .

When a player, in his excitement, seeks to retrieve the fortunes of a match, or to outdo a brilliant stroke, by forcing additional strength into his swing, he is said technically to "press". Nothing is more fatal to steady play than his pressing; it throws the golfer, during the sweep of his club, from the moment off his equilibrium, and this renders the hitting very uncertain. Besides, it is a curious fact that, even when the ball chances to be correctly struck with this additional impetus, the distance is but a little increased; bearing out an assertion . . . that an excess of lead (which is the equivalent to an increased rapidity of the swing) does not tend to give much greater momentum to a ball when hit with a correctly executed sweep. Pressing one's play to recover a lost stroke is also radically wrong in principle; for it is very evident that the stroke must be made up if at all by some mistake committed by the opposite party, rather than by an extraordinary achievement which shall cover two good shots of the adversary.

Excitement is liable likewise to influence the short game; we can only advise in such case coolness and deliberate play. But of all other things let not the young player get irritated, by the luck of the green being apparently against him. Perhaps he finds his ball after a well-calculated stroke, lying in a narrow rut; at another time when he chances to draw his ball among some whins, he discovers he has the additional misfortune to be down a rabbit hole; then, a beautiful long putt promising to be dead by the lip of the hole, is midway thrown at right angles off its course by an unremarked stone; let him bravely defy his luck, and if he be a philosopher, even thank the fate that has given him some useful experience. The golfer should never give up a hole. This is a capital maxim, and has done wonders on a links where hazards abound.

Indecision should be overcome boldly and promptly by the player. He must have confidence in himself. If he is conscious of having a tolerably correct theory of the game in his head, backed by some experience, he should never seek advice from his caddie. Should he play correctly, his merit is greater, and the success encourages him; should he fail, he has himself to blame, and his idea he finds erroneous of his own showing—a very conclusive and convincing argument.

A single is perhaps the best match for a novice to make his *debut* in. He has the play all to himself, and therefore gets a more rapid knowledge of the various predicaments of the game; and besides, if fortune declares against him, there is no partner to hint wrathfully that if he had done so-and-so the result would have been widely different.

When two players of unequal game engage, the match is usually equalized by the given of what is termed "odds" by the stronger to the weaker party. This consists in allowing a certain number of extra shots to be deducted from the number played by the golfer receiving them. . . . There is another way of giving odds in a match, by allowing the party receiving the difference so many holes ahead to start with. Now this kind of odds, although very tempting, is very insidious, and does not by any means equalize the chances of a match, especially if the party giving the odds is a much superior player to his adversary. . . . By all means therefore, let the novice . . . take strokes instead of holes.

In a match with odds, both parties should play with extreme coolness, avoiding pressing and hazardous strokes; for he who gives the odds cannot afford to run dangerous risks, and he who receives them, is only benefited by their use when he keeps his ball safely on the course. The fact of an extra shot occurring in a hole should be, as much as possible, ignored on both sides; it should occupy no place in the calculations of their play; the only time, indeed, that it should be remembered is, when the balls lie dead, or nearly so at the hole. . . .

In foursomes, coolness and command of temper cannot be too much enjoined on the unsteady player, for in addition to the reasons we have already urged against the indulgence of excitement, he has a partner whose interests and enjoyment he is bound to consult as much as his own, and it's doubtful whether this can be accomplished by wild driving or haphazard play. This species of match is a favorite one among oldsters, as the subdivision of labor enables them to enjoy all the excitement of a contest with one-half the usual fatigue.

The great match, however, on the golfing course is the periodical contest for a club medal. . . . Just let the reader picture the awe-inspiring preparations; the deserted green, waving with flags, tabooed from pressure of the competitors' foot, till the word be given; the whispering circles of stalwart golfers, all soon to be engaged in friendly combat; and most dread sight of all—alas! that it should be so—the waving silks of beauty and fashion, flitting around the starting point, like the fair dames of the ancient tournament. What can an unfortunate fellow, with nervous tendencies, do, but miss his ball, and start away with a tingling sensation of shame! Many a medal has been lost by a very champion of golf in consequence of this fatal miss at the start.

While repeating our somewhat monotonous advice of playing coolly and deliberately, we would caution good golfers against a fault they glide into unwittingly; that is, extreme caution in putting. We have repeatedly seen old hands, who were first-rate performers, lose their chance of coming in at the top by this seeming prudence, after making their long game in the most masterly style. . . . The cause is simply this: An indifferent player knowing his chances are feeble . . . rushes his ball at the hole when he gets on the putting green, seeking by a steal or gobble to gain a stroke or more on the hole. The more evenly couples are matched . . . the better the play will be; nothing distracts the good performer more than seeing continual missing and wild play; in the latter case, indeed, he has to wait . . . till his unlucky opponent tracks his wandering stroke among the whins. . . .

In playing for club honors, we only need say in conclusion, avoid pressing, and by all means try and give your irons a holiday.

From *The Golfer's Manual—Being an Historical and Descriptive Account of the National Game of Scotland*, by "A Keen Hand" (H. B. Farnie). Whitehead & Orr, Cupar, Scotland.

The Psychology of Golf

1913 · JEROME D. TRAVERS

Long before Jerome Travers was a four-time U.S. Amateur champion, it became obvious that even the greatest golfers, other than Allan "the Unbeaten" Robertson, tasted defeat on occasion, and it wasn't always due to a dodgy swing. At the time Travers penned his book, the "mental game" was an increasingly hot topic among golf writers. Travers claimed that the head and hands complement each other, as do talent and reasoning, encouraging golfers to "think before you play" and do "head work." With advice that Jack Nicklaus and a bevy of sports psychologists would preach years later, Travers told golfers to understand the subtleties of shot and club selection. Many current golfers and teachers also agree with his counsel to play conservatively after taking an early lead—the opposite of what is usually taught in baseball, football, and other sports.

Golf is a game of the head as well as a game of the hands. The golfer who does not use his head will never achieve any great proficiency in the sport. A really clever player takes note of everything about him that may have an influence on the result of his strokes and does his best to use it for his benefit. When the wind is dead against him on the tee, and the bunker ahead is likely to trap his shot because of the adverse wind, he plays short if there seems small chance of carrying the bunker because little distance will be sacrificed, and because a trapped shot is certain to cost him one stroke and possibly two or three. In match play this misfortune would cost him the hole and in medal play it might cause him to lose the day's competition. . . .

The old adage, "Look before you leap," when applied to the royal and ancient game of golf, should read, "Think before you play." There is no virtue, no success in walking up to the ball and hitting it blindly. Study the lay of the land ahead, remember the condition of the ground, plan to avoid the traps along one side of the course, or the other, make allowance for the wind, canvass all these things quickly and then make your shot. I have seen noted experts devote over a minute to the study of a putt before the putt was made. When they were badly bunkered, I have seen them play back so that the second shot would safely clear the obstruction and give them good distance. I have seen them slice or hook a ball deliberately so that it would pass round a tree in the line of play and roll to the putting green. I have seen so much backspin applied to a mashie shot that when the ball struck the putting green it actually rolled toward the man who played it.

A player must be fairly expert to do some of these things, and in such instances mere thought will be of little value unless it be backed by skill, but from the first drive to the last putt the player should make good use of his reasoning powers. Suppose, for example, that the drive is along the edge of the links and the wind is apt to carry a straight or hooked ball out of bounds to the left. How easy it is for the player to take this fact into consideration and drive a little further to the right than usual, or slice the ball a trifle to counteract the force of the wind. Suppose that the player knows he cannot reach the green in one shot and has a bad brassy lie. The thoughtless player will play the brassy and, doubtless, get a poor shot and poor distance. The player who thinks will play the safer mid-iron, get good distance and reach the green on his next shot, lying 3 as against the brassy player's 4. Often, in medal play, have I seen golfers refuse to take advantage of the rule which permits them to lift and tee up the ball with a loss of two strokes only to lose stroke after stroke in unsuccessful attempts to get out of trouble and finally, in disgust, pick up the ball, thereby disqualifying themselves. A moment's thought would have convinced them that the safe and wise thing to do was to lose two strokes rather than risk such a disaster.

Often during a 36-hole match, the condition of the ground undergoes a remarkable change and the player should note this and make allowance for it. For example, owing to a heavy rain overnight the links are soft and slow and the ball gets only a fair amount of roll in the morning. The sun is hot and by 1:30 P.M., when the afternoon round is to start, the ground has become well dried-out and the ball gets a long roll, consequently much less power is needed to duplicate the approach shots of the morning. The player must remember this from the moment he makes his first tee shot in the afternoon round, or a few strokes or a few holes will be lost before he wakes up and adjusts his play to the new condition of the links.

Beyond a doubt, there is greater opportunity for head work in match play than in medal play. In the latter the golfer is playing against the entire field, and he is doing his best to turn in the lowest possible score—so many strokes for the entire eighteen holes. There is no direct competition. He and his companion are not playing against each other except in a general sense, and each man's interest in the other largely consists in his duty to see that the other plays the game according to the rules governing medal play contests, counting every stroke, holing out each putt, etc., etc. If he fails to do this he is a traitor to every other player in the competition and is himself disqualified, as a matter of honor, no matter whether or not the committee learns of his failure. In match play the contest is man against man. The two players go out together, and each hole is a separate battle in itself. Smith wins the first hole, and is 1 up. Jones makes a desperate rally and captures the second hole, and the match is all-square. They tie the third hole. All square. Smith wins the fourth and fifth holes and is 2 up, and thus, hole after hole, the battle rages. Such matches often go 18 holes, 36 holes, yes, even 50 holes before one contestant or the other wins.

In a hand-to-hand struggle of this character the golfer who keeps perfectly cool, holds his temper no matter what happens, plays with thoughtful deliberation and carefully studies his opponent, will have a decided advantage over an adversary who gets nervous, loses his temper because [of] bad luck or a bad shot, plays hastily and devotes but little thought to his shots and to the temperament of the man he is playing. While it is highly improper and against the etiquette of golf to say or do any un-sportsmanlike thing that will annoy or irritate your opponent, there are legitimate acts that may prove useful in breaking down his nerve and making him "go up in the air," to use the expressive metaphor of the streets. Suppose, for example, that your opponent particularly prides himself concerning the great distance he secures in driving, and that you know he confidently expects to out-drive you from start to finish in the match. If you have specialized a bit in the psychology of golf you will guess shrewdly that if you equal or surpass his drives from the first, second, and third tees his confidence will receive a severe jolt, worry will set in and he will at once commence pressing every tee shot beyond the limits of prudence. In the game of golf confidence is a great helper. Let a player lose it and he is marked for slaughter.

On the other hand, an attack of over-confidence is apt to be fully as disastrous. Overconfidence and carelessness are teammates. If you can do so, break down your opponent's nerve by out-driving him and by setting a heart-breaking pace from the first tee, but simply because you have him a few holes down do not hold him too cheap and ease up in your efforts. As every experienced golfer knows, the little ball is tricky and eccentric. It will "roll for you" hole after hole as if it were bewitched in your favor. You will drive out of bounds and the ball will hit a tree or a rock and come back into bounds again. Your approach shot will strike the green three feet off the line to the hole, yet the ball will deliberately turn to the right or left, make straight for the cup as if pulled by an invisible string and drop in as if there were no other place for it to go. Then, after "rolling for you" for a time it will "roll against you" with the perversity of the evil one. You will top your drive, foozle your approach, and miss your two-foot putt, and before you quite realize it your opponent will have squared the match and be leading you by a hole or two. Consequently it behooves you to keep on playing golf with all the skill at your command until your man is actually beaten. . . .

Another important thing the real golf psychologist remembers is to refrain from playing a hazardous shot when he is a stroke or two ahead of his opponent through the green and there is no necessity for doing so. . . .

The golfer who wishes to secure health and happiness from the sport should be a philosopher. He should strive to play his best, but if that be none too good, he should not permit the fact to worry, irritate, or anger him. . . .

A man who gets into a rage, swears, and breaks his clubs, and petulantly drives the inoffensive ball off into the woods should either reform or give up the game. He is reaping no benefit mentally, morally, or physically. Let him go beat carpets! No true lover of golf will mourn his loss.

From *Travers' Golf Book*, by Jerome D. Travers, published by The MacMillan Company, New York, copyright © 1913, by the MacMillan Company.

DO IT BETTER

Teaching pro Manuel de la Torre said he got his best mental tip from his father, a club pro in Spain who immigrated to America with the help of Ernest Jones. "If you know what you are doing, and it works," he wrote in *Understanding the Golf Swing*, "spend the rest of your life perfecting it" and never second-guess yourself when you hit a bad shot or assume you need to completely revamp your approach to playing. Just go back to what you do correctly, he added, and focus on making that even better. ◈

The Eight-Inch Golf Course

1 9 2 4 ✑ E D D I E   L O O S

Playing tournaments, the New York City–born Eddie Loos usually made substantially less than the $2,200 in prize money he earned in his best year, 1930. But he won titles like the California, Missouri, and Illinois Opens, and, memorably, he and Leo Diegel defeated Harry Vardon and Ted Ray in 1920, and he and Cyril Walker became the first Americans to conquer Arnaud Massy and Archie Compston in 1926. He spent years as a club pro in California and Illinois and was one of the first golf professionals to offer group lessons, sometimes averaging 820 one-hour sessions a year. In this famous essay, one of the first to promote a pre-shot routine, Loos wrote about how golf should be played between the ears. His main point is central to all sports: The smart golfer thinks what must be done before execution, but then leaves it to muscle memory—the key to an automatic swing.

———◆———

Every game of golf that has ever been played—whether the medal was 68 or 168—has taken place on a golf course that measured eight inches—more or less.

The dimensions of this golf course, I arrived at by the more or less crude method of taking a ruler and measuring my own head from back to front.

Of course—that's just what I mean—every game of golf is played—every shot is played—in your mind before the ball actually starts on its way.

You've heard before about golf being a mental game. So have I. But my objections to most articles on the mental side of golf have been that the nut or kernel of the message seems to be that the mental side is vital, then—???

. . . If a woman wants to cut a dress—if a foundry wants to make a casting—if an architect starts to design a building—the basis of the finished product is a plan or pattern. The finished product, properly erected, is an exact reflection of the original plan or "pattern."

If you wanted to learn a verse—wanted to learn to speak it effectively—you would commit it to memory, with every inflection and emphasis necessary to make a good delivery.

This would be your "pattern."

And—when you wanted to deliver the verse—mentally you'd fish out your "pattern" and go ahead—practically the same every time, gaining skill, ease, and certainty with repetition.

It is exactly the same thing with the game of golf—every shot, successful or otherwise, is the result of a "mental pattern."

Of course, in speaking the verse, your voice is the vehicle through which the pattern is reproduced.

And your voice is more or less easily controlled.

On the other hand, the "mental patterns" used in the golf shot express themselves through many, many muscles.

So, the "patterns"—the *right* patterns—must be slowly and painstakingly built up, so that their part is so impressed upon your "muscular memory" that their execution requires no conscious thought.

Here is what I mean. The "mental patterns" of the professional are so set that when he steps up to his ball, his only conscious thought should be where he wants it to go, and then the decision to send it there.

Ask any professional you know if he carries any thought besides these after he has decided upon the playing of his shot.

The stance must be built upon a "mental pattern." When that pattern is developed, you are able to step up to your ball and—without conscious thought—know where the ball is going as the result of the position you assume in relation to it.

The "grip" of the club is the subject of another "mental pattern."

When you have the right "mental pattern" of your grip, you know that the face of the club is not going to turn over or turn up when it comes to the ball—it's fair, square, and true.

The arc of your swing—the timing—the "feel" of the clubhead—all of these things are basic "mental patterns" which find execution through your "muscular memory."

In the putt—short or long—direction is simpler than distance—the better the "mental pattern" of the proper force of the blow—the closer the ball comes to the cup.

I know this sounds complicated. I don't believe that, once understood, it will be so.

On the contrary, I firmly believe that it is the greatest step possible toward simplification of golf instruction. . . .

The oldest golf instruction extant in the early days of the paid professional coach was to take the beginner and make him swing a club without a ball for days before he actually hit one. Then—to make him hit shots with the various clubs various distances without actually playing the game—this for a month or so.

This system, a wonderful one, was based—although I never heard it so explained—upon the building in the beginner's mind of proper "mental patterns," free from the obstructing strain of actual play.

I learned to play golf with the flat swing of Willie Anderson, my youthful idol.

I created my "mental patterns" upon this method of play.

When I changed to the "upright swing" and the "game through the air," I was forced to completely change my train of "mental patterns," those relating to the arc of the swing, the stance, and the timing.

Of course, my grip and my "club feel" patterns remained the same.

My game went back. But once the new "mental patterns" were correctly established, by experiment and practice, my game became better than ever before.

Here is the way "mental patterns" evince themselves.

I stand up with an iron. My usual shot would be a high, long ball to drop dead upon the green.

A strong wind is blowing against me.

I call to mind my "mental pattern" of a push shot, get my direction, and execute it.

You must realize that these "mental patterns" are not—decidedly not—a set of directions memorized on "how to play the shot."

They are "muscular memories"—the "physical repetition" of the way previous successful shots of this character have been played.

John M. Sellers of Chicago, a great golfer and a keen student of the game, has—I understand—made an observation that is very interesting.

He says in effect that the fancy, full, free swing of the professional in casual play or practice is a decidedly different thing from the "money shot" that he settles down to where there's a stake up. . . .

While the professional is playing a casual round, he feels that he can take a chance—experiment perhaps.

So his "mental patterns" are of the kind of swing he thinks his fellow players like to see—the slashing, bold, take-a-chance set of "patterns."

On the other hand, when there's a cup or a prize at stake, the average professional calls up, or tries to call up, that set of "patterns" that minimize the chance of error—the "mental patterns" where every bit of unnecessary flourish, of useless motion is eliminated—the "money shot."

I firmly believe that one of the things that holds back hundreds of professionals from far better scoring is the possession of these two sets of "mental patterns."

Men like Walter Hagen have only one set of "mental patterns"—the "money shot"—the shot that minimizes chance results is the one that their "muscular memory" reproduces.

I do not mean that they do not take chances, but I do mean that their chance taking lies in the daring of the shot—not in its execution.

Concentration in golf, to my mind, is simply a matter of eliminating all outside matters from the successful reproduction of the "mental pattern" of the shot about to be played. . . .

Permitting noise, movement, fear of water, or hazards to spoil shots can all be traced back to the interruption of the execution of the duplication through "muscular memory" of the proper "mental pattern" for the shot.

Build your "patterns"—increase your skill in executing them—distance, direction, and a handicap that takes the winter thermometer drop will be your reward.

That eight-inch golf course in your head will do wonders if you'll take the time to plant the seed of proper "mental patterns." And the longer you own them, the better they are.

From *The American Golfer* (March 22, 1924), by Eddie Loos.

The Mental Hazards of Golf

1929 ⚑ CHARLES W. MOORE

During the 1920s, a number of books were devoted exclusively to what Seymour Dunn called "Golf Psychology." Long forgotten are such works as Charles William Bailey's *The Brain and Golf: Some Hints for Golfers from Modern Medical Science*, Jack Hackbath's *The Key to Better Golf: The Mental Plan*, and Theodore B. Hyslop's *Mental Handicaps in Golf*. Charles W. Moore's *The Mental Side of Golf* got more attention than the others, partly due to a foreword by Gene Sarazen, but also because Moore's writing was less obscure, he identified "mental hazards" all golfers could recognize, and he gave solid advice on how they could think their way past them. Perhaps his topics are so simple and obvious that most other writers never felt the need to discuss them, but they are a great starting point for those who are baffled by the cruel tricks golf plays on the mind.

azards form an integral part of golf the same as the tee, the fairway, and the green. And hazards exist not only in traps, bunkers, ponds, streams, shrubs, bad lies, rub of the green, the rough, the out-of-bounds margins, but in such personal traits as haste, inattention, carelessness, indecision, fright, overwrought temper, and the like. Golf architects have placed hazards in strategic localities along the fairway and about the green; and it is only now and then that a player comes upon a trap or bunker or stream. But the golfer carries mental hazards about with him all through the game; and these mental hazards seem to have a "working agreement" with the physical hazards to play into their hands. . . .

The very existence of the physical hazard is a standing challenge to your mental and physical equipment, whether you actually fall prey or not. The risk and peril which these jeopardies suggest often go much further than merely warning you to "keep out!" They may insinuate themselves into your consciousness as to utterly blind you in what you are trying to accomplish. The Hazard of Worry is one of the most destructive enemies of golf. For worry can put a heavier handicap on the player than ten traps along the course. The golfer is in danger of bringing to the golf course something out of his complicated life that interferes sadly with his game. Even if he is not easily upset, but takes his ups and downs more calmly, still, the very nature of the care may so occupy the center of his thought, it will make a strong bid for his attention while he is trying to fix his mind on his game.

One of the things that makes worry the menace of the golfer that it is, is that it seems to be harder to get rid of than many other kinds of hazards. . . . [I]t very frequently happens that a certain worry brought up out of business or personal life is able so to intrench itself in the golfer's consciousness that it seems to stand by his side when he is on the tee, to dim the fairway itself. It will tug at his arms as he makes his swing. It will fatigue the finer parts of his shotmaking mental mechanism. It will take the bloom off his game. In his chip shots to the green, which call for such an extreme degree of nicety, worry grips at his nerves and muscles. When he tries to make his putt, he seems to be looking at the ball through a haze and film of this ever-present and annoying worry. . . . However, there is one method of overcoming the influence of worry, and that is the friendly method of substituting some thought in the place of the worry! A substitute thought will help keep the worry from distracting you. Otherwise it can so fill your mind and nerves as to blur or even divert your attention from what you are trying to do.

The Hazard of Haste in your mental golf course drives you into pressing in your swing. It whips you into an eagerness to see what has become of the ball . . . before you have hit it! It spurs you to shoot before attention has had time to focus fairly; and before observation has had opportunity to bring you the facts which reason and judgment and association and imagination must have, to help you to choose the most useful club to use, or the most intelligent shot to make.

The Hazard of Inattention lures you to put your mind on something not present, at that critical moment in the shot when the club is coming on the ball, to decide its fate. It clouds your eyes in looking down the fairway, with your thoughts miles away. It blinds you to all important undulations on the putting green. It asks you to "hit the ball with memory!" It afterward apologizes to you for the trouble it has drawn you into.

The Hazard of Distraction has a bag full of stimulations to entice you away from the business of sinking your putt; or of timing your drive. Its playground by preference is the putting green, but it is not above following the willing subject to a sand trap, or even along the easy fairway.

The Hazard of Fear leads you to doubt whether, after all, you have chosen the driver that "just fits you." It crouches in the ball, not only when it lies sullenly in some heel-track or pit, but when teed up nicely on its throne on the tee. It tries to persuade you that your opponent will win in spite of all that you can do. It is often successful in making you believe that your game has advanced as far as is in the reach of your ability. On the other hand, this hazard is not all against you. For the warning which it gives you makes you more careful in avoiding trouble; besides, your anxiety lest you lose the hole or game kindles your emotions just enough to "warm up" your "fighting fire" and, so, to put on more steam.

The Hazard of Discouragement convinces you that when the enemy has you two down and five to go, you might as well concede him the game. It shows you the worst side of a bad lie; and when you are trying to heave the ball out, it gives you a picture of failure. It tells you that your opponent does not have half the bad rub of the green that you do. That this is not your day, anyway.

The Hazard of Indecision has an awkward way of sidetracking your singleness of purpose. It starts you out on one idea, then checks you while you are in the act of carrying it through. On the tee, and while the driver is coming on the ball, it makes you feel that you are going to slice your shot, and foozle; so, it pulls your club across the ball and thus forces you to do just what you were trying to avoid. It has a habit of making your arms fall between two purposes, even when you seem to be struggling desperately to carry out only one. It convinces you that your sense-perceptions have misinformed you as to distance to the green; so, you check the force of your club in the dangerous "hitting arc," and end by falling far short!

The Hazard of Temper leads you into fixing the blame for a poor shot on your caddy, or your club, or an earthquake in Siam! . . . when the real cause of the mischief is all above your neck. It is so full of self-assertion that the Reason and Attention and Poise are driven out before its storm, so that the club is in the hands of a mutiny force, and is guided more by avenging anger than the calm, controlled temperament needed to produce results. But, this hazard of temper, like that of fear, is often the golfer's ally. For when purpose is hindered, and plans balked, either by physical conditions or by the opponent, the kindling of the right degree of temper thrice arms the player. When his good shot is set at naught by a better one from his opponent; when the attitude of triumph settles on the countenance of the enemy; when a won game seems to be slipping; all this often has the effect of so augmenting the player's determination, perseverance, and will-to-win that his temper helps sweep him to victory!

The Hazard of Fatigue strikes at the mental golfer as well as the physical. Tenseness as to the outcome of the game can tire the brain to such an extent that attention is handicapped, judgment is made unsafe, and will power is weakened. Mental fatigue is also due to over-strenuous concentration, which may burn up the finer skill in play.

THE FINE ART OF RECOVERY

To possess the ability to overmaster the "hazard idea" in the mental golfer; and to stay out of hazards, or to get out of them when a victim, is a valuable asset just as real as the putting touch, or the timing of a shot. The golfer of "recovering ability" is marked by his cool courage, his mettlesome will, his calm staying qualities, his control of temperament, his utter refusal to allow a bad shot or the rub of the green to fuss him. See how hard it is to get him to haul down his flag! He will never strike colors till his opponent's winning putt is sunk, and there is no more ground on which to stand and give fight! His unafraid resources of mind and muscle seem to come to his aid most confidently and readily when in a tight place. . . .

WAIT FOR THE REST OF YOUR BRAIN TO ARRIVE!

When confronted by a problem in golf, do not jump at a conclusion before your whole brain has had time to judge. To decide on a hair trigger is to use only a small part of brain-skill. Let the decision come from a balanced mind. Train yourself to withhold judgment till the rest of the brain "arrives." . . . Few things are commoner in a game than a golfer's premature anxiety for a shot whose outcome is uncertain. The temperamental player, on seeing the ball diving into a hazard, will begin, long before he reaches the ball, to anticipate all sorts of difficulty. As he approaches the hazard, his imagination exaggerates the disaster, and his nerves grow tense in preparation for the dreaded ordeal. However, it frequently happens that when he comes to the ball, the situation is not nearly so bad as he figured. Until his whole brain has "arrived" to reason a way out, he must not permit his first impression to alarm him and disarm him. Let him wait for the "whole mind" to catch up with the fast-running impulse, so that a calmer judgment may protect him from the wild disaster which an untimely impulse would have brought on him.

From *The Mental Side of Golf* by Charles W. Moore. Copyright © 1929 by Horace Liveright, Inc.

A Famous Star Discusses
the Mental Side of Competition

1931 ⚬ JOYCE WETHERED

It's definitely reassuring to high-handicap players that as great a champion and tough a competitor as Joyce Wethered would admit to battling nerves in the heat of close competition, to experiencing "fear in my heart, the match slipping away, the club feeling strange and useless in my hand." Her assertion that "a calm and placid exterior" can conceal churning emotions brings to mind John Feinstein's recent *A Good Walk Spoiled*, in which he shed light on the pressures felt by seemingly detached PGA golfers. Wethered advised acknowledging weak moments and the "fear of failure"— a modern concept also advanced by Charles W. Moore—and offsetting that with concentration, confidence, and a sense of humor. She advised playing your own game, as would Annika Sorenstam, but differed by saying that with the game on the line you need to shift into competitive mode with your opponent and scramble to the finish.

———

The strain of competitive golf can mean one thing and one thing only, a call upon tensely-strung nerves. However much a player may apparently be blessed with a calm and placid exterior, appearances are generally deceptive; the odds are that there is a tumult of emotions surging beneath the surface that onlookers rarely suspect.

The consolation is that this is an experience common to the majority of those who have to face what is generally and erroneously termed "the music." The music may be felt, if not expressed, when one steps off the last green. But while the ordeal is in progress, the discords are varied and numerous. Yet I am certain that no one can excel at any game without having to suffer from the sensations inseparable from "nerves."

The only resource one has to fall back on is to try to understand and develop a philosophy which will cope with them, and her experiences will naturally differ. I know perfectly well the two qualities which have helped me most: the first is honesty with oneself and the other is a sense of humor. We have to recognize our weaknesses, and unless we realize them and refuse to make allowances for them they will catch us out every time in a crisis. When, however, we have learned them all and recognized that we are going to suffer them always, it is worth a great deal to be able to feel amused by our own peculiar idiosyncrasies.

I know the feeling of standing on a tee with real fear in my heart, the match slipping away, the club feeling strange and useless in my hand; and yet I have fortunately been able to laugh at the ridiculous side of my feelings and the way they are apt to behave on these occasions. This reflection is, after all, perfectly sane and rational, and perhaps by this method of persuading oneself of its value it may be possible to regain a more normal balance.

As the mind governs the whole of our actions, everything will go to pieces, unless it is working on the right lines. Set a thief to catch a thief: set the mind to watch the mind. It becomes in moments of excitement full of fancies, fears, or useless wandering ideas and it may be no easy task to tie it down to the matter at hand. Concentration is at the root of success, if the mind can be made to concentrate on the right idea. If it will persist in thinking of harmful ideas, the execution of the shot is bound to suffer. If the mind is full of the fear of failure—a dread of the next approach, a persistent thought of three putts although the green is still far away—then, in my experience, there is but one thing that can at all help and that is to see the humor of the situation.

If one is really amused (and I must admit that one rarely is) at the absurdity of one's thoughts and anticipations, he can, and frequently does, respond by changing and coming back to a more practical and firm outlook on things. Otherwise if you cannot direct your thoughts into more suitable channels, they will grow worse and worse with the result that the horrible feeling that you are "cracking" badly becomes a certainty.

Confidence undoubtedly is a great asset, perhaps the greatest of all. But it must be genuine and based on facts. For myself I can never manufacture it; I can only keep it, if I know that I am hitting the ball correctly. If my method is working rightly, then I know that I can have confidence in producing the shot— and that is everything.

Of course, confidence depends on the avoidance of distraction. Big occasions are very apt to scatter thoughts in every direction. The only safeguard is to create your own little world and for the time being to live in it. I used to play my matches with one definite idea, to be entirely engrossed in my own shots and to be oblivious, so far as I could be, of what my opponents were doing; also to concentrate for the first part of the game entirely on figures and to let the match take care of itself until

it took a definite form. I am convinced that to play a match hole by hole right away from the first tee is an unnecessarily wearing process. It will, more often than not, make you play down to your opponents if they happen to be off their game. On the other hand, if they are playing well, your best figures are all you can hope for in any case. The scramble will probably come toward the finish.

And while speaking of scrambles, it may be an unusual experience of my own, but I find the moments of greatest strain to be when I have succeeded in building up a really promising position—say, two up and five to go, or one up and three to go. If at this critical moment you have birdies shot at you, the situation is altered without any need to blame yourself. But when it is just a matter of steady figures to win, then there can come the biggest strain of all.

Playing against Miss Cecil Leitch at Troon in 1925, after a most grueling and exhausting battle, I at last became two up and three to go, with an excellent chance of winning the sixteenth to finish the match. Instead of that, I faltered and only halved it. To make things worse, I was unable to halve either of the last two holes, dropping a stroke at each. These were the most trying holes I have ever had to play. That I won at the thirty-seventh has always seemed to me a most unjust tribulation for my opponent.

It is just that final clinching of a match that can, with some people, be so difficult. Here what little philosophy one may possess is apt to desert one. The end is just appearing in sight; one is so near and yet so far from being secure. I have often wondered how Miss Glenna Collett felt during our match at St. Andrews in 1929. I wonder if at any time she felt quite as uncomfortable or unhappy as I did when I stood two up and four to play, or as utterly incompetent as when I had to run my ball up on to the narrow shelf of the Road Hole green to win!

It can be the greatest fun to look back on thrilling encounters that are past. But how fortunate also it is that we cannot know what trials and ordeals the future holds for us—on the links or off!

From *The American Golfer* (April 1931), by Joyce Wethered.

Relaxation

1 9 3 9   K E N N E T H R. T H O M P S O N

That Charles W. Moore's *The Mental Side of Golf* had disappeared from the public view a decade after its publication is confirmed by Kenneth R. Thompson's decision to give his book the same title. Thompson's work is still regarded as the most significant of the era to deal with the "psychology of golf," but, though it has recently been reissued, it doesn't have much new to offer current golfers who have read the vast amount of material on the topic published in the last thirty years. The one exception is this essay. Every instructional writer advises golfers to relax and get rid of tension, but Thompson told readers how to do it, physically and mentally. His most welcome concept was that a golfer can achieve relaxation during the setup by filling the mind with images of "an easy-flowing backswing and a leisurely start down," an idea stated frequently by Bobby Jones.

You can just picture to yourself the tenseness of the player who takes his stance with the idea that he must "rest on his heels," or that he must "rest on his toes," or that he must "bend his knees." The legs, before starting the golf swing, must be in a relaxed position. As the weight shifts, some muscles are relaxed and others tensed to take care of the proper order of the swing. . . . Relaxation comes from the thought of smooth-flowing motion. A sense of ease and balance must prevail. The player's posture over the ball should be as little bent as possible. It must not be a strained position.

If you fill your lungs with a deep breath you feel a certain tenseness in the area of the lungs. Now if you exhale and think in terms of relaxation you will find the tenseness gone. The forcing out of the air seems to bring on a state of relaxation. Some of us who have domestic animals can perhaps learn a lot from the way they relax. One can often see a little Scottie trot into a room, throw himself on the rug, inhale and then exhale rather forcibly, and render the muscles of his legs limp. A true lesson in complete relaxation.

Freeing the shoulder muscles in the region of the neck—between the shoulder blades and the areas around the armpits—does a great deal to carry out the smoothness of a full swing. Relaxing these muscles aids the flow of the swing.

You will notice that some champions while addressing the ball on the tee—as well as on the green—place their weight on the left leg and relax the right leg. This has much to do with cutting down tension. By so doing all the leg muscles are not tensed at the same time. Having the full weight evenly distributed on both legs may account in some part for overactive nerves in putting.

Tenseness, it must be realized, is not purely a physical matter. Mental tenseness is just as bad as a physical tenseness. When a person "tries too hard" to do a thing this also brings on tenseness. To go about a task easily breeds an atmosphere of relaxation. If there is any desire to "hit the cover off the ball" it certainly has no place in the backswing. We do not hit on the backswing. The mind filled with the thought of an easy-flowing backswing and a leisurely start down will do much to aid one in relaxing.

It is not necessary to contract a muscle in order to relax it, and it is bad practice to contract it in order to relax it. You start relaxation from whatever state you find your body or muscles in. Relaxation comes about by letting the muscle grow limp, letting it "go" and permitting the mind to disregard it as useless for the time being and until needed for action. Cultivating a state of lassitude, a phlegmatic tendency, is the proper method to encourage relaxation and foreclose tension.

We have all seen how the person who is learning to control an automobile often clutches the wheel with a "death grip." As times goes on he relaxes. His grip on the wheel becomes firm but relaxed, and the muscles of the hands, arms, shoulders, and body contract and relax as occasion demands. So it should be with the golf swing.

The person who is playing golf with relaxed muscles is less troubled by sudden sounds or noises made while he is swinging his club. If the noise is continuous, the player takes it into his consciousness, so to speak, and it no longer becomes a disturbing factor; but in the case of an unexpected or sudden noise, if the muscles are not relaxed there is a decided effect on the swing which may result in a bad shot.

We take recreation for the purpose of relaxing from the strain of business. It is important that genuine relaxation should come from one's golf game, because if it does not the mind and body will not be truly refreshed. Continual or habitual tenseness in sport brings on fatigue just as much as deep and applied concentration in business. With this in mind, one can easily realize the double value of the art of relaxing. Physicians will tell you that during periods of worry a person's systolic pressure may rise as high as forty points but again settle back to normal after the person has relaxed. Practicing the ability to relax the muscles aids us to throw off mental activity in the form of worry. It involves the avoidance of undue excitement and the exercise of constant mental control by frequently exhorting yourself to relax.

It must be realized that there will always be some residual tension in a golf muscle that is not in use at the time, but the aim of the player must be to reduce this to a minimum under any and all circumstances.

The art of relaxing is a study worth pursuing until it is mastered. It must be cultivated and practiced until it has become a component of the golf stance and swing. . . . The power to relax under pressure is what aids in making champions, and, as we all know, champions are not made overnight. They have practiced the art of relaxation as faithfully as the rudiments of the proper swing.

From *The Mental Side of Golf: A Study of the Game as Practised by Champions,* by Kenneth R. Thompson. Copyright © 1939 and 1947 by Funk & Wagnalls Company.

If profanity had an influence on the flight of the ball, the game of golf would be played far better than it is.

HORACE G. HUTCHINSON

Concentration

1941 ✦ PATTY BERG
AND OTIS DYPWICK

No one had more impact on the growth of women's golf than Patty Berg. As a player she won around ninety amateur and professional tournaments; as a pioneer, she became one of the first women pros in 1940 and cofounded the LPGA in 1948. Moreover, she conducted countless clinics over five decades, usually representing Wilson Sporting Goods. She also wrote *Golf*, one of the first instructional books by a female professional. In this essay, she distanced herself from Joyce Wethered's idea to visualize the outcome of shots by saying that to get a good shot the golfer must do one thing: focus on properly striking the ball. It's likely that Berg, who played quarterback as a kid and spent time as a Marine lieutenant, surveyed the course and strategized before every shot—*unless* she was struggling. Slumping golfers as well as those with inexperience are the ones who would benefit most from Berg's advice.

Occasionally, while playing golf you will hear a player excuse a partially-missed shot by saying, "I looked up."

I believe this common error could be very briefly explained in these words, *Lack of concentration*. Chances are that he was thinking more of the result than of the execution of the shot itself.

It is my opinion that our very finest golfers have a definite mind-picture of how they are going to swing. I believe no one can hit the ball well merely from memory.

It seems to me that every golfer has some weakness which is particularly apt to show up under stress. The one effective way to check this erring tendency and its disastrous consequences is to *concentrate* on the swing.

Isolate each step of your golf game so that every shot becomes a separate unit within itself. Then devote your entire mental process to the proper execution of that particular shot, with no thought of what the results may be. If you are utterly oblivious of what goes on about you, then you are concentrating correctly.

Many times I have observed players actually looking at the green before they hit the ball. In contrast, most of the prominent amateurs and professionals seem to be in a sort of "trance." They are totally unconcerned about galleries or incidents transpiring around them, for they are concentrating intensely on the work at hand.

I see men step out on to the first tee after leaving their office. Business matters rather than their golf game are uppermost in their minds. They experience all kinds of difficulties with their game, and begin to think their game has "gone on the rocks." It is their concentration, and not their mechanical ability that is lapsing.

The great Patty Berg was almost obsessive when it came to "concentration."

Fortunately, the power of concentration has come to me quite naturally in connection with my golf. It may have been due to my previous participation in other sports requiring concentration. In spite of this I experience days when this power seems to leave me. My game suffers on such occasions.

And so I say, *"Practice concentrating on the work at hand. Do not think of the result, but only of the shot."*

From *Golf,* by Patty Berg and Otis Dypwick. Copyright © 1941 by A. S. Barnes and Company, Incorporated. Reprinted with permission from Patty Berg, LPGA founder and Hall of Fame member.

Make Use of Your Imagination

1954 JACK BURKE

Jack Burke, Jr., rose to prominence with two runaway victories in the 1951 Ryder Cup, leading to four more appearances. In 1952, he won four consecutive events, second only to streaks by Byron Nelson and Ben Hogan at the time; and in 1956 he captured the first televised Masters and the PGA, and was selected PGA Player of the Year. Overall he'd win seventeen PGA titles. For years, *The Natural Way to Better Golf* was considered merely a mandatory instructional book by a hot golfer. Today it is referenced often because Burke went on to become one of golf's most respected swing teachers, like his father in the 1920s. This chapter on the mental process, however, is overlooked still. Elsewhere Burke has said he uses visualization techniques and has pointed his club at targets, yet here he echoed Patty Berg by insisting that when the pressure's on and he can't afford distractions the only thing he thinks about at address is hitting the ball.

W hether you want it or not, your imagination is entering into every shot you play. You might just as well give it free rein. This golf imagination can be made use of if you confine your thinking on the course to golf. . . .

In the 1952 Los Angles Open I needed only two putts to win, first prize being $4,000. Before I hit the first one I had an acceptance speech already phrased and $3,800 of my prize money spent.

When I finally got around to hitting it, I knocked the putt four feet past the cup. This shocked me so much that I missed the next one coming back. In the play-off the next day I lost to Tommy Bolt.

Then and there I decided that every round of golf I played in the future wouldn't be finished mentally until I had also finished it physically. You could do a whole lot worse.

To some extent this experience has happened to every golfer.

Elementary as it may be, we fail to keep in mind that there are eighteen holes to a game of golf—not seventeen and a half. The last putt must be played as deliberately as the first drive.

Never underestimate the power of suggestion in a round of golf. How often have you seen a golfer being painfully careful not to hit a ball out of bounds who ended by doing just that?

Few people shank a ball who did not have a shank in mind before they hit it. Few people are chronic slicers who do not have the fear of a slice, who do not have an apparition of it parade across their imaginations before each and every shot they hit.

Discipline your thoughts to the type of shot you want to play. You don't care to have your opponent suggest you are about to shank the ball. Why, then, suggest it to yourself?

The sort of thinking I have been outlining . . . is subsidiary, in any shot, to one paramount thought— hitting the ball. Thinking is preparation for the shot, not part of the shot itself. The thinking you preface each address with is prologue to hitting the ball. But you have to hit it. Nothing can be more important in your mind than that.

I have never played a good round of golf with more than one thought in mind as I address the ball. Two, and I'm dead. That one thought is always the same: "Hit the ball."

From *The Natural Way to Better Golf,* by Jack Burke. Illustrations by Norman Todhunter. Copyright © 1954 by Jack Burke. Used by permission of Doubleday, a division of Random House, Inc.

Stylish Jack Burke warned golfers against their own power of suggestion.

"Put All Yer Attention on the Feelin' o' Yer Inner Body"

1972 · Michael Murphy

Michael Murphy's disarming, never-out-of-print excursion into the mysticism of golf is the game's equivalent of Eugen Herrigel's *Zen in the Art of Archery*, but a lot more fun. Its appeal is so widespread that its back cover featured blurbs from the likes of Herbert Warren Wind, John Updike, and Joseph Campbell, who correctly predicted it "should have a long and prosperous life." The book is about Murphy stopping off in Scotland while on his way to India and discovering that golf is a life-transforming experience "whilst" taking brief lessons from a mysterious, heavy-drinking teacher-philosopher named Shivas Irons. This excerpt, in which Murphy is taught to swing while in a state of grace by focusing on sensations in his "inner body," is pure fiction, but it likely influenced the teaching methods of future instructors and writers who believe a clear mind and positive energy is essential for a good golf swing.

He picked up the balls and led me back to our imaginary tee. "Michael come heer," he said. "I want to show ye somethin'." He had me take my customary golf stance in front of a ball he had put on the ground. "Now, I want ye to try somethin' slightly different this time, will ye do it?" He looked at me hopefully, cocking his head to one side. His large blue eyes caught the flickering firelight. I could see my reflection in them, he was standing so close, a distorted image of my entire body wavering like a flame. "Would ye like to try it?" he repeated the question, fixing me with that slightly cross-eyed double-angle look. I could now see two images of myself in the mirror of his eyes, each one slightly different from the other. I nodded that I was willing. "Awright, now," he said quietly, raising a long finger. "When ye swing, put all yer at-

tention on the feelin' o' yer inner body—*yer inner body*." He whispered these last words as if he were telling me a secret.

I looked at the shifting reflection in his eyes. To this day I can vividly remember my reaction. It was as if an immediate split occurred in my mind. A part of me instantly knew what he meant; another part began to question and puzzle. I looked at him dumbly, without answering, as the two attitudes formed themselves.

He leaned toward me and took my arms in his hands. "Close yer eyes," he said soothingly. Then he lifted my arms, I was still holding the shillelagh like a golf club, and moved them through the arc of an imaginary swing as a golf professional does with a student, whispering again the words, "feel yer inner body." My questions and puzzlement quieted and I fell into the rhythm of his movements, slowly swinging the club and sensing what he meant. It was like the state I had discovered that afternoon during our round of golf—a growing power, rhythm, and grace, a pleasure that had no apparent cause. Yes—perhaps you have had that sense of it—a body within a body sustained by its own energies and delight, a body with a life of its own waiting to blossom.

"Do ye see what I mean?" he murmured as he swung my arms back and forth. I nodded and he backed away. "Now try to hit the ball tha' way," he said.

I adjusted my stance and waggled the club, focusing my attention on the sense of an inner body. When I swung I topped the ball and it bounced high in the air.

He nodded with approval. "Good, good," he said loudly, "ye stayed right in it, now try another."

I took my stance and swung again. This time the ball flew toward the target but fell short. "Ye did it again. Good!" he said decisively. "Now stay wi' tha' feelin'." We found the balls and repeated the exercise. He seemed oblivious to the results as he studied my attitude and "energy." He claimed that my state of mind was reflected in an aura around me which he could sense. "Yer energy was good that time," he would say, or "it wavered on that one." He was as definite about these statements as he was about my physical form.

Our lesson continued for half an hour or more, some twenty or thirty shots, while I practiced that indubitable awareness of my "inner body."

The experience went through stages. At first there was a vague yet tangible sense that there was indeed a body closer to me than my skin, with its own weight and shape. It seemed to waver and bounce and subtly change its form, as if it were elastic. Then—I can still remember the feeling so clearly—it changed to an hourglass: my head and feet were enormous and my waist was as small as a fist. This sensation lasted while we looked for the balls and returned to our tee, then it changed again. My body felt enormously tall, I seemed to look down from a point several feet above my head. I told him what I was feeling. "Now come down heer," he said, calmly putting a finger on my breastbone. "Just come down heer." I returned to my ordinary size and shape, and continued swinging.

I was aware that part of my mind had suspended judgment, that many questions were simmering still. But it felt marvelous to swing that way, so absorbed in the pleasure and feel of it. And it was a relief not to worry about the results. I could have gone on for hours.

But he ended the lesson abruptly. "Enough for now," he said, putting a finger on my chest, "rimember the feelin'. Yer inner body is aye waitin' for yer attention." We added some branches to the fire, which had almost died out, and leaned back against a pair of rocks. I glanced up the cliff, but no face was there, just the writhing shadows on the canyon walls. I felt marvelously alive, as if I were floating in some new field of force, but the questions that had been suspended began rising like vapors. This state I was in was too good to be true, too easily come by, I began to wonder how soon it would fade after Shivas and his colorful admonitions were gone. Anyone would feel good around him, getting so much attention, being led into adventures like these. Dark and true premonitions, I felt an edge of sadness.

He must have sensed what was going through my mind. "Wha' ye thinkin' there?" he asked with a fatherly tone in his voice. "Tell me wha' ye're thinkin'." I told him some of my doubts. I especially remember asking him if all his talk of inner bodies and subtle energies wasn't a mere device for helping concentration. I told him about the Hawthorne experiment in which a group of social psychologists had found that workers in a factory had improved their output every time a change was made in their routine, no matter what that change might be. I asked him if he was running a Hawthorne experiment on me.

He leaned back with his genial grin and shook his head in mock exasperation. "They're two Michaels, I can see; Michael the plunger and Michael the doubter," he chided. "Wha' a shame it is tha' ye canna' even go five minutes heer without yer good skeptical mind intrudin'. Yer good skeptical mind, tha's a problem for ye." He raised his finger like a wand and shook it at me. "Watch out for yer good mind," he said. . . .

How to Be Your Own Best Coach

1978 / DR. GARY WIREN AND
DR. RICHARD COOP WITH LARRY SHEEHAN

Dr. Gary Wiren is a PGA Master Teacher; the founder of Golf Around the World, Inc.; a regular contributor to *Golf Digest*; and a golf historian who has authored numerous instructional books. Wiren, who once conducted classes with Jack Burke, Jr., is probably the foremost "holistic" golf teacher, putting equal emphasis on the mental and physical aspects of golf. A mental game consultant to *Golf Magazine*, coauthor Dr. Richard Coop, of the University of North Carolina, has worked on "Mental Skills Training and Performance Enhancement" with numerous golf pros, including the late Payne Stewart, Corey Pavin, Mark O'Meara, and Nick Faldo. Despite their imposing credentials, Wiren and Coop wrote, as this excerpt illustrates, a witty, reader-friendly book. They realize that when pupils play a round, they become their own teachers and tend to be hard on themselves. Positive thinking, they say, will help them have more fun and play better.

When good teaching pros give clinics, they frequently find themselves making shots that they know they can't normally make during an actual playing round. If they're demonstrating wood play, they'll start fading and drawing their drives on command so well they'll wonder why they're not on tour. If they're demonstrating bunker play, they'll hole out tricky sand shots. If they're showing aspects of the short game, they'll hit the flagstick on chips and run putts in from improbable distances.

The power of positive suggestion accounts for this phenomenon, which coaches and instructors in many sports, not just in golf, experience.

The teachers talk as they demonstrate, and in trying to create a clear and coherent communication channel between teacher and pupil about the subject, they simultaneously create the ideal *analyzer/integrator* relationship within their own minds.

One of us had a chance to play with the legendary Oklahoma State golf coach, Labron Harris Sr. and, knowing his reputation as a putter, we looked forward to picking up a few tricks on the greens. Well into the round we decided that there was nothing special about his technique. Finally, we realized it was his attitude, not his method, that let him sink so many putts. His faith in himself on the greens was total. He said he was a great putter, he believed it. And he was. . . .

Harris believed in practice partly because it built the good stroke, as he himself had learned, partly because it built a more favorable self-concept. He insisted on positive talking as well as positive thinking. If he heard one of his players say "three-putt" or "shank," he'd chase them off the course or out of the room.

According to educational psychologists, the trouble with negative language in teaching—"That's a mistake," "This is wrong," "Don't do that"—is that it does not automatically foster the behavior you do want, and sometimes promotes just the opposite. . . .

The analogy has been overused, but in certain ways the human mind really does function like a computer. Just as a computer is programmed to understand and respond to key words, so we light up at the sound of some words and not others. We may tell ourselves, "Don't slice" but the manner in which the mind receives that data is: "Don't *SLICE*." "Don't" is a weak, negative helping verb. "Slice" is a powerful, image-provoking action word.

The thousands of "don'ts" that comprise low-level golf instruction can be ineffectual and often destructive.

Swaying is a commonly heard diagnosis of a mis-hit among high-handicappers. But if you tell yourself, "Don't sway!" you may stand so rooted to the ground that you lose all weight transfer in your swing.

If, however, you say, "Brace that right knee!" you may eliminate the sway without interfering with the rhythm of the swing.

The *analyzer* is good at pinpointing the things that go wrong in our golf game and announcing them to us, but it requires a lot of work for it to be *constructively* analytical—to figure out a corrective measure for the situation.

Negative instruction doesn't always have "nos" or "don'ts" in it. For example, "Keep your head still!" can be a form of negative instruction in the sense that it does not necessarily promote *golf-appropriate* behavior. Almost all good golfers move their heads when they swing. Following the advice to keep your head rock-steady could result in a stiff, inhibited swing.

A more positive way of encouraging golf-appropriate behavior in this instance might be: "Keep yourself centered over the ball!" or "Swing around your center!" These phrases would allow for rotation, even of the head, around a center and so would free up the swing.

How do you address yourself during your various internal dialogues on the course? Do you use names like these?

BUM	BLOCKHEAD
DONKEY	DUMMY
IDIOT	JERK
TURKEY	KLUTZ
IGNORAMUS	STUPID
HACKER	DIMWIT

If we added the obscenities, the list could run for pages. The point is, such names automatically tarnish the self-concept, whereas your own name, affectionately intoned, does not. Nor do these:

ARNIE	BUDDY
PARTNER	GUY
PAL	AMIGO
TIGER	SWEETHEART
PRO	BABY
BIG FELLOW	JACK

A study of gymnasts preparing for the Olympics showed clearly that the most successful performers were the ones who talked to themselves constantly and always in favorable, positive terms.

Golfers can get into the habit of coaching themselves in the same way, on the practice tee and out on the course. . . .

We can't always get good results by talking to ourselves positively. If there are mechanical flaws in our swing, no amount of sweet talk is going to help.

All we're saying is that the extent to which we can slant our internal dialogues on the golf course favorably and optimistically . . . the better are our chances of playing our best possible shots.

Talking to yourself negatively is in some cases the articulation of the negative expectations we

He who would attain self-knowledge should frequent the links.

ARNOLD HAULTAIN

mentioned earlier, which pave the way for unwanted results. But golfers with high expectations also make the mistake of choosing negative language to urge themselves on, not realizing the language itself can cause their downfall.

Tell yourself, "Play to the center of the green!" rather than "Stay out of that bunker on the left!" and you'll be less likely to pull the shot into the sand.

Tell yourself, "Let's see if we can par this hole," rather than "Let's not get another double-bogey," and you'll improve your chances of ending up with a par or birdie.

Say, "Let's get the ball up to the hole," rather than, "Don't leave it short, stupid," and you're more likely to sink the putt.

If you're a 90 shooter, you're not going to break 80 just by coaching yourself through your next round of golf with positive language. But you won't soar to 100, either. And if you really get a strongly positive internal dialogue going whenever you do play, you are bound to pick up a few strokes—the strokes you have traditionally lost to the "can't-do" voice inside you.

Overtightness:
The Most Common Cause of Error

1981 ✦ W. Timothy Gallwey

Harvard grad Tim Gallwey came up with a premise that applied to sports and other activities— "There is always an inner game being played in your mind no matter what outer game you are playing"—and has spent thirty years writing and lecturing (even to corporations) about it. *The Inner Game of Golf*, following successful "Inner Game" books on tennis and skiing, had its genesis as a three-part series in *Golf Magazine* that was eaten up by readers, including golfers needing an excuse for why their physical talents weren't enough to deliver low scores. Like Wiren and Coop, but using self-help jargon, Gallwey contended the critical, order-giving mind interferes with our body's natural muscular activity during the swing. And in this essay, Gallwey told readers how to relax, but in different ways than Kenneth R. Thompson, suggesting that humming and the tightening and then loosening of the grip should be added to pre-shot routines.

The single most common physical cause of error in golf, and perhaps in all sports, is *overtightness*. It is generally understood by golfers with even a little experience that the overtightening of muscles in an effort to produce power is responsible for many poor drives. "Don't try to hit the ball so hard, dummy," is a familiar criticism from Self 1 [the verbalizing, thought-producing self] on the course.

But it is equally true, though less recognized, that tightened muscles cause most slices, hooks, topped balls, and fat shots. Overtightening of the shoulders prevents a full backswing and follow-through, and overtightening of the hands turns the putterblade closed or keeps it open at contact, sending the ball off course. Involuntary tightening lies behind the dread "yips" in both chipping and putting.

Commonly, the observation of a beginning golfer watching the pros is, "Wow, they make it look so easy. They don't seem to be swinging hard at all." On almost any driving range the muscled jerkiness of the average golfer's swing is in obvious contrast to the pro's powerful fluidity.

Yet overtightness need not plague even the most inexperienced golfer. . . .

Humming Your Swing

One day, quite by accident, I discovered an exercise that is remarkably effective in reducing overtightness. I was out late one afternoon hitting seven-irons on the driving range while waiting for Tom Nordland, with whom I was going to do an Inner Game practice session. I was not concentrating on anything in particular, simply hitting balls and humming to myself. Suddenly something struck me. I could *hear* differences in my humming, depending on how I was swinging the club. The experience was such a surprise that I wish everybody could become aware of it as spontaneously as I did. The next time you're on the practice tee, take a few swings and try humming to yourself while swinging. *Listen to the humming.*

I hadn't considered my swing particularly tight, but my humming told me differently. I could actually hear the tightness of my swing in the sound. While going back the sound would be nice and smooth, but during the change of direction my voice would become strained, and at contact my throat would constrict and the humming would increase in volume, pitch and, most noticeably, in tightness. Sometimes, when I really went after the ball, the hum would stop after contact, and I would notice that I had also cut off my follow-through. Using a tape recorder, I later recorded the sound of my practice swing and compared it with a recording of a swing at a ball. The increase in tension was painfully obvious.

This phenomenon turned out to be very practical. I realized that I was amplifying feedback from my body by the use of sound. Overtightness that I previously was not very aware of now became glaringly apparent. The audible alterations in sound while swinging told me a lot about what was happening to my body. What to do? The answer was easy: Simply keep swinging and humming. Use this humming as a biofeedback machine to increase control. . . .

The sound method works in the same way. The sound amplifies the feedback you are receiving from the overtightening of muscles. By listening to changes in the sound, you can soon gain more control over subtle muscular tightness than you might have thought possible by simply trying to relax, or to hit smoothly—efforts that often impel you to swing too loosely, and with low clubhead speed. The best way to use this exercise is to make no effort to swing more smoothly, and to simply keep listening while you hit balls on the range. Automatically, and in specific ways you won't understand—and don't need to understand—your swing will start changing. You will begin to hear less tightness in your humming, will notice that you are making better contact with the ball, and will get more distance while making no conscious effort to get those results. Simply accept them and don't ask too many questions about how they happen. Otherwise you will start thinking you know how to relax and giving yourself instructions about how to do it—which is one of the ways the overtightness was created in the first place. A name for this exercise might be "singing your swing"—or, if you don't mind bad puns, "hum, hum, on the range."

It should be noted that although it is useful to hum loudly enough to make variations in sound easily audible for the sake of giving maximum feedback when first experimenting with the use of "singing your swing," later on I found it sufficient to hum in a voice audible only to myself. Even if the hum is very quiet, overtightness in the swing will usually change the sound. Muscles in the throat constrict with bodily overtightness, and the sound is choked off, giving you the necessary feedback. The principle behind this exercise has nothing to do with sound per se. It is *awareness* that is the curative and controlling factor. . . . The sound simply serves as a device to increase awareness of what is happening, just as a biofeedback machine does.

Maximum Tightness

There is one other practical and time-tested method of decreasing overtightness. Paradoxically, it has to do with a tightening to the maximum. I first learned of this method in a beginner's class in hatha yoga, and have since learned that it has been used for thousands of years by those whose knowledge of the relation between body and mind is in many ways more sophisticated than our own. *To gain maximum relaxation in the body, first tighten it to the maximum extent, and then let go.* For total body relaxation this exercise can be done on each part of the body from foot to head, holding the muscles in each part as tightly as possible for five or ten seconds before releasing them. In a golfing situation you may not have the time to do all this, but it might help to tighten the stomach muscles and then let go, and perhaps do the same with the arms and shoulders. The tightening will make it easier to relax many muscle units that might otherwise not let go, thereby giving the swing more flexibility and fluidity. An added benefit of this exercise is that it increases circulation of the blood and makes it easier to feel movement. There is one final benefit. When you tighten *before the swing*, you reduce some of your tendency to do so *during* it. A lot of our tightening comes from anger and frustration that build up at an unconscious level. By providing an escape hatch for these emotions, you reduce the chances of letting tension destroy your swing. . . .

Golf Is Not a Game of Perfect

1995 / Dr. Bob Rotella
with Bob Cullen

Dr. Robert Rotella is recognized as golf's foremost sports psychologist. A contributing editor to *Golf Digest* and *Sports Psychologist*, he has produced a number of successful books and audio tapes, and has consulted with the PGA, LPGA, and Senior LPGA Tour. The former Director of Sports Psychology at the University of Virginia also earned the moniker "the Mental Coach of the Stars," working with Tom Kite, David Duval, Nick Price, Darren Clarke, Davis Love III, Pat Bradley, and many others. This excerpt from his shrewdly titled best-seller makes it clear why his professional and amateur pupils swear by him. By nature, competitive golfers unrealistically strive for perfection and are too self-critical when they don't achieve it, so Rotella eases their minds by reminding them that golf is a game of mistakes—a Ben Hogan mantra. By forgiving and forgetting mistakes, says Rotella, golfers will stay upbeat and play better.

———◆———

I find it amusing and ironic that players like Tom [Kite] and Nick Price, who are among the best ball strikers in the world, who practice regularly, can learn to accept their bad shots, while the high-handicappers I see in pro-ams and clinics often cannot. . . . If Price or Kite pushes one into the woods, which he occasionally does, he accepts it as something that is going to happen in golf and he calmly plans his next shot. . . .

But the high-handicapper, who's got a loop in his swing the size of the Washington Beltway, who practices twice a year if the weather is good, will fume and curse and berate himself if he hits one into the woods. . . .

I've had guys in pro-ams turn to me after a tee shot that wiped out two squirrels and a woodpecker and say, "I don't hit the ball that way."

To which I am tempted to reply, "That's funny, I thought I just saw that you did."

No one likes to hit a bad shot. . . .

But the question is, does it do any good to get angry?

Getting angry is one of your options. But if you choose to get angry, you are likely to get tighter. That's going to hurt your rhythm and your flow. It will upset you and distract you. It will switch on your analytical mind and your tendency to criticize and analyze anything you do that falls short of perfection. It will start you thinking about the mechanical flaws in your swing and trying to correct them.

You will very likely play worse.

Alternatively, you could train yourself to accept the fact that as a human being, you are prone to mistakes. Golf is a game played by human beings. Therefore, golf is a game of mistakes.

The best golfers strive to minimize mistakes, but they don't expect to eliminate them. And they understand that it's most important to respond well to the mistakes they inevitably make.

Chip Beck has one of the best attitudes toward bad shots. When he hits it into the woods, he walks toward the ball and all he says is, "You gotta love it. This is what golf is all about."

And he's right. Golf is indeed all about recovering from bad shots. It's about getting up and down from sand traps. It's about knowing when it's smart to pitch sideways out of the rough and do your best to save par or bogey with your wedge and putter. It's about the exhilaration that comes from spotting a narrow path through the trees and threading your ball through it to the green. Viewed this way, any round you play will be enjoyable.

But if you bring a smothering perfectionism to the golf course, you will probably leave with a higher handicap and a lousy disposition, because your game will never meet your expectations. . . .

The first thing to do is throw away your expectations as soon as you step onto the golf course, and just play. It's very difficult to do. But I have never worked with a golfer who could play anywhere close to his potential unless he shed his expectations before the first shot.

Expectations are great if you confine them to long-range considerations. It's fine, for example, to expect that if you work at your game intelligently for an extended period of time, you will improve. But expectations can hurt you if they are narrowly focused on the results of a particular stroke, hole, or round. . . .

This is not to say that you should not think about hitting every ball to the target and believe that every shot will do just that. You should. But there is a fine difference between believing that the ball will go where you want it to go and expecting that it will and being upset if it doesn't. You have to put expectations out of your mind by the time you get to the first tee.

On the first tee, you should have two immediate goals. One is to have fun. The other involves the process of playing, not the results. This goal is to get your mind where it's supposed to be on every shot. If you do that, you'll shoot the best score you're capable of shooting that day, whether it's a 67 or 107.

Having fun shouldn't be so difficult. You are, after all, out in the fresh air. You are playing in what amounts to an emerald park. Clipped grasslands, according to one theorist, have been the most soothing and emotionally satisfying habitat for man since the first humans dropped out of the trees. You are, presumably, in good company, the company of other golfers. You have a chance to strike a little ball and send it flying straight and true against the sky, an act that seems to resonate pleasantly somewhere deep within the human brain. These are the reasons you initially liked golf even though you couldn't play it very well. Savor all of them as you play. Let the joy of the game come to you. . . .

You [also] have to be nonjudgmental. You have to forgive and forget and be compassionate toward yourself. But in our culture, people, particularly high achievers, are taught to judge themselves harshly. They're taught that being compassionate toward oneself is weak and indulgent. There is a kernel of truth in this. There is a time and place for tough self-evaluation, and you will not improve as a golfer unless you honestly examine your game and work on its weaknesses.

But don't do it on the golf course.

When a shot is done, it's done. The only constructive thing you can do about it is to hit the next shot as well as you can. That requires that you stay optimistic and enthusiastic.

If you must have expectations about results, expect to make some mistakes. Walter Hagen once said that he expected to make seven mistakes per round. When he hit a bad shot, he wasn't bothered. It was just one of the expected seven.

Acceptance allows a golfer to be patient, and patience is one of the necessary virtues in golf. Sometimes, players tell me they are sick and tired of hearing me say that they must be patient and keep believing that if they do all the right things, the results they want will follow. That's just one more thing they have to learn to be patient about.

If you remember to have fun, it shouldn't be too hard. When was the last time you were impatient when you were having fun?

Remember too, that golf is not a game of justice. A player can practice properly, think properly, and still hit a bad shot. Or he can hit a good shot and watch a bad hop or gust of wind deposit the ball in a sand trap.

A golfer can't force results to happen. He can only do everything possible to give those results a chance to happen. As Tom Watson once put it, to become a really good golfer, you have to learn how to wait. But you have to learn to wait with confidence.

Golf is a game that creates emotions that sometimes cannot be endured with the club still in your hands.

BOBBY JONES

Think Like Tiger: Course Preparation

2002 · JOHN ANDRISANI

Much of Tiger Woods's success can be contributed to what's on top. He is not only the most mentally tough competitor since Jack Nicklaus, but also seems to be on a different plane than other golfers when conceiving shots. Prolific, astute writer John Andrisani says that prior to hitting the ball, Woods visualizes good shots, allowing no negative thoughts, and relaxes with deep breaths and practice swings. Whereas Patty Berg and Jack Burke concentrated fully on hitting the ball, Woods focuses primarily on the swing, going along with Timothy Gallwey's belief that if you swing well you should trust that the ball will be hit properly. Similarly, he believes in thinking of the shot and letting the score take care of itself. To keep emotions in check, he, like Walter Hagen once did, accepts bad shots and stays patient—soothing advice attributed to both Dr. Bob Rotella and Tiger's Buddhist-trained mother.

———

Earl Woods, Rudy Duran, John Anselmo, and Butch Harmon . . . taught Tiger how to strengthen his mental game by following a set of sophisticated rules that go beyond the basic steps. . . . Study these rules, because they will make you a more confident golfer and allow you to cut strokes off your score.

RULE #1: BE MENTALLY CONFIDENT ABOUT YOUR SWING

To fight off any anxiety about making a good swing, particularly on the first tee, copy Tiger. Make a smooth (not slow) practice swing until you feel the sensations of the clubhead reaching the top and swishing through impact. If you are unable to employ the right actions the first time, take a couple of deep breaths, or open and close your eyes slowly, as Tiger does, to induce a relaxed state of mind. Next, make a couple more swings until you find the one that you want to match when it comes time to hit the ball. Once you discover your ideal swing, set up to the ball. As you will discover, you will feel confident and experience no first-tee jitters.

RULE #2: BE POSITIVE ABOUT THE SHOT YOU ARE ABOUT TO HIT

All Tiger's coaches, including his former psychologist, Dr. Jay Brunza, have taught Tiger the value of putting a positive thought into his mind when standing over a shot. You should, too. Whatever shot you are about to hit, pick a target and say to yourself: "That's where I'm going to hit the ball." The more positive you are about hitting your target and the clearer your mental image of the ball flying toward it, the better the chance that you will succeed.

"Visualization enables us to conjure up confidence, boosting alignments or scenarios that assist us in freeing our minds from doubt, anxiety, or other inhibiting negative thoughts," says Larry Miller, golf teacher, spiritual coach, and author of *Golfing in the Zone.*

You'll also find it easier to stay positive if you favor your natural shot or the one you bring to the course on a given day. If you usually hit a fade, don't try to hit a draw. If on the practice tee before the round you notice that you are hitting a controlled draw, however, don't try to switch back to a fade. Take the new draw shot with you to the course, as long as you can repeat it over and over.

RULE #3: THINK ABOUT SWINGING THE CLUB TO ALLEVIATE ANXIETY ABOUT HITTING THE BALL

"Trust allows you to think straight, and you must trust that the ball will be hit," says Timothy Gallwey, the author of *The Inner Game of Golf.*

Something Duran impressed upon Tiger, from the day he started taking lessons at age four, was to stand to the ball and realize that his short-term goal was to imagine himself swinging the club and not hitting the ball.

The old adages "The ball gets in the way of a good swing" and "Swing the force; don't force the swing" certainly apply. Drum these statements into your head when taking your address. Also, remember this: If you set up to the ball properly, make a timed takeaway action, turn your body on the backswing, and uncoil your hips on the downswing, the swing will take care of hitting the ball—automatically.

RULE #4: DON'T FOCUS ON QUICK SWING FIXES; FOCUS ON WHAT YOU KNOW WORKS

One of the most common mistakes amateur golfers make is analyzing their swing during the round, usually in between shots. They look for a new and quick way to fix a fault, such as turning the clubface inward to correct a slice.

If you run into a problem during a round, forget about what's wrong and focus your attention on what to do right. That's what Tiger has been trained

Tiger Woods plays with intensity, but sometimes his emotions spill over.

to do. When standing over the ball, revert back to the basics, concentrating on a good grip, square setup, smooth backswing, and full follow-through rather than searching for a quick fix. This is the only true shortcut to hitting good shots and restoring your confidence.

If for some reason you still experience trouble, spend time on the practice tee after the round, ideally with your instructor, to pinpoint your faults and correct them. Keep practicing until you recapture that "I got it" feeling.

RULE #5: CONCENTRATE ON PERFORMANCE, NOT SCORE

To alleviate tension and play with positive energy, focus on the shot at hand. After grinding hard mentally to hit a good tee shot, Tiger walks to the ball to play his next shot. Once he reaches the ball, he starts focusing his attention on what he will do next. This entails looking at the hazards near the green, the slopes in the putting surface, and the position of the pin to get a jump-start on the right strategy.

Give each shot full concentration, and the good scores will come.

Rule #6: Stay in Control of Your Emotions

Tiger is much more levelheaded than he used to be, learning that it is best to go with the flow and not overreact to a bad shot or get super-excited over a good shot. "No matter what happens with any shot you hit, accept it," says performance consultant to the pros Dr. Bob Rotella, author of *Golf Is Not a Game of Perfect.*

Drastic emotional swings negatively affect your concentration and thus hinder the way you play the upcoming shot. If you overreact to a bad shot and hold on to that mental baggage, chances are you will make a faulty fast swing and hit a bad next shot. If you overreact to a good shot, the tendency is to become lackadaisical on the next shot and hit it left or right of target.

According to the Buddhist religion, when you gain wisdom you learn not to expect anything, good or bad—which is precisely how Tiger's mother taught him to be patient on the course. Furthermore, by disciplining yourself to let go like Tiger and Buddhist Zen masters, you will alleviate pressure, not just deal with it, and make fewer unforced errors.

Excerpted from "On-Course, Off-Course Prep Work," from *Think Like Tiger: An Analysis of Tiger Woods' Mental Game,* by John Andrisani. Copyright © 2002 by John Andrisani. Used by permission of G. P. Putnam's Sons, a division of Penguin Group (USA) Inc.

I have never been troubled by nerves in golf because I felt I had nothing to lose and everything to gain.

Harry Vardon

ACKNOWLEDGMENTS

The two of us might have tried doing this book ourselves, but we wisely decided to enlist the help of more than one hundred individuals from around the world. So without having to wait until the twenty-second century, we are happy that our dream project is now in your hands. We can't properly express our gratitude to the people who helped us, including a lot of new friends, but if they enjoy this book, they have themselves to thank. It truly was a joint effort.

Foremost we would like to acknowledge Gary Player for lending his words and name to *Great Golf*. During his more than forty-five years in the public eye no one has better exemplified what is great about golf. We sincerely say that it is an honor to have his name on our cover and his foreword to begin our book.

We wish to convey our tremendous appreciation to our editor, Anne Kostick, who had faith in the book from the start and made sure it exceeded everyone's expectations. She was our director, our cheerleader, our referee, and our calm captain who refused to let the unsteady ship sink under her watch. We couldn't have imagined working with anyone else. She also was shrewd enough to put together a crack team: illustrator John Burgoyne, designer Anna Christian, copyeditor Lara Comstock, and photo editor Anne Kerman. Special thanks to them for their special work.

Also at the top of our list is Leslie Stoker, our supportive publisher at Stewart, Tabori & Chang, and the other person who got the book off the ground, Jennifer Unter, our problem-solving agent at RLR Associates, Ltd. Without them, there would be no book. Thank you both.

Thank you, Robert L. Rosen, for always being there, and everyone else at RLR, particularly Tara Mark, Walton Shepherd, Gail Lockhart, Maury Gostfrand, Craig Foster, and Barbara Hadzicosmas. We acknowledge the entire crew at STC, but we must single out Kate Norment, Andrea Glickson, Galen Smith, Dervla Kelly, Cynthia Crippen, and Kristen Latta. You always made us feel we were in good hands.

Very special thanks to Gida Campbell, the media director of the Gary Player Group, for her enormous help. And to Frank Thorp, for researching copyrights at the Library of Congress in Washington.

We spent countless hours doing research at the USGA Library in Far Hills, New Jersey. We would have been lost if it weren't for Doug Stark, USGA Librarian and Curator of Archival Collections; Rand Jerris, the extremely knowledgeable director of the USGA Museum and Archival Collections; unsung heroine Patty Moran, the Archives Research Assistant whose work on our behalf was far beyond the call of duty; and Nancy E. Stulack, Registrar, Museum and Archives. We thank everyone there for their kindness. If you want to research golf, there is no better place.

Also extending invaluable help on background research and in reaching individuals were: Mark Cubbedge, Peyton Taylor, Tammy G. Smith, and Jack Peter of the World Golf Hall of Fame; Samantha Groves, the curator of the British Golf Museum in St. Andrews, Scotland; Bill Cioffoletti and Una Jones of the PGA of America; Kathy Widick and Dana Von Louda, of the LPGA; and Dr. Gary Wiren, PGA Master Professional.

For their help and patience answering a multitude of questions about the game of golf and the methods of various golfers, we thank Frank A. Cisterino, PGA Golf Professional/Owner, and Anthony D. Cisterino, assistant teaching pro at Willow Creek Golf Club in Vermilion, Ohio; Beverly Lewis, European PGA teaching pro and captain of the British PGA; George Lewis of Golfiana, PGA Master Professional, Mamaroneck, New York; Chris Meadows, European PGA teaching pro, golf mentor, teacher, and friend; Ryan Spicer, PGA teaching pro of Thunderbird Hills Golf Club in Huron, Ohio; Christopher Toulson, PGA, Corporate Director of Instruction at Jim McLean Golf School; Ned Vare, teaching pro, author, and son of Glenna Collett Vare;

Vance Levin, PGA, head pro at E. Gaynor Brennan Golf Course in Stamford, Connecticut, and teaching pro at Sterling Farms Golf Course, Stamford, Connecticut; and Rob LaRosa, Patrick Robertson, and Boris Busljeta, PGA teaching pros at Sterling Farms. We also extend gratitude to Tom Kokoska for his insight on the science and technology of the game.

Acquiring permissions for so many articles was a daunting task, but we were given exceptional treatment by a number of people on both sides of the Atlantic. For your next permissions party, we recommend you invite: Carol Christiansen, Deborah Foley, Rebecca Heisman, Alicia Torello, Caryn Burtt, Michael Greaves, Bette Graber, and Lisa Phillips of Random House; Catherine Trippett and Nicole Gross of Random House Group, London; Rose Marie Cerminaro, Jeniqua Moore, Lydia Zelaya, Marie Florio, and Nicole Albers of Simon & Schuster; Florence B. Eichin of Penguin Group (USA) Inc.; Melinda Lin-Roberts of Human Kinetics; Julie DiMarco and Bob Carney of *Golf Digest*; W. L. Pate, Jr. of the Babe Didrikson Zaharias Foundation, Inc.; Kate O'Hearn and Briar Silich of Hodder and Stoughton, Ltd.; Jack and Ann Snead; Sidney L. Matthew; Melvin Powers of Wilshire Book Company; Patty Berg and her assistant Toby Hingson; Mrs. Armen C. Boros; Martin J. Elgison, of Alston & Bird, and the family of Bobby Jones; Albert Zuckerman, Susan Ginsburg, and Emily Saladino of Writers House LLC; Grace Anderson Smith of *Time*; Faith Freeman Barbato of HarperCollins; Laura Scott of HarperCollins, England; Michelle Irwin of Golden Bear International; Jimmy Ballard and Laurie L. Ensor of J. B. Golf Enterprises; Jon M. Bradley, CPA of Weaver and Tidwell LLP, representing Byron Nelson; Byron Nelson; Jack Nicklaus; Ken Bowden; Patrick Shearer, Scott Plikerd, and Ebony Rosa of McGraw-Hill Education; Colin Webb of Palazzo Editions Limited; David Grossberg, attorney representing Alistair Cooke; Richard Myers of Thinkandreachpar.com; Pauline Zline of Taylor Trade Publishing; Esther Robinson of St. Martin's Press; Kellie Stenzel; Rosanna Bruno of Russell & Volkening, Inc.; MaryKate Roberts of Time Warner Book Group; Butch Harmon and his assistant Carole; Mary Kay McGuire-Willson and the family of Johnny Farrell; Bev Norwood and Jennifer Bassett of IMG: Christine Duggan of Gerald Duckworth & Co.; Gerardine Munroe: Katy Smith; Erick McClenahan of Icon Sports Management; Chi Chi Rodriguez; Ilene Tannen of Pennie and Edmonds, LLP; Tara Gavel and Lorin Anderson of *Golf Magazine*; Andrew Clark of Harlequin, Mills & Boon, Ltd.; Hilary Doan of AP Watt; Mimi Ross of Henry Holt & Co.; Paul Williams and Steve Kendall of *Country Life*/IPC Country & Leisure Media; Beth Doty, Robyn Schwartz, Carolan Workman, and Walter Weintz of Workman Publishing; John Jacobs; Kathryn Bradwell of Callaway Editions; Leigh Gensler; Maria Bohman of Nick Faldo Enterprises; Peter Tummons of Methuen & Company; Scott Rowan of Triumph Books; Monique Riedel of St. Remy's Media; Julie Kacala; Gail Blackhall; Jessica Napp; Margaret L. Kaplan; Robert Sidorsky: Susan Friedland; and, again, Gida Cambell, Beverly Lewis, and Dr. Gary Wiren. Thank you all for being so attentive and generous.

We are compelled to thank the nearly one hundred authors, dead and alive, whose fascinating writing fills the pages of our book. You are the book, and we salute you.

And finally, for their encouragement we wish to express our heartfelt gratitude to Fred and Joan Baum, John and Valerie Bell, Dr. Robert Brody, Amy Byronette, Tom Clavin, Lance and Mardi Cone, Al and Susan Daniels, Jeanie Dooha, Cory Gann and Sharon Holt, Roy Greenberg, Wendy Hirschhorn, Philip and Mayda Idone, Cindi Kane, Joan Kokoska, Bob Kouffman, Bob Nowacki, Melissa Kay Rogers, Daniel Rubinstein, Carol Summers, Mary Tiegreen, and Donna Villani. And to loving family members Karen Curry, Samantha Richardson, Cody Greenoe, Roberta Greenoe; Gerald Peary, Amy Geller, Suzanne Rafer, Zoë Weaver Ohler, Gene Ohler; and our dear moms, Nancy Richardson and Laura Peary.

CREDITS

The editors are grateful for permission to reprint articles from the following publishers, estates, and individuals:

Alpha Books, an imprint of Penguin Group (USA) Inc., for excerpts from *The Complete Idiot's Guide to Improving Your Short Game*, by Jim McLean. Copyright © 2000 by Jim McLean.

Jimmy Ballard, for excerpts from *How to Perfect Your Golf Swing: Using "Connection" and the Seven Common Denominators*, by Jimmy Ballard, with Brennan Quinn. Golf Digest/Tennis Inc., a New York Times Company. Copyright © 1981 by Jimmy Ballard.

Patty Berg, LPGA founder and World Golf Hall of Fame member for excerpts from *Golf*, by Patty Berg and Otis Dypwick. Copyright © 1941 by A. S. Barnes and Company, Incorporated.

Armen Boros, for excerpts from *Swing Easy, Hit Hard*, by Julius Boros, Harper & Row Publishers Inc., New York, New York. Copyright © 1965 by Julius Boros and Lealand R. Gustavson.

Broadway Books, a division of Random House, Inc., for excerpts from *How to Find Your Perfect Golf Swing*, by Rick Smith; edited by John Andrisani. Copyright © 1998 by Smith Management, Inc.

Callaway Editions, Inc., for excerpts from *Breaking 90*, by Johnny Miller. Copyright © 2000 by Callaway Editions, Inc.

The Estate of Alistair Cooke for excerpts from "Nicklaus: 22 Years of Hard Labor," by Alistair Cooke, from *The New York Times Magazine*, July 9, 1972.

Michael Corcoran, for excerpts from *The PGA Tour Complete Book of Golf*, by Michael Corcoran. Henry Holt and Company. Reissued in condensed form as *Shotmaking Techniques*. Copyright © 1999 by Mountain Lion, Inc.

Gerald Duckworth & Co. Ltd. for excerpts from *The Key to Golf*, by Dai Rees. Copyright © 1961 Dai Rees.

Doubleday & Co., a division of Random House, Inc., for excerpts from: *Golf for Women*, edited by Louise Suggs. Chapter by Marlene Bauer Hagge. Copyright © 1960 by Rutledge Books; *Dave Pelz's Putting Bible*, by Dave Pelz, with James A. Frank. Copyright © 2000 by Dave T. Pelz; for excerpts from *The Natural Way to Better Golf* by Jack Burke. Copyright © 1954 by Jack Burke.

The family of Johnny Farrell for excerpts from *If I Were in Your Golf Shoes*, by Johnny Farrell. Copyright © 1951 by Johnny Farrell.

Golf Digest® for excerpts from: *How to Solve Your Golf Problems*, by the Professional Panel of *Golf Digest*, Jack Burke, Jr., Byron Nelson, Johnny Revolta, Paul Runyan, and Horton Smith. Copyright © 1963 Golf Digest, Copyright © 2004 The Golf Digest Companies; "How to Square Your Putterface and Hole More Putts," by Tiger Woods, with Pete McDaniel. (May 2003); "I Dare You: Try My Killer 2-Iron," by Tiger Woods, with Pete McDaniel (April 2000). Reprinted with permission from Golf Digest®. Copyright © 2005 The Golf Digest Companies. All Rights Reserved. Golf Digest is a Registered Trademark of The Golf Digest Companies, which is a subsidiary of Advance Magazine Publishers, Inc.

Golf Magazine for: "Cut It Out. . .," by Ken Venturi (October 1991). Copyright 1991–2005, Time4Media, Inc.; "How to Psych-Out Your Opponent" by Lee Trevino (October 1978). Copyright © 1978–2005, Time4Media, Inc.

Butch Harmon and Golf Digest® for "The Eight Stupid Mistakes Every Golfer Makes," by Butch Harmon (December 1999).Copyright © 2005 The Golf Digest Companies.

HarperCollins Publishers Inc. for excerpts from: *The Only Golf Lesson You Will Ever Need*, by Hank Haney, with John Huggan. Copyright © 1999 by Hank Haney; *The Eight-Step Swing*, by Jim McLean. Copyright © 1994 by Jim McLean; *From 60 Yards In—How to Master Golf's Short Game*, by Ray Floyd, with Larry Dennis. Copyright © 1989 by Raymond Floyd Enterprises;

HarperCollins Publishers Ltd. for excerpts from *The Golf Swing*, by David Leadbetter, with John Huggan, foreword by Nick Faldo. Copyright © 1990 by David Leadbetter; *The Complete Short Game*, by Ernie Els, with Steve Newell. Copyright © 1998 by Tee-2-Green Enterprises.

Hodder and Stoughton Ltd., for excerpts from *Essentials of Golf*, by Abe Mitchell, edited and arranged by J. Martin (Verulum Golf Club of St. Albans).

The family of Robert T. Jones, Jr., for excerpts from *Golf Is My Game*, by Robert Tyre (Bobby) Jones, Jr. Copyright © 1959, 1960 by Robert Tyre Jones, Jr.; *Bobby Jones on Golf*, by Robert Tyre (Bobby) Jones, Jr. Copyright © 1966 by Robert Tyre Jones, Jr.

John Jacobs, for excerpts from: *Practical Golf*, by John Jacobs, with Ken Bowden. Copyright © 1972 John Jacobs and Ken Bowden; *Practical Golf*, by John Jacobs, with Ken Bowden. Copyright © 1972 John Jacobs and Ken Bowden.

Alfred A. Knopf, a division of Random House, Inc., for excerpts from *On Learning Golf*, by Percy Boomer. Copyright © 1942, 1946 by Percy Boomer.

Beverly Lewis, for excerpts from *Golf for Women*, by Beverly Lewis. Copyright © 1989 Sackville Books Ltd.

Little, Brown and Co., Inc. for excerpts from *Golf by Design, How to Lower Your Scores by Reading the Features of a Course*, by Robert Trent Jones, Jr. Copyright © 1993 Robert Trent Jones, Jr.

McGraw-Hill Book Company, for excerpts from: *Swinging into Golf*, by Ernest Jones and Innis Brown. Copyright © 1946 by Robert M. McBride & Company; *Nancy Lopez's The Complete Golfer*, by Nancy Lopez, with Don Wade. Contemporary Books, Chicago, Illinois. Copyright © 1987 by Nancy Lopez.

Richard Myers and New South Media, LLC, for excerpts from *Johnny Revolta's Short Cuts to Better Golf*, by Johnny Revolta and Charles B. Cleveland. Copyright © 1949 by Johnny Revolta and Charles B. Cleveland.

Sidney L. Matthew for excerpts from *Bobby Jones on Golf*, by Robert Tyre (Bobby) Jones, Jr. Copyright © 1929–1930 by Bell Syndicate, Inc. Revised in 1997 by Sidney L. Matthew, Sleeping Bear Press, Chelsea, Michigan. Copyright © 1997.

Jack Nicklaus and Ken Bowden for excerpts from *Jack Nicklaus' Lesson Tee*, by Jack Nicklaus, with Ken Bowden, Copyright © 1972, 1973, 1974, 1975, 1976, 1977, and renewed © 1992 by Golden Bear, Inc.

Byron Nelson, individually, and Byron Nelson, Trustee, of the Byron Nelson Revocable Trust, for excerpts from: *Shape Your Swing the Modern Way*, by Byron Nelson, with Larry Dennis. Published 1976 by Golf Digest, Inc.; *How to Score Better than You Swing*, by Byron Nelson.

Pocket Books, a division of Simon & Schuster Adult Publishing Group, for excerpts from: *Tom Watson's Getting Back to Basics,* by Tom Watson, with Nick Seitz. Copyright © 1992 by Tom Watson; *Tom Watson's Strategic Golf,* by Tom Watson, with Nick Seitz. Copyright © 1993 by Tom Watson.

Gary Player Group, Inc., for excerpts from *Play Golf with Player,* by Gary Player. Copyright © 1962 by Gary Player.

Melvin Powers and the Wilshire Book Co., for excerpts from *The Secret of Holing Putts!,* by Horton Smith and Dawson Taylor. Copyright © 1961 by A. S. Barnes & Company. Reissued as *The Secret of Perfect Putting!* in 1963 by Wilshire Book Company, North Hollywood, California.

Arnold Palmer Enterprises, for excerpts from *Go For Broke, My Philosophy of Winning Golf,* by Arnold Palmer, with William Barry Furlong. Copyright © 1973 by Arnold Palmer (with William Barry Furlong).

G. P. Putnam's Sons, a division of Penguin Group (USA) Inc., for "On-Course, Off-Course Prep Work," from *Think Like Tiger: An Analysis of Tiger Woods' Mental Game,* by John Andrisani. Copyright © 2002 by John Andrisani.

Random House, Inc., for excerpts from *Getting Up and Down: How to Save Strokes from Forty Yards and In,* by Tom Watson and Golf Digest, with Nick Seitz. Copyright © 1983 by Thomas S. Watson and *Golf Digest; The Inner Game of Golf,* by W. Timothy Gallwey. Copyright © 1979, 1981 by W. Timothy Gallwey.

The Random House Group, Ltd., for excerpts from *Golf—The Winning Formula,* by Nick Faldo, with Vivien Saunders. Copyright © 1989 by Nick Faldo.

Chi Chi Rodriguez Management Group, Inc., for excerpts from *101 Supershots—Every Golfer's Guide to Lower Scores,* by Chi Chi Rodriguez, with John Andrisani. Copyright © 1990 by Chi Chi Rodriguez, with John Andrisani.

Russell & Volkening for *The Bogey Man: A Month on the PGA Tour,* by George Plimpton. Copyright © 1967 by George Plimpton, renewed in 1995 by George Plimpton.

Simon & Schuster Adult Publishing Group for excerpts from: *And if You Play Golf, You're My Friend,* by Harvey Penick, with Bud Shrake. Copyright © 1993 by Harvey Penick, Bud Shrake, and Helen Penick; *Golf My Way,* by Jack Nicklaus, with Ken Bowden. Copyright © 1974, and renewed © 2002, by Jack Nicklaus; *Par Golf for Women,* by Louise Suggs. Copyright © 1953 by Prentice-Hall, Inc.; *How to Play Your Best Golf All the Time,* by Tommy Armour. Copyright © 1953 by Thomas D. Armour. Copyright renewed © 1981 by John Armour and Benjamin Andrews; *How I Play Inside Golf,* by Doug Ford. Copyright © 1960 by Prentice-Hall, Inc.; *Advanced Golf,* by Cary Middlecoff. Copyright © 1957 by Prentice-Hall, Inc.; *Golf Is Not a Game of Perfect,* by Dr. Bob Rotella, with Bob Cullen. Copyright © 1995 by Robert Rotella.

Jack Snead, for excerpts from *The Education of a Golfer,* by Sam Snead, with Al Stump. Copyright © 1962 by Sam Snead and Al Stump.

Annika Sorenstam, for her excerpt from *LPGA's Guide to Every Shot,* edited by the Ladies Professional Golfers Association. Human Kinetics, Champaign, Illinois. Copyright © 2000.

St. Martin's Press, LLC. For excerpts from *The Women's Guide to Golf,* by Kellie Stenzel. Copyright © 2000 by Kellie Stenzel.

Taylor Trade Publishing Co., from *Play Golf the Wright Way* by Mickey Wright, with Joan Flynn Dreyspool. Copyright © 1962, 1990 by Mickey Wright and Joan Flynn Dreyspool.

Three Rivers Press, a division of Random House, Inc., for excerpts from: *How to Feel a Real Golf Swing,* by Bob Toski and Davis Love, Jr., with Robert Carney. Copyright © 1988 by Golf Digest/Tennis, Inc.

The Golf Handbook for Women: The Complete Guide to Improving Your Golf Game, by Vivien Saunders. Copyright © 2000 by Marshall Editions Development Ltd.

Times Books, a division of Random House, for excerpts from *How to Play Double Bogey Golf,* by Hollis Alpert, Ira Mothner, and Harold C. Schonberg. Copyright © 1975 by Quadrangle/The New York Times Book Co.; Copyright © 1990 by Hollis Alpert, Ira Mothner, and Harold C. Schonberg.

Time, Inc., for "This is My Secret," by Ben Hogan, from *Life* magazine (August 8, 1955). Copyright © 1955 Time Inc.

Viking Penguin, a division of Penguin Group (USA) Inc., for excerpts from *Golf in the Kingdom,* by Michael Murphy, Copyright © 1972 by Michael Murphy.

Villard Books, a division of Random House, Inc., for excerpts from *On Golf: Lessons from America's Master Teacher,* by Jim Flick, with Glen Waggoner. Copyright © 1997 by Jim Flick.

Gary Wiren and Golf Digest® for excerpts from *The New Golf Mind,* by Dr. Gary Wiren, PGA Professional, and Dr. Richard Coop, Educational Psychologist, with Larry Sheehan. Copyright © 1978 by Gary Wiren, Richard Coop and Lawrence Sheehan. Copyright © 2005 The Golf Digest Companies.

Writers House, LLC, as agent for the Ben Hogan Estate, for excerpts from: *Ben Hogan's Power Golf,* by Ben Hogan. Copyright © 1948 A. S. Barnes and Company, Inc.; *Ben Hogan's Five Lessons, The Modern Fundamentals of Golf,* by Ben Hogan, with Herbert Warren Wind. Copyright © 1957 by Ben Hogan.

The Babe Didrikson Zaharias Foundation, for excerpts from *Championship Golf,* by Mildred Didrikson Zaharias.

For permission to reproduce photographs:

AP/Wide World Photos: p. 51, Jack Nicklaus; p. 151, Babe Didrikson Zaharias; p. 193, Johnny Revolta; p. 196, Gary Player; p. 217, Bobby Locke; p. 221, Horton Smith; p. 303, Payne Stewart; p. 314, Lee Trevino; p. 336, Patty Berg; p. 337, Jack Burke, Jr.; p. 348, Tiger Woods.

Historic Golf Photos/The Ron Watts Collection: p. 161, Johnny Miller; p. 308, Sam Snead.

Kellie Stenzel: p. 245, Kellie Stenzel.

Library of Congress, Prints and Photographs Division: p. 145, Harry Vardon.

USGA Archive: p. 44, Joyce Wethered; p. 232, Abe Mitchell; p. 311, Arnold Palmer.

INDEX